T0295595

The Credit Investor's Handbook

Founded in 1807, John Wiley & Sons is the oldest independent publishing company in the United States. With offices in North America, Europe, Australia, and Asia, Wiley is globally committed to developing and marketing print and electronic products and services for our customers' professional and personal knowledge and understanding.

The Wiley Finance series contains books written specifically for finance and investment professionals as well as sophisticated individual investors and their financial advisors. Book topics range from portfolio management to e-commerce, risk management, financial engineering, valuation, and financial instrument analysis, as well as much more.

For a list of available titles, visit our Web site at www.WileyFinance.com.

The Credit Investor's Handbook

Leveraged Loans, High Yield Bonds, and Distressed Debt

MICHAEL A. GATTO

WILEY

Published by John Wiley & Sons, Inc., Hoboken, New Jersey.
Published simultaneously in Canada.

For general information on our other products and services or for technical support, please contact our Customer Care Department within the United States at (800) 762-2974, outside the United States at (317) 572-3993 or fax (317) 572-4002.

Wiley also publishes its books in a variety of electronic formats. Some content that appears in print may not be available in electronic formats. For more information about Wiley products, visit our web site at www.wiley.com.

Library of Congress Cataloging-in-Publication Data is Available:

ISBN 9781394196050 (Cloth)
ISBN 9781394196036 (ePDF)
ISBN 9781394196043 (ePUB)

Cover Design: Wiley
Cover Image: © oxygen/Getty Images; Xuanyu Han/Getty Images
Author Photo: Courtesy of the Author

SKY10066208_013024

To my wife, Mary Kay, thank you for all your support during the past 25 years. I could not have done any of this without you.

To my children, Gabriella and Matthew, it has been my greatest joy watching you grow into kind and caring young adults. You inspire me to be a better person.

To my dad, I miss your guidance and wish you were still here.

To my mom, I love you for how you raised me, Carolyn, Laura, and Julia. You taught us by example how to deal with the curve balls life throws our way. You are the best mom ever!

To my sisters, to be clear, this makes me unambiguously mom's favorite until one of you writes a book and dedicates it to her.

Finally, to all my students, you have been my inspiration to write this book.

Contents

CLOSING COMMENT

APPENDIX

Disclaimer

Views Expressed. All views expressed herein are those of Michael Gatto (the "Author") as of the date set forth on the cover and do not represent the views of his current or former employers, or any entity with which the Author has ever been, is now, or will be affiliated, including without limitation, Silver Point Capital, L.P. and its affiliates (collectively, "Silver Point").

Except as otherwise specified herein, the information contained herein is believed to be accurate as of the date set forth on the cover. No assurance is made as to its continued accuracy after such date and neither the Author nor John Wiley & Sons, Inc. (the "Publisher") has any obligation to update any of the information provided herein. All information and views contained herein are subject to change without notice.

Informational Only; No Investment Advice; Not an Offer. The views expressed herein are for informational purposes only, and are not intended to be, and should not be, relied upon by you as an investment recommendation, in connection with any investment decision related to any investment, including investment in any investment fund or other product, or for any other purpose. This book is not intended to, and does not, constitute legal, tax, or accounting advice. This book is not an offer to sell, or a solicitation of an offer to buy, any security. Prior performance is not any form of guarantee as to future results.

References and Examples Illustrative Only. Any and all examples included herein are for illustrative and educational purposes only, and do not constitute recommendations of any kind, and are not intended to be reflective of results you can expect to achieve. Case studies of investments have been provided for discussion purposes only. As a result, any factual information, including price levels and company financial information, may be altered or changed, should not be relied upon, and is presented solely for informational and teaching purposes. These investments may be illustrative of potential investment strategies. The case studies do not discuss (and should not be interpreted to discuss) the amount of any profits or losses, realized or unrealized, in connection with the investments. There can be no assurance that the processes or analyses described can be successfully applied to other investments. None of these case studies are indicative of Silver Point's investment strategies, prior investment performance, or investment portfolios of the funds it manages. Such strategies, performance and portfolio do not reflect those of the select examples set forth herein. There can be no assurance that similar investment opportunities will be available in the future or, even if they were, that such investments would be successful. Differences in, among other things, the timing of transactions and market conditions prevailing at the time of investment may lead to different results. It should not be assumed that any of the investments discussed herein will be profitable or that other investments will have traits similar to the investments presented herein.

Information Accuracy. The Author cannot and does not guarantee the accuracy, validity, timeliness, or completeness of any information or data (including information and data provided by third parties) made available to you for any particular purpose. Neither the Author nor the Publisher will be liable or have any responsibility of any kind for any loss or damage that you incur in the event of error, inaccuracies, or omissions.

Risk. Investments involve a high degree of risk and should be considered only by investors who can withstand the loss of all or a substantial part of their investment. No guarantee or representation is made that the investments and investment strategies discussed herein will be successful, and investment results may vary substantially over time. Investment losses occur from time to time. Nothing herein is intended to imply that the investments and investment strategies discussed herein may be considered "conservative," "safe," "risk free," or "risk averse." PAST PERFORMANCE OF AN INVESTMENT IS NEITHER INDICATIVE NOR A GUARANTEE OF FUTURE RESULTS. NO ASSURANCE CAN BE MADE THAT PROFITS WILL BE ACHIEVED OR THAT SUBSTANTIAL LOSSES WILL NOT BE INCURRED.

No Reliance. Neither the Author nor the Publisher will be liable, whether in contract, tort (including, but not limited to, negligence), or otherwise, in respect to any damage, expense, or other loss you may suffer arising out of or in connection with any information or content provided herein or any reliance you may place upon such information, content, or views. The information presented should not be relied upon by you. Any investments you make are at your sole discretion and risk.

Disclaimer of Warranty and Limitation of Liability. In no event will the Author, the Publisher, their affiliates, or any such parties be liable to you for any direct, indirect, special, consequential, incidental, or any other damages of any kind.

Intellectual Property. "Silver Point" and "Silver Point Capital" are registered trademarks owned by Silver Point and/or its affiliates. Any recipient of the information contained herein has no right to use the trademarks, service marks, logos, names, or any other intellectual property or proprietary rights owned by Silver Point and/or its affiliates. This presentation constitutes copyrighted material and cannot be used, reproduced, or transmitted, in whole or in part, without the prior written consent of Silver Point. This presentation does not grant any patent, copyright, trademark, or other proprietary right or license to any recipient of the information contained herein.

Foreword

David Solomon, CEO Goldman Sachs

Long before I was the CEO of Goldman Sachs, I was a first-year analyst in a credit training program, unaware of how important what I learned there would be to my career.

It wasn't part of the plan. When I graduated from college in May 1984, I was thinking of going to law school. But I was busy during my senior year, the idea of studying for the LSAT wasn't all that appealing to me, and once I saw my score, I decided it was time to get a job. I was rejected by most of the places I applied, including Goldman Sachs, but eventually I landed at a commercial bank called the Irving Trust Company, where for the first year my fellow recruits and I received extensive financial training.

Only later did I realize how fortunate we had been. When I first walked into Irving's New York offices in the ornate One Wall Street building, all I had was an undergraduate degree in political science. I had no formal business education to speak of, and I was more than a little intimidated. But luckily for me, we spent most of that first year taking classes taught by professors from the University of Virginia's Darden School of Business. We were essentially getting paid to get an MBA.

It was in that program that I learned how to perform credit analysis, a foundational skill for any finance professional, and I proceeded to use it at every stage of my career. After a little less than two years at Irving, I worked in high yield sales at Drexel Burnham, and later I went to Bear Stearns to lead a piece of its junk-bond business. Then, in 1999, I joined Goldman Sachs to co-head the Global High Yield Business Unit, leading the firm's high yield bond and bank-loan underwriting, trading, and sales. That job put me on the path to becoming the co-head of the Investment Banking Division.

Today, there's a huge demand among finance professionals for a do-it-yourself guide to credit analysis because many banks have scaled back or eliminated their training programs, and we all should be grateful that my friend Michael Gatto has answered the call. What I like about *The Credit Markets Handbook* is that it covers the fundamentals as well as more advanced topics such as bankruptcy and distressed debt investing, all while being easy to understand and fun to read.

You'd be hard-pressed to find someone better qualified to write this book than Michael. I worked with him during my early years at Goldman, and I've always been impressed by his clear, analytical mind. He developed and taught credit training for several years before joining Goldman's leveraged finance division, first on the bank loan trading desk and then in the distressed debt proprietary trading business. In addition, he taught various credit courses to Goldman professionals in the US and Europe.

But perhaps his best recommendation is what he did next. In 2002, Michael left the firm to join two former Goldman partners, Ed Mule and Bob O'Shea, in launching one of the world's most successful credit investment funds, Silver Point Capital.

And now he's written a first-rate textbook. After 39 years in finance, I can't stress enough the importance of a firm grounding in credit analysis, and if you're wondering whether this book has what you need, take it from me: you're in good hands.

David Solomon

Acknowledgments

For the last year and a half, every business call I had ended with some version of the following:

Hey, did I mention I'm writing a credit training textbook? I will send you a couple of chapters, and I would love to get your opinion.

For those with value-added comments, it became a "no good deed goes unpunished" scenario in which I rewarded thoughtful readers with . . . more chapters to review. This continued until someone stopped responding to book-related emails, which was fine because by then I had latched on to others.

In light of how many people I asked to contribute their time, feedback, and input to this book, it is inevitable that I will inadvertently leave someone out of these acknowledgements, and I apologize to any of you whose names should be here but are not.

My heartfelt thanks go out to the following people.

1. **Ed Mulé and Bob O'Shea,** the founders of Silver Point.
   Every concept covered in this book has been learned or refined during my 25 years working for you, first at Goldman Sachs and then at Silver Point. I can never thank you enough for all you have done for me, including supporting me in writing this book.
2. **David Reganato,** Silver Point Partner and Global Head of Restructuring.
   My kids joke that you are my third and favorite child, to which I respond that they are partially wrong. You took the brunt of the "Can u do me a favor?" inquiries for this book.
3. The other Silver Point partners:
   John Abate, Partner and Co-Head of Trading;
   J.T. Davis, Partner and Head of Public Desk; and
   Eve Teich, Partner and Head of Investor Relations and Marketing.
4. **Stefania Mazzuoccolo,** my amazing and wonderful assistant. Thank you for all your help, especially in designing all the graphics.
5. **Paul Alzapiedi,** Co-Head of Trading, Silver Point Capital
   Ara Lovitt, Managing Director and Head of Research, Silver Point Capital
   Steve Weiser, General Counsel, Silver Point Capital
   I cannot thank each of you enough for your help throughout the process.

6. **Ellen Carr,** my editor.
   I thank you for all your hard work and contributions. Working with you was fun. I enjoyed debating how to explain complex concepts, and the only time you were wrong was your incorrect belief that my reference to *Fight Club* in Chapter 10 was not funny.
7. **Josh Pearl,** coauthor of *Investment Banking*. Thank you for your guidance throughout the process.
8. **Paul Johnson,** coauthor of *Pitch the Perfect Investment*. Thank you for convincing me to write a book.
9. The Wiley team:
   - **Bill Fallon,** acquisition editor, who was a champion of this book.
   - **Stacey Rivera, Purvi Patel, Lori Martinsek, Aldo Rosas, ArunRaj Arumugam, and Rahini Devi.** I appreciate your patience, guidance, and support throughout the process of publishing.
10. Various industry professionals who provided quotes, floated ideas, read chapters, and gave honest feedback. This book benefited greatly from the input of:
    - **Daniel Aronson,** Senior Managing Director, Restructuring and Liability Management, Evercore
    - **Carla Casella,** Managing Director, JP Morgan
    - **Adam Cohen,** Managing Partner and Portfolio Manager, Caspian Capital
    - **Paul Degen,** Global Head of Credit Sales, Barclay's
    - **Phil Desantis,** Portfolio Manager, Soros Fund Management
    - **Jack Devaney,** Partner and Head of Leveraged Finance Sales, Goldman Sachs
    - **Rio Dhat,** Head EMEA of Leveraged Credit Trading, Citi
    - **Dennis Dunne,** Partner and Head of Financial Restructuring, Milbank
    - **James Ely III,** CEO, PriCap Advisors LLC
    - **Fred Fogel,** Partner & General Counsel, The Baupost Group
    - **Jeff Forlizzi,** Head of Corporate Credit, Security Benefit / Eldridge Industries LLC
    - **Bob Franz,** Chief Investment Officer and Co-Founder, Arbour Lane Capital Management
    - **Avi Friedman,** former Co-Head Credit Investing, Davidson Kempner Capital and Adjunct Professor, Columbia Business School
    - **Nathaniel Furman,** Partner, Oak Hill Advisors, L.P.
    - **Kumail Gangjee,** my first TA at Columbia Business School
    - **Mitch Goldstein,** Partner and Co-Head of Credit Group, Ares
    - **RJ Grissinger,** Senior Managing Director, Centerbridge Partners
    - **David R. Hility,** Managing Director & Co-Head Global Restructuring, Houlihan Lokey
    - **Donna M. Hitscherich,** Senior Lecturer and Director of the Private Equity Program, Columbia Business School
    - **Mark Horowitz,** Managing Director, Distressed Sales, Jefferies
    - **Matt Kahn,** former Founding Member of the Private Equity and Second Lien Lending Business, Gordon Brother Group
    - **James Russell Kelly,** Director of the Gabelli Center for Global Security Analysis and Senior Lecturer, Fordham Gabelli School of Business

- **Alan Kornberg,** Of Counsel and former Co-Chair of the Restructuring Department, Paul, Weiss, Rifkind, Wharton & Garrison LLP
- **Michael Kramer,** CEO and Founding Partner, Ducera Partners
- **Matthew Kretzman,** Managing Director, Global Head of PE Capital Markets, H.I.G. Capital
- **Daniel Krueger,** Partner and Managing Director, Owl Creek Asset Management and Adjunct Professor of Business, Columbia Business School
- **Howard Levkowitz,** Founder and Managing Partner, Signal Hill Holdings
- **Richard Maybaum,** Managing Director and Co-Head of Credit Strategies, Littlejohn & Co
- **Drew McKnight,** Co-Chief Executive Officer, Fortress Investment Group
- **Bruce Mendelsohn,** Partner & Head of Restructuring, Perella Weinberg Partners
- **Michael Meyer,** Head of Global Sales and Trading, Seaport Global Holdings
- **Justin Murfin,** Associate Professor of Finance, Cornell University
- **Michael Patterson,** Governing Partner, HPS Investment Partners
- **Jacob Pollack,** Global Head of Credit Financing & Direct Lending, Credit Markets, J.P. Morgan
- **Bill Raine,** Senior Managing Director and Co-Portfolio Manager, Contrarian Capital Management
- **JP Rorech,** Managing Director, Head of Distressed, Stifel Financial Corp.
- **Chris Santana,** Managing Principle, Co-Founder, Monarch Alternative Capital
- **Damian Schaible,** Partner, Co-Head Restructuring Group, Davis Polk
- **Roopesh Shah,** Senior Managing Director, Restructuring and Capital Markets Advisory, Evercore
- **Eric Siegert,** Senior Manager and Global Co-Head of Financial Restructuring, Houlihan Lokey
- **Derron Slonecker,** Founding Partner, Ducera Partners
- **Steve Starker,** Co-Founder, BTIG
- **Christine Victory,** my former assistant
- **Rob Thomas Symington,** Adjunct Professor Cornell University
- **Parag Vora,** Founder, HG Vora Capital Management LLC
- **Alan Waxman,** Co-Founding Partner and CEO, Sixth Street
- **Harry Wilson,** Founder and CEO, MAEVA Group, LLC
- **Steven Zelin,** Partner, Global Head of Restructuring and Special Situations, PJT Partners
- **John Zito,** Senior Partner and Deputy CIO of Credit, Apollo Management

11. Silver Point employees who proofed chapters and provided significant input:
    - **Nick Aynilian,** Director, Silver Point Capital
    - **Matt Chilewich,** Managing Director, Consultant Relations, Silver Point Capital
    - **Hayden Choi,** Associate, Silver Point Capital
    - **Anthony DiNello,** Managing Director and Head of Private Credit Silver Point Capital
    - **Joseph Fallon,** Managing Director, Silver Point Capital
    - **Zane Feldman-Isaksen,** Associate, Silver Point Capital
    - **Nate Goodman,** Associate, Silver Point Capital
    - **Carter Hass,** Director, Silver Point Capital
    - **Kyle Hyland,** Associate, Silver Point Capital

- **Michael Jordan,** Managing Director, Silver Point Capital
- **Eric Karp,** Senior Advisor, Silver Point Capital
- **James Kasmarcik,** Chief Compliance Officer, Silver Point Capital
- **David Koziol,** Managing Director, Silver Point Capital
- **Matt Landry,** Vice President, Silver Point Capital
- **Sherman Lee,** Director, Silver Point Capital
- **Conor Mackie,** Director, Silver Point Capital
- **Alyssa Mehta,** Director, Silver Point Capital
- **Josh Milgrom,** Director, Silver Point Capital
- **Taylor Montague,** Managing Director and Head of Capital Markets, Silver Point Capital
- **Paul Morris,** Associate, Silver Point Capital
- **Jaclyn Mulé,** Associate and "grammatical genius," Silver Point Capital
- **Parker O'Shea,** Associate, Silver Point Capital
- **Tom O'Connor,** Senior Trader, Silver Point Capital
- **Manjot Rana,** Managing Director, Silver Point Capital
- **Max Sahlins,** Associate, Silver Point Capital
- **Austin Saypol,** Chief Operating Officer, Silver Point Capital
- **Matt Sheahan,** Managing Director and Head of Underwriting, Silver Point Capital
- **Billal Sikander,** Managing Director, Silver Point Capital
- **Derek Staples,** Managing Director, Silver Point Capital
- **Anthony Van Dervort,** Associate, Silver Point Capital
- **Lu Wang,** Associate, Silver Point Capital
- **Jared, Weisman,** Managing Director, Silver Point Capital
- **Genna Zaiman,** Managing Director, Silver Point Capital
- **Jon Zinman,** Managing Director, Silver Point Capital

12. Finally, thank you to my spring 2023 Advanced Credit Class students at Fordham, who were my guinea pigs. You read my first drafts and spotted calculation errors. If there are any mistakes, it is your fault!
    - **Olivia Bezzone**
    - **John Bollish**
    - **Grace L. Ciccone**
    - **Matthew F. Forlenza**
    - **Benjamin Goodrich**
    - **Ashley Hassell**
    - **Ricardo He**
    - **Tamar Hovsepian**
    - **Daniel Kelly**
    - **Natalia Kimmelshue**
    - **John Koutsonikolis**
    - **Richard Lazzaro**
    - **Aidan Lezynski**
    - **Matthew M. Mai**
    - **Diego MunozLedo**
    - **Henrik Murer**
    - **William Murphy**

- Emma Nance
- Joe Nussbaum
- Declan O'Donnell
- Chris Owen
- Patricio Pulla
- Wynne Scheffler
- Mitchel Selitsky
- Emme Simning
- Alex S. Simon
- Bobby Singh
- Elaine Sionov
- David Smeriglio
- Billy Smith III
- Lois Van Weringh
- Freddy von Knobelsdorff
- Leo Wackerman

About the Author

Michael Gatto
Partner, Head of the Private Side Businesses
Silver Point Capital
Adjunct Professor
Columbia Business School
Fordham University's Gabelli School of Business

Michael Gatto was one of the first employees at Silver Point Capital, a credit-focused hedge fund. After joining the firm in April 2002, he became the first non-founding partner in January 2003 and helped grow the business from $120 million of investable capital in 2002 to approximately $23 billion. Today, he heads the firm's Private Side Businesses.

From 1999 to 2002, Michael worked at Goldman Sachs on the bank loan trading desk and then in the Special Situations Investing Business, where he focused on distressed credit.

Before joining Goldman, Michael designed and taught credit training programs for banks and investment banks. He taught at some of the world's leading financial institutions, including Citibank, CSFB, Union Bank of Switzerland (UBS), American Express Bank, Fleet, and Barclays in global financial centers such as New York, Boston, London, and Singapore, as well as more remote locations, including Bangladesh, Manila, and Cairo. Before becoming a professional credit instructor, he was a credit analyst and head of Global New Entry Training at Citibank.

Michael is also an adjunct professor at Columbia Business School and Fordham University's Gabelli School of Business, where he teaches courses on credit analysis, distressed value, and special situation investing.

Michael received an MBA from Columbia Business School and a BA in Economics from Cornell University.

To Contact the Author:
Please feel free to contact the author with any questions, comments, or suggestions at gatto@creditinvestorshandbook.com or connect with him on LinkedIn.

About the Editor

Ellen Carr
Principal, Portfolio Manager
Barksdale Investment Management
Adjunct Professor
Columbia Business School

Ellen Carr is a principal and high yield bond portfolio manager at Barksdale Investment Management (BIM), a majority-women-owned investment management firm focused on investment grade and high yield fixed income. Prior to joining BIM in 2013, Ellen spent 11 years at The Capital Group as a leveraged credit analyst and portfolio manager.

Ellen is also an adjunct professor of finance at Columbia Business School, where she teaches courses on the credit cycle and cash flow forecasting. She is a regular contributor to the *Financial Times* and the coauthor of a book on women in investment management, *Undiversified: The Big Gender Short in Investment Management.*

Ellen received an MBA from the Kellogg Graduate School of Management at Northwestern University and a BA in literature from Harvard.

Preface

MY STORY

This book aims to prepare you for an investment career in the credit markets or, if you are already in the business, to enhance your skill base.

While there is a multitude of books on investing in equities, there are few books on investing in the credit markets, and to my knowledge, none as comprehensive as this one.

My unique background allows me to combine a teacher's approach with real-world experience. For the past 25 years, I have invested in the credit markets through multiple economic cycles and global crises alongside some of the world's most successful credit investors. I have had the opportunity to learn from, mentor, teach, and manage dozens of Wall Street's brightest minds. Along the way, I developed a systematic methodology for analyzing credit.

After graduating from Columbia Business School in 1993, I started my career at Citibank, a global commercial bank just breaking into the more lucrative investment banking business that was then dominated by the likes of Goldman Sachs, Morgan Stanley, Merrill Lynch, Lehman Brothers, and Bear Stearns. Citibank's main attraction was its well-regarded credit training program: a six-month course in the fundamentals of credit analysis that every new corporate finance hire was required to take.

In 1994, Citibank's senior management wanted to revamp its credit training program and set out to find a recent graduate of the program to spearhead the project. When asked to spend six months working on this assignment, I worried that it would set back my career. I believed the quickest path to success at the bank and on the Street was by working on deals. However, management assured me that if I did this assignment, I could choose my next rotation, so I agreed to focus on revamping Citibank's credit training program.

The project was a wonderful experience that piqued my interest in a career as a professional instructor. Once the revamp was completed, I was asked to run the training program, which I did for three years across Citibank's global footprint. I left Citibank to become an independent consultant, designing and teaching credit analysis for other financial institutions. I teamed up with Barry Frohlinger, a veteran in the bank training world whom I had previously worked with on revamping the Citibank program. Barry was a charismatic instructor, and I was fortunate to spend the next two years designing programs and teaching credit analysis with him. We taught at some of the world's leading financial institutions, including Citibank, CSFB, Union Bank of Switzerland, American Express Bank, Fleet, and Barclays. We ran courses in global financial centers such as New York, Boston, London, and Singapore, as well as more remote locations, including Bangladesh, Manila, and Cairo. Over time, I became a "credit expert," despite having never done any actual deals.

Meanwhile, my former students were beginning to populate a growing number of credit investing seats across Wall Street, as the asset class grew rapidly, spurred by the burgeoning leveraged buyout (LBO) market. And then, in 1997, I received a call that would change my life.

A former student of mine was working for Bob O'Shea, a young partner at Goldman Sachs, and had mentioned to Bob that I was the best credit investor he had ever met, as evidenced by the multitude of banks that had hired me to teach their analysts (hilarious given my lack of real deal experience). On my former student's recommendation, Bob cold-called me to interview for a job on Goldman's loan trading desk. I was intrigued; while I loved teaching credit analysis, I felt I would be better positioned professionally if I had real deal experience. He explained that while Goldman had always dominated in M&A and IPOs, the bank had only recently begun growing its credit business and developing a new market in trading illiquid bank loans. Bob had joined Goldman from Bear Stearns in 1990 to develop this business and had teamed up with Ed Mulé, another young partner, to build out Goldman's broader credit investing business.

Bob did not fit the typical Ivy League, white-shoe, Goldman mold. He was a scrappy kid from New Jersey and, like me, came from a modest background. His grandmother was a maid at the Waldorf Astoria hotel, and his father was a New York City cop. After attending Fordham on a track scholarship, he joined Security Pacific Bank and later Bear Stearns. Bear was known to recruit young, aggressive professionals who were poor, hungry, and driven, referred to as "PHD" candidates. Bob became one of the pioneers of Bear's bank loan trading business. Before the loan trading market developed, loans sat on the balance sheets of the original syndicate of banks, meaning banks had no ability to monetize these loans or move them off their balance sheets if they needed access to liquidity or if their risk tolerance or the underlying credit quality of the borrower changed. Bob recognized an opportunity to develop a market to trade loans similar to the high-flying "junk bond" market effectively created by Michael Milken.

In 1990, Goldman Sachs recruited Bob from Bear Stearns to build the firm's bank loan business. During the recruiting process, Bob pitched Goldman on a strategy to become the number one market maker in the secondary bank loan market *before* launching its corporate bank loan underwriting business. Goldman embraced Bob's plan, knowing that the global money center banks would fight to retain their leading market position in the profitable business of underwriting leveraged loans. Bob was hired as a vice president at the very young age of 24 and was the only employee in this new group until he could prove out the business model, which over time called for Goldman to commit billions of capital.

Bob's plan worked, as his group became the market leader in trading loans. Goldman used its number one market position in trading loans in the secondary market to become the first investment bank to penetrate the commercial banks' dominance in the leveraged loan underwriting business. As Bob built the business in North America and Europe, he earned the reputation of being a visionary leader and business builder. In addition to partnering with Ed to build the firm's proprietary credit investing business, Bob also ran other groups at Goldman, including the global high yield bond business, which included managing all sales, trading, capital markets, research, and the firm's CLO business while also running the international bank loan business. Goldman made him a partner in 1994 at the age of 29—the second-youngest partner in the firm's history.

Like Bob, Ed Mulé came from modest means (i.e., he was a "PHD" in Bear Stearns' speak). Ed graduated from a public high school in a primarily rural, working-class area of upstate New York. He was admitted to the University of Pennsylvania's Wharton School despite handwriting his application (he did not know that typing was the standard method). Ed funded his studies with financial aid and a government Pell Grant. While at Wharton, he was admitted into the selective Wharton joint BS/MBA program, which accepted only 4 of the 600 students in his class. Ed completed the BS/MBA program in four years instead of the usual five, graduating *magna cum laude* with both a BS and an MBA at the age of 21.

Ed's grit and determination paid off. Upon graduating in 1984, he joined Goldman Sachs's highly respected M&A department. Navigating the shift from his no-frills roots to working at a white-shoe investment bank was not easy, but Ed excelled, building a reputation for being thoughtful and analytical as well as a highly commercial investment banker. Ed had an unusual ability to exercise sharp judgment in complex situations by tying together granular company-level analysis with an appreciation of the macro-level factors shaping a situation. It was this approach that allowed Ed to see things that others missed. For instance, when most M&A departments viewed the telecom sector as a low-priority backwater, Ed correctly anticipated that regulatory and technological forces would drive a boom of strategic M&A and private equity activity. With that foresight, Ed helped position Goldman to take advantage of the telecom sector's rising tide.

After seven successful years in Goldman's M&A department, Ed was recommended by Hank Paulson (future Goldman CEO and US Treasury Secretary) to work with Goldman's then co-CEOs on firmwide strategy. Three years later, Ed was elected a partner in the same class as Bob, at the young age of 31, and was soon asked to move again, this time into the private equity investment area. But Ed believed that his skill set, experience, and intellectual curiosity could have the highest impact on Goldman's emerging distressed debt business. The firm agreed and eventually tasked Ed and Bob with jointly building what ultimately became Goldman's proprietary credit investing operation.

When I got that initial call from Bob, it was a good thing that I did not know how brutal the interview process to join his and Ed's team would be. I had five intense meetings with Ed and Bob, followed by ten other meetings with various Goldman professionals, followed by five rigorous case studies. Eventually, Goldman made me an offer, and I accepted on the condition that I could take 6 to 12 months to wind down my teaching commitments.

During that wind-down period, global markets suffered an economic downturn resulting from the 1998 Asian Financial crisis. Goldman's macro proprietary trading desk was hit particularly hard, and significant mark-to-market losses caused the bank to put in place a temporary hiring freeze. Barely two weeks before my first day there, my phone rang in London, where I was finishing up my last assignment for Citibank. It was Bob, who told me there was no longer a job waiting for me at Goldman. The timing couldn't have been worse; I had just given up all my teaching clients, no one was hiring, as most Wall Street firms were dealing with losses, and my wife was pregnant with our first child. I was ecstatic to be a father—just not an unemployed father with limited savings.

Although there was no longer a role for me at Goldman, as a gesture of good faith, the firm committed to paying half my annual guaranteed compensation. Contractually, I was owed nothing. I suggested to Bob that it was a terrible deal for Goldman to pay me with nothing in return and offered to work for six months effectively for free, as the original offer was to pay me this amount not to show up. I was gambling that the world would be a better place in six months, and I would position myself to be offered a permanent job at the firm. Goldman was reluctant to take me on for "free," as it did not want additional headcount—even if having me work for six months cost nothing. But after refusing to take no for an answer, I struck a deal to join the firm through a temp agency so as not to impact Goldman's official headcount.

My gamble paid off with a full-time offer on Goldman's loan trading desk. I eventually moved to the Special Situations Group ("SSG"), led by Ed. I initially focused on distressed retailers and made a name for myself at the firm through luck and a lot of hard work. In addition, for the first time in my life, my bank account was starting to grow.

Goldman had a culture of risk-taking, and the firm was a breeding ground for some of the best investors of all time, including David Tepper of Appaloosa, Cliff Asness of AQR, Eddie Lampert of ESL, Tom Steyer of Farallon, and Leon Cooperman of Omega Advisors. Eleven of the original 15 desk analysts and traders I worked with ended up either starting their own firms or heading a group at a well-established firm, including Adam Cohen, cofounder of Caspian Capital; Alan Waxman, cofounder of Sixth Street; Jason Colodne, cofounder of Colbeck Capital; Bruce Mendelsohn, head of restructuring at Perella Weinberg; Jody LaNasa, founder of Serengeti Asset Management; Kevin Ulrich and Tony Davis, co-founders of Anchorage Capital; Jim Gillespie and Jonathan Savitz, cofounders of Greywolf Capital; Damien Dwin, founder of Lafayette Square; Mark DeNatale, head of distressed trading at CVC; and Vivian Lau, founder of One Tusk Investments.[1]

After four years at Goldman, I faced another career choice. Ed and Bob retired from Goldman in 2001 and 2000, respectively. In 2002, Bob joined Ed, who was launching a new credit investing firm. I had three options: stay at Goldman Sachs, join Ed and Bob, or return to teaching. As with many decisions on Wall Street, greed and ambition played a prominent role. Joining on the ground floor of a new fund could lead from a seven-figure net worth to eight figures, maybe even nine! And if it didn't work out, teaching would still be there. I decided I would join Ed and Bob and return to teaching no more than five years later.

Silver Point Capital launched in January 2002 with $120MM of capital to invest. I joined the firm in April and became the firm's first non-founding partner in January 2003. I initially continued the work I was doing at Goldman Sachs, but as the firm grew, I moved off the trading desk to build out Silver Point's private businesses, which grew to include (i) "off-the-run" strategies, (ii) real estate investing, (iii) a restructuring group, and (iv) corporate lending. Today, I continue to oversee Silver Point's private side activities and mentor the next generation of investors at the firm.

[1]Not all of these professionals are still at the firms mentioned.

As it turns out, navigating my Goldman job offer was good training for a career in which tough negotiations feature prominently. Either personally or through people who worked for me, I have negotiated some of the most exciting and complex bankruptcy and restructuring deals around the globe, including the restructuring of Quinn Industries, an Irish industrial company; Novasep, a French biochemical business; Steinhoff, a South African retailer; Codere, a Spanish gaming company; Studio City, a Macau gaming company; Delphi, the world's largest auto supplier; and Hostess, the iconic manufacturer of Wonder Bread and Twinkies, to name just a few.

Over its 20-year history, Silver Point has consistently generated highly attractive returns, and as of the writing of this book, the firm manages approximately $23 billion of investable capital across both public and private credit strategies. Silver Point has received multiple industry accolades and is recognized as one of the world's top credit investing firms.

Obviously, I did not follow my plan of returning to full-time teaching within five years of joining Silver Point. While I enjoyed helping my partners build a world-class credit firm, I missed teaching. I reentered the academic world as an adjunct professor at Fordham's Gabelli School of Business in 2013 and Columbia's Graduate Business School in 2016, where I teach courses on credit and special situations investing. Furthermore, in 2021, Bob and I sponsored the establishment of the Fordham O'Shea Center of Credit Analysis and Investment to address the growing need for well-trained credit analysts. I serve as director of the Center, which has three goals:

1. To offer students a secondary concentration in credit that helps them obtain and prepare for top-tier jobs;
2. To provide networking opportunities and foster ongoing professional learning;
3. To establish a "Giving Back" program for underserved communities in the Bronx.

My students often ask if there is a textbook they can use to supplement class discussions and case studies. I have thus far failed to find one. Part of my inspiration for writing this book was to fill this void by creating a textbook I could assign for my courses and recommend to colleagues in both the investing and academic realms.

I have included as close to everything I know about credit analysis in these pages. I hope and believe that you will find here the tools to succeed in a career that involves analyzing and investing in leveraged credit.

Introduction: Structure of the Book

The goal of this book is simple: to prepare you for a career investing in corporate debt or, if you are already in the business, to enhance your skill base.

Corporate debt falls into three risk categories:

1. ***Investment grade:*** low risk of default, usually issued by the largest and most stable companies;
2. ***Non-investment grade*** (also known as high yield or junk bonds and leveraged loans/credit): higher risk of default;
3. ***Distressed debt:*** highest risk of default, sometimes already in bankruptcy.

Investors tend to specialize in one type of debt defined by its underlying riskiness. Debt investors evaluate risk by assessing the probability of a payment default (i.e., the potential that the company cannot pay its interest or principal when due) and the severity of loss in the event of a default (i.e., the estimate of how much of the investment will be lost if the company defaults).

This book focuses on investing in the non-investment grade and distressed debt markets, where the greatest opportunity for return exists.

In preparing to write this book, I interviewed virtually everyone I know in the credit space with experience managing new credit analysts. I did this to find out what skills they wished their new hires had. Three themes stood out:

1. Analysts hired directly from undergraduate and MBA programs were not prepared to do relevant, real-life, real-time analysis on actual companies. It was common for their professors to use fictitious companies and hypothetical situations. Students learned the basic concepts of investment analysis; however, when they landed a job, they lacked an understanding of how to analyze companies using actual financial disclosures, such as a 10-K. A company's financial disclosures are complex and confusing; an analyst needs to be comfortable comprehending and gathering relevant information from them.
2. Even when new hires could put together a proper analysis, they were often not able to draw conclusions from their work. They typically learned the ratios used to analyze a company's profitability, leverage, etc. However, they did not always know how to translate their work into investment recommendations. At best, they performed helpful analysis, but readers of their research needed to draw their own conclusions, reducing the value of the work.
3. Finally, new hires tended to lack a framework for writing a concise investment memo. Most firms have an investment committee that approves new investments going into a portfolio. Before the investment committee meets to debate

the merits of an idea, an analyst will prepare and circulate a memo that includes the high-level investment thesis, a detailed description of the company, the risks of the investment, and all supporting **relevant** analysis. I bolded and underlined relevant because, in my experience, many analysts want to include everything in an investment memo to demonstrate the depth of their work. But an investment committee is made up of experienced employees, and their time is precious. An analyst does a significant amount of analysis and due diligence, but rather than incorporating everything, the best analysts include only the critical inputs needed to debate the merits of the investment. In fact, one of the most important parts of the analyst's job is distilling a tremendous amount of information into a concise investment memo used to debate and make buy and sell decisions.

My goal in this book is to address these three deficiencies. While fictitious companies will be used to illustrate some concepts, I will also perform each step of the analysis on real-world companies. Furthermore, the book will give real-life examples of investment memos and trade recommendations that can serve as a template.

BOOK STRUCTURE

Part One: Building Blocks of the Leveraged Credit Markets, Chapters 1–4

These chapters provide a basic background of the credit asset class, including:

1. A history of the leveraged credit markets;
2. An overview of credit cycles;
3. A primer on credit trading terminology, including a review of price, yield, and spread; and
4. A primer on leveraged buyouts.

Part Two: The Seven-Step Process of Evaluating a Debt Investment, Chapters 5–13

Part Two is Credit Training 101 using my seven-step process. In this section you will learn to analyze and make investment recommendations for performing (i.e., non-distressed) debt instruments, supported by all relevant analyses.

Traditional credit training programs often focus on the "5 Cs of Credit:"

1. Character: a view on the leadership of the borrower, its reputation, and its strategy;
2. Capacity: a focus on the borrower's ability to generate enough cash flow to service its debt (interest and principal);
3. Capital: a review of how much equity the business has relative to its debt;
4. Conditions: an analysis of the firm's competitive environment; and
5. Collateral: an evaluation of the quality of the assets securing the borrower's debt.

While my seven-step approach incorporates the 5 Cs, this book will introduce you to a more comprehensive set of analyses used by the world's top investors to evaluate debt instruments. Although the focus of this book is credit investing, this framework can be useful in assessing any corporate investment, from debt to equity.

In all credit analysis, the investor needs to have an informed view of default risk (i.e., the likelihood that the company will get into financial trouble) and the recovery prospects for the company's various types of debt if it gets into financial trouble (often referred to as "severity of loss"). While excellent credit analysis by no means takes a cookie-cutter approach, I have developed an organized, routinized process to guide an investment decision. Part Two of the book will follow this seven-step approach to investing in corporate debt instruments (see Figure I.1).

Step 1 Sources and Uses (only applicable to originations)
- (a) Why is the company seeking financing?
- (b) What are the proposed sources of capital to fund the financing need?

Step 2 Qualitative Analysis
- (a) Industry analysis
- (b) Business strategy
- (c) Management assessment
- (d) ESG concerns

Step 3 Financial Statement Analysis
- (a) Profitability
- (b) Cash flow and liquidity
- (c) Capital structure

Step 4 Forecasting
- (a) Identification of key business drivers and assumptions
- (b) Development of base, upside, and downside cases

Step 5 Corporate Valuation
- (a) Comparable company analysis
- (b) Precedent transactions (M&A comps)
- (c) Discounted cash flow analysis
- (d) Liquidation analysis

Step 6 Structuring and Documentation
- (a) Economic points
- (b) Structure and collateral
- (c) Covenants

Step 7 Preparing an Investment Recommendation and Credit Committee Memo
- (a) Investment thesis and recommendation
- (b) Risks and mitigants
- (c) Relative value analysis

FIGURE I.1 The Seven-Step Process of Evaluating a Debt Instrument

Part Three: Distressed Debt Investing, Chapters 14–19

Part Three is more advanced and focuses on distressed debt investing along with the nuances of bankruptcy. After completing Part Three, you will appreciate the complexity of distressed debt analysis and the different strategies used to profit from these situations.

Two other considerations: You will notice many of the companies analyzed are retailers. There are three reasons for this:

- First, retail is a simple industry to understand—not least because we all (still) shop in stores for various goods.

- Second, a retailer often experiences multiple operating challenges in its lifecycle, which are representative of the situations and resulting investment opportunities a credit analyst might encounter.
- Third, retailers' financial statements illustrate many of the more esoteric concepts discussed in the analysis section, including working capital swings, trade relationships, and off-balance sheet liabilities.

This book is meant to be a workbook. We will use JCPenney (JCP) during one of its distressed periods (2012) as a case study for the seven-step credit analysis process outlined above. Each of the chapters in Part Two ends by performing the relevant analysis on JCP. I suggest you refer to JCP's financial statements[1] and attempt the analysis outlined in each of the seven-step chapters on your own before looking at the solution at the end of the chapter. In Chapter 19, the JCP analysis will be used to make investment recommendations. I encourage you to reach your own conclusions before reading the JCP section of the chapter, and then compare your trade ideas to those of professional investors.

The best way to develop credit analysis skills is . . . to do credit analysis. You probably won't get all the case studies right the first time you tackle them, but with practice, the process and analyses outlined in this book will become second nature. A model that took days to build will gradually require only hours, and your conclusions will come more easily as pattern recognition takes hold. Everything you need to know about analyzing leveraged loans, high yield bonds, and distressed debt is in these pages—it's up to you to practice the tools outlined here to become a top-notch credit analyst.

[1]Download JCP's 2012 10-K using the free Edgar search at https://www.sec.gov/Archives/edgar/data/1166126/000116612613000016/jcp-20130202x10k.htm. The company's search term on Edgar is Old Copper Company, Inc., not JC Penney.

PART One

Building Blocks of the Leveraged Credit Markets

CHAPTER 1

Description and History of the Leveraged Finance Markets

To set the stage for analyzing corporate debt, let's start with a history of the leveraged finance asset class (this chapter) and credit cycles (Chapter 2).

FINANCING A COMPANY: WHY USE DEBT?

Debt financing is as old as human society, although it has enjoyed varying levels of acceptance over the centuries. To choose one of many famous historical references to debt, Shakespeare's play *Hamlet* includes the well-known quote, "Neither a borrower nor a lender be." If all companies heeded this advice, there would be no debt markets and thus no need for this book. While Shakespeare was a brilliant playwright, a few courses in corporate finance might have changed his one-sided view of debt.

The concept of borrowing and lending dates back to 3000 BC in ancient Mesopotamia. Farmers borrowed seeds and would pay back what they owed with a share of their crops when the spring harvest came. The Code of Hammurabi, an ancient legal text, shares some of the conditions of the loans at the time: if the harvest was ruined by poor weather, the debt was void. But if a farmer failed to pay his debt for any other reason, he was forced to work for three years to settle it. While today we borrow and lend money instead of seeds and crops, debt continues to be a backbone of the modern economy, with most companies using a combination of debt and equity to finance their assets and operations. Therefore, an analyst must understand the pros and cons of each source of financing.

The primary benefit of debt financing to the issuer is that, unlike equity, it does not require giving up an ownership stake in the business. An added bonus is that interest payments are tax-deductible, whereas stock dividends are not.[1]

The downside of debt is that it entails contractual interest and principal payments, whereas equity is permanent capital that never has to be repaid by the company. If a company cannot meet the cash burden of these payments, it might have to file for bankruptcy. Fundamentally, the trade-off between giving up ownership (equity financing) and increasing the probability of financial distress (debt financing) is at the core of a company's financing decisions and informs the optimal mix of debt and equity.

[1]In 2017, the Tax Cuts and Jobs Act (the Act) reduced some of the tax benefits of debt financing. Before the Act, companies were unrestricted in the amount of interest they could deduct. After the Act, companies were limited to deducting up to 30% of their 12-month EBITDA. After 2021, the cap became 30% of EBIT.

WHAT IS LEVERAGED CREDIT?

Simply put, the leveraged credit market is composed of corporate bonds and loans with a below investment grade credit rating. Leveraged credit is also referred to as high yield (HY), sub-investment grade, speculative grade, or junk. As discussed in the book's introduction, corporate debt is broadly categorized into three risk categories, summarized in Figure 1.1.

Category	Risk of Default
Investment grade (IG)	Low
Non-investment grade	Moderate to high
Distressed debt	High or already in default

FIGURE 1.1 Risk Categories of Corporate Debt

Whether a company's debt falls into the investment grade or high yield rating category depends on the credit ratings agencies' views of its probability of default. Credit rating agencies came into existence more than a century ago[i] to provide a third-party evaluation of credit quality for a range of entities, from companies to sovereigns to municipalities. The most well-known and utilized rating agencies are Moody's, Standard and Poor's (S&P), and more recently Fitch. As shown in Figure 1.2, the rating agencies have "letter grades" for credit quality; a company is viewed as investment grade if it has a rating of Aaa to Baa3 from Moody's or a rating of AAA to BBB- from S&P/Fitch.

Bond Rating Scale

	MOODY'S	STANDARD & POOR'S	FITCH
Investment Grade	Aaa	AAA	AAA
	Aa1	AA+	AA+
	Aa2	AA	AA
	Aa3	AA-	AA-
	A1	A+	A+
	A2	A	A
	A3	A-	A-
	Baa1	BBB+	BBB+
	Baa2	BBB	BBB
	Baa3	BBB-	BBB-
Non-Investment Grade	Ba1	BB+	BB+
	Ba2	BB	BB
	Ba3	BB-	BB-
	B1	B+	B+
	B2	B	B
	B3	B-	B-
	Caa	CCC	CCC
	Ca	CC	CC
	C	C	C
		D	D

FIGURE 1.2 Bond Rating Scale

With any investment, the higher the risk, the higher the return required by an investor. This book focuses on investing in the leveraged finance (non-investment grade/high yield) and distressed debt markets, where the greatest risk and opportunity for return exist.

The non-investment grade market is further divided into three sub-markets, shown in Figure 1.3 and discussed in greater detail later in this chapter.

- High yield bonds (HY)
- Broadly syndicated loans (BSL)[a]
- Private credit or direct loans

[a]BSLs are also referred to as leveraged loans, bank loans, bank debt, or simply loans. This book will use these terms interchangeably.

FIGURE 1.3 Leveraged Credit Sub-Markets

GROWTH IN THE LEVERAGED CREDIT MARKET

The non-investment grade debt markets have grown by roughly 7x over the last 20 years (Figure 1.4). There are several reasons for this growth, including growing acceptance of more-levered companies in the public equity markets, the growth of private equity (an asset class requiring leverage to achieve target returns), and investor demand for a higher rate of return to counterbalance the long-term trend of lower Treasury rates since the 1980s. This growth continues to drive increasing demand for well-trained credit analysts.

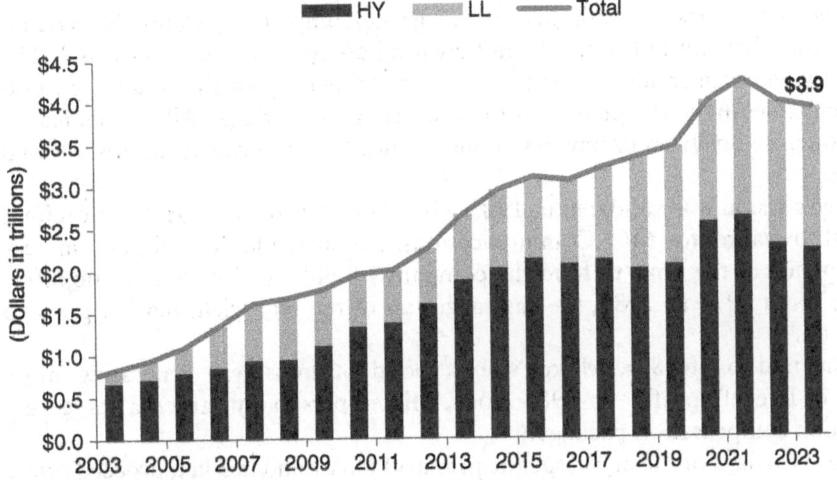

FIGURE 1.4 Total High Yield and Leveraged Loan Market Size
Sources: Bank of America Merrill Lynch (high yield data), LCD (leveraged loan data), Silver Point Capital (graph)

THE HIGH YIELD BOND MARKET

As shown in Figure 1.5, bonds and loans with a high yield rating have a significantly higher probability of default than investment grade bonds. They are commonly referred to as "junk," or more forgivingly as "speculative grade" or "non-investment grade." Their higher risk means that these bonds must provide higher yields to investors.

Global Corporate Average Cumulative Default Rates (1981–2021)										
	Percent of Credits That Defaulted									
(%)	Time Horizon (Years)									
Rating	1	2	3	4	5	6	7	8	9	10
Investment-Grade	0.08	0.23	0.40	0.61	0.83	1.05	1.26	1.45	1.63	1.81
Speculative-Grade	3.60	6.97	9.86	12.23	14.16	15.75	17.06	18.16	19.14	20.04
All rated	1.50	2.93	4.17	5.22	6.10	6.83	7.45	7.97	8.43	8.86

FIGURE 1.5 Global Corporate Average Cumulative Default Rates (1981–2021)
Sources: S&P Global Ratings Research and S&P Global Market Intelligence's CreditPro®

In the 1970s, the non-investment grade bond market was predominately comprised of "fallen angels," formerly investment grade–rated companies downgraded to high yield at some point after they were issued due to financial underperformance. Since fallen angel bonds were such a small part of the corporate bond market, the so-called "bulge bracket" investment banking firms did not focus on trading them.

Michael Milken of Drexel Burnham Lambert established himself as the go-to trader in the non-investment grade secondary bond market. After dominating the secondary trading market, he realized the fastest way to grow his business was to open up the new issue market to non-investment grade companies (essentially expanding the market beyond fallen angels and creating an entirely new asset class). The opportunity was tremendous as, at the time, only 6 percent of the roughly 11,000 public companies in the US qualified for investment grade ratings.[ii] All Milken had to do was convince investors to buy new bonds issued by non-investment grade–rated companies.

Milken's vision was validated in 1983 when Drexel brought a $1.1 billion junk bond deal to market for MCI Communications, one of the largest telecommunication companies at the time, to fund the company's buildout of its fiber optic infrastructure. From 1977 to 1989, the capitalization of the high yield market grew to $189 billion.[iii]

By the mid-to-late 80s, Milken's junk bond business was generating more than half of Drexel's profit.[iv] In 1986 alone, Milken personally earned a staggering $550 million compensation package.[v]

In the early days of the new issue (or primary) junk bond market, proceeds were used to fund business operations. However, by the mid-1980s, junk bonds were increasingly used to fund leveraged buyouts (LBOs) of public companies, a structure discussed in detail in Chapter 4, giving rise to the private equity (PE) industry. PE firms targeted some companies that had no interest in being sold. This became known as a hostile takeover, and the firms and individuals behind these types of takeovers were referred to as "corporate raiders."[2]

Carl Icahn and Ron Perelman are two famous corporate raiders. The 1987 Oliver Stone movie *Wall Street* featured a main character named Gordon Gekko, who was loosely based on a composite of Carl Icahn and disgraced arbitrageur Ivan Boesky. Today, hostile takeovers and corporate raiders are rare; however, activist investors are the modern version, taking meaningful stakes in public companies to force changes in management strategy and/or balance sheet structure. Carl Icahn, 87 years old in 2023, is a name that can still send shivers down a management team's spine when he takes a stake in their company.

The first, but by no means last, high yield bubble popped in the late 80s and early 90s. The 1989 LBO of RJR Nabisco by private equity firm KKR is widely considered the peak of this cycle. A must-read for those interested in learning more about the first LBO heyday is *Barbarians at the Gate* by Bryan Burrough and John Helyar.

However, the bubble began to deflate in 1986, when federal authorities started investigating insider trading allegations against one of Milken's clients, corporate raider Ivan Boesky, nicknamed "Ivan the Terrible" for his ruthless takeover strategies. Later that year, federal prosecutor Rudy Giuliani led an aggressive prosecution of Milken, charging him with racketeering, insider trading, and securities fraud. Giuliani, who would later become the mayor of New York City, a presidential candidate, and a personal lawyer and adviser for President Donald Trump, invoked the Racketeer Influenced and Corrupt Organization Act of 1970 (RICO) to pressure Milken into pleading guilty. Historically, RICO had been used to pursue organized crime and mobsters, not white-collar criminals. In April 1990, Milken pleaded guilty to only regulatory violations after Giuliani indicted his brother and sent the FBI to interrogate his 92-year-old grandfather.[vi] Many believed the case against Milken was weak and politically motivated and that he only pleaded guilty to protect family members. The government dropped all charges against his brother as part of his plea bargain. The judge sentenced Milken to 10 years in prison, later reduced to two years.

Milken's contribution to the financial world was substantial. Put simply, the market of Milken's making ushered in a new era of financing for corporate America. Figure 1.6 summarizes the positive impacts of the high yield / junk bond market. A must read for those interested in learning more about Milken is *Witness to a Prosecution: The Myth of Michael Milken* by Richard Sandler.

- Created a new source of capital for the huge universe of companies without investment grade ratings.
- Fueled economic growth and job creation by enabling companies to invest in growth initiatives.
- Provided investors, including endowment and pension funds, with higher-yielding investment opportunities.
- Provided a catalyst for corporate governance improvements by facilitating takeovers of undermanaged companies.

FIGURE 1.6 Benefits of the High Yield Market

[2]While there were occasional takeovers and corporate raiders before the inception of the high yield bond market, its development, brought the hostile takeover concept into the mainstream of corporate finance.

While the financial community remembers him for his career on Wall Street, Milken's reputation with the broader public is for both philanthropic and financial innovation. More than just a major donor, he substantially changed the medical research process to make it more efficient and effective. In 2020, Milken received a presidential pardon.

Subsequently to the junk bond market's first bubble and burst, there have been several credit cycles, which are discussed in detail in the following chapter. The early history of high yield bonds is instructive, as it created the foundation for a volatile market fueled by strong risk appetite and excessive leverage (in the boom) followed by extreme risk aversion and balance sheet restructuring (in the bust). As you will learn in this book, the hallmark volatility of the junk bond market provides interesting investment opportunities.

THE BROADLY SYNDICATED LOAN MARKET

While the high yield bond market's origin is filled with riveting tales, the loan market's inception is less exciting. Like their junk bond counterparts, leveraged loans are non-investment grade rated. Loans began as a sleepy asset class dominated by banks with a focus on capital preservation as compared to investment management firms with a focus on total returns. Historically, leveraged loans were underwritten by commercial banks with the intention of holding them to maturity or refinancing.

There are three significant differences between high yield bonds and leveraged loans. First, loans are less liquid, meaning they are more difficult to buy and sell. In fact, unlike high yield bonds,[3] leveraged loans can only be purchased by qualified institutional buyers (QIBs), making them inaccessible to individual investors and smaller institutional investors outside of fund structures. Second, leveraged loans are generally secured and therefore sit higher in the company's capital structure. This security lowers the risk of leveraged loans relative to high yield bonds; if a loan defaults, its investors typically receive much higher recoveries than unsecured bond investors. Third, bonds are classified as "securities," while loans are not. This has implications for the applicability of securities laws, such as rules relating to insider trading. As of 2023, a legal challenge pending before the Second Circuit Court of Appeals is seeking to classify loans as securities.[vii] Chapter 12 provides more detail about these and other structural differences between leveraged loans and high yield bonds.

In the 1990s, Goldman Sachs and other investment banks started to make markets in (that is, trade) leveraged loans, facilitating the development of a secondary trading market. An LBO funded with a $1 billion leveraged loan might be held by

[3]High yield bonds are increasingly being issued as 144A securities, making them off-limits to individual investors as well; however, before 2010, most HY bonds were "registered" and available to all investors (individual as well as institutional) for purchase.

10 large lenders. Initially, if one of the lenders wanted to reduce its exposure, it was dependent on a bid from another holder. The buildout of trading desks opened the asset class to non-bank investors, including pension funds and hedge funds. It also allowed original lenders to sell out of problematic loans, which gave rise to the distressed debt market.

The evolution of a bank's economic model from holding a loan on its balance sheet and earning the resulting interest to charging fees for arranging loans and selling the risk to others led to the development of the broadly syndicated loan (BSL) market.

As the BSL market emerged, the leveraged loan market expanded further with the development of structured or asset-backed products called collateralized loan obligations (CLOs). A CLO manager purchases and bundles together 100 or more leveraged loans. To fund the purchases of these loans, the CLO manager raises money from outside investors in different risk tranches. The CLO market came into its own in the run-up to the Global Financial Crisis (GFC) of 2008. While it shut down for a period of time after the GFC, today the CLO market is larger than ever.

As shown in Figure 1.7, the creation of a collateralized loan obligation has the following steps:

1. The CLO manager raises capital from investors. Each investor chooses a risk tranche that meets its individual risk and return expectations. Like corporate debt, the CLO tranches obtain credit ratings from the rating agencies. The Aaa/AAA debt tranche provides the lowest risk of impairment and the lowest return. On the other end of the spectrum, the equity tranche (sometimes referred to as "last out" or "first loss") has the highest risk of losing money and therefore the highest potential return. This "tranching" of risk into various ratings categories is used in virtually all asset-backed transactions (MBS, CMBS, ABS, etc.) and serves to broaden the pool of investors and thus the amount of capital available to underwrite the asset class underlying the structure. Put differently, many investors cannot buy leveraged loans because of their non-investment grade ratings, but virtually all investors are able to invest in the AAA-rated securities that compose most of a CLO.
2. The CLO manager uses the funds raised by selling different risk tranches to invest in non-investment grade new loan issues and/or attractive secondary loan offerings.
3. The interest and principal from purchased loans is used to pay interest and principal to the CLO investors. The cash flows go first to servicing the interest and principal of the senior tranche (Aaa/AAA), then to the next tranche (Aa2/AA), until, by a prearranged final maturity date, all the tranches are repaid. Any residual proceeds are paid to the equity tranche. Given this waterfall, losses from defaults on any loans purchased by the CLO manager are absorbed first by the equity, then by the lowest rated tranche. This continues up to the Aaa/AAA tranche—which, again, has very low risk of loss.

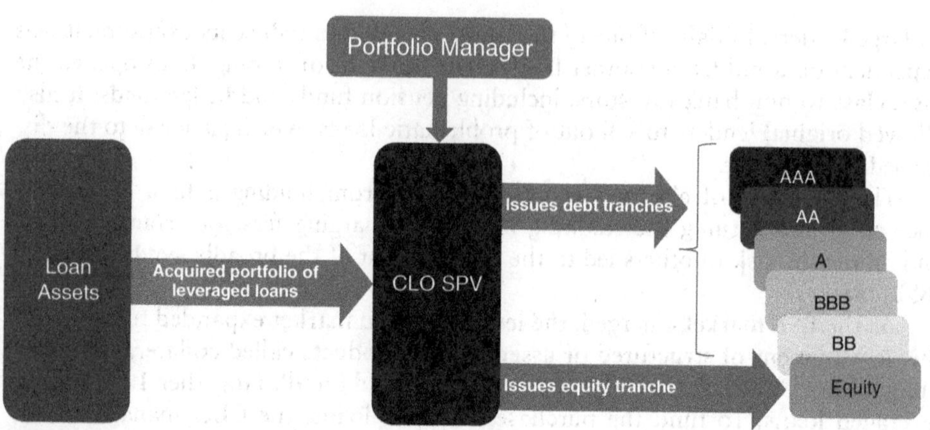

FIGURE 1.7 CLO Transaction Summary

CLOs by no means invented the magic of securitization, but they enjoy its benefits. The typical CLO is spread across 100 or more corporate loan issues with an average rating well below investment grade (e.g., low-BB). Yet 80 percent of a typical CLO's liabilities are rated AAA. How can this be? Two reasons: first, diversification across many issuers greatly reduces risk. And second, the 20 percent of the structure below the AAA piece, referred to as credit enhancement, acts as an absorber of loss. Think of this as putting 20 percent down on your mortgage—if you sell the house for 80 percent of what you bought it for, the bank does just fine, but you have lost your down payment.

The importance of CLOs to the leveraged loan market cannot be overstated. CLO structures own roughly two-thirds of leveraged loans today. The health, or lack thereof, of the CLO market (or "the CLO bid") is a major consideration for PE sponsors when they are evaluating the all-in financing rate for an LBO.

THE PRIVATE CREDIT OR DIRECT LOAN MARKET

The most recent significant development in the leveraged credit market is the massive growth of private credit, including direct loans, as an alternative to the BSL market. Increasingly, non-bank lenders such as private loan funds and business development companies (BDCs) underwrite these loans. In the aftermath of the GFC, bank regulations intensified, leading to increased capital charges associated with banks engaging in non-investment grade lending. Simply put, non-investment grade lending became less profitable for banks. As banks stepped back from leveraged lending, loans "institutionalized," that is, became their own asset class, managed by non-bank investment firms with dedicated teams of analysts and portfolio managers. Figure 1.8 shows the growth in private credit over the last decade.

There are now hundreds of private credit funds, ranging in size from under $100 million to mega funds with over $50 billion in assets. I know principals at three of these mega private credit firms quite well—Ares Management Corporation

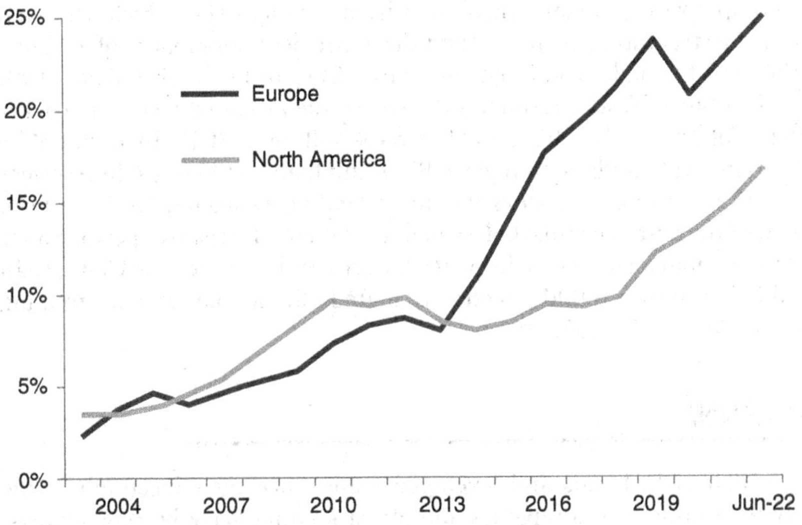

FIGURE 1.8 Private Credit as a Share of Leveraged Finance
Source: Courtesy J.P. Morgan Chase & Co., Copyright 2023

(~$380 billion in assets), HPS Investment Partners (~$100 billion in assets), and Sixth Street Partners (over $70 billion in assets).[4]

I went to Columbia Business School with Mitch Goldstein, co-head of credit at Ares; worked with Michael Patterson, governing partner of HPS, when he was part of our team at Silver Point; and started my career with Alan Waxman, CEO and co-founder of Sixth Street, on Goldman's bank loan trading desk. They are three of the smartest and hardest-working people I know, and each has taken tremendous advantage of the shift in leveraged credit origination from traditional banks to investment funds. All three believe that significant growth opportunity exists for the private credit market, as direct lenders continue to take share from traditional banks. This share shift is driven by many factors, including private credit's ability to provide speed and certainty of closing.

These industry veterans foresee increasing demand from institutional investors for private credit driven by three key attributes of the asset class:

1. Senior secured debt has provided excellent risk-adjusted returns through various market cycles.
2. The floating-rate structure of private credit insulates investors from increasing interest rates.
3. Well-structured senior secured debt has historically fared better than most asset classes in a recession.

In addition to replacing some of the BSL market, private credit has also stolen share from the high yield bond market. This new breed of investors is willing to go

[4]Asset values are approximate as of 2023.

deeper into a company's capital structure—that is, take more risk—which has given rise to a unitranche structure, which can fund the entire debt component of an LBO, eliminating the need for high yield bonds in many LBOs. In his book *Private Debt*, investment advisor Steve Nesbitt estimates the size of the private direct loan market at $1.0 trillion as of March 31, 2022, up from $400 billion in 2019. In addition, he believes direct loans will continue to replace BSLs and high yield bonds. In response to demand from institutional investors for direct lending exposure, Nesbitt's firm, Cliffwater, created the first benchmark designed to evaluate the relative performance of US direct lending managers. The Cliffwater Direct Lending Index, or CDLI, is an asset-weighted index of over 8,000 directly originated middle-market loans totaling $223 billion as of March 31, 2022.[viii]

CHAPTER CONCLUSION

The growth in high yield bonds and leveraged loans since their inception in the 1980s is likely to continue, as companies and investors alike have become increasingly comfortable with leveraged capital structures. More recently, the growth of private credit as an asset class has super-charged career opportunities for those trained to analyze corporate credit. The next chapter introduces the concept of the credit cycle, which is characterized by the waxing and waning of company access to and investors' interest in the leveraged credit markets.

NOTES

i. Moody's Investors Service. (Accessed June 18, 2023). https://ratings.moodys.io/ratings.

ii. Taggart, Robert A., Jr. (1988). "The Growth of the 'Junk' Bond Market and its Role in Financing Takeovers." In: *Mergers and Acquisitions* (ed. Alan J. Auerbach), p. 9. Chicago: University of Chicago Press.

iii. Jark, Daniel. (September 26, 2022). "The History of High Yield Bond Meltdowns." Investopedia. https://www.investopedia.com/articles/investing/022616/history-high-yield-bond-meltdowns.asp.

iv. "Michael Milken." Encyclopedia Britannica. (Accessed April 5, 2023). https://www.britannica.com/biography/Michael-R-Milken.

v. Ibid.

vi. "Michael Milken Deserved a Pardon, but Didn't Need One." Bloomberg Opinion by Joe Nocera. February 19, 2020.

vii. Greenberg Traurig, LLP (2023). "Are Syndicated Term Loans Securities Under Reves v. Ernst & Young? 2nd Circuit Solicits SEC Views." *The National Law Review.* https://www.natlawreview.com/article/are-syndicated-term-loans-securities-under-reves-v-ernst-young-2nd-circuit-solicits.

viii. For more information on the CDLI, see https://www.cliffwaterdirectlendingindex.com/.

CHAPTER 2

Credit Cycles

To become a great credit investor, you must understand the credit cycle, which refers to the degree of difficulty companies have in accessing the debt markets based on changes in market participants' appetite for risk.

Howard Marks is the co-founder of Oaktree Capital, a credit-focused firm with approximately $180 billion in assets under management (AUM).[1] He has written extensively about the importance of credit cycles. In his book *The Most Important Thing*, he writes:

> *The credit cycle deserves a special mention for its inevitability, extreme volatility, and ability to create opportunities for investors attuned to it. Of all the cycles, it's my favorite . . .*
>
> *The longer I'm involved in investing, the more impressed I am by the power of the credit cycle. It takes only a small fluctuation in the economy to produce a large fluctuation in the availability of credit, with great impact on asset prices and back on the economy itself.*[i]

As Marks observes, economic cycles impact credit availability, and credit availability impacts the economy. Banks tend to tighten their lending standards when the economy goes into recession. This tightening of credit affects the economy directly, by restraining access to the funding needed for corporate profit growth, and indirectly, through job creation's trickle-down effect. In other words, since companies need access to credit to sustain and grow their businesses, where we are in the credit cycle is inextricably linked to the health of the economy. Figure 2.1 summarizes the stages of a typical credit cycle.

Each phase of the credit cycle presents different types of investment opportunities.

1. **Expansion phase.** Lending standards become lax, and access to credit is easy and cheap. Companies tend to increase leverage during this phase.
2. **Downturn.** This phase usually begins when the economy slows and enters a recession. Defaults increase, as companies' profitability, cash flow, and debt servicing capacity are negatively impacted. As lenders deal with troubled loans, they tighten lending standards. Greater risk aversion leads investors to demand higher returns, resulting in higher borrowing costs, and access to debt capital is curtailed for all but the highest-quality companies.

[1]AUM approximate as of 2023.

3. **Repair phase.** Defaults start to decline. Companies focus on cash flow generation by cutting costs and growth-oriented capital spending. Some companies take advantage of the bankruptcy process to restructure with more manageable balance sheets post-Chapter 11.
4. **Recovery phase.** At the beginning of this phase, companies direct cash flow toward debt paydown. Once they regain confidence in the economy, their growth prospects, and their ability to service their debt, they gradually return to using free cash to fund growth opportunities and payouts to shareholders. Confident the worst is behind them, lenders relax their credit standards, and the debt markets reopen, which allows companies to re-lever their balance sheets.

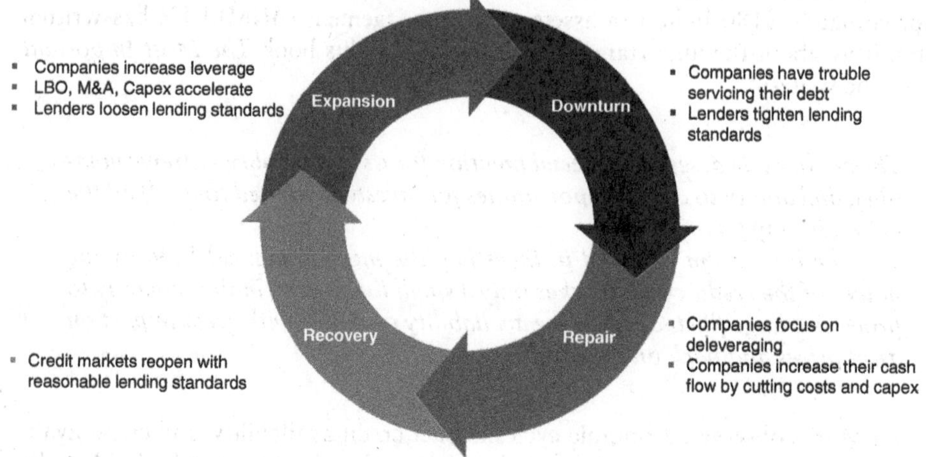

FIGURE 2.1 Phases of the Credit Cycle

As Marks writes, "It's my strong view that, while they may not know what lies ahead, investors can enhance their likelihood of success if they base their actions on a sense for where the market stands in its cycle."[ii] For example, toward the end of an expansion period, the fear of missing out ("FOMO") mentality in the market permits some "dumb" deals (that is, those that provide inadequate compensation for the underlying risk of the investment) to get done, as greed overwhelms risk aversion. These deals often create future opportunities for distressed debt investors because when the cycle turns, they have the chance to buy the debt from these transactions at a significant discount to the price at issuance. To Marks's point, if you don't know where you are in the credit cycle, it's difficult to avoid getting caught up in the market psychology that makes poor risk-reward deals possible.

During the downturn phase, fear dominates investor psychology. Default expectations rise, and investors lose money, at least on paper. Growing risk aversion creates a supply-demand imbalance as the number of investors willing and able to lend to companies or buy high yield bonds and loans in the secondary market shrinks at exactly the point when companies most need access to capital. This lack of risk appetite has three drivers:

1. Lenders decrease new loan originations as they prioritize workouts of their existing problematic loans.
2. With diminished capital to make new investments, many lenders are dealing with their own liquidity issues.
3. Fear replaces greed as the primary emotion in the investment process.

This supply-demand imbalance is challenging for most market participants, but it provides lucrative investment opportunities for those investors with the capital and conviction to act.

The description of the credit cycle and its four phases might sound predictable, measurable, rational, and even obvious. Any experienced credit investor, however, will tell you that the credit cycle is not linear; zigzags and bumps are inevitable in each of the four phases. For example, an expansion may see a mini-correction as bloated new issuance is absorbed, only to recommence and ultimately result in an even deeper downturn later (for example, the fall of 2007). Likewise, a dramatic downturn may spend very little time in repair and recovery before heading back to expansion (for example, the pandemic downturn of 2020). You won't understand the credit cycle until you have lived through a few—and, to borrow a popular phrase, "If you've seen one credit cycle, you've seen one credit cycle."

PAST CREDIT CYCLES

Figure 2.2 outlines the four downturns that I have lived through and learned from during my decades in the leveraged credit markets.

Downturn	Description
1997–1998	The Asian Financial Crisis and Contagion Effect
2000–2002	The Bursting of the Dot-Com/TMT Bubble
2008–2009	The Global Financial Crisis/Great Recession
2020	The Global Pandemic

FIGURE 2.2 Past Credit Cycles

To provide context, I've included returns (from Barclays) and defaults (from JP Morgan) for each crisis period.

THE ASIAN FINANCIAL CRISIS AND CONTAGION EFFECT (1997–1998)

You may wonder what an overseas economic crisis has to do with high yield bonds and loans issued by US-based companies. As you will see, the domestic credit market is not insulated from crises in other markets. As a "risk" asset class, leveraged credit acts somewhat like the stock market in periods of extreme risk aversion.

In the summer of 1997, the Thai baht devalued as the Thai government was forced to float its currency, which was previously pegged to the US dollar.

The collapse of the baht quickly spilled over to other parts of East Asia, especially the Philippines, Malaysia, South Korea, and Indonesia, all of which had high foreign debt–to-GDP ratios. By early 1998, those frontline Asian currencies had devalued by nearly half, triggering substantial asset deflation and plummeting stock prices and property values. This became known as the Asian Financial Crisis.

The Asian Financial Crisis became a global crisis when it spread to Russia. In August 1998, the Russian government devalued its currency, defaulted on its ruble-denominated bonds, and suspended payments to foreign creditors. The default surprised the investor community, which had largely viewed Russia's local currency-denominated sovereign debt as a safe bet given the government's ability to print this currency. This led to a systemic reassessment of credit and sovereign risk and a rush to buy liquid, high-quality assets, such as US Treasury bonds, while depressing the prices of lower-quality, less liquid investments. Commonly referred to as a "flight to quality," this is a standard feature of the downturn phase of the credit cycle.

One notable victim of the heightened volatility and subsequent contagion across a broad spectrum of global financial assets was Long-Term Capital Management (LTCM). LTCM was a renowned hedge fund founded and run by seasoned financial practitioners and Nobel Prize winners, including John Meriwether, who built Salomon Brothers' bond arbitrage group. Michael Lewis's book *Liar's Poker* made Meriwether famous. Lewis, a junior analyst at Salomon at the time, recounts how John Gutfreund, the bank's CEO, challenged Meriwether to a hand of liar's poker for $1 million. According to the book, Meriwether (widely considered the firm's best player) didn't want to beat the CEO, but, equally, didn't want the trading desk to think he was scared to play. He responded to the challenge by accepting, but only if they played for $10 million. Gutfreund declined.

LTCM's top talent included Nobel Prize–winning academics Robert Merton and Myron Scholes, who created the Black-Scholes-Merton option pricing model. In February 1994, LTCM set the record for the largest launch of a new hedge fund, raising $1.25 billion. Its AUM rose to $140 billion over the next two years. LTCM managed to borrow a massive amount of money to fund its investments, which normally would be challenging for a deliberately opaque firm—but it benefited from the halo effect of its impressive management team. At the end of 1997, LTCM's assets-to-capital ratio was 28-to-1. To put this into context, traditional banks have regulatorily determined maximum assets-to-capital ratios (as measured by the reverse of the Tier 1 capital equation) of ~17-to-1, and most operate well below that level.[iii] Thanks at least in part to this substantial leverage, LTCM generated annual returns of over 40 percent in 1995 and 1996, and 17 percent in 1997.[iv]

However, in August 1998, when Russia defaulted on its debt, LTCM's fortunes changed dramatically. In one day, the fund lost $553 million, 15 percent of its capital. It was forced to liquidate some of its positions at depressed prices, as banks demanded repayment on the credit lines they had extended to LTCM. The firm ultimately lost more than 50% of its capital in less than four months.

The Federal Reserve worried that a bankruptcy of LTCM could trigger a downfall of the banking system by dragging its counterparty banks into default along with it. In September 1998, the Fed organized a bailout in which LTCM handed over its ownership and operational controls to 14 financial institutions. *When Genius Failed* by Roger Lowenstein is a must-read for those interested in the rise and fall of LTCM.

An interesting sidenote: Bear Stearns refused to participate in the bailout of LTCM, believing it was not the role of the Fed to bail out financial institutions. It was thus a karmic irony that in 2008 Bear Stearns would itself need a government-sponsored bailout to avoid bankruptcy.

The 1998 Asian crisis, Russian default, and LTCM unwind provoked a credit cycle in the US. The S&P 500 index decreased almost 20 percent from its peak in mid-July to its trough in early October 1998. While the high yield index posted a modest positive return of 1 percent over this period, the index price declined almost 9 percent, meaning that virtually all of the coupon income generated by the index was offset by capital loss.

Two lesser-known impacts of the 1998 credit crisis: my career almost ended before it started, as Goldman pulled my job offer (see Preface: "My Story" for details); and Silver Point Capital, at its launch, rented the space previously occupied by LTCM at 600 Steamboat Road in Greenwich, Connecticut. Some people don't like to move into houses where people died, but distressed debt investors relish the corporate analog if the rent is a bargain.

By 1999, the credit markets had moved into the recovery phase—but it was short-lived.

THE BURSTING OF THE DOT-COM/TMT BUBBLE (2000–2002)

During this downturn, I learned the benefit of maintaining a capital reserve that allows investment when most investors are scared and in "risk-off" mode.

Under the heading "timing is everything," Silver Point launched in January 2002, and I joined in April, during one of the worst downturns in the credit market since the Great Depression. Little did we know how insignificant that downturn would be compared to the 2008 Global Financial Crisis.

High yield bond defaults spiked to 9 percent and 8 percent in 2001 and 2002, respectively, and the credit markets faced a historic number of bankruptcy filings, the largest of which are shown in Figure 2.3. The average trading price of the high yield bond index troughed below $76 in October 2002. From its peak in February 2001 to trough in October 2002, the S&P 500 was down 42 percent, and the high yield index was down 11 percent.

Company	Date of Bankruptcy	Total Assets
Worldcom	7/2/2002	$104B
Enron	12/2/2001	$ 66B
Conseco	12/7/2002	$ 61B
PG&E	4/6/2001	$ 36B
Global Crossing	1/28/2002	$ 30B
Kmart	1/22/2002	$ 17B

FIGURE 2.3 Largest Bankruptcies of the 2000–2002 Credit Cycle
Source: Adapted from bankruptcy filings

On the surface, declines in the stock and high yield bond markets in the 2001–2002 downturn look like the deflation of a bubble. In the stock market, high-profile darlings such as Pets.com received toppy valuations despite unproven, cash-burning business models. The corporate bond market was not immune to this euphoria, although it had a different complexion; the communication sector's share of the high yield bond market (including media and telecommunications) swelled from 26 percent in 1996 to 39 percent by the beginning of 2001, as credit investors underwrote questionable business models, such as unfunded wireless start-ups and paging.

A loss of confidence in the integrity of markets was also responsible for the bust. After the initial tech crash of 2000, Eliot Spitzer, then the attorney general of New York, initiated an investigation into the practices of the large Wall Street investment banks. After a year-long investigation, Spitzer negotiated a payout of $1.4 billion in fines from the 10 largest firms on Wall Street, which rested on several conflicts of interest. Spitzer's focus was on the pressure felt by analysts employed by investment banks to have a "buy" rating on a company's stock to help win lucrative investment banking business. He also took on the practice of "spinning" in which banks offered preferred customers, such as the CEOs of large public companies, allocations in "hot" IPOs that would lead to investment banking business.

In an ironic twist of fate, Spitzer's own ethical lapses led to his downfall several years later (coincidentally, as the next credit cycle was entering its downturn). On March 10, 2008, the *New York Times* reported that Spitzer had patronized a high-priced escort service called Emperors Club VIP and met with a $1,000-an-hour call girl for two hours.[v] Investigators alleged that, while serving as attorney general and then governor, Spitzer paid up to $80,000 for prostitutes over several years.[vi] For an in-depth documentary on Spitzer's rise and fall, check out *Client 9: The Rise and Fall of Eliot Spitzer*.

If the Spitzer investigations were not enough to dent investor confidence in the markets, early 2002 also saw some of the largest accounting scandals in history. The biggest was energy company Enron's use of off-balance sheet partnerships to hide losses and debt obligations.

Enron generated $100 billion in revenue annually. *Fortune* named it "America's Most Innovative Company" for six consecutive years and ranked it 18th on the list of the nation's 535 "Most Admired Companies." Enron's downfall was rapid; it went from an investment grade–rated company to bankrupt in less than a year. The severity of the situation began to emerge in mid-2001 and intensified in October, when Enron announced a $638 million loss for the third quarter. Shortly after that, the Securities and Exchange Commission (SEC) began investigating Enron's off-balance sheet transactions. As that investigation ensued, some of the partners at Enron's external accounting firm, Arthur Andersen, shredded documents related to Enron audits.

Enron's stock price plummeted from a high of $90 per share in mid-2000 to less than $12 per share by November 2001, when Enron attempted to avoid bankruptcy by agreeing to be acquired by energy company Dynegy. Dynegy then backed out of the deal, forcing Enron to file for Chapter 11 in December 2001. Many Enron executives were indicted on various charges; in 2006 two of the company's CEOs leading up to the bankruptcy, Jeff Skilling and Ken Lay, along with CFO Andrew

Fastow, were convicted on various conspiracy and fraud charges and sentenced to time in prison.

Arthur Andersen did not escape scrutiny. In March 2002, the US Department of Justice indicted the firm for obstruction of justice, and in June, Arthur Andersen was found guilty of shredding evidence and lost its license to engage in public accounting. Two must-reads for those interested in Enron's rise and fall and the role played by Arthur Andersen are *The Smartest Guys in the Room* by Bethany McLean and Peter Elkind and *Conspiracy of Fools* by Kurt Eichenwald.

The terrorist attack of September 11, 2001 deserves more than a postscript, but we will leave it at that in our discussion of this turbulent period in the credit markets. Suffice it to say that for a period of a couple of months, global risk appetite evaporated.

The credit markets finally started to normalize toward the end of 2002 in response to a combination of factors:

(i) **Monetary Policy:** The Federal Reserve reduced the federal funds rate from 6% in January 2001 to 1.8% in December 2001.
(ii) **Fiscal Policy:** President Bush proposed and signed the Economic Growth and Tax Relief Reconciliation Act in 2001. The legislation reduced tax rates for every American, including creating a new 10% tax bracket, and increased the child tax credit, with the goal of doubling it to $1,000 by 2010.
(iii) **Diminishing Fear of a Follow-On Terrorist Attack:** As further attacks failed to materialize, risk appetite gradually returned.
(iv) **Enhanced Regulation:** In response to widespread accounting scandals and incidents of corporate fraud, such as Enron, the government enacted waves of bipartisan new regulation and legislation designed to increase the accuracy of financial reporting for publicly traded companies. The most important of those measures, the Sarbanes-Oxley Act in 2002 ("Sarb-Ox"), imposed, among other things, greater oversight over the accounting profession (through the creation of the Public Company Accounting Oversight Board, the PCAOB), new standards for auditor independence, enhanced financial disclosure obligations, and federal criminal penalties for destroying, altering, or fabricating financial records. Sarb-Ox restored some confidence in the integrity of companies' financial reporting and in the stock and debt markets.

THE GLOBAL FINANCIAL CRISIS/GREAT RECESSION (2008–2009)

The 2008 downturn dwarfed previous historical downtowns. High yield bond defaults were 12% in 2009, as defaults typically lag in the economic cycle. Even greater distress occurred in the leveraged loan market, which experienced a default rate of 13% in 2009. The S&P 500 declined 54% from its peak in October 2007 to its trough in early March 2009, while the high yield index declined 28% and the loan index declined 25% over that same period. The average trough trading prices of high yield bonds and leveraged loans were $58 and $63, respectively. As shown in Figure 2.4, four of the ten largest corporate bankruptcies in history occurred during this cycle.

Rank	Company Name	Date of Bankruptcy	Total Assets
#1	Lehman Brothers	9/15/2008	$691B
#2	Washington Mutual	9/26/2008	$328B
#3	Silicon Valley Bank	3/10/2023	$209B
#4	Signature Bank	3/12/2023	$110B
#5	WorldCom	7/2/2002	$104B
#6	General Motors	6/1/2009	$82B
#7	Pacific Gas & Electric	1/14/2019	$71B
#8	CIT	11/1/2009	$71B
#9	Enron	11/2/2001	$66B
#10	Conseco	12/17/2002	$61B

FIGURE 2.4 Largest Corporate Bankruptcies in History
Source: Adapted from Statista.com[vii]

To understand the underpinnings of the 2008–2009 credit cycle, it's helpful to contextualize the systemic increase in risk appetite leading up to it. Coming out of the previous credit cycle, banks started lending again, first conservatively, then aggressively. This time, they had a new group to underwrite: "subprime" mortgage borrowers with FICO scores below 600 and high default risk.[2] A confluence of factors led to a massive increase in subprime loans.

First, low interest rates encouraged investors to "reach for yield," i.e., to take more risk in search of higher returns. Since subprime borrowers are charged higher rates of interest to compensate for their higher default probability, increased risk appetite from investors meant that lower-quality borrowers could access mortgage loans more easily. Because mortgage brokers are paid based on originations rather than credit quality, they came up with increasingly creative ways to get loans to lower and lower quality borrowers. Adjustable rate mortgages ("ARMs") and very low (or even zero) down payments along with relaxed documentation requirements (e.g., "liar loans" and "no-doc" loans), helped subprime borrowers obtain financing they would have been denied in normal underwriting environments.

The banks didn't keep most of the subprime loans they originated on their own balance sheets. Instead, they packaged them into subprime mortgage-backed securities (MBS). This structure allowed for "tranching" of risk into different securities rated AAA, AA, and on down the ratings spectrum. Since most of the tranches were investment grade–rated, the MBS structure created the illusion of safety. The misleading high investment grade ratings enticed many investors to buy BBB subprime MBS under the assumption they would never experience impairment.

Additionally, since mortgages are collateralized by the underlying houses, many purchasers of MBS believed they would not lose money even if default rates increased because as long as property values continued to rise, the value of the collateral underlying the MBS would continue to exceed the amount of the investment. This belief created a vicious cycle: as lenders issued more credit to risky borrowers, the demand for housing increased, housing prices rose, and the next borrower could get a bigger loan for the same house. The music stopped when mortgage defaults

[2]A FICO score measures an individual's ability to repay a loan and ranges from 300 to 850. A FICO score below 600 is considered sub-prime and at high risk of default.

accelerated, and the aggressive lending that fueled the subprime bubble ground to a halt. This, in turn, depressed housing demand, at exactly the same time that banks flooded the market with foreclosed properties.

There were 2.3 million mortgage defaults in 2008, an 81% increase versus 2007, and 2.8 million defaults in 2009. Residential mortgage delinquencies peaked at 11.5% in March of 2010 (a lagged effect).[viii] From its peak in mid-2006, the Case-Shiller housing price index fell by 20% before stabilizing in March 2009.[ix] Many of the hottest markets saw worse declines. For instance, in Cape Coral–Fort Myers, Florida, which had the third-highest rate of foreclosure filings in the nation, average home prices fell by *half*.[x]

While the banks and credit rating agencies seemed oblivious to the dangers of subprime, several hedge fund managers, such as John Paulson, saw the disaster coming and shorted MBS. A short position in a security pays off if its price declines. A must-read for those interested in the subprime crisis is *The Big Short* by Michael Lewis.

Why is this detour into subprime lending important to understanding this credit cycle? Because the meltdown of the subprime mortgage market in 2007 led to the 2008–2009 Global Financial Crisis (GFC), also referred to as the Great Recession. Although there were early signs of distress, such as the bankruptcy filing of mortgage originator New Century Financial, in April 2007, the demise of Bear Stearns in early 2008 was the first systemic event of the crisis. Bear Stearns managed several hedge funds that owned large positions in subprime MBS, and rumors of its counterparties' problems led clients to move their money out of these funds. As other financial institutions became worried about doing business with Bear, and the unimaginable collapse of this 85-year-old institution became a reality, the US government stepped in to prevent a domino effect from Bear's failure. The government brokered a deal for JP Morgan to acquire Bear Stearns at a price of just under $2 per share (the price was later adjusted to $10 per share) plus the assumption of its debt. Bear Stearns' stock had traded over $170 per share as recently as January 2007.[xi] A must-read on the collapse of Bear Stearns is *House of Cards: A Tale of Hubris and Wretched Excess on Wall Street* by William D. Cohan.

JP Morgan's purchase of Bear Stearns did not stabilize confidence in US banks, and by the fall of 2008, it was Lehman Brothers' turn to fail. Once again, the government tried to broker a deal over a tumultuous weekend in mid-September. While at first it appeared Lehman might avoid bankruptcy through a takeover by Barclays, a British investment bank, the latter ultimately pulled out of the deal, forcing Lehman Brothers to file for bankruptcy on September 15, 2008. As you will learn in Section III, Lehman's filing created one of the largest distressed debt buying opportunities in history. That same weekend, the government brokered the purchase of Merrill Lynch by Bank of America and bailed out financial giant AIG. Both transactions were aimed at shoring up the global financial system. A must-read on that fateful weekend is James B. Stewart's in-depth article "Eight Days" in *The New Yorker*.

As the chaos in the financial system accelerated, massive financial frauds came to light, as they often do when asset price bubbles burst. The most infamous of these involved well-known investment advisor Bernie Madoff. The Madoff fraud ended up being the largest Ponzi scheme in history, and its perpetrator was given an effective life sentence of 150 years in jail.

Another financial fraud hit closer to home, and I will share the story as a cautionary tale of the potential consequences of a search for yield without adequate due diligence.

Marc Dreier was a prominent lawyer with an impeccable bio, including attending Yale University for his undergraduate degree and Harvard Law School. He was the sole equity partner of a law firm with 175 lawyers and offices across the US.

In September 2006, Dreier acquired a bankruptcy law firm occasionally used by Silver Point. Early in 2008, I was introduced to Dreier by the founding partner of the acquired law firm. Dreier's office at 499 Park Avenue was decorated with expensive art, including Picassos and Warhols, worth an estimated $30 million. Dreier lived an over-the-top lifestyle, which included a luxury apartment on the Upper East Side, multiple properties in the Hamptons, an impressive art collection, and a 121-foot yacht valued at $18 million. Dreier, divorced at the time, hosted late-night parties on the yacht, attended by business clients and fashion models.[xii]

Dreier told me he was doing deals with many of our competitors and wanted to increase his business with Silver Point. He had a client who had made a short-term, unsecured loan to Solow Realty, a real estate development firm. This client had a liquidity crisis and was willing to sell the note at a discount if we could close quickly. After some back and forth, we agreed on a price subject to reviewing the loan documents and some confirmatory due diligence. But Dreier became annoyed with our diligence requests, saying no one else he worked with asked for all this additional information. Dreier ultimately informed us he had sold the note to another hedge fund, but we agreed that he would come to Greenwich for dinner because of his insistence on establishing a relationship with Silver Point.

Dreier was arrested in Canada a week before our scheduled dinner.

It turned out that the Solow Realty loans, along with several others marketed by Dreier, were fake. Dreier had been selling notes that did not exist and pocketing the money. As the notes came due, he would either convince the holder of the notes to extend the maturity or sell new (also fake) notes to pay earlier investors. Dreier's scheme ended in Toronto in December 2008, when he secured a $50 million commitment from Fortress Investment Group to buy a note issued by Ontario Teachers' Pension Plan. Fortress insisted on closing in a face-to-face meeting with Ontario Teachers. This requirement put Dreier in a bind, given that the note was fake. However, Dreier did happen to know people at Ontario Teachers and set up an unrelated meeting, in which he asked if he could use one of its conference rooms for the rest of the day. Dreier posed as an Ontario Teachers lawyer to meet with the Fortress executive, but when the latter got suspicious and asked the receptionist who was in the conference room, the jig was up. Canadian authorities held Dreier for four days before he returned to New York and was taken into custody. Needless to say, our previously scheduled dinner never took place. In hindsight, it is clear why Dreier was so put off by our due diligence. A must-see documentary for those interested in the Dreier scandal is *Unraveled*.

The Madoff and Dreier stories are colorful examples of the unfortunate endgame for some investors who eschewed due diligence. Most investments that went south during the GFC did not involve fraud but rather financial distress—and there was plenty of that to go around, both in corporate America and the banking system that typically provided liquidity to it. It's impossible to exaggerate the dire state of the credit markets during this time. The financial meltdown was global, and many believed the banking system around the world was insolvent. There was a desperate attempt to save other financial institutions from Lehman's fate, and the only way to avoid the domino effect was for the strongest institutions to acquire weaker ones with government intervention and financial backing. Within weeks of Lehman's filing for Chapter 7 liquidation, JP Morgan acquired Washington Mutual, Wells Fargo acquired Wachovia, and Goldman Sachs accepted a $5 billion equity infusion from Warren Buffett.

The credit markets were as unstable as anyone could remember because this was no ordinary downturn. The banking system was broken and facing a liquidity crisis. Overnight, the lubrication it provided to the credit markets dried up, and bonds and loans went into free fall as the counterparties that normally facilitate trading backed away from market-making to preserve liquidity.

It was impossible to end this crisis without stabilizing the banking system. If banks could not lend, the global economy would end up in a depression. Central banks around the world were forced to divert billions of dollars into shoring up the liquidity of global financial institutions. The Fed cut interest rates to help stimulate the economy in the US, reducing the Fed Funds rate from 5.25 percent in September 2007 to a range of 0–0.25 percent in December 2008.

To help stabilize the banking system, President Bush and Secretary of the Treasury Henry Paulson proposed the Emergency Economic Stabilization Act of 2008 (EESA) concurrent with the Lehman filing and the other transactions discussed above. EESA sought to restore liquidity to credit markets by authorizing the Secretary of the Treasury to purchase up to $700 billion in mortgage-backed securities and other troubled assets from the country's banks, as well as any other financial instruments the Secretary deemed necessary "to promote financial markets stability." I was on the Silver Point trading desk with one eye on the TV coverage of the House vote on EESA and the other watching the market on my Bloomberg screen. As the votes were being tallied it became clear that the bill would not pass on its first try. The reaction of the stock market was swift and sharp, as the S&P 500 fell 8 percent. After several amendments, and in part in response to the stock market's swoon, the bill was passed with a vote of 74-25 in the Senate and a vote of 263-171 in the House, and it was signed into law by President George W. Bush on October 3, 2008.

The backbone of EESA was the $700 billion Troubled Asset Relief Program (TARP), which the Secretary of the Treasury used to restore liquidity and stability to the US banking system. In addition to stabilizing the banking system, the government turned its attention to US car manufacturers. The US auto industry was hard hit by the recession and, in November 2008, Chrysler, Ford, and General Motors (GM) traveled to Washington to ask for $25B in emergency loans from the government. Their initial meeting was a public relations disaster, as the CEOs were unprepared for the scrutiny they received—down to their use of private jets to fly to Washington, DC, to request taxpayer bailout money.

As car sales continued to plunge in early 2009, it became clear that GM and Chrysler would run out of money. President Obama established the Auto Task Force, led by Steven Rattner, a former investment banker and private equity manager. Rattner concluded that without government intervention, GM and Chrysler would have to liquidate, devastating a web of workers, suppliers, and communities, especially in the Midwest. Rattner put it simply: GM was "too big, too important" to let it fail.[xiii]

In March 2009, Rattner brought in Harry Wilson, a former partner at Silver Point, renowned for his intensity, restructuring prowess, and ability to thrive on a mere three hours of sleep per night. The automakers found out about Wilson's approach and work ethic the hard way when he was setting up a meeting with top management at GM for ten o'clock. The executives assumed he meant 10 a.m. the following day, until he clarified, "No, I mean we are meeting at 10 p.m. tonight." He led a small group of people within the auto task force known internally as the "deals and diligence team," which performed much of the analysis that underpinned the task force's policy decisions, conducting interviews, touring auto plants, and poring over financial records.[xiv]

The auto task force followed two major principles: first, the government would inject money into the troubled companies only if they could be restructured to become viable; and second, there would have to be "shared sacrifice" among all stakeholders—meaning creditors, shareholders, and unionized auto workers.

Perhaps unintuitively, the task force put GM and Chrysler into bankruptcy, where the companies could overhaul operations and balance sheets with money from TARP approved by Congress to rescue the financial sector. "Team Auto" slashed the carmakers' costs and debt by shutting plants and laying off workers, eliminating dealers, shedding brands, and negotiating concessions from creditors and the United Autoworkers Union. The auto task force whisked GM through bankruptcy in approximately 40 days[xv]—which as you will see in the chapter on bankruptcy is a very quick exit.

The auto task force was considered a success and one of the key reasons the US avoided a depression. During his months leading negotiations, Wilson worked harder than ever. However, public service was important to him, and he was grateful for the opportunity to serve his country.

While Wilson oversaw all the auto task force's diligence, he personally led the US Treasury's General Motors restructuring. I asked Harry how he and his team managed such a large, complicated, and high-profile bankruptcy in a very short period of time. He indicated there were a lot of skeptics at the outset, as GM had seen its market share shrink since 1954 and had been flirting with bankruptcy for the previous 20 years. While most industry observers felt it couldn't be fixed, Wilson was certain it could be, but that fixing it would require a fundamental restructuring with far harder decisions than a "Band-Aid" approach. The team sought not only to address GM's problems at the time but also to position it for success in the years ahead. With the benefit of hindsight, Wilson's lofty goals have been realized. In the 14 years since its emergence from bankruptcy, GM has seen its market share stabilize and has generated strong profits.

While government intervention in a myriad of forms allowed the US to avoid a depression, this was the worst credit cycle experienced since the Great Depression. The economic recession began in December 2007 and ended in June 2009. Labor market conditions improved, albeit slowly. The economy didn't return to pre-2008 unemployment levels until 2015.

For those interested in learning more about the GFC and the related bailouts, a must-read is *Too Big to Fail: The Inside Story of How Wall Street and Washington Fought to Save the Financial System—and Themselves* by Andrew Ross Sorkin.

With a couple of hiccups, including the oil and gas exploration and production (E&P) industry bear market of 2015, the credit cycle recovery and expansion period lasted from the end of the recession in June 2009 to the Covid crisis of 2020, marking the longest post-war period of growth on record. Historically, a recession happens on average every five years. Many economists started to argue that the business cycle was a thing of the past and that there might not be another downturn, using Australia, which experienced economic growth for 28 consecutive years, as a reference point.

Silver Point disagreed. In fact, during the latter part of this long period of expansion, we raised our first "dry powder fund." The concept we marketed to our investors was that after a prolonged period of economic growth, it was inevitable that the credit markets would experience another cycle and that funds sitting on unused capital (i.e., "dry powder") would be best positioned to react quickly at the right point in the cycle. That opportunity came in 2020.

THE GLOBAL PANDEMIC (2020)

The historic 11 years of economic growth and predictions that there would never be another downturn ended abruptly in 2020, as Covid-19 created both a public health crisis and an economic crisis with severe and far-reaching repercussions across the world.

To put some numbers to the pandemic headlines:

- US GDP decreased by over 9% in the second quarter of 2020 (from the first quarter).
- Unemployment increased from 3.5% in February 2020 to over 14% in April 2020.
- The S&P 500 index decreased over 33% from mid-February to late March 2020.
- The Barclays High Yield Bond Index decreased in price by 21% while its yield increased from 5.1% to 11.7% during the same period.

The human suffering created by the Covid crisis was a tragedy. But the pandemic also created an incredible, albeit short-lived, opportunity for investors. There was panic selling, sending the price of debt of healthy companies without material Covid exposure down meaningfully. With few offsetting buyers, Silver Point was able to deploy its dry powder to buy debt at large discounts to par. We also provided emergency loans to companies that our analysis showed would survive the crisis. Finally, we bought deeply discounted debt of carefully researched companies that we thought would have to file for bankruptcy because we believed that debt would be converted into the company's equity—and that we stood to make excellent returns as the post-reorganization shareholders. (You will learn more about this "distressed for control" strategy in Chapter 19.)

In response to the economic hardship, the US government introduced the Coronavirus Aid, Relief, and Economic Security (CARES) Act in late March 2020, a $2.2 trillion economic stimulus package that provided one-time cash liquidity to individuals, small businesses, corporations, and state and local governments. This was the largest economic stimulus package in US history, dwarfing the $830 billion stimulus package in response to the Great Recession in 2008.

The US Federal Reserve, led by Chair Jerome Powell, also supported the US economy and the financial markets in several ways:

- It cut the federal funds rate by 1.5% in the span of a few short weeks in March 2020, bringing the fed funds rate down to a range of 0% to 0.25%, while implicitly promising the markets that rates would stay low for as long as needed for the economy to heal.

- It purchased massive amounts of securities via quantitative easing (QE) programs, lent to primary dealers, backstopped money market mutual funds, and expanded the scope of its repurchase agreement operations.
- It supported corporations and businesses via lending directly to major corporations, purchasing commercial paper, and supporting loans to small and mid-sized businesses and non-profit institutions. It also supported households and consumers, and state and municipal borrowers.

Due to the massive fiscal and monetary stimulus, the 2020 buying opportunity was short-lived, which made our dry powder idea even more strategic, as we had capital on hand to take advantage of the opportunity immediately. The stimulative government policies combined with encouraging news about vaccines brought buyers back into the credit markets, and pricing quickly normalized. In less than a year, the credit cycle was in the recovery phase.

THE NEXT DOWNTURN? INFLATION, FED TIGHTENING, AND REGIONAL BANKING CRISIS

> "Cycles will never stop occurring. If there were such a thing as a completely efficient market, and if people really made decisions in a calculating and unemotional manner, perhaps cycles (or at least their extremes) would be banished. But that'll never be the case."
>
> —Howard Marks, *The Most Important Thing*

As I write this book in 2023, the inevitability of the credit cycle is on display. Indeed, 2022 was the worst bear market for high yield bonds in a decade and a bad year for stocks as well. The S&P was down 18%, the Barclays High Yield Bond Index declined 11%, and the JP Morgan leveraged loan index was flat for the year.

The cause of this latest downturn is not a recession but rather the Federal Reserve's response to a spike in inflation, which in 2022 touched a level not seen in the US since the 1980s. Many investors had not experienced inflation in their lifetimes, much less in their investing lifetimes. The Fed Funds rate started 2022 at 0.25%, and as of May 2023 stood at 5–5.25%, with more increases ("tightening") expected at the time.

The divergence in the returns of the bond and loan indices, which have historically moved in tandem, is emblematic of what happened in 2022. As you will learn in the next chapter, since loans are floating rate investments, meaning their coupons adjust based on an underlying risk-free rate of interest, they are more sheltered from interest rate increases. On the other hand, bonds are fixed-rate instruments; therefore, bond prices decrease as interest rates rise. (Chapter 3 provides a primer on the price/yield relationship.)

The previous credit cycles resulted primarily from macroeconomic conditions (typically, a recession). As discussed, the classic presentation of a credit cycle is that a recession collides with toppy valuations, risk appetite and access to capital decline, and prices of high yield bonds and loans decline as well. But so far in 2023, the economy and corporate profitability are in reasonably good shape, despite inflationary pressures. Unemployment remains low, and demand for services is still benefiting from a hangover of Covid-driven pent-up demand (e.g., for travel). The traditional credit investing playbook doesn't apply—yet.

However, there are signs of distress in the lowest-quality parts of the credit markets. First, the broadly syndicated loan market essentially shut down in 2022 and has been slow to reopen. As a result, banks got stuck with billions of so-called hung bridges on their books. Hung bridges are capital commitments made early in 2022 to finance LBOs that cannot be sold to credit investors because yields have increased so sharply. Twitter is the best-known of these names, but there is a host of others, such as technology company Citrix.[xvi]

Second (and related), risk appetite has dried up for the lowest-rated and highest-risk debt instruments. At the start of 2023, the average yield of the Barclays CCC Index, which returned −16% in 2022 (versus −11% for BBs), stood at 14%, and its average price at $74. This is either a great buying opportunity or a warning signal of more price downside as a default wave builds.

Compounding the fractures in the lower-quality parts of the credit market, the banking sector—which many believed to be "fixed" after regulatory reforms post-GFC—is experiencing its own crisis. The failure of Silicon Valley Bank in March 2023, along with the government-mandated takeover of Credit Suisse by competitor UBS, spooked investors in bonds issued by banks, particularly the subordinated securities issued as quasi-equity (e.g., AT1 bonds like those issued by Credit Suisse that were wiped out in the takeover by UBS). Some experts estimate that the mark-to-market losses in bank portfolios in the spring of 2023 are roughly equivalent to the total equity capital in the banking system,[xvii] which implies impairment of many theoretically safe, or at least investment grade–rated, bank bonds. In tandem, the Treasury bond market has experienced some of its wildest swings since the GFC as investors try to guess the Federal Reserve's next moves.[xviii] Market volatility and investors' shift to a risk-off mentality have presented some excellent buying opportunities.

Where do we go from here? Of course, even the savviest credit investor can't say with certainty. The goal of this book is not to predict credit cycles but to give you the tools you need to identify good credit opportunities in all kinds of markets and to keep you out of bad ones. As you become familiar with the structural features and pricing of the investments analyzed in the pages to come, you will also start to recognize typical behaviors of investors at each phase of the credit cycle.

NOTES

i. Marks, Howard. (2011). *The Most Important Thing*. New York: Columbia Business School Publishing.

ii. Marks, Howard. (September 26, 2018). "The Seven Worst Words in the World." Oaktree Capital website. www.oaktreecapital.com/docs/default-source/memos/the-seven-worst-words-in-the-world.pdf?sfvrsn=6dc9dd65_4.

iii. Hayes, Adam. (November 20, 2020). "Tier One Capital Ratio: Definition and Formula for Calculation." Investopedia. https://www.investopedia.com/terms/t/tier-1-capital-ratio.asp.

iv. Fleming, Michael, and Weiling Liu. (November 22, 2013). "Near-Failure of Long Term Capital Management." federalreservehistory.org. https://www.federalreservehistory.org/essays/ltcm-near-failure.

v. Hakim, Danny, and William K. Rashbaum. (March 10, 2008). "Spitzer Is Linked to Prostitution Ring." *New York Times.* https://www.nytimes.com/2008/03/10/nyregion/10cnd-spitzer.html.

vi. Thomson, Katherine. (August 14, 2008). "Spitzer Prostitute Details: $80,000 Spent, Mood Music, Multiple Prostitutes, up to a Decade of Use and an Ever-Present Security Detail." *Huffington Post.* https://www.huffpost.com/entry/spitzer-prostitute-detail_n_91116 .

vii. "Largest bankruptcies in the United States as of July 2023, by assets at the time of bankruptcy." Statista. (Accessed August 24, 2023). https://www.statista.com/statistics/1096794/largest-bankruptcies-usa-by-assets.

viii. "Delinquency Rate on Single-Family Residential Mortgages, Booked in Domestic Offices, All Commercial Banks." FRED Economic Data. (Accessed August 24, 2023.) https://fred.stlouisfed.org/series/DRSFRMACBS.

ix. "S&P/Case-Shiller U.S. National Home Price Index." FRED Economic Data, accessed August 24, 2023. https://fred.stlouisfed.org/series/csushpinsa.

x. Christie, Les. (February 12, 2009). "Home prices in record plunge." CNNMoney.com.

xi. Reuters staff. "Timeline: A dozen key dates in the demise of Bear Stearns." Reuters.com (17 March 2008). https://www.reuters.com/article/us-bearstearns-chronology-idUSN1724031920080317.

xii. Burrough, Bryan. (September 29, 2009). "Marc Dreier's Crime of Destiny." *Vanity Fair.* https://www.vanityfair.com/news/2009/11/marc-dreier200911 .

xiii. Shao, Maria. (March 1 2011). "Steven Rattner: The 2009 U.S. Auto Bailout Was Necessary." Insights by Stanford Business.

xiv. "Harry Wilson (businessman)." Wikipedia.

xv. Reuters Staff. "TIMELINE: GM emerges from bankruptcy." Reuters.com (July 10 2009).

xvi. Wirz, Matt. (November 13, 2022). "JPMorgan Dodges a Buyout Loan Bullet." *Wall Street Journal.* https://www.wsj.com/articles/jpmorgan-dodges-a-buyout-loan-bullet-11668340804.

xvii. Jiang, Erica Xuewei, Gregor Matvos, Tomasz Piskorski, and Amit Seru. (April 2023). "Monetary Tightening and U.S. Bank Fragility in 2023: Mark-to-Market Losses and Uninsured Depositor Runs?" Stanford Business School, Working Paper #4080. https://www.gsb.stanford.edu/faculty-research/working-papers/monetary-tightening-us-bank-fragility-2023-mark-market-losses.

xviii. Rennison, Joe. (March 24, 2023). "'Bonkers' Bond Trading May Be Sending a Grim Signal about the Economy." *New York Times.* https://www.nytimes.com/2023/03/24/business/treasury-market-swings-economic-signal.html?searchResultPosition=6.

CHAPTER 3

A Primer on Leveraged Credit Trading Terminology

Before diving into credit analysis, I will introduce some important terminology and concepts associated with trading and valuing leveraged credit. While some of these concepts might sound very technical, they are critical to making good investment recommendations. This primer is divided into nine sections (see Figure 3.1).

---

1. New issues versus secondary trades
2. Components of debt investment returns
   - Risk-free rate
   - Credit spread
3. Investment returns
   - Internal rate of return (IRR) and yields
   - Price and yield inverse relationship
4. Calculations
   - Yield
   - Multiple of money (MOM)
5. Pricing dynamics (why a debt instrument might trade below/above its issuance price)
6. Calculating the price of a bond when the required yield changes
   - Concept of duration
7. Trading levels
   - Price
   - Yield
   - Spread
8. Trading lingo for secondary trades
   - Hit the bid
   - Lift the offer
9. Investing concepts
   - Concept of risk-adjusted returns
   - Expressing a negative view by shorting
   - Generating alpha versus beta

FIGURE 3.1 Primer on Leveraged Credit Terminology and Concepts

NEW ISSUES VERSUS SECONDARY TRADES

Credit investments occur via new issues/originations (the primary market) or secondary trades.

(a) *New issues/originations* occur when a company is borrowing money (issuing debt) right now, and therefore the investor can be involved in structuring the debt at the outset by negotiating key terms, such as coupon, maturity, and covenants. This is discussed in detail in Chapter 12. High yield bonds and broadly syndicated loans are generally "originated to distribute" by investment banks, which syndicate (sell) the debt to a wide array of investors. This is referred to as the primary market. New issues are much more common in the credit markets than the equity markets, where initial public offerings (IPOs) definitionally only happen once, and secondary equity offerings are less common than debt offerings. This is due mainly to the fact that, unlike equity, bonds and loans have explicit maturity dates, which results in frequent refinancing.

(b) ***Secondary trades*** occur after bonds or loans are syndicated, and investors buy and sell debt issued in the past from each other. These transactions go through a broker-dealer, usually one of the large investment banks with a debt trading desk. The trading desk matches a buyer with a seller and takes a small fee, referred to as the bid-ask spread (discussed in more detail below), for executing the order. More recently, electronic trading exchanges (e.g., MarketAxess) have facilitated secondary trading.

COMPONENTS OF DEBT INVESTMENT RETURNS

The core principle of investing in anything—debt, equity, real estate, etc.—is the time value of money: a dollar is worth more today than that same dollar in the future. Investors who don't want to take default risk invest in "risk-free" government bonds (US Treasury bonds), which theoretically have no default risk.[1] However, most investors seek to generate returns higher than the risk-free rate, which requires taking on incremental risk. Therefore, the return demanded by an investor can be disaggregated into two components (see Figure 3.2).

Component	Description
Risk-free rate	The rate that rewards the investor for the time value of money
Plus the credit spread[a]	Component of return to compensate investors for taking credit risk (the chance that the company will not pay all coupons and principal), also referred to as the risk premium
Equals Return	Required yield that adequately compensates an investor for both components (time value of money and credit risk)

[a] Credit spreads are commonly quoted in basis points (bps). Every 100 bps is equal to 1%.

FIGURE 3.2 Components of Return

If a debt instrument is trading at 100% of the outstanding amount of debt (also referred to as trading at par), then the return is equal to the coupon.

There are two types of coupons: floating rate and fixed rate.

[1] I say "theoretically" because the US government could default. As of the writing of this book, Congress has narrowly voted to raise the debt ceiling, but leading up to this contentious vote, some market participants speculated that the US government could default on its debt—an extremely low probability event but theoretically possible.

Floating Rate

The coupon of a floating rate bond or loan moves ("floats") at a spread negotiated at the time of issue to an underlying risk-free rate; as this base rate moves, so does the coupon. Historically, the base rate for US dollar loans[2] was typically the London Interbank Offered Rate (LIBOR); however, in 2020, the Secured Overnight Funding Rate (SOFR) replaced LIBOR. For example, if a bank debt coupon is SOFR + 500 bps, and SOFR is 2%, then the coupon is 7% (the 2% SOFR rate plus the 5% credit spread). If SOFR increases to 3%, the coupon rises to 8% (the 3% SOFR rate plus the 5% credit spread). Loans typically have floating rate coupons.

Fixed Rate

Most high-yield bonds are fixed-rate debt instruments, meaning the coupon does not change with the underlying risk-free rate.

IRR AND YIELDS

Internal rate of return (IRR) and yield are calculations used to assess the returns of investments. While they are fundamentally different calculations, credit investors at times use them interchangeably when expressing the forecast or actual return of a credit instrument.

IRR corresponds to the discount rate used in a discounted cash flow (DCF) analysis that results in a net present value (NPV) of all cash flows from an investment that equals zero. NPV, like time value of money, is a foundational concept of financial theory; if you are not familiar with it, Chapter 11 provides an overview of NPV and the DCF analysis used to calculate it. For now, I will simplify IRR to mean the return of an investment.

Yield is the compounded annual return an investor would receive by holding the bond until maturity. The calculation assumes all coupons are reinvested at the same yield of the debt instrument.

Price and Yield Inverse Relationship

As discussed above, the yield of a debt instrument trading at par is equal to the coupon. However, if the investor buys the debt below par (at a discount), the yield is higher than the coupon, and conversely the yield is lower if the price is over par. This inverse relationship between price and yield (see Figures 3.3 and 3.4) should make intuitive sense. The company pays a set of cash flows to the lender (the coupons throughout the life of the debt and the amount borrowed at maturity). If you can buy that stream of cash flows at a discount, your yield and implied return must go up, and if you pay a premium, your yield and implied return must go down. In the next section, I will discuss reasons for debt to trade up or down.

[2]For non-dollar loans, the base rate is typically Euribor (Euro Interbank Offered Rate), which was not affected by the LIBOR phase-out.

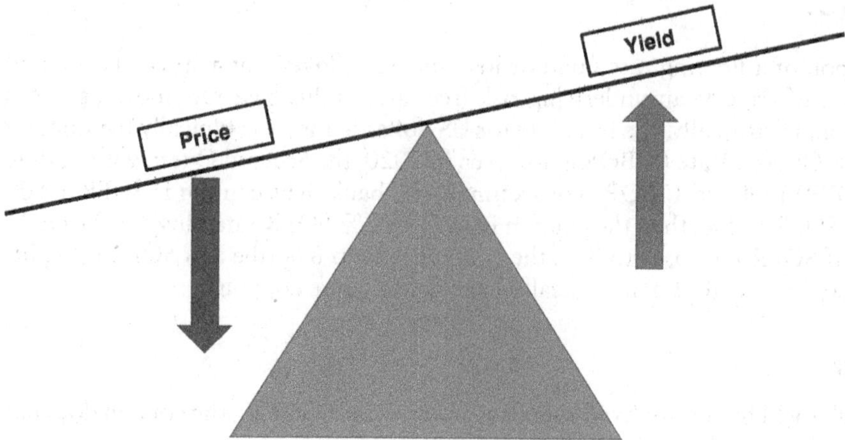

FIGURE 3.3 Relationship between Price and Yield

Terminology	Trading Level	Yield vs. Coupon
Trading at a discount	Investor pays < $100	Yield > Coupon
Trading at par	Investor pays par	Yield = Coupon
Trading at a premium	Investor pays > $100	Yield < Coupon

FIGURE 3.4 Price and Yield Dynamics

CALCULATING RETURN AND MULTIPLE OF MONEY

Return Calculations

An Excel worksheet is the easiest way to calculate the return of a debt instrument trading at a price different from par. Below is an example.

On January 1, 2023, an investor buys $1,000 face value of bonds trading at 88% or $88 with a 12% coupon paid semiannually (i.e., half of the coupon is paid every six months). The bond is held until its maturity in two years. As shown in Figure 3.5, return can be calculated in Excel using either the "Yield" or "IRR" functions.

The investor would earn a return of 19.53% on this investment. If the investor bought the same bond at par, the return would equal the coupon of 12%; the extra 7.53% comes from buying the bond at a discount to par.

For simplicity, I annualized the 6-month month IRR calculation by multiplying it by two. Another approach would be to compound the 6-month IRR, resulting in a slightly higher return using the formula ((1+6-month IRR) ^2)-1. Furthermore, some firms prefer to use the XIRR[3] function versus IRR. I recommend taking your firm's approach to calculating returns.

[3] The main difference between Excel XIRR and IRR functions is that IRR assumes all the periods in a series of cash flows are equal. XIRR gives you the flexibility to assign specific dates to each cash flow.

	A	B
1	**Return using Excel's yield formula**	
2	Settlement Date	1/1/2023
3	Maturity Date	1/1/2025
4	Coupon	12%
5	Purchase Price	88
6	Redemption Price (amt paid at maturity)	100
7	Payment Frequency (semi-annual coupon pymts)	2
8	Yield	=YIELD(B2,B3,B4,B5,B6,B7)
9		
10	**Return using Excel's IRR function**	
11		Cash Flows
12	Purchase Date	(880)
13	Coupon Month 6	60
14	Coupon Month 12	60
15	Coupon Month 18	60
16	Principal & Coupon Month 24	1,060
17	6-month IRR	=IRR(B12:B16)
18	Annualized IRR	=B17*2

FIGURE 3.5 Calculating Return Using "Yield" and "IRR" Functions in Excel

Multiple of Money (MOM) or Multiple of Invested Capital (MOIC) Calculations

In addition to yield, some investors use multiple of money (MOM) to evaluate an investment. MOM is sometimes referred to as cash-on-cash return or multiple of invested capital (MOIC) and is calculated by dividing all cash flows received by the investor by the total cash invested.

The MOM of the above trade is calculated by summing cash inflows and dividing them by the up-front dollar investment. The cash inflows are the four semiannual $60 coupons plus the repayment of the $1,000 bond at maturity, or $1,240. The initial investment was $880 ($1,000 face value × 88% to reflect the $880 purchase price). The MOM of this investment is $1,240/$880 or 1.41x.

IRR or yield has the benefit of considering the time value of money, whereas MOM does not. However, IRR can be distorted for short holding periods since it reflects an *annualized* return. For instance, if you buy a 12% coupon bond at $99 and sell it one day later at par, you will achieve an incredibly high IRR (over 350%) since you made $1 in one day, and the IRR calculation assumes this return for the other 364 days in the subsequent year. However, the MOM of 1.01x (= [100 + one day of accrued coupon]/99]) would be extremely low.

PRICING DYNAMICS—WHY A DEBT INSTRUMENT MIGHT TRADE BELOW/ABOVE ITS ISSUE PRICE

With a few exceptions (e.g., zero-coupon bonds), debt is issued at a price of par, ($100) or close to it. The coupon of debt issued at par is the rate that adequately compensates the investor for the time value of money and the credit risk of the investment at the time the company borrowed. However, the debt will trade below the issue price if investors no longer feel that the initial coupon adequately compensates them. As discussed above, for the investor to get a higher yield on a debt instrument, she will need to buy it at a lower price (recall the inverse relationship between price and yield).

Figure 3.6 describes three reasons for an increase in the required return of a credit investment, each of which will result in a decrease in its trading price.

1. *The risk-free rate increases.* If the risk-free interest rate (e.g., US Treasury yield) increases, new debt must be issued with a higher coupon than existing debt. Investors reprice existing debt to reflect the higher yield that the market now demands. Note that this only holds true for fixed rate debt, since the coupon of a floating rate debt instrument adjusts with movements in the risk-free rate.
2. *The overall level of credit spreads (credit risk premium) in the market increases.* In times of broad financial distress or economic uncertainty, such as during the GFC, investors require a higher return (credit spread) for the same credit risk. Prices must decrease so that the resultant yield reflects increased risk aversion.
3. *The company's idiosyncratic risk increases.* If a company underperforms expectations, the probability of default has increased, and investors require a higher return. This is accomplished via a decrease in the prices of the company's debt instruments.

FIGURE 3.6 Reasons for Debt to Trade Down in Price

The inverse of the scenarios outlined above applies as well. A decrease in the risk-free rate, market spread, or issuer risk reduces the yield demanded by investors, and the price of the debt instrument increases with a corresponding decrease in yield.

CALCULATING THE PRICE OF A BOND WHEN THE REQUIRED YIELD CHANGES

Price Calculations

An Excel worksheet is the easiest way to calculate the trading level of debt instruments as their required yields change. Below is an example.

A company's performance has significantly deteriorated since it issued its 12% coupon bond, which has two years until maturity. Due to the higher risk of the bond, an investor requires a 19.53% yield.

As shown in Figure 3.7, the price that corresponds to a 19.53% yield can be calculated in Excel using either the "Price" or "PV" function.

	A	B
1	**Price using Excel's Price formula**	
2	Settlement Date	1/1/2023
3	Maturity Date	1/1/2025
4	Coupon	12%
5	Yield (What investors require to buy the bond)	19.530%
6	Redemption Price (amt paid at maturity)	100
7	Payment Frequency	2
8	Price	=Price(B2,B3,B4,B5,B6,B7)
9		
10	**Price using Excel's PV function**	
11		Cash Flows
12	Rate (Yield investors require to buy bond / 2)	9.765%
13	Nper (2 yrs until maturity x 2 pymts per yr)	4
14	Pmt (Coupon pymt / 2 = pymt made every 6-mos)	6
15	Redemption Price (amt paid at maturity)	100
16	Type (pymt coupon made at end of period)	-
17	Price	=-PV(B12,B13,B14,B15,B16)

FIGURE 3.7 Calculating Price Using "Price" and "PV" Functions in Excel

The bond would trade down to $88 based on the new required yield. If you refer back to Figure 3.5, you will see that the yield and price match the outcome here; the difference is that the earlier example started with a price, which was used to calculate yield, while this example starts with yield and backs into price.

Bond Analytics/Duration

Fixed-income investing may incorporate complex analytics and modeling, including concepts such as Macaulay duration, modified duration, gamma, valuation of embedded options, and convexity. Most of this higher-end analysis is more relevant to higher-quality securities, such as investment grade corporate bonds, asset-backed securities, and Treasuries, than for leveraged credit investments. However, duration is a critical concept in all fixed income markets. As a general rule, for every 1% increase or decrease in interest rates, a bond's price will change approximately 1% in the opposite direction for every year of duration. For example, if a bond has a duration of four years and interest rates increase by 1%, the bond's price will decline by approximately 4%. In its simplest terms, duration is how long it takes, in years, for an investor to be repaid a bond's price by the bond's total cash flows (coupon and principal). The duration of a bond is primarily driven by its maturity (the longer, the higher the duration) and coupon (the higher, the lower the duration—because more of the total cash flows from the bond are received up front). While duration can be calculated manually, the easiest way to find the duration of a bond is using the YAS screen on Bloomberg.

For those interested in a comprehensive overview of all fixed-income markets, of which leveraged credit is a small part, and complex bond analytics, *The Handbook of Fixed Income Securities* by Frank Fabozzi provides a deep dive into the valuation, modeling, and forecasting techniques used for debt instruments.

TRADING LEVELS: PRICE, YIELD, AND SPREAD

Price, yield, and spread can all express the trading level of a debt instrument. Let's go back to the Excel example used to calculate yield (Figure 3.5). When the analyst was evaluating the bond, the two-year Treasury had a yield of 3.5%. Figure 3.8 summarizes three ways to describe the trading level of the bond.

- The bond is trading at a price of $88.
- The bond is trading at a yield of 19.53%.
- The bond is trading at a 1,603 bps spread over Treasuries.[4]

FIGURE 3.8 Measures Used to Describe Bond Valuation

TRADING LINGO FOR SECONDARY TRADES

Credit traders at intermediary banks match buyers and sellers. If they quote "96," the loan trades at 96% of face value (e.g., an amount of $1 million face value in bonds trades for $960,000).

Traders "make markets," meaning they give investors a price at which they are willing to buy the debt instrument (bid price) as well as a price at which they are willing to sell the debt (ask, or offer, price). Figure 3.9 summarizes a trader's quote of 94/96 2x3. The bid price is $94, the ask, or offer, price is $96, and the 2x3 represents the size of both the bid and offer (i.e., the trader would buy $2 million face value of the loan at $94 and would sell you up to $3 million face value of the loan at $96). If you want to sell the loan to the trader at $94, the market convention is to tell the trader you will "hit the bid." Conversely, if you want to buy the loan from the trader at $96, you tell the trader you will "lift the offer." The bid price is always lower than the offer price because the trader needs to be compensated for his role in the transaction (referred to as "making a spread"). In times of market volatility, bid-ask spreads increase to provide incremental compensation to the intermediary trader for the increase in risk aversion, which might leave him stuck with bonds he cannot sell. In the example above, the bid-ask spread is $2 (the difference between $94 and $96).

[4]While I have included the spread to illustrate the example, in practice bonds and loans trading at a significantly discounted dollar price (< 90% of face) and/or very high implied spread (> 1,000 bps) are rarely quoted in spread terms. Spread conventions are largely used for bonds and loans trading at prices reasonably close to par and spreads below +1,000.

Term	Definition	Example
Bid price	The price at which the investor can sell the debt to the trader	Quote of $94/$96 2x3: $94 is the bid price
Ask, or offer, price	The price at which the investor can buy the debt from the trader	Quote of $94/$96 2x3: $96 is the ask/offer price
Hit the bid	When an investor sells at the trader's bid price	Quote of $94/$96 2x3: Investor sells $2 million at $94
Lift the offer	When an investor buys at the trader's offer price	Quote of $94/$96 2x3: Investor buys $3 million at $96
Bid-ask spread	Difference between the trader's bid and ask/offer price	Quote of $94/$96 2x3: $2 is the bid-ask spread

FIGURE 3.8 Terminology for Secondary Trades

US bond prices are typically quoted as "clean" prices, meaning they do not include accrued interest. As a result, the trader's offer price is not the total cash outlay for the bond, as you are also responsible for compensating the seller for any accrued interest. In the example above, if the bond coupon is 6% paid semiannually, and you buy the bond three months before its next coupon payment, your total cash outlay is:

96% × $3 million = $2.88 million

Plus: 6% divided by 4 (i.e., one quarter of interest) × $3 million = $45,000

Total cash outlay = $2.925 million

Unlike the US market, in Europe traders quote bond prices "dirty," which includes accrued interest. So in Europe, the above bond would be quoted "dirty" at $97.50. The quote includes the accrued interest cost.

Another pricing convention is for the bonds of very distressed companies to trade "flat," that is, without expectation that the buyer will pay accrued interest, or the seller will receive it. Bonds are quoted flat when the market believes a bankruptcy filing is imminent and additional coupon payments are unlikely.

INVESTMENT CONCEPTS

Risk-Adjusted Return

Credit analysis involves analyzing companies to determine their risk profiles. Debt investors define risk by the probability the company will experience a payment default (i.e., the company cannot pay its interest or principal when due) and the severity of loss in the event of a default, also referred to as loss given default (LGD), which is an estimate of how much of the investment will be lost if the company defaults. The inverse of LGD is recovery, that is, what the investor can expect to recover in a default scenario, which is discussed in detail in the distressed section.

Relative value analysis compares the expected returns of corporate debt investments with a similar risk profile. The focus is on "risk-adjusted return" rather than absolute return. For instance, a debt instrument trading at a 10% yield is not necessarily a better investment than another at 8% if the latter investment has a lower risk profile. A critical component of credit analysis is making good risk-adjusted recommendations. This concept will be explored further in Chapter 13.

Expressing a Negative View by Shorting

If you believe the market underestimates the risk associated with a company, you can express your negative investment view by *shorting* the company's equity or bonds (loans cannot be sold short). Selling short, or shorting, a stock or bond means betting its price will go down.

The steps in short-selling shares and bonds are outlined in Figure 3.10.

- Borrow the security from a broker-dealer.
- Sell the borrowed security at the current market price.
- Pay dividends (if an equity short) or coupons (if a bond short) that the company makes during that period.
- Close the short sale by buying the shares or bonds to replace the borrowed ones.

FIGURE 3.10 Short Selling Process

For a short to be profitable, the price of the shorted security must have decreased more than any dividends or coupons paid. A "synthetic" short of a bond can also be created by purchasing a credit default swap (CDS), as discussed in Chapter 18.

Alpha versus Beta

At the portfolio level, investors disaggregate returns into beta and alpha components. Beta refers to the return of the overall credit market, and alpha refers to the return above the market. Any return above an investor's benchmark or index return is alpha.

Alpha can be generated in several ways but typically arises from some "edge," (i.e., an advantage over other investors) such as superior credit analysis or differentiated portfolio construction. Active investment managers attempt to generate alpha and charge fees for their stated ability to do this. However, many active investment managers do not consistently generate alpha and thus do not justify their fees; this is one reason for the shift to "passive" investment strategies over the last decade. Passive strategies promise only beta by mirroring the composition of the reference market. For example, a passive high yield bond fund seeks to replicate the return of a high yield bond index. One of the goals of this book is to impart the skills needed to create alpha in credit portfolios.

CHAPTER CONCLUSION

While some of the terminology in this chapter might sound like a foreign language, it will become second nature throughout the course of your credit investing career.

CHAPTER 4

A Primer on Leveraged Buyouts (LBOs)

Since the inception of the so-called junk bond market in the 1980s, LBOs and leveraged credit have gone hand in hand. As a large portion of the leveraged finance market is driven by LBO activity, it is critical to understand this financial construct.

WHAT IS AN LBO?

An LBO is the acquisition of a company by a private equity (PE) firm using a significant amount of debt relative to equity. As with most areas of finance, LBOs have their own set of terminology, which Figure 4.1 summarizes.

Key Term	Meaning
1. Financial sponsor, sponsor, or financial buyer	1. PE firm acquiring the company
2. The target	2. The company being acquired
3. LBO	3. The acquisition or purchase of the target
4. Sponsor financing or acquisition financing	4. The debt raised to fund the LBO
5. Portfolio company	5. A company acquired by a PE fund

FIGURE 4.1 Key Terminology

The amount of debt used will depend on the riskiness/volatility of the company being bought and the state of the debt markets at the time of the acquisition. While debt is used to fund 60%–75% of a typical LBO purchase price, I have been involved in transactions where the amount of debt was as low as 40% and as high as 90%.

Since LBOs have substantial debt, strong and predictable cash flow to service this debt was historically viewed as critical to the success of an LBO. Figure 4.2 lists the traditional characteristics of a strong LBO candidate.

- Leading and defensible market position
- Non-cyclical and stable customer demand
- Limited capital requirements (capital expenditures, or "capex," and working capital)
- Strong tangible asset base
- Proven management team

FIGURE 4.2 Traditional Characteristics of a Strong LBO Candidate

However, the LBO industry has evolved since its early days, and the old rules no longer apply. Today's PE sponsors will consider buying any company they think is attractively valued and will use more equity as needed to make those acquisitions. Some PE funds now specialize in acquiring companies that would not fit traditional LBO criteria. For instance, tech-focused LBO firms such as Thoma Bravo and Francisco Partners buy growth companies that are burning cash.

The credit markets have also evolved to include debt financing options with lower cash servicing requirements and fewer borrower restrictions, such as:

- Paid-in-kind (PIK) coupons that allow the borrower to defer cash interest payments by paying with new debt rather than cash, thus preserving liquidity;
- Covenant-light ("cov-lite") loans, which do not require maintenance of financial ratios such as leverage and coverage; and
- Recurring revenue loans, where the lender focuses on revenue rather than cash flow.

Chapters 5, 9, and 12 will discuss these and other debt structures in detail.

HOW DOES A PE FUND GENERATE RETURNS FOR ITS INVESTORS?

A PE firm raises multiple funds to make investments. Each fund typically has a 10-year life. The PE firm acquires companies in the first four to six years (the investment period). During the last four to six years, it monetizes those investments (the harvest period).

In the investment period, the PE sponsor has the goals summarized in Figure 4.3.

1. Identifying/sourcing investment opportunities
   - Auctions
   - Proprietary deals
2. Negotiating the acquisition
3. Financing the debt component and closing the deal

FIGURE 4.3 PE Goals during the Investment Period

1. Identifying/sourcing investment opportunities (i.e., potential acquisition targets) takes place in two ways:
   - *Participating in auctions.* In an auction, the owner of the company hires an investment bank (IB) to act as the seller's advisor (sell-side advisor). The job of the IB is to get the highest price for the business. As discussed below, a good IB creates a competitive process to sell the business.
   - *Sourcing proprietary deals.* These are less competitive than auctions. Often the PE firm approaches the owners of the target directly and builds a relationship over time, sometimes for years. In most instances, these are smaller, privately held and/or family-owned businesses whose owners do not have a fiduciary duty to other shareholders to maximize price. The existing owner often rolls a significant portion of their current equity into the deal and remains a meaningful but minority owner of the LBO'd business. Since proprietary deals are less competitive, the sponsor can typically buy the company at a lower price

than at auction. However, it is a much more time-consuming process generally limited to smaller, privately held companies.

2. Negotiating the acquisition with the seller to get the best possible terms is critical to deal success.
3. Financing the debt component of the deal involves discussions with bankers and credit investors regarding pricing and structure. Analysis of the types of debt instruments used in LBOs is the focus of this book. Below we will discuss the financing of an LBO in more detail.

After making an acquisition, the sponsor focuses on harvesting in two ways, summarized in Figure 4.4.

1. Improving the company
   - Upgrading management and the board
   - Executing operational improvements
   - Pursuing growth initiatives
2. Returning capital to investors
   - Dividend recapitalizations
   - Sale of the business
   - Initial public offering and subsequent secondary share sales

FIGURE 4.4 PE Goals during Harvest Period

1. Improving the company typically includes one or more of the following:
   - *Upgrading management and the board of the company.* The sponsor puts a new board of directors in place to ensure better business oversight. In addition, the sponsor often replaces some or all of the management team.
   - *Executing operational improvements*, including creating a culture of cost discipline (i.e., removing the "fat"). Many PE firms draw on a network of operating partners and consultants during due diligence to identify business improvement opportunities. Once the acquisition is completed, these experts are often embedded in the company to execute these operational improvements.
   - *Pursuing growth initiatives*, including "tuck in" acquisitions (that is, small acquisitions of related businesses), with a focus on maximizing returns on all investments made.
2. Returning capital to investors usually begins three to seven years from the acquisition date, typically in one of three ways:
   - *Dividend recapitalization (recap).* If the company has generated cash flow during the harvest period and used it to pay down debt, it might re-lever the balance sheet (i.e., issue new debt) and use those debt proceeds to pay a dividend to the sponsor. This transaction, referred to as a dividend recap, allows a partial return of cash before fully monetizing the investment.
   - *Sale of the business.* The PE sponsor can hire an IB to market and sell the business to another financial buyer (PE fund) or a strategic buyer (e.g., a competitor).
   - *Initial public offering (IPO) and subsequent secondary share sales.* If the business is large enough, the sponsor might sell shares to the public on a listed exchange such as the NYSE or NASDAQ.

WHAT IS A SELL-SIDE M&A PROCESS?

Figure 4.5 summarizes the typical steps in the M&A process.

1. The target selects a sell-side advisor.
2. The investment bank performs due diligence, including a preliminary valuation of the business.
3. The investment bank in consultation with the company identifies a buyer universe.
4. The bank prepares and distributes marketing materials to the buyer universe.
5. The bank runs the auction.
6. The target and its advisor pick a winner.
7. The acquisition closes.

FIGURE 4.5 The M&A Process

1. The target selects a sell-side advisor.

The selling company hires an investment bank (sell-side advisor), often after considering multiple banks for the job during a process referred to as a bake-off, in which banks pitch for the engagement. The ultimate choice is usually a function of three criteria:

(i) Expertise, industry knowledge, and contacts to create the most competitive dynamic and get the best price;
(ii) Fees charged to the seller; and
(iii) Overall firm relationships.

2. The investment bank performs due diligence, including a preliminary valuation of the business.

Once the target hires a sell-side advisor, the IB performs due diligence to ensure the business is marketable. The bank has both legal and reputational risk if it sells a company relying on false or misleading information provided by management. In addition, the bank performs valuation analysis to determine a reasonable range of prices. Chapter 11 covers corporate valuation methods.

3. The investment bank in consultation with the company identifies a buyer universe.

The potential buyer universe typically includes strategic and financial buyers. The more inclusive the universe, the more likely the process will achieve the highest price. However, in some cases, the seller might prefer a more targeted approach due to confidentiality concerns (for example, the seller might be unwilling to disclose proprietary information to a competitor).

4. The bank prepares and distributes marketing materials to the buyer universe.

The marketing process starts with a teaser describing the business without confidential information. Potential buyers interested in doing due diligence will sign a confidentiality agreement (CA), also referred to as a nondisclosure agreement (NDA), to receive a complete set of marketing materials referred to as a confidential information memorandum (CIM). The CIM usually includes the following:

(i) Industry overview;
(ii) Company overview, including strategy;
(iii) Historical financial information including audited financial statements;
(iv) Financial forecast/projections; and
(v) Investment considerations.

5. The bank runs the auction.

After parties that received the CIM reconfirm their interest in pursuing the acquisition, they receive access to an online data room with detailed information needed to make a bid such as critical contracts, outstanding litigation, customer and supplier information, third-party reports such as industry analysis, and quality of earnings reports.

After initial due diligence and review of the CIM, potential acquirers submit nonbinding bids for the company. The IB then selects buyers to invite to the second round of bidding, which includes management meetings and site visits. The bank creates as much competitive tension as possible to maximize bid prices; there are multiple check-ins with buyers to reconfirm or update their nonbinding bids. The bank usually spends the most time with a small subset of the two to five bidders it believes will submit the highest price and actually close the deal. After some period, any party still in the bidding will be asked for a final bid, including a markup of the purchase and sale agreement, the legal document needed to close the transaction.

6. The target and its advisor pick a winner.

The company and IB must "pick a horse" at this point, based on multiple considerations including:

(i) Purchase price;
(ii) Purchase price consideration (i.e., type of currency: cash, stock, take back notes/seller financing, contingent payouts based on performance, etc.);
(iii) Conditions to close: is the buyer ready to close, or are there due diligence outs, material adverse change (MAC) clauses, anti-trust or other regulatory approvals, financing contingencies, shareholder approval, etc.?
(iv) Other terms, including (a) seller representations (reps) and warranties and (b) seller indemnifications:
   (a) Reps and warranties are the seller's explicit confirmation in the purchase and sale agreement of certain material facts. If the information is not valid, the buyer could walk from the deal and, in certain situations, sue the seller for damages (see indemnification below). The broader the information covered by the reps and warranties, the more risk for the seller. For instance, there could be knowledge-based reps and warranties, such as the seller having no knowledge of potential litigation or environmental issues, which protect the buyer from the omission of a material known liability in the CIM or data room.

(b) A seller indemnification clause outlines the monetary compensation to which the buyer is entitled for any losses or damages suffered from breach of a rep and warranty. A closing document with no or very limited seller indemnifications is much better for the seller than one with many.

7. The acquisition closes.

Once the company picks the winning bid, the IB closes the deal as soon as possible. If there are any conditions to closing, the bank also tries to keep the losing bidders "warm" as a backup.

HOW DO PE SPONSORS MAKE MONEY?

Figure 4.6 depicts a typical PE fund structure. The owners of the PE firm are the firm's general partners (GPs). The GPs raise capital to invest in LBOs from a combination of high-net-worth individuals and institutions such as endowments and pension funds, referred to as limited partners (LPs). The PE fund has access to the LPs' "committed capital" during the investment period. This committed capital is the equity portion of the LBO and is in place before the transaction occurs. Since the equity component of an LBO financing is already in place, once a deal is struck the PE fund only has to raise the debt capital to fund the LBO. A company acquired by a PE fund is referred to as a portfolio company.

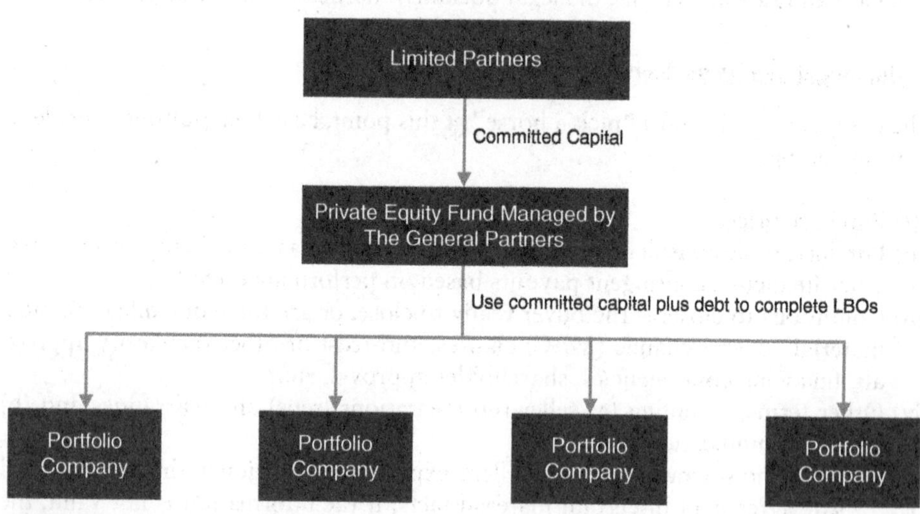

FIGURE 4.6 PE Fund Structure

PE funds typically target a 20%+ IRR and a 2.0x+ MOIC to their investors or limited partners (LPs). Refer back to Chapter 3 for a primer on IRR and MOIC.

The PE firm makes money by charging its LPs management fees and "carried interest."

- Management fees are usually in the range of 1.5%–2.0% of LPs' committed capital.
- Carried interest is the sharing of deal profits (i.e., the returns generated by the fund) between the fund's GPs and LPs. Once the LPs have recouped their initial investment, all profits are shared; usually 15%–20% of the profits go to the PE firm and the remainder to the LPs.[1]

This arrangement can be highly lucrative to successful PE firms. Let's use the example of a fund with, on average, $10 billion of investments charging two and twenty, meaning a 2% management fee and 20% carried interest. As shown in Figure 4.7, if this fund's investments yield an 18% net annualized return to its LPs, the GP (i.e., the PE firm) earns $560 million per year before expenses.

	In $ Millions
Average committed capital	$10,000
× Annual management fee	2.0%
Annual management fee	$200
Amount of investments	$10,000
× Annual IRR of those investments	18.0%
Profits from the investments	1,800
GP's share of the profits	20%
Carried interest per year	$360
Revenues to GP before expenses (mgmt. fee + carried interest)	**$560**

FIGURE 4.7 General Partner's Profits

In addition to management fees and carried interest charged to LPs, many PE firms charge their portfolio companies an annual management fee, transaction fees, and other miscellaneous fees. Furthermore, PE funds receive favorable tax treatment due to the carried interest tax loophole. The loophole allows for PE fund income generated by carried interest to be taxed at the lower capital gains rate.[2]

HOW ARE LBOs FINANCED?

A broad array of different types of debt and equity instruments can fund an LBO. Figure 4.8 breaks these into six categories based on their relative risk. Differences among these financing options will be discussed in detail in future chapters.

[1] Most funds need to meet a hurdle rate before they can earn carried interest.

[2] In 2017 the tax law changed so only investments held for at least three years enjoy the preferential capital gains treatment of carried interest. However, the change had little impact since most PE funds hold their investments for over three years.

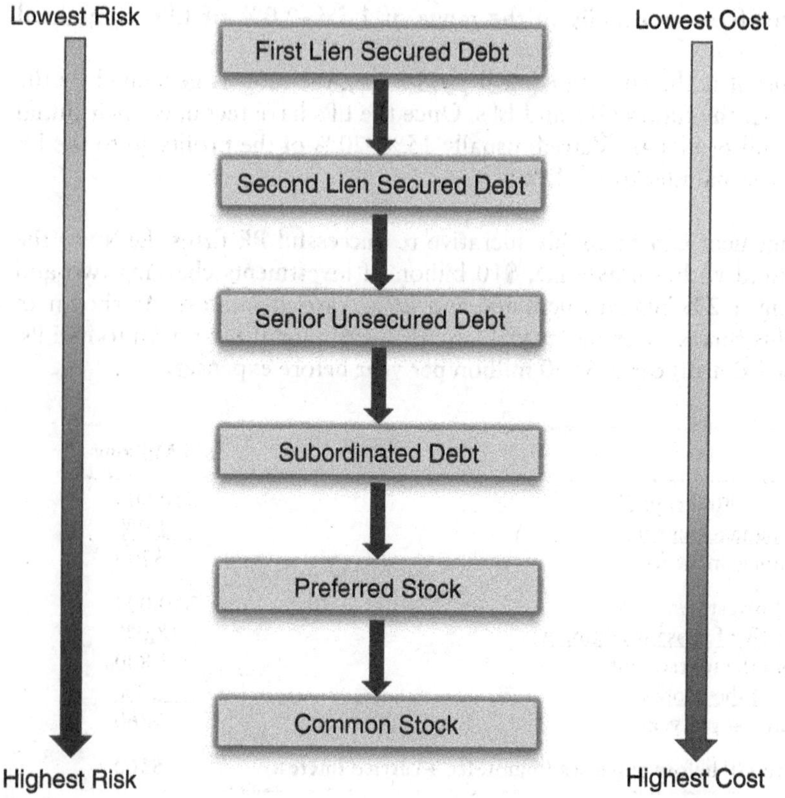

FIGURE 4.8 Types of Financing Used in LBO Transactions

Since the PE fund uses committed capital from its LPs to fund the equity component of an LBO,[3] the sponsor only needs to raise the debt component of the bid. The terms of this debt are critically important to the economics and ultimate success of any LBO. The PE sponsor must know how much the debt will cost (that is, what interest rate the target company will have to pay) to determine whether the deal math works. High interest rates on the loans and bonds used to finance a transaction can crowd out the returns to the equity, while onerous restrictions in the debt indentures (discussed in detail in Chapter 12) can prevent the company from making important investments or paying dividends to its sponsors.

As discussed in Chapter 1, there are several sources of debt financing, the two largest of which are:

1. The secured loan market:
   - Broadly syndicated loans (BSLs); and
   - Private credit.
2. The high yield bond market.

[3]If the equity check is too big for the PE fund, it might bring in other PE funds or passive coinvestors, sometimes referred to as "sidecar" investors.

The first step for the sponsor is to decide between the BSL and the private credit market. This usually involves a trade-off between price and structure versus speed and certainty. The private debt market tends to be more expensive with more restrictive terms than the BSL market. But since private debt funds predominantly use their own balance sheets, they can fully commit to a deal, providing certainty to the borrower. These firms are also willing to lend at a higher leverage multiple than traditional banks, which are regulatorily disincentivized from making loans to companies with leverage greater than 6x Debt/EBITDA. And for all but the largest deals, the private loan market can finance the whole transaction, thus removing the need for a high-yield bond component. For these reasons, as of the writing of this book, private credit firms continue to gain market share at the expense of the BSL and high yield bond markets (see Figure 4.9).

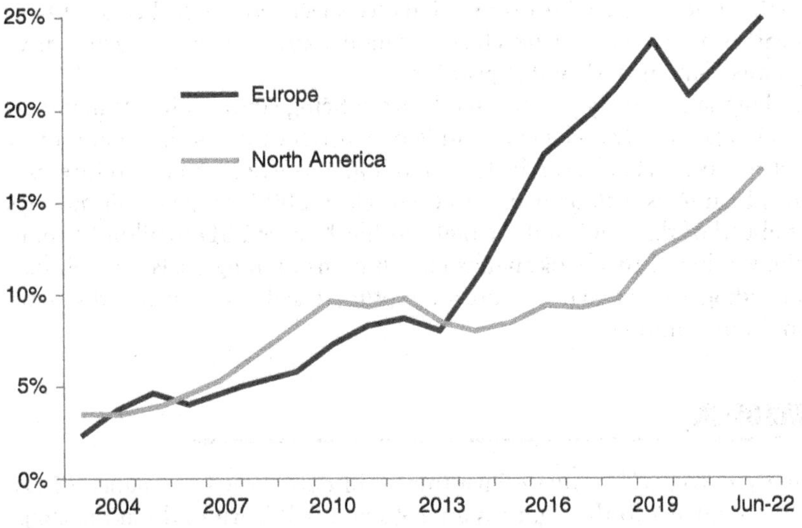

FIGURE 4.9 Private Credit as a Share of Leveraged Finance
Courtesy J.P. Morgan Chase & Co., Copyright 2023

If the PE firm plans to use the BSL and high-yield bond markets, raising debt will take more time and have less certainty of completion. Typically, the sponsor will get a "market read" from an investment bank. The sponsor's bank will use comparable trading levels on other debt and informal conversations with significant key investors to determine a clearing level along with the necessary terms (structure, covenants, etc.) for the new debt issues. But the loan and bond issues can't go to market or price until the deal to buy the target company is struck—which means that the pricing offered by the banks is only an estimate.

The lead banks present two categories of financings for LBOs:

1. *Best effort.* If the banking syndicate cannot sell the loan or bond issue at the "market read" levels, the deal might be re-struck with different pricing and terms.

2. *Fully underwritten or "bought" deal.* The lead bank or consortium of banks agrees to make the loans or buy the bonds—that is, fund them and keep them on their balance sheets—if they cannot place them in the market. However, even a fully unwritten deal seldom includes actual pricing and terms. In most cases, the banks have "flex" language, meaning they can change the terms of the agreement up to a ceiling ("cap") interest rate. For instance, the banking syndicate might give a market read of a coupon of SOFR + 625 bps with 150 bps of flex, meaning if they can't syndicate the loan, the coupon can increase up to SOFR + 775 bps.

If the banks cannot sell the debt at a rate lower than the cap, they are on the hook to fund the deal themselves—a situation referred to as a "hung deal." Due to regulatory-driven carrying costs and risk management, banks generally seek to move exposure to highly leveraged credits off their balance sheets once a deal closes. Owning a "hung deal" is not part of a bank's business model and is an extremely negative event for any bank that ends up in this position.

While flex language usually protects banks from being stuck with a deal, if market conditions change rapidly and meaningfully between the time of the commitment letter and the deal closing, banks can be forced to hold more debt, and therefore risk, than they want. Examples include many deals struck in 2007, as the credit markets began to shut ahead of the GFC, and the high-profile Twitter LBO by Elon Musk in 2022. As of the writing of this book, banks have billions in hung deals on their balance sheets, including Twitter, that they are attempting to sell, typically at a discount, as market conditions improve.

CHAPTER CONCLUSION

As a credit analyst, you will evaluate investments in debt issued to finance LBOs. The "L" in LBO is subject to the rigorous analysis you will learn to do in the chapters ahead. LBO-related debt is risky—but that is where the opportunity lies. As you develop your credit analysis skills, you will learn to differentiate between peak-market LBOs (such as Twitter) with substantial downside and good LBO financings with attractive risk-reward profiles (such as the 2006 LBO of HCA, which will be discussed in Chapter 13).

PART Two

The Seven-Step Process of Evaluating a Debt Investment

CHAPTER 5

Step 1 of the Credit Analysis Process: Sources and Uses

Let's assume you get a job at a credit hedge fund. On your first day, your boss says XYZ Company is in the market for debt financing and forwards you all the information she has on the company. She asks you to lay out your thoughts so that you can discuss it next week. While this may sound overwhelming, it is the type of assignment you will likely get early in your career.

Rather than hyperventilate at the enormity of your task, let's take Mark Twain's advice: "The secret of getting ahead is getting started. The secret of getting started is breaking your complex, overwhelming tasks into small, manageable tasks and starting on the first one." Section II of this book breaks credit analysis into seven steps, with each step containing smaller sub-steps. While I have laid out the seven steps sequentially below in Figure 5.1, the process is iterative rather than purely linear. For example, when we analyze the company's strategy (step 2), we will need to incorporate financial statement analysis (step 3) to assess if the strategy has worked in the past. The following chapters will take you through the seven steps in granular detail.

The reason for beginning with sources and uses is that many credit investment opportunities come via the new issue or primary market. This is different from stocks, which are rarely "new issues," since an initial public offering (IPO) takes place only once, and secondary/follow-on equity offerings are rare. In contrast, bonds and loans are often analyzed concurrently with being issued—which means that your credit analysis is effectively a decision on whether to lend money to the company on current market terms.

New issues offer several advantages over secondary trades. They typically price at a discount to existing loans/bonds for a company with other debt outstanding. They also offer the opportunity to negotiate terms. Lastly, they provide an opportunity to purchase a large amount of debt at once that can be lacking in the secondary market.

Because it deals with the types of debt issued by companies, this chapter will introduce you to several capital structure concepts that we will cover in granular detail in Chapters 9 and 12. Don't worry if terms such as "secured loan," "senior unsecured bond," and "mezz debt" haven't gelled in your thinking by the time you finish this chapter—we will return to them later in the book. For the purposes of step one, the key learning objective is to create a sources and uses table, two examples of which are included at the end of the chapter, as a starting point for the intensive credit analysis that follows in Chapters 6–13.

Step 1	**Sources and Uses (only applicable to originations)** **(a) Why is the company seeking financing?** **(b) What are the proposed sources of capital to fund the financing need?**
Step 2	Qualitative Analysis (a) Industry analysis (b) Business strategy (c) Management assessment (d) ESG concerns
Step 3	Financial Statement Analysis (a) Profitability (b) Cash flow and liquidity (c) Capital structure
Step 4	Forecasting (a) Identification of key business drivers and assumptions (b) Development of base, upside, and downside cases
Step 5	Corporate Valuation (a) Comparable company analysis (b) Precedent transactions (M&A comps) (c) Discounted cash flow analysis (d) Liquidation analysis
Step 6	Structuring and Documentation (a) Economic points (b) Structure and collateral (c) Covenants
Step 7	Preparing an Investment Recommendation and Credit Committee Memo (a) Investment thesis and recommendation (b) Risks and mitigants (c) Relative value analysis

FIGURE 5.1 The Seven-Step Process of Evaluating a Debt Instrument

The first step in analyzing a new origination is to answer two questions up front:

(a) Why is the company seeking financing?
(b) What are the proposed sources of capital to fund the financing need?

WHY IS THE COMPANY SEEKING FINANCING?

Figure 5.2 outlines seven reasons companies might seek to access the credit markets.

1. To fund a leveraged buyout (LBO)
2. To fund seasonal inventory fluctuations
3. To fund growth (including purchases of property, plant and equipment [PP&E], referred to as capital expenditures, or capex)
4. To fund an acquisition
5. To fund shareholder-friendly initiatives, such as a share repurchase or dividend recapitalization
6. To fund operating losses, such as when a cyclical business hits a deep recession
7. To refinance existing debt as the company approaches the maturity date

FIGURE 5.2 Seven Primary Reasons a Company Issues Debt

WHAT ARE THE PROPOSED SOURCES OF CAPITAL TO FUND THE FINANCING NEED?

Figure 5.3 summarizes the most common types of debt instruments in order of seniority/security/safety from least risky (top) to most risky (bottom).

- Secured revolving credit facility
- Secured term loans (first lien, second lien, and unitranche)
- Senior unsecured high yield bonds[1]
- Subordinated, or mezzanine debt

FIGURE 5.3 Common Types of Debt Instruments

Below is a brief overview of each debt instrument. Chapters 9 and 12 will provide a deeper dive into capital structures and where each of these fits in.

REVOLVING CREDIT FACILITY

A secured revolving credit facility (also referred to as a revolver or RCF) allows the borrower to draw on the facility when the company needs cash, repay it when the company has excess cash, and redraw as needed. You can think of it as the company's credit card. Revolvers have floating rate coupons, indexed to an underlying "base rate" of interest (typically the Secured Overnight Financing Rate, SOFR). Unlike other types of debt, RCFs can be reborrowed, just like your credit card once you've paid off some of it.

Figure 5.4 outlines the three primary purposes of a revolver.

1. To fund seasonal working capital needs
2. To backstop letters of credit (LCs)
3. To serve as liquidity insurance

FIGURE 5.4 Three Primary Purposes of a Revolver

[1]While most high yield bonds are unsecured, some companies issue secured bonds, particularly when the bond market is more hospitable than the loan market. For simplicity we will refer to loans as secured and high yield bonds as unsecured when discussing sources and uses.

Fund Seasonal Working Capital Needs

The sales and profits of seasonal businesses experience regular and predictable fluctuations that recur annually. For example, the peak of most retailers' sales occurs in the fourth quarter during the holiday season, which includes Christmas, Hanukkah, Kwanzaa, and Festivus (for fans of the TV show *Seinfeld*). Leading up to the holiday season, retailers increase their inventory levels. This results in a short-term liquidity need; the inventory will be sold during the holiday season, but since retailers typically pay their suppliers before merchandise is sold, the temporary increase in inventory requires temporary funding. A revolver is the ideal instrument for this seasonal need. The company can borrow as seasonal inventory builds and repay the facility once the holiday season ends and the seasonal inventory is monetized. Revolvers typically have a maturity of three to seven years, so the company does not need to renegotiate the facility every year.

Backstop Letters of Credit (LCs)

A backstop LC creates a secondary source of funds in case the primary source is insufficient to meet current needs. For instance, a vendor might be unwilling to extend payment terms to a specific retailer due to concerns about its financial health, in which case the vendor might demand payment in advance or at the time of purchase ("cash on delivery," or COD, terms). Rather than accept these punitive financing terms, the retailer can offer the vendor a letter of credit (LC) from its revolving credit provider. The LC is an agreement in which the bank guarantees payment for the inventory. So if the retailer does not pay the vendor for the inventory, the bank pays instead. This eliminates the retailer's credit risk for the vendor, as the bank is on the hook if the company fails to pay. Any LC outstanding reduces the amount that the retailer can borrow from its revolver. In Chapter 8, we will review how to incorporate undrawn LCs into liquidity analysis using footnote disclosures.

Liquidity Insurance

In addition to funding seasonal working capital needs or acting as a backstop, a revolver also serves as backup liquidity. In Chapter 8, we will analyze a company's liquidity in detail, including the role of the revolving credit facility. For now, think of an undrawn revolver as a kind of insurance policy that provides access to capital in case of an unforeseen event.

Types of Revolvers

Revolvers for highly levered companies typically take one of two forms. The first is an asset-based loan (ABL), which has the lowest risk of impairment of any debt instrument. In the event of default, an ABL has priority over all other debt instruments, including any secured term loans, with respect to the company's most liquid assets: the working capital accounts. The maximum amount drawn on the revolver is limited by a borrowing base formula, which restricts borrowing to an amount typically less than the liquidation value of the company's inventory and receivables. Even if the company fails and must liquidate, the ABL should be covered—that is, lenders will receive 100 cents on the dollar back. A typical borrowing base formula would limit ABL borrowing to 90% of eligible (no more than 30 days past due) receivables and 85% of the orderly liquidation value (OLV) of the company's inventory.

The second type of revolver is a facility pari passu with the secured term loans. "Pari passu" is a Latin term that means "without partiality" or "at an equal rate or pace." This type of revolver has more impairment risk than an ABL because it shares collateral with the term loan versus having a first lien on the liquid working capital assets, and there is no borrowing base formula restricting the maximum amount outstanding to a percentage of liquid working capital assets (although every revolver has a contractual maximum capacity).

TERM LOANS

Moving down the capital structure from the revolver, a secured term loan is senior debt with a lien on some or all of the borrower's assets. Term loans are also floating-rate instruments. As explained above, they are riskier than ABLs and revolvers with a senior lien and often cannot be fully repaid by the liquidation value of their collateral.

Since term loan lenders are effectively lending against the "franchise value" or cash flow generation potential of the underlying business, term loan lending is also known as cash flow lending.

Secured term loans are described based on their priority of repayment (first lien, second lien, and so forth). The lower the priority of repayment, the riskier the loan and the higher the rate of return demanded by the investor. If a company cannot repay all its debt, the first lien debt will have priority—that is, will be repaid in full before the second lien. Unitranche term loans combine first and second lien debt into one facility with a single blended interest rate.

HIGH YIELD BONDS AND MEZZANINE ("MEZZ") DEBT

High yield bonds are typically unsecured and thus higher risk than revolvers and term loan facilities because secured debt has a higher priority claim than unsecured debt on the value of the collateral in bankruptcy.

Mezzanine debt is the most junior, and therefore the riskiest type of debt. It is often contractually and/or structurally subordinated to all other debt. In Chapter 17, we will discuss the mechanics of contractual and structural subordination. Given the higher risk of impairment relative to other forms of debt, mezzanine lenders require the highest yield in the capital structure. Sometimes they also receive equity or warrants packaged with this debt instrument.

In Part III of the book, we will work through recovery analysis in bankruptcy to quantify the risks associated with each debt instrument.

SOURCES AND USES SECTION OF A CREDIT MEMO

If your firm is considering investing in a new loan or bond, the sources and uses table is the first section of your credit committee memo. In Chapter 13, "Step 7 of the Credit Analysis Process: Preparing an Investment Recommendation and Credit

Committee Memo," I have included two sample memos based on actual transactions. Figures 5.5 and 5.6 are the sources and uses tables for these two transactions, which are incorporated into each memo.

Sources		Uses	
New $20MM revolver	0.0	Refinance existing secured debt	188.7
New secured term loan	200.0	Est. lender fees	5.0
		Other transaction fees & expenses	4.5
		Cash to balance sheet	1.8
Total sources	200.0	**Total uses**	200.0

FIGURE 5.5 Sources and Uses for VCC Loan Origination (in $ millions)

Sources		Uses	
$2 billion ABL facility	1,750	Cash purchase price	21,279
$2 billion revolving credit facility	188	Refinance existing bank debt	3,275
Senior secured term loan A	2,750	Rollover of existing debt[a]	7,702
Senior secured term loan B	8,800	Cash on balance sheet	141
Euro term loan	1,250	Transaction fees/expenses	743
Legacy secured debt[a]	230		
2nd Lien-cash-pay notes	4,200		
2nd Lien PIK toggle notes	1,500		
Legacy unsecured notes[a]	7,472		
Contributed equity	5,000		
Total sources	33,140	**Total uses**	33,140

[a]HCA's LBO was partially financed by $7.7 billion in debt outstanding at the time of the LBO that was kept in place (rolled over) because it did not have protective covenants.

FIGURE 5.6 Sources and Uses for HCA LBO (in $ millions)

The first transaction, VCC, is an example of a private loan origination, where the proceeds of the loan were used to refinance existing debt.

The second transaction, HCA, is an example of an LBO financing. In this example, a consortium of private equity sponsors (Bain Capital, KKR, and Merrill Lynch Global Private Equity) is acquiring HCA for $33 billion.

CHAPTER CONCLUSION

While the credit analysis outlined in the next several chapters will be the same whether you're evaluating a new issue or a secondary trade, creating a sources and uses table is unique to originations. It is a mechanical, straightforward process that sets the stage by outlining the debt instruments you will have the chance to evaluate and recommend for purchase. The capital structure concepts you've started to master in this chapter will show up again in Chapter 9, where you will create a capital structure matrix that builds on the sources and uses table.

CHAPTER 6

Step 2 of the Credit Analysis Process: Qualitative Analysis

When evaluating a company for the first time, credit analysts often rush into quantitative analysis, such as financial statement review, modeling, and valuation. However, it is crucial to start by developing a qualitative, big-picture view of the industry, the business, management, and potential ESG concerns. Whether analyzing debt or equity, your research should start with assessing the industry dynamics and the company's basic business model—that is, qualitative analysis—as shown in Figure 6.1. Since debt investors do not have the same upside potential as equity investors, we tend to be most focused on identifying potential risks in our qualitative analysis.

Step 1	Sources and Uses (only applicable to originations) (a) Why is the company seeking financing? (b) What are the proposed sources of capital to fund the financing need?
Step 2	**Qualitative Analysis** **(a) Industry analysis** **(b) Business strategy** **(c) Management assessment** **(d) ESG concerns**
Step 3	Financial Statement Analysis (a) Profitability (b) Cash flow and liquidity (c) Capital structure
Step 4	Forecasting (a) Identification of key business drivers and assumptions (b) Development of base, upside, and downside cases
Step 5	Corporate Valuation (a) Comparable company analysis (b) Precedent transactions (M&A comps) (c) Discounted cash flow analysis (d) Liquidation analysis
Step 6	Structuring and Documentation (a) Economic points (b) Structure and collateral (c) Covenants
Step 7	Preparing an Investment Recommendation and Credit Committee Memo (a) Investment thesis and recommendation (b) Risks and mitigants (c) Relative value analysis

FIGURE 6.1 The Seven-Step Process of Evaluating a Debt Instrument

QUALITATIVE ANALYSIS—INDUSTRY AND BUSINESS RISK ANALYSIS

The first component of qualitative analysis is to identify industry and company-level risks that might result in a deterioration in cash flow and profitability. Once these risks are identified, you must determine the analyzability of each risk factor. Risk alone does not rule out an investment opportunity—but the more quantifiable and analyzable the risk, the more likely you can get comfortable with it.

Figure 6.2 lists eight common risks. While this list is not comprehensive, it is a good starting point. In Chapter 13, "Step 7 of the Credit Analysis Process: Preparing an Investment Recommendation and Credit Committee Memo," you will learn how to summarize this component of your analysis in the "key investment risks and mitigants" section of an investment committee memo.

- Secularly declining industry
- Adverse competitive dynamics
- Cyclicality
- Government regulation: the probability and impact of potential regulatory changes
- Customer concentration risk
- Product concentration risk
- Fad/fashion risk
- Commodity risk

FIGURE 6.2 Common Qualitative Risks

Let's discuss each of these eight risks.

SECULARLY DECLINING INDUSTRY

An industry in secular decline is shrinking due to new business models and competitive threats. Some examples of secularly declining industries are:

- Print newspaper publishing (disintermediation by online news delivery models);
- Movie theaters (disintermediation by streaming video);
- Department stores (disintermediation by e-commerce); and
- Wireline telecommunications (disintermediation by wireless).

Credit analysts need to be particularly comfortable analyzing companies and industries in secular decline, since the high yield bond and leveraged loan markets tend to have a disproportionate number of them. Many "fallen angels" (formerly investment grade–rated companies) get downgraded to high yield due to deteriorating industry dynamics.

Some critical areas of due diligence are:

1. Understanding and quantifying the industry's annual decline rate and developing a view on whether the revenue of the company you are evaluating will decline in line with, faster, or more slowly than its peer group.
2. Determining the percentage of fixed versus variable costs. The greater the proportion of fixed costs, the higher the risk to cash flow since it is difficult to cut fixed costs as sales decline.

3. Quantifying the minimum amount of capex needed.
4. Evaluating management's strategy (if any) to address shrinking sales (e.g., cost-cutting).

These due diligence points will inform step four, forecasting, in which you will model different decline assumptions.

While investing in a company's debt in secular decline is risky, it can offer attractive returns. For example, in 2009, Silver Point was approached by Blockbuster's investment bank to refinance debt that was maturing later that year. Blockbuster was the largest movie rental retailer at the time—an industry in secular decline, as new entrants such as Netflix were reinventing the business model. After performing the analysis outlined in this book, we believed that if management froze new store openings, cut capex to the bare minimum, and reduced costs such as advertising, it would produce a tremendous amount of cash flow. Furthermore, we estimated that the decline in movie rentals would take place over many years rather than falling off a cliff, as streaming technology was very early stage.

Given Blockbuster's declining business, lenders needed to be compensated appropriately. As a result, Blockbuster entered into a $250 million loan that included a $25MM up-front fee and a 13.25% coupon. In addition, the loan was structured with a short-dated maturity and required amortization (repayment) over the loan's life to mitigate risk. The resulting loan was done at a massive premium to the average 7%–10% returns in the leveraged loan market. While its accelerating business deterioration eventually forced Blockbuster to liquidate, the loan's tight structure and heavy amortization resulted in payoff in full before the company's demise.

ADVERSE COMPETITIVE DYNAMIC

It may seem obvious, but it bears repeating: the more competitive an industry is, the riskier the investment. Figure 6.3 classifies industries based on the level of competition.

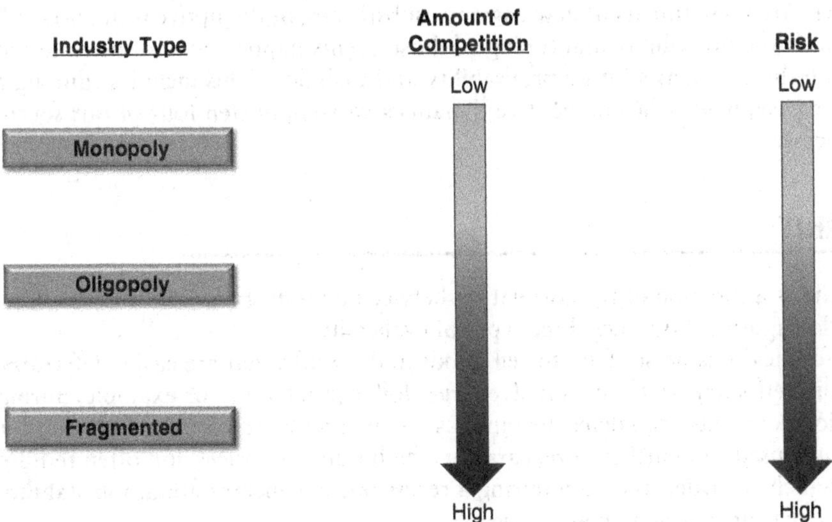

FIGURE 6.3 Industry Classification by Level of Competition and Risk

Monopoly: In a monopoly, only one company provides the good or service. There is no competition. There are virtually no true monopolies in the US; however, some industries come close. For example, Luxottica owns almost all the major brands of sunglasses. Since the company maintains multiple names and brands, this creates the illusion of variety for the consumer. Luxottica produces more than 80 percent of worldwide eyewear. More recently Ticketmaster's parent company, Live Nation, has been under investigation for exhibiting monopolistic powers.

Oligopoly: In an oligopoly, sustainable barriers to entry exist, allowing a few players to dominate. These industries tend to be price-rational (i.e., they do not engage in price wars). The computer operating software industry is an oligopoly: Apple, Windows (Microsoft), and Linux open-source command almost 100% of the global market. Another example is credit cards: Master Card and Visa facilitate more than 75% of the country's credit card transactions. Some would argue this oligopoly looks more like a monopoly, as evidenced by staggering profit margins of around 50%, making Master Card and Visa two of the most consistently profitable companies in the world.

Fragmented: A fragmented industry has many competitors. When analyzing a company in a fragmented industry, it is crucial to focus on market share, cost to produce relative to competitors, and potential synergies if combined with other players. It is not uncommon for fragmented industries to consolidate; if the industry experiences declining sales, weaker players fail and liquidate, and stronger competitors merge or acquire one another. Take the recycled board industry. Before 2017, the sector had approximately 10 prominent players and many small mom-and-pop competitors. Recycled board manufacturing has high fixed costs, and its products are highly commoditized, making it vulnerable to exogenous shocks. In 2017, a significant market dislocation driven by the combination of record high input prices and a decrease in demand resulted in multiple bankruptcies and restructurings. As a result, many small, independent mills either shut down or were acquired by larger competitors. Today the industry is an oligopoly, with four companies controlling 90% of the market.

In addition, you should develop a view of the likelihood of changing competitive dynamics. Are there threats of new entrants, substitutes, or disruptive technology? If so, evaluate the probability and timing of those events happening and the resultant impact on the company's future profitability and cash flow. This includes running a downside case, where the competitive dynamics worsen, in step four of our seven-step process.

CYCLICALITY

Cyclicality is a function of the correlation between an industry's sales and the business cycle. Figure 6.4 outlines three types of cyclicality.

Pro-cyclical businesses tend to sell goods and services that are easily deferrable and/or discretionary, and some involve large dollar purchases. For example, during a recession consumers can defer the purchase of an auto by repairing an existing car or buying a used car. Furthermore, cars have high purchase prices and often require a loan, which is harder to obtain during a recession, so concerns about job stability and future earnings weigh on auto sales.

Type	Description	Examples
Pro-cyclical	Flourishes when the economy is growing and does poorly in a recession	Autos, restaurants, housing
Non-cyclical	No correlation to the economy	Healthcare, consumer staples, supermarkets
Counter-cyclical	Performs better when the economy is in a recession and worse when the economy is growing	Repair and maintenance businesses, bankruptcy advisory firms, collection agencies

FIGURE 6.4 Types of Cyclicality

Examples of non-cyclical businesses are essential goods and services, such as healthcare and pharmaceuticals. If your appendix ruptures, you are going to a hospital, no matter how the economy is doing.

Counter-cyclical businesses outperform during a recession. It's a commonly held belief that alcohol sales are counter-cyclical, but alcohol is non-cyclical; people consume it equally during good and bad times. Examples of counter-cyclical businesses are auto repair and maintenance firms, bankruptcy advisory firms, and collection agencies. Even cyclical industries might have segments that are counter-cyclical; for example, the dollar store segment tends to outperform during a recession, as consumers downshift to cheaper products.

If you identify a business as cyclical, the next step is to develop a view of how the company will perform during a recession. When you get to step three, financial statement analysis, you will analyze how the company and its peers did during past recessions. Then, in step four, forecasting, you'll model a recession case.

Understanding a cyclical company's cost structure is critical. As mentioned earlier, companies with mostly fixed costs have little room to cut costs in a recession. The automobile industry illustrates the devastating impact of a fixed cost structure in a highly cyclical business. During the recession of 2008, auto sales fell by 40 percent. The US auto manufacturers had a predominately fixed cost structure with unionized labor, which limited their ability to cut costs. As discussed in Chapter 2, by the fall of 2008, the Big Three US car companies (Ford, General Motors, and Chrysler) were hemorrhaging cash and required a government bailout of $80 billion. Despite government assistance, General Motors and Chrysler had to file for bankruptcy, and Ford came close.

GOVERNMENT REGULATION

Some industries are highly regulated, and changes in the regulatory environment can dramatically impact cash flow. For example, new casinos require a government license, which is a substantial barrier to entry. However, if the government increases the number of licenses available in a market close to an existing casino, this impacts incumbents negatively.

If you are considering an investment in the gaming sector, you must consider the potential for the government to grant new licenses and the associated impact by performing the due diligence outlined in Figure 6.5.

1. Using outside legal firms and political consultants, identify any proposals to grant new licenses that could compete for the same customers.
2. Understand the process for obtaining a new license and develop a view on the timing of a new casino's opening once licensed.
3. Run a downside case showing the potential impact on the incumbent's cash flow and profitability.

FIGURE 6.5 License Due Diligence in the Gaming Sector

The progression of Atlantic City illustrates the impact of changing regulation. In 1976, Atlantic City became the first jurisdiction to legalize gaming outside of Nevada. The city enjoyed a monopoly on East Coast gaming for almost two decades. Its initial success was driven by day trippers who could bus in from surrounding areas to play slot machines before heading home the same day. In 2004, Pennsylvania legalized slot machines at 14 locations that would be operational by 2006. Due to these and other regulatory changes, Atlantic City's gaming revenues have fallen more than 50% from their peak 2006 levels, and of the 12 casinos thriving there in 2006, only seven remain today.

Healthcare is another heavily regulated industry. Many healthcare providers are at least somewhat dependent on Medicare and Medicaid reimbursement rates. If you are considering an investment in a healthcare provider, include the due diligence summarized in Figure 6.6.

1. **Compliance:** Healthcare companies must follow stringent government rules to be adequately reimbursed for care provided. If an error in billing is uncovered, the company's receivables have write-down/collection risk. You also need to get comfort that the company is not engaging in Medicare or Medicaid fraud (e.g., inflating billing or performing unnecessary services).
2. **Potential reimbursement rate changes:** Use outside legal firms and consultants to identify any proposals to lower reimbursement rates.
3. **Incorporate findings:** If you determine that there could be regulatory or reimbursement changes, attempt to quantify and incorporate these into your downside scenario.

FIGURE 6.6 Government-Related Due Diligence in the Healthcare Sector

A real-life example of healthcare regulatory change is Rotech, one of the largest providers of home respiratory therapy and durable medical equipment and services in the US through 425 locations, mainly in nonurban markets. The company's primary business lines are:

1. Respiratory therapy and equipment services (88% of sales): Rents oxygen delivery systems to patients with breathing disorders (mainly COPD).
2. Durable medical equipment (DME) and others (12% of sales): Rents and sells durable medical equipment, including wheelchairs, hospital beds, walkers, patient aids, and other ancillary supplies.

In 2013, Medicare introduced competitive bidding as the rate-setting mechanism for Medicare reimbursements of all respiratory therapy and durable medical equipment. This reduced reimbursement rates by approximately 40% (great for the government but awful for the industry). As a result, many players in the industry went out of business, and others, such as Rotech, had to restructure in bankruptcy.

CUSTOMER CONCENTRATION RISK

If any customer or small group of customers makes up a significant amount of a company's sales, Figure 6.7 summarizes the three required follow-up analyses.

1. Customer creditworthiness
2. Probability of losing the customer
3. Impact on cash flow and profitability if the customer is lost

FIGURE 6.7 Follow-Up Analysis for Customer Concentration

Customer creditworthiness: If you are investing in a company with customer concentration, you are effectively also investing in its customers, which means that you need to develop a view on their long-term viability. Obtaining credit ratings for any large customers is a good starting place, since investment grade–rated companies are generally safer than high yield–rated companies.

Probability of losing the customer (i.e., it stops buying from the company): You can analyze this by answering the following questions:

- Are there long-term contracts?
- What is the switching cost?
- Is the company delivering a *commodity* or a *specialized/customized* good or service? (Commodity-like products are easier to replace.)
- How easy is it for the customer to find alternative suppliers?

Impact on cash flow and profitability if the customer is lost (i.e., a downside forecast): If the company has more variable than fixed costs, it is more likely to survive as costs will decline with revenue. If the company has capacity issues that historically led it to turn away other customers, it should also fare better as it could likely replace at least some of the lost business.

Based on your work, you might be comfortable investing despite significant customer concentration risk. For example, Silver Point recently underwrote a $200 million loan to a company whose largest customer made up 40 percent of the borrower's revenues. Furthermore, the customer's contract expired in a year, leading many competing lenders to classify the loan as a "quick pass." However, our due diligence and the structuring of the loan got us comfortable based on the following considerations:

1. The large customer was an investment grade–rated company experiencing 20% annualized revenue growth, making us comfortable with its credit quality.
2. The service provided was mission-critical software integrated into every aspect of the customer's business. We hired an IT expert to analyze how easy it would be to replace the software. His conclusion: it would be extremely difficult, and the customer would need at least a one-year transition plan during which time it

would probably want the company as a backup for another six months in case of any glitches.

3. The proceeds of our loan were going toward refinancing existing debt and an acquisition that would bring customer concentration down from 40% to 25%.
4. 80% of the company's costs were variable, so if revenue declined, costs would decline commensurately.
5. Although our research led us to believe there was an extremely low probability of nonrenewal, we underwrote the loan assuming a 20% price reduction and a 25% volume reduction with this customer. With these base case assumptions, our forecast showed that the company would be able to service the loan, including the first year's 5% amortization and 10% annually thereafter.
6. We ran a draconian downside scenario of nonrenewal. Our downside model showed that the company would be cash flow positive before debt service but would not be able to pay the full coupon in cash and, therefore, would not be able to amortize the loan. However, even in this low-probability case, we believed that the value of the company would still cover our loan, with minimal potential for impairment.
7. Due to limited competition and the company's need to close quickly to complete the acquisition, we were able to negotiate premium pricing and a very tight structure.

Sometimes due diligence leads to the opposite conclusion. For example, we passed on the LBO financing of a manufacturer and distributor of home improvement products. The company was highly dependent on sales to Home Depot and Lowes, each making up approximately 40% of sales. Otherwise, there were several positives. Leverage was moderate at only 50% percent of the purchase price, and historical performance was impressive, with 15%+ annual revenue growth from 2010 to 2020. Our base case forecast showed the company could easily service the LBO-related debt, but we could not get comfortable with our downside scenario for several reasons:

1. The company's growth was driven by product innovation. While a new product permitted premium pricing for a couple of years, copycats quickly replicated the innovation, resulting in either a loss of market share or a significant price reduction.
2. The company was not a critical supplier to Home Depot and Lowes. Its products constituted less than 2% of their sales. Furthermore, there were no contracts between the company and its major customers, so they could stop ordering anytime.
3. 60% of the company's costs were fixed.
4. In the event of a downside case, we believed our investment would be meaningfully impaired.

PRODUCT CONCENTRATION RISK

Companies with product concentration risk don't have a portfolio of products to offer their customers; instead, they have "all their eggs in one basket." To determine the likelihood that demand for that product changes materially in the future, consider the questions summarized in Figure 6.8.

1. Is the product vulnerable to changes in consumer demand?
2. How long has the company been around, and has its primary product maintained market share?
3. Are there barriers to entry that might disappear in the future (e.g., patents that are expiring)?
4. Is the company earning excess profits that will attract competitors?

FIGURE 6.8 Product Concentration Questions

Based on your work, you might be comfortable investing in a company with significant product concentration risk. For example, Silver Point underwrote a $70MM loan to a single-product company that produced equipment used for high-end skin care. It had a large, established base of equipment at spas, dermatologist offices, and plastic surgeon practices, resulting in two sources of revenue: sales of the machines and sales of the tips containing serum, which were replaced after every treatment. This was effectively a "razor/razor blade" model with a substantial component of recurring revenue from the tip replacements. We viewed the biggest risks as lower-cost copycats and the introduction of a competing, better product. These risks were significant given the lack of product diversification.

The meaningful investment required for the machines mitigated these risks. It would be uneconomic for the existing client base to switch to a new machine until the end of its useful life. But recognizing the potential for a new entrant, we ran our downside scenario as a "harvest case" in which sales of new equipment went to zero, with a long tail of tip replacement revenue. Based on the remaining life of the installed base of machines and the ability to cut R&D and advertising expenses in this draconian downside case, we believed that the company could service the loan.

On the other hand, we did not invest in the LBO debt of a manufacturer and installer of a product that prevented debris from accumulating in a house's gutter. This company had the number one market share with a very high rate of revenue growth. However, unlike the prior example, there was no recurring revenue source, and thus no downside protection if a lower-cost copycat or a better product emerged. This company has continued to do exceptionally well after the LBO and looks as if it will be a great deal for the private equity sponsor. This is a good example of the difference between debt and equity analysis; as lenders, we would not have the chance to participate in the upside but would have experienced meaningful impairment in a downside case.

FAD/FASHION RISK

Companies that are vulnerable to changes in consumer tastes and preferences have fad and fashion risk, which require answers to the questions summarized in Figure 6.9.

1. How diversified is the product mix? If one offering goes out of style, does the company have other products that would limit the impact on sales and profitability?
2. Who are the company's customers, and is their buying pattern relatively predictable?
3. How does the company source its product, and how long is the lead time in building inventories? (The longer the lead time, the higher the risk of missing changing consumer trends.)
4. How much inventory does the company carry? The critical measurement is inventory days, discussed in Chapter 8, which is a measure of how long the company holds inventory before it is sold. The longer the inventory days, the more risk of inventory write-downs, particularly for "faddish" items.

FIGURE 6.9 Fad/Fashion Risk Questions

Teen apparel is an example of an industry with significant fad and fashion risk. It is tough to get comfortable lending to a teen apparel company unless the loan is fully covered by the liquidation value of its hard assets (inventory, receivables, and owned real estate). The concept of "cool" changes often in the teen demographic, and it is hard to keep up with these trends. It's not unusual for teen retailers to experience high growth when they get a fashion trend right but then to miss the next fashion trend entirely. Examples of once high-flying teen retailers filing for bankruptcy include Wet Seal, Rue 21, Forever21, Quicksilver, Aeropostale, and American Apparel. Here again, identifying the teen retailer with the "coolest" fashion is an equity play. You get paid for getting this right if you're invested in the company's stock, but with limited upside, the debt of the company can't adequately compensate you for its downside risk.

COMMODITY RISK

Companies with profitability and cash flow tied to commodity prices, such as oil and gas, have commodity risk. Companies can have commodity risk related to selling price or cost structure.

- Selling price risk exists when the company produces the commodity. For example, exploration and production (E&P) companies produce oil.
- Cost structure risk exists for companies that rely on a commodity to produce their product or service. For example, airlines use jet fuel.

If commodity risk exists, the analysis summarized in Figure 6.10 is required.

1. If the company is facing cost structure risk, can it pass along changes in commodity cost to its customers?
2. Does the company have a hedging strategy, and does it differ from that of its key competitors?
3. Based on statistical analysis, how volatile is the price of this commodity?
4. In step four, forecasting, how does commodity risk translate into downside cases to reflect adverse moves in the commodity price?

FIGURE 6.10 Commodity Risk Questions

QUALITATIVE ANALYSIS—SUMMARY OF INDUSTRY AND BUSINESS RISK ANALYSIS

To summarize, a comprehensive industry and business risk analysis includes three primary steps:

1. Identify big-picture concerns for the company. The eight risks discussed above are not comprehensive. Your job is to identify the three to five most substantial risks related to the specific company you are analyzing.
2. Decide if you can get comfortable with the identified risks. This requires follow-up analysis and due diligence.
3. Finally, incorporate these risks into step four, forecasting. For instance, if a company has cyclicality risk, your model will include a downside recession case. One of the most challenging parts of the analyst's job is to translate the qualitative analysis laid out here into quantitative inputs into your model. We will spend time on this in the forecasting chapter.

QUALITATIVE ANALYSIS—BUSINESS STRATEGY ANALYSIS

Although there are myriad individual business strategies, they all generally fall into three buckets, which Harvard Business School Professor Michael Porter defines in his book *Competitive Advantage*. His thesis is that a company must choose among three strategies, shown in Figures 6.11 and 6.12.

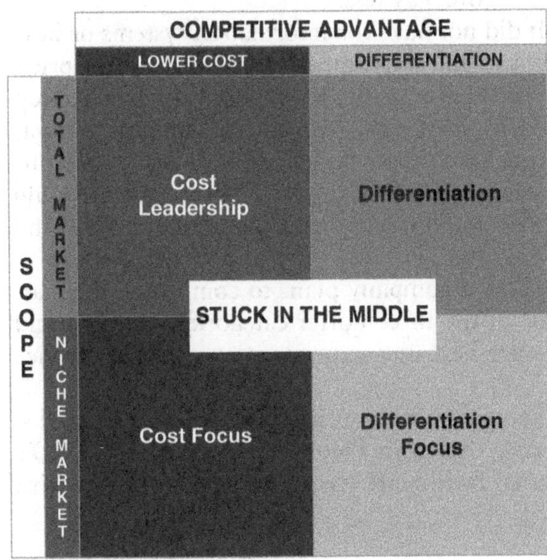

FIGURE 6.11 Michael Porter's Three Strategies

- **Differentiation:** The company produces a unique product or service. As a result, the company can price its product at a premium. Examples include Apple, Harley-Davidson, and Lego.
- **Cost Leadership:** The company delivers its product more economically to the consumer. These companies tend to have a dominant market share resulting from economies of scale and superior productivity. Examples are Amazon, Walmart, and McDonald's.
- **Focus:** This strategy is sometimes referred to as a niche strategy, in which the company targets a narrower, less competitive market. Within their niche, these companies choose either a differentiation or cost leadership approach. Examples include retail category killers such as Best Buy (electronics) and Staples (office supplies), specialty chemical manufacturers such as Avient, and niche healthcare delivery models such as DaVita (stand-alone renal care facilities).

FIGURE 6.12 Michael Porter's Three Strategies (Descriptions)

Companies stuck in the middle are likely to fail. For example, Kmart was one of the first retailers in the discount store segment and dominated this form of retailing through the 1970s, but its competitive advantage waned as Walmart and Target gained share with more defined strategies.

Walmart became the low-price leader. Heavy investment in technology and strong buying power allowed it to dominate the everyday low price (EDLP) segment. In addition to low prices, Walmart provided a better shopping experience than Kmart. It invested in clean, well-lit stores and hired greeters to create a friendly and customer-focused atmosphere. Target differentiated itself by being more upscale. Its simple tagline highlighted this: "Expect more. Pay less."

Kmart was stuck in the middle. It did not have the information systems or buying power of Walmart, which meant it could not compete with Walmart on price. It also lacked the brand cachet of Target. Eventually, Kmart filed for bankruptcy. Although Chapter 11 allowed Kmart to shed legacy liabilities, ultimately it was forced to liquidate several years after its bankruptcy filing, despite a last-gasp effort by one of its major shareholders to merge it into Sears. Even consolidation could not save Kmart in the face of Walmart and Target's better operating models and customer propositions.

An effective strategy must define how a company plans to compete in the markets it serves. It might begin with one of the three Porter categories, but it should expand beyond that. Some examples are best user experience or customer service and most innovative products.

Another approach to analyzing a company's strategy is SWOT analysis (strengths, weaknesses, opportunities, and threats), shown in Figures 6.13 and 6.14. SWOT analysis focuses on internal and external factors affecting a company's competitive position in an industry.

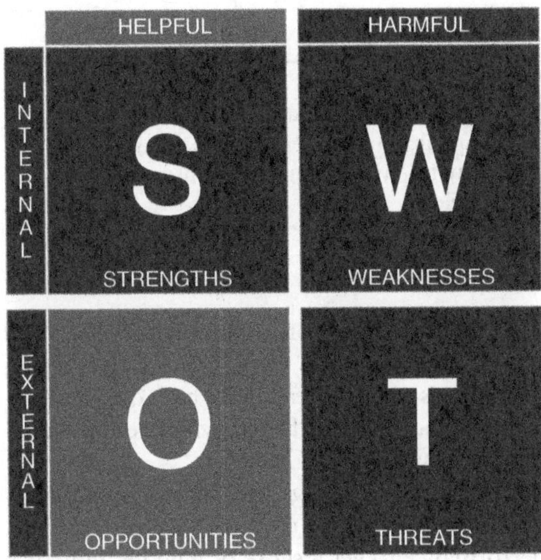

FIGURE 6.13 SWOT Analysis

- **Strengths (internal):** What does the company do well versus its competitors?
- **Weaknesses (internal):** What does the company not do well versus its competitors?
- **Opportunities (external):** What opportunities in the marketplace is the company trying to capitalize on?
- **Threats (external):** What obstacles or competitive threats does the company face?

FIGURE 6.14 SWOT Analysis (Descriptions)

Whether you use Porter's competitive advantage framework, the SWOT framework, or another methodology to analyze a company's business strategy, the key objective is to answer two questions:

1. Does the company have a clear strategy for competing in its industry?
2. Do you believe in the company's strategy and its ability to execute it?

QUALITATIVE ANALYSIS—MANAGEMENT ASSESSMENT

An assessment of management is critical to any investment. However, in my experience, most analysts overestimate management because the typical forums for investors to interact with management are somewhat cursory. It's difficult to evaluate management after a few phone calls, a formal company presentation, and/or a single private meeting in a roadshow format or at a conference. And if you work for a smaller firm, you may not have access to management outside of publicly available presentations (e.g., earnings calls).

The first step in evaluating management is understanding who the critical managers of a business are and what role each plays. Figure 6.15 describes the key members of the management team of most companies.

Position	Responsibilities
1. Chief executive officer (CEO)	1. Driving vision and strategy
2. Chief financial officer (CFO)	2. Maintaining accounting records and raising capital to fund operations (debt and equity)
3. Chief operating officer (COO)	3. Day-to-day running of the business
4. Other C-suite members	4. Various

FIGURE 6.15 Key Members of Management Team

The next step is to evaluate key managers' track records. Start with a list of all historical jobs/roles. How long was their tenure at each firm? Constantly moving around can be a red flag. During the employee's tenure at each job, how did the company perform? Try to contact people who used to work for or with the individual using LinkedIn or an outside consultant firm, such as GLG.

The next step is to review transcripts from past earnings calls, which public companies typically host on a quarterly basis. Keep track of the guidance provided on these calls and compare it to actual performance to get a sense of whether guidance skews conservative or aggressive. A history of earnings "misses" (i.e., failure to meet guidance) can be a red flag and might downgrade your confidence in management.

The final step is to look at how much ownership senior management has in the company and whether they have been buyers or sellers of their company's stock. If the company is public, this is a required disclosure found in public filings. While ownership levels do not tell you how good management is, knowing how much skin they have in the game is a helpful insight. In addition, when available, research compensation information such as target financial metrics management needs to achieve to earn bonuses. This information will also be helpful in step four, forecasting.

The critical questions that need to be answered are:

- Does the company have the right people to execute its strategy?
- Does management have the skills and flexibility to evolve its strategy as needed in response to changes in the industry?

QUALITATIVE ANALYSIS—ENVIRONMENTAL, SOCIAL, AND GOVERNANCE (ESG) CONCERNS

ESG has become a critical issue for virtually all investments. Analyzing environmental concerns, social issues such as diversity, equity, and inclusion (DEI), and corporate governance is now a routine part of credit analysis, which must answer two critical questions related to ESG:

- Is the investment opportunity consistent with the ESG policy of the firm that employs the analyst?
- Will your investors react negatively to the investment due to ESG concerns?

ESG strategies have gained share in both equity and bond markets. However, ESG investing has also become a political landmine. For example, in February 2023, the Senate passed a bill to disallow investment managers to consider ESG criteria in retirement plans.[i] The bill was vetoed by President Biden, but the debate rages on at the state level.

ESG concerns can be emotional. There is no absolute right or wrong answer in most situations that trigger ESG concerns. Often, your evaluation of an ESG issue depends on the beliefs embraced by your firm and any client considerations/constraints/exclusions. Ultimately, creditors should analyze all the risks of a company—and for companies across a wide range of industries, various E, S, and/or G issues have the potential to impact financial performance both positively and negatively. Once the analyst understands how ESG considerations might impact a company's profitability and cash flows, the investment committee must also deal with the gray area of deciding whether the investment is consistent with the firm's ESG policies.

Below are some real-life deals with controversial ESG considerations, along with the pro and con arguments for each from an ESG perspective. All of these financings ultimately got done but with less participation in many cases due to ESG concerns.

Would you lend to JUUL, an e-cigarette company?

This ESG issue relates to the potential targeted marketing to teenagers of a product that is highly addictive. Tobacco/nicotine use among teenagers had declined significantly over the last several decades, until e-cigarette products such as JUUL emerged and reversed this trend. But there are offsets to the perceived negatives of the vaping business model. First, JUUL's marketing practices no longer target teens. Additionally, most studies have shown that JUUL is less harmful than smoking regular cigarettes.[ii]

Would you lend to Playboy Industries?

This ESG issue relates to the objectification of women and what some would argue is pornographic content. The counterargument is that Playboy has transitioned its business; it ceased publishing Playboy Magazine in 2020.

Investors in Playboy argue that Playboy's revenue today comes from licensing the Playboy name, the rabbit head design, and other trademarks, as well as from its direct-to-consumer ("DTC") and retail businesses that focus on the sexual wellness space.

Would you lend to a coal company, such as Consol Energy?

Coal is the poster child for ESG concerns related to the environment (the "E" in ESG). Coal is generally considered the most harmful fossil fuel. While coal produces 44% of US electricity, it accounts for 80% of power plant carbon emissions. Burning coal leads to soot, smog, acid rain, global warming, and carbon emissions.

The counterargument is multifaceted. Some deny that global warming is an issue; some cite the impact on employment in communities reliant on coal mining as an offsetting "S" positive; some maintain that boycotting coal is economically ineffective.

Would you buy Russian government bonds?

After Russia invaded Ukraine, many funds would not buy Russian government bonds in the secondary market, arguing that it is wrong to support Russia and/or to profit from the conflict.

One counterargument is that these bonds have already been issued, so none of the proceeds go directly to Russia; transactions are cash transfers from one investor to another in the secondary trading market. A further counterargument is that some buyers in the secondary market are aggressive distressed debt funds, which are more likely to go after Russian assets outside the country in the event of a sovereign default.

There are no right or wrong answers to the five examples above, or to most ESG-related investment situations. Credit analysts need to understand the ESG implications of all investments, as well as how their firm and its clients strive to incorporate ESG considerations, if at all.

QUALITATIVE ANALYSIS SUMMARY

Figure 6.16 below summarizes the types of qualitative analysis required for any credit investment.

Analysis	Key Considerations
Industry and Business Risk Analysis	■ Secularly declining industry risk ■ Adverse competitive dynamics risk ■ Cyclicality risk ■ Government regulation risk ■ Customer concentration risk ■ Product concentration risk ■ Fad/fashion risk ■ Commodity risk
Business Strategy Analysis	■ Strategy for competing - Porter's competitive advantage model (differentiation/cost leadership/focus) - SWOT analysis (strengths, weaknesses, opportunities, threats) ■ Likely success of the company's strategy ■ Company's ability to execute its strategy
Management Assessment	■ Assessment of key members of the management team - Reference checks - Track record - Management's ownership of equity in the company and recent transactions in the stock ■ Compensation metrics
ESG Concerns	■ Identification of any ESG concerns - Internal firm policies and ESG framework - Client guidelines/sensitivity to ESG considerations

FIGURE 6.16 Qualitative Analysis Summary

JCPENNEY CASE SETUP

At the end of each of the next several chapters, we will practice the credit analysis step outlined in the chapter on JCPenney (JCP), using its 2012 financials and position as our starting point.

The 2012 era was a pivotal time for JCP, which had attracted the interest of an activist investor, someone who believes a company's stock price is meaningfully undervalued and has substantial upside with a meaningful change in strategy. In late 2010, Bill Ackman's hedge fund Pershing Square acquired 17.8% of JCP's stock at approximately $25 per share, a huge discount from its 2007 peak of $86.35. As is typical for activist investors, Ackman joined the board of JCP and convinced the other board members that dramatic changes were required. At the end of 2011, the board replaced CEO Mike Ullman with Ron Johnson. Johnson was a pioneer in the retail world, having created and launched the Apple store and Genius Bar concepts, before which he oversaw a successful rebranding of Target. Johnson fired many of JCP's incumbent executives and replaced them with his own hires, including COO Michael Kramer, who followed him from Apple.

In early 2011, Johnson unveiled his strategic plan to transform JCP. There were two key components of this plan:

1. *Clearer pricing and reduced promotions*
   - Johnson felt that promotional activity at JCP was excessive and confusing. He thought that JCP's pricing strategy of offering items at a high initial price and then marking them down by having sales or supplying 10%–30% off coupons was "insulting" to the customer, who preferred clearer and more consistent pricing.
   - Johnson wanted to move to a "fair and square everyday pricing" strategy, similar to Walmart's EDLP strategy. Rather than start with high initial markups and then incentivize customers to make purchases by putting items on sale and distributing coupons, he wanted the initial list price to represent good value on day one, thereby eliminating the excessive use of promotions and coupons.
2. *New store design*
   - Johnson believed JCP's stores were dated, and he wanted to do a massive renovation of each store.
   - Stores would prominently feature a social area in the center called a "Town Square," a place for consumers to gather to grab a bite to eat, attend an event, or enjoy a coffee with a friend.
   - In the shopping areas, Johnson envisioned 100 "store within a store" concepts featuring brands such as Sephora, Liz Claiborne, Levi's, and Izod.

In 2012, JCP rolled out these initiatives, and it was an unmitigated disaster.

END OF CHAPTER: QUALITATIVE ANALYSIS OF JCPENNEY[1]

- *Industry: Department store retail:* The industry is extremely competitive. The competitor peer group has expanded to include not only traditional department stores such as Macy's, but also off-mall competitors such as Kohl's, online retailers such as Amazon, category killers such as Best Buy, and discounters such as Walmart and Target. Since traditional department store shoppers skew older age, department stores are in secular decline. The business is cyclical with a moderately high fixed cost structure driven by labor costs (a portion of which are fixed) and lease expense.
- *Business strategy:* JCP historically catered to a lower price customer than competitors such as Macy's and Nordstrom. The company decided to change its pricing, coupon strategy, and store layouts—which resulted in a disastrous sales decline of 25%.
- *Management assessment:* JCP's senior management is new and unproven. Its strategies to date have resulted in dismal performance.
- *ESG:* No material ESG concerns.
- *Summary:* Qualitative analysis shows JCP in a very challenging position. The department store industry faces substantial secular and cyclical challenges; JCP's competitive position within its industry is weak; and its management team is new, albeit with a strong background in other retail verticals, which might not be transferable to JCP's business.

NOTES

i Bykowicz, Julie, and Angela Au-Yeung. (February 26, 2023). "Conservatives Have a New Rallying Cry: Down with ESG." *Wall Street Journal.* https://www.wsj.com/articles/conservatives-have-a-new-rallying-cry-down-with-esg-2ef98725?mod=Searchresults_pos1&page=1.

ii Turner, Ashley. (June 14, 2019). "Juul-Sponsored Study Shows Secondhand Vaping Emissions Are Much Less Toxic than Cigarette Smoke." CNBC. https://www.cnbc.com/2019/06/13/juul-study-shows-secondhand-vaping-emissions-are-less-toxic-than-cigarette-smoke.html.

[1]Download JCPenney's 2012 10-K (fiscal year ended February 2, 2013) at the SEC Edgar website for public company filings, https://www.sec.gov/edgar/searchedgar/companysearch, using the search term "Old Copper Company." The company's search term on Edgar is Old Copper Company, Inc., not JCPenney.

CHAPTER 7

Step 3(a) of the Credit Analysis Process: Financial Statement Analysis—Profitability

As shown in Figure 7.1, analyzing profitability is the first step in financial statement analysis.

Step 1	Sources and Uses (only applicable to originations) (a) Why is the company seeking financing? (b) What are the proposed sources of capital to fund the financing need?
Step 2	Qualitative Analysis (a) Industry analysis (b) Business strategy (c) Management assessment (d) ESG concerns
Step 3	**Financial Statement Analysis** **(a) Profitability** **(b) Cash flow and liquidity** **(c) Capital structure**
Step 4	Forecasting (a) Identification of key business drivers and assumptions (b) Development of base, upside, and downside cases
Step 5	Corporate Valuation (a) Comparable company analysis (b) Precedent transactions (M&A comps) (c) Discounted cash flow analysis (d) Liquidation analysis
Step 6	Structuring and Documentation (a) Economic points (b) Structure and collateral (c) Covenants
Step 7	Preparing an Investment Recommendation and Credit Committee Memo (a) Investment thesis and recommendation (b) Risks and mitigants (c) Relative value analysis

FIGURE 7.1 The Seven-Step Process of Evaluating a Debt Instrument

If you've taken any financial accounting and financial statement analysis courses, chances are you'll be familiar with at least some of the principles we'll explore in the following chapters. A detailed analysis of financial statements is essential to anyone investing in a company, whether debt or equity. Warren Buffett sums it up well in the following quote:

> *You have to understand accounting and you have to understand the nuances of accounting. It's the language of business and it's an imperfect language, but unless you are willing to put in the effort to learn accounting—how to read and interpret financial statements—you really shouldn't select stocks yourself.*[i]

While ripping apart financial statements and seeing what others don't is important for any successful investor, it's critical for credit investing. Unlike equities, where an investor can offset bad trades with home runs (i.e., one "ten-bagger," a stock that has a 10x return, can offset a lot of losses), in credit investing, you do not have that luxury. Outside of distressed investing, the upside on a credit investment is generally limited to "clipping your coupon" (receiving interest payments) and getting par ($100) at maturity.

This chapter starts with the basics, laying out a summary financial statement, including calculating the last twelve months (LTM) of results, and then moves to spotting potential red flags in the financial disclosures. While it's not possible to capture all the ways companies can misrepresent their financial standing—both intentionally and inadvertently—my decades in the credit markets are a "living laboratory" for nefarious corporate behavior. The following chapters will give you a guided tour of a company's financial statements—let's call this the interstate—to navigate to an economically honest picture of a company's financial position. The good news is, in most cases, the interstate will take you where you need to go. But when it doesn't, my goal is to provide a map of the backroads you must take, including analysis of relevant footnotes in the financial statements, along with follow-up questions and due diligence to arrive at a true understanding of a company's financial health.

PROFITABILITY ANALYSIS: SIX SUB-STEPS

We will begin by analyzing a company's financial statements: (i) the income statement, (ii) the cash flow statement, and (iii) the balance sheet, all of which are found in a company's quarterly and annual report filings (10-Qs and 10-Ks). This book assumes a baseline level of knowledge/understanding of financial accounting. Our examples will use US generally accepted accounting principles (GAAP), which are similar to other standards such as International Financial Reporting Standards (IFRS). What you learn here should be broadly applicable to non-US companies/filers. The sub-steps to analyze profitability are summarized in Figure 7.2.

1. Adjust the reported income statement to remove nonrecurring gains and losses using data from the income statement, footnotes, and management's commentary. Adjustments for nonrecurring gains and losses will be an exhibit to your investment memo.
2. Create a summary adjusted income statement as shown in Figure 7.6. For a noncyclical business, three to five years of historical information is adequate. For a cyclical industry, you should include enough history to capture a complete economic cycle, including at least one recession.
3. Analyze earnings quality. Are there any red flags that make you question the GAAP income statement? Is the reported income statement a good reflection of economic reality, or is it potentially misleading?
4. Create summary adjusted income statements for the company's most direct peer group /competitors.
5. Draw conclusions:
   - Did the company make, beat, or miss expectations (yours and the analyst community's)?
   - How did the company perform relative to its peer group?
   - Are results good or bad in an absolute sense?
   - What are the critical drivers of performance?
   - What other conclusions can you draw that are potentially important to making an investment recommendation?
6. Make a list of follow-up questions for management and other due diligence items.

FIGURE 7.2 Sub-Steps to Analyze Profitability

PROFITABILITY SUB-STEP #1

In this sub-step, the credit analyst adjusts the income statement to eliminate the impact of nonrecurring contributions to income and expenses. These adjustments will become an exhibit to the investment memo.

How do you figure out if an expense or income component is truly nonrecurring? This is an art, not a science, and will become easier as you analyze more companies. To identify nonrecurring charges, you must carefully review the company's full set of financial disclosures, including the management discussion and analysis (MD&A) section and footnotes to the 10-Ks (annual financial statements) and 10-Qs (quarterly financial statements). Examples of nonrecurring items are summarized in Figure 7.3.

- Cash restructuring charges, including severance pay and cost of factory closings
- Non-cash restructuring charges, including asset impairment charges and write-offs
- M&A or divestiture-related expenses
- Gains or losses from the sale of assets
- Litigation expenses

FIGURE 7.3 Nonrecurring Items

Cash restructuring charges, including severance pay and cost of factory closings: When a company is in "shrink" mode, it incurs costs to shut down facilities. It's not as simple as turning off the lights in a factory. These are real cash costs, but unless the company is in a secularly declining industry (for example, wireline telecommunications) with chronic rationalization, it's an accepted practice to treat these charges as nonrecurring.

Non-cash restructuring charges, including asset impairment charges and write-offs: These are non-cash and virtually always added back to arrive at adjusted income. But since they reflect an impairment of the valuation of the company, it is important to understand why they happened, and whether this is a pattern of poor decision-making by management. For example, impairment charges may result from a series of overvalued acquisitions or investments in new plants that did not generate the anticipated return on invested capital (ROIC). Some impairments occur regularly, just not every year. For example, an "on-trend" retailer might have to record a significant write-down of its inventory every few years because part of the business model is taking fad and fashion risk—and from time to time, the company gets the trend wrong. For this company, you might argue that inventory write-downs are part of the business model and should not be added back to income. However, including infrequent inventory write-downs makes year-over-year comparisons difficult. My recommendation is to add back those write-downs, and account for this in step two, qualitative analysis, by noting that there is fad and fashion risk, and in step four, forecasting, by modeling a downside scenario in which the company gets a fashion trend wrong. Later in this chapter, we will discuss ways to identify companies at high risk of inventory write-downs.

M&A or divestiture-related expenses: When a company acquires another company or disposes of assets, there are transaction-related expenses (e.g., investment banking /advisory fees). Generally, these are assumed to be one-time in nature and added back to arrive at adjusted income. However, a company may bury other operational expenses in these costs. When possible, ask for a detailed breakout of all costs associated with M&A so you can determine for yourself what to include.

Gains or losses from the sale of assets: These are typically one-time in nature and added back to arrive at adjusted income.

Litigation expenses: While these are typically added back since they are generally one-time in nature, litigation costs are common in some industries. For example, litigation to defend patents is typical for pharmaceutical companies, and some analysts do not adjust for (add back) this cost.

Often, management provides an adjusted income number to "help" analysts. Beware: management might err on the side of describing items that are in fact regular costs of doing business as "nonrecurring" to inflate income. An adjusted income reconciliation provided in an earnings release is only a starting point for your calculation. For example, we analyzed a company that included an add-back for a large portion of its advertising expense because it was not planning to use that type of advertising again. However, we did not add back this expense, because even if one ad strategy proved ineffective, the company regularly tested new advertising forms. Our analysis suggested that total advertising expense was unlikely to decline meaningfully as new ad campaigns replaced ineffective ones. Furthermore, we could not verify whether ineffective advertising or other factors drove the company's underperformance.

Let's walk through an adjustment for nonrecurring items. Figure 7.4 is the income statement of hypothetical MGEC Corp and a footnote to the financial statements, while Figure 7.5 shows how to adjust for nonrecurring charges.

	Historic		
$ in 000s	**Year 1**	**Year 2**	**Year 3**
Reported Sales	$145,210	$155,120	$150,780
Cost of Goods Sold (COGS)	65,345	69,980	76,160
Gross Profit	79,865	85,140	74,620
Selling General & Administrative (SG&A)	36,303	37,229	40,711
Gain on Sale of Real Estate[a]	-	-	(520)
Restructuring Expense[a]	-	-	25,000
Operating Profit or EBIT[b]	43,562	47,911	9,429
Interest Expense	10,891	11,500	11,555
Pretax Profit	32,671	36,411	(2,126)
Tax Expense	9,801	10,923	(638)
Net Income	$22,870	$25,488	$(1,488)

[a] In year 3 the company implemented a long-term restructuring program. The company took a $25,000 restructuring charge for severance expense and asset impairment as part of this restructuring. In addition, the company took $5,000 of obsolete inventory write-off charges, included in cost of goods sold (COGS). As part of the year 3 restructuring, the company divested one plant for a profit of $520. To implement the restructuring, the company spent $2,000 on consulting and legal expenses, all of which was included in reported SG&A.

[b] EBIT stands for earnings before interest and taxes. It is used interchangeably with operating earnings or operating profit.

FIGURE 7.4 MGEC Corp Income Statement

	Adjusted Historic		
$ in 000s	Year 3	Adjustments	Adj. Year 3
Reported Sales	$150,780		$150,780
Cost of Goods Sold (COGS)[a]	76,160	−5,000	71,160
Gross Profit	74,620		79,620
Selling General & Administrative (SG&A)[b]	40,711	−2,000	38,711
Gain on Sale of Real Estate[c]	(520)	+520	0
Restructuring Expense[d]	25,000	−25,000	0
Operating Profit or EBIT	9,429		40,909
Interest Expense	11,555		11,555
Pretax Profit	(2,126)		29,354
Tax Expense[e]	(638)	+6,611	5,973
Net Income	$(1,488)		$23,381

[a] Adjusted for $5,000 of inventory write-down included in COGS
[b] Adjusted for $2,000 one-time consulting and legal expenses included in SG&A
[c] Removed $520 gain on sale of real estate
[d] Removed $25,000 restructuring charges
[e] Adjusted taxes by multiplying the marginal tax rate of 21% × total adjustments of $31,480. If the company did not record the items we deemed as nonrecurring, the pretax income would have been $31,480 higher, so the company would have had $6,611 more in tax expense. Note this assumes all nonrecurring items were taxed at the marginal rate. This assumption is reasonable, but we would put this on our follow-up due diligence list.

FIGURE 7.5 Worksheet for Year 3 Adjustments to Remove Nonrecurring Charges

PROFITABILITY SUB-STEP #2

Figure 7.6 shows a summary historical adjusted income statement template. For a noncyclical business, three to five years of history is adequate. However, you should include a complete economic cycle for a company in a cyclical industry, including at least one recession.

	Historic			
	Year 1	Year 2	Year 3	LTM
Sales				
Sales Growth				
Sales Growth Ex Impact of M&A and F/X				
Adjusted Gross Profit				
Adjusted Gross Profit Margin				
Adjusted SG&A Expense				
Adjusted SG&A/Sales				
Adjusted EBITDA				
Adjusted EBITDA Margin				

FIGURE 7.6 Summary Adjusted Income Statement Template

The summary table introduces a non-GAAP term, EBITDA, which stands for earnings before interest, taxes, depreciation, and amortization. It is the company's adjusted operating profit plus depreciation and amortization, which are non-cash expenses. Depreciation expense is the portion of a fixed asset, such as property, plant, and equipment (PP&E), that is considered to be consumed in the current period. This charge gradually reduces the carrying amount of fixed assets as their value is consumed over time. For instance, if you own a piece of equipment with a 10-year expected life, the value of that asset decreases over time. The depletion of this wasting asset is a cost of doing business, and the company records an annual associated expense. While depreciation expense lowers the amount of operating profit, there is no associated cash outflow; this occurred when the company bought the asset. We will discuss this in the next chapter on cash flow and liquidity; for now, hold the thought that the original cash outlay is reflected in the cash flow statement as a capital expense rather than on the income statement as an operating expense. The same argument holds for adding back amortization expense, which reflects the annual decrease in value of intangible assets.

In the world of credit analysis, EBITDA is a fundamental financial metric. It is also the metric that bond indentures and credit agreements use to calculate compliance with covenants (discussed in Chapter 12). Since EBITDA is a better measure of cash flow than operating profit, some credit analysts refer to it as a proxy for cash flow. The calculation is straightforward: add D&A back to the operating income you adjusted in sub-step #1 above. Note that while D&A expenses lower income, many companies do not break out these expenses separately on the income statement, rather lumping them in either with COGS or SG&A. You can always find D&A as an add-back in the operating section of the cash flow statement.

Staying with the previous example, let's calculate the EBITDA of MGEC Corp. To do this calculation, we will use the adjusted income statement above and the company's cash flow statement shown in Figure 7.7. Figure 7.8 shows the adjusted EBITDA calculation.

	Historic		
$ in 000s	Year 1	Year 2	Year 3
Net Income	$22,870	$25,488	$(1,488)
Depreciation and Amortization	5,120	5,500	5,350
Non-Cash Restructuring Charges	0	0	15,000
Gain on Sale of Real Estate	0	0	(520)
Changes in Inventory	125	(400)	(1,000)
Changes in Receivables	10	80	(45)
Changes in Payables	5	15	8
Changes in Other Op Assets & Liab	5	(12)	9
Cash Flow from Operations (CFO)	**$28,135**	**$30,671**	**$17,314**
Capital Expenditures	$(22,500)	$(28,400)	$(27,900)
Divestment of Businesses	0	0	3,000
Acquisition of Businesses	0	0	(32,000)
Cash Flow from Investing Activities	**$(22,500)**	**$(28,400)**	**$(56,900)**
Proceeds from Issuance of Debt	$0	$0	$100
Repayment of Debt	(250)	(250)	(250)
Dividends Paid	(50)	(50)	(50)
Cash Flow from Financing Activates	**$ (300)**	**$(300)**	**$ (200)**
Change in Cash	**$5,335**	**$1,971**	**$(39,786)**

FIGURE 7.7 MGEC Corp Cash Flow Statement

	Adjusted Historic		
$ in 000s	Year 1	Year 2	Year 3
Reported Operating Profit from Figure 7.5	$43,562	$47,911	$9,429
Inventory Write-Down Adjustment	0	0	+5,000
One-Time Consulting and Legal Fee Adjustment	0	0	+2,000
Gain on Sale of Real Estate Adjustment	0	0	−520
Restructuring Charge Adjustment	0	0	+25,000
Adjusted Operating Profit	43,562	47,911	40,909
Plus Depreciation and Amortization	5,120	5,500	5,350
Adjusted EBITDA	**$48,682**	**$53,411**	**$46,259**

FIGURE 7.8 Worksheet to Calculate Adjusted EBITDA

The next calculation is LTM (last twelve months), which refers to the time frame of the most recent twelve-month period. This calculation incorporates the most recent quarterly financial results into the analysis.

LTM = Last Year's Income Statement + YTD (Year-to-Date) Income Statement − Prior YTD Income Statement

Calculating LTM numbers requires the most recent YTD financial statements, which can be found in the 10-Q. As with annual numbers, you must adjust for the impact of any nonrecurring items. For this example, let's assume all the nonrecurring charges were in the fourth quarter, so there were no adjustments needed in the first three quarters. Figure 7.9 shows the year 4 YTD income statement and D&A expense through the third quarter (the most recent quarterly statement available), while Figure 7.10 shows the calculation for LTM numbers.

	Historic	
	YTD 3rdQ	YTD 3rdQ
$ in 000s	Year 3	Year 4
Sales	$98,007	$100,005
COGS	46,254	45,002
Gross Profit	51,753	55,003
SG&A	25,162	26,701
Operating Profit	26,591	28,302
Interest Expense	7,511	7,558
Pretax Profits	19,080	20,744
Tax Expense	4,007	4,356
Net Income	$15,073	$16,388
Operating Profit (from above)	$26,591	$28,302
D&A Expense (from CF)	3,531	3,605
EBITDA	$30,122	$31,907

FIGURE 7.9 MGEC Corp Quarterly Income Statement in $000s

	Adjusted LTM			
	Last Year	(+)	(−)	(=) LTM
	Figure 7.6	Figure 7.9	Figure 7.9	LTM
$ in 000s	Adjusted Year 3	YTD 3rdQ Year 4	YTD 3rdQ Year 3	Through 3rdQ Year 4
Sales	$150,780	$100,005	$98,007	$152,778
COGS	71,160	45,002	46,254	69,908
Gross Profit	79,620	55,003	51,753	82,870
SG&A	38,711	26,701	25,162	40,250
Operating Profit	40,909	28,302	26,591	42,620
Interest Expense	11,555	7,558	7,511	11,602
Pretax Profits	29,354	20,744	19,080	31,018
Tax Expense	5,973	4,356	4,007	6,322
Net Income	$23,381	$16,388	$15,073	$24,696
Operating Profit (from above)	$40,909	$28,302	$26,591	$42,620
D&A Expense (from CF)	5,350	3,605	3,531	5,424
EBITDA	$46,259	$31,907	$30,122	$48,044

FIGURE 7.10 Worksheet to Calculate LTM Financials

Figure 7.11 is the summary adjusted income statement for profitability sub-step #2. This table will be included in the investment memo, while the supporting worksheets will be backup exhibits to the memo.

	Adjusted Historic			
$ in 000s	Year 1	Year 2	Year 3	LTM
Sales	$145,210	$155,120	$150,780	$152,778
Sales Growth	NA	6.8%	–2.8%	1.3%
Sales Growth Ex Impact of M&A and F/X[a]	NA	NA	NA	NA
Adjusted Gross Profit	$79,865	$85,140	$79,620	$82,870
Adjusted Gross Profit Margin	55.0%	54.9%	52.8%	54.2%
Adjusted SG&A Expense	$36,303	$37,229	$38,711	$40,250
Adjusted SG&A/Sales	25.0%	24.0%	25.7%	26.3%
Adjusted EBITDA	$48,682	$53,411	$46,259	$48,044
Adjusted EBITDA Margin	33.5%	34.4%	30.7%	31.4%

[a]We will discuss this concept in sub-step #3.

FIGURE 7.11 Summary Adjusted Income Statement for MGEC Corp

PROFITABILITY SUB-STEP #3

This sub-step analyzes earnings quality to identify red flags in the GAAP income statement. The goal is to determine whether the reported income statement is a good reflection of reality by identifying times when GAAP accounting might make financial statements misleading. Figure 7.12 summarizes four categories of concerns.

1. Attempts to pass off recurring operating expenses as nonrecurring to make the company look more profitable than it is (as discussed in sub-step #1).
2. Intentional overstatement of expenses when earnings are already set to disappoint/miss consensus estimates, sometimes referred to as "taking a big bath" or "kitchen-sinking." For example, a company writes inventory down more than necessary so that in the future, when the marked-down merchandise is sold, there is a correspondingly larger profit. In effect, the company is booking future costs on the current income statement to improve future earnings.
3. Other accounting tricks to mislead investors, such as booking future revenues today as receivables ("channel stuffing") or improperly capitalizing operating expenses.
4. Instances in which GAAP accounting does not tell the full story.

FIGURE 7.12 Key Accounting Concerns

For private debt and equity originations and acquisitions, it's standard to hire a third-party firm to do a quality of earnings ("Q of E") report. In these instances, the Q of E consultant has full access to the company's management team and accounting team. However, you won't have this level of access when analyzing a secondary trade.

As a credit analyst, you need to question every line on the income statement and ask yourself, "Does this reflect economic reality?"

PROFITABILITY SUB-STEP #3 CONTINUED—WHEN REPORTED SALES ARE MISLEADING

Figure 7.13 summarizes four items that might result in a mismatch between reported sales and economic reality.

1. Potential dealer dumping
2. Sales growth versus order growth
3. Impact of foreign exchange (F/X) movements
4. Impact of acquisitions

FIGURE 7.13 Sales Red Flags

Sales Red Flag #1: Potential Dealer Dumping

Dealer dumping, also referred to as channel stuffing, inflates sales by shipping more goods to a distributor than the distributor can sell to the end user. Let's examine a footnote from Deere & Company's 1995 10-K.

> *Deere & Company 1995 Footnote:*
> *Dealer accounts and notes receivable arise primarily from sales to dealers of John Deere agricultural, industrial, and lawn and grounds care equipment. Generally, terms to dealers require payments as the equipment which secures the indebtedness is sold to retail customers.*

The first sentence of this footnote tells the reader that Deere does not sell directly to the end user (the farmer) but through a third party (the dealer). However, the dealer does not pay Deere until the dealer sells the product. The GAAP accounting for this on Deere's income statement is as follows: Deere gets a $100,000 order from one of its dealers, which shows up on Deere's income statement when the inventory ships to that customer. But since the inventory has not yet been sold to an end user, Deere does not receive any cash from this transaction. Instead, Deere's accounts receivable balance increases by $100,000 with the expectation of receiving cash from the dealer in the future.

Given this accounting, it would be easy for Deere to inflate its sales at the end of a quarter to hit its revenue guidance by asking one or more dealers to order more of its product. Since the dealer does not pay for the product until it is sold to the end user, as long as the physical space to store the product exists, it does not cost the dealer anything to do Deere this favor.

When I teach the concept of dealer dumping, some students express doubt that a company would do this, or confidence that auditors would catch the inflated revenue. But many blue-chip companies have channel-stuffed. For instance, in 2008, Coca-Cola agreed to pay $137.5 million to settle a shareholder lawsuit that claimed the world's largest soft-drink maker artificially inflated sales.[ii] The lawsuit, filed in October 2000, claimed that in 1999 Coca-Cola had forced some bottlers to purchase hundreds of millions of dollars of unnecessary beverage concentrate to make its sales seem higher. According to court documents, without admitting any wrongdoing, Coca-Cola agreed to a settlement on June 26, 2008. In 2005, Coca-Cola settled a similar issue over selling excess beverage concentrate to bottlers in Japan between 1997 and 1999. The Securities and Exchange Commission (SEC) claimed that, at or near the end of each reporting period between 1997 and 1999, Coca-Cola implemented an undisclosed channel stuffing practice in Japan known as "gallon pushing" to pull sales forward into a current period.[iii]

In August 2004, the SEC announced the filing of an enforcement action against the pharmaceutical company Bristol-Myers Squibb. The complaint alleged that Bristol-Myers perpetrated a fraudulent earnings management scheme by, among other things, selling excessive amounts of pharmaceutical products to its wholesalers ahead of demand, improperly recognizing revenue from $1.5 billion of such sales to its two largest wholesalers.[iv] In its settlement with the SEC, Bristol-Myers agreed to pay $150 million and perform numerous remedial undertakings, including the appointment of an independent adviser to review and monitor its accounting practices, financial reporting, and internal controls.[v]

As a financial analyst, you can distinguish yourself from your peers by spotting dealer dumping and incorporating your findings into your investment recommendation. Here are some ways to do this:

- Determine whether the company's customer is a distributor/dealer/broker, or the end user. Dealer dumping can only take place when companies don't sell directly to their end users. For example, a retailer such as JCPenney sells directly to the customers in its stores, which eliminates the possibility of dealer dumping.
- Read the company's footnotes to get a sense of how easy it would be for the company to ask its distributors for favors. Above we looked at Deere's 1995 footnote disclosure; in 2012, that footnote changed. The change in accounting policy discussed below made it harder for Deere to channel-stuff, as now the "favor" would have an actual cost to the distributor in the form of interest payable to Deere.

Deere & Company 1995 Footnote:
Dealer accounts and notes receivable arise primarily from sales to dealers of John Deere agricultural, industrial, and lawn and grounds care equipment. Generally, terms to dealers require payments as the equipment which secures the indebtedness is sold to retail customers.

Deere & Company 2012 Footnote:
Trade accounts and notes receivable primarily arise from sales of goods to independent dealers. Under the terms of the sales to dealers, interest is primarily charged to dealers on outstanding balances from the earlier of the date when goods are sold to retail customers by the dealer or the expiration

of certain interest-free periods granted at the time of the sale to the dealer, until payment is received by the company. Dealers cannot cancel purchases after the equipment is shipped and are responsible for payment even if the equipment is not sold to retail customers. The interest-free periods are determined based on the type of equipment sold and the time of year of the sale. These periods range from one to twelve months for most equipment. Interest-free periods may not be extended. Interest charged may not be forgiven, and the past due interest rates exceed market rates. The company evaluates and assesses dealers on an ongoing basis as to their creditworthiness and generally retains a security interest in the goods associated with the trade receivables.

- Determine who has more power in the relationship: the company you are evaluating or its distributors. It is easier for a company to dealer-dump if it has the upper hand with its distributors, while it's harder if the company is not a significant supplier to its distributor(s). For instance, a textile manufacturer that sells to Walmart will find it challenging to dealer dump, as Walmart exercises substantial control over the terms of its vendor relationships.
- Monitor the trend of the company's receivable days and compare it to its peer group. Receivable days are a measure of how long it takes a company to collect cash from its customers. If a company is dealer-dumping, receivable days would be increasing year-over-year and would be greater than peers'. The formula to calculate receivable days is 365 × (average receivables / LTM sales).

  Coca-Cola's receivable days consistently averaged approximately 30 days in the 1990s and then increased roughly 20% in 2000—the year after the alleged dealer dumping. An increase in receivable days does not necessarily mean the company is channel-stuffing, but it is a red flag to be investigated.
- Finally, if you are concerned about dealer dumping, you can do "channel checks." Put together a list of distributors and check in with them regularly. Channel checks may sound mundane, but you can learn quite a bit from this kind of due diligence. If dealers consistently tell you they have so much inventory that they are running out of space to store it, that's a red flag.

While these avenues of analysis are relatively straightforward, you'd be surprised how few analysts pursue them.

Sales Red Flag #2: Sales Growth versus Order Growth

Most companies recognize sales upon shipping their products, not upon receipt of an order. However, monitoring order growth is essential, especially if it deviates materially from sales growth. While orders are generally not disclosed in a company's financial statements, they can be estimated by reading the backlog footnote disclosures. Backlog refers to orders received but not yet shipped. A company's backlog increases with new orders and decreases with shipments.

$$\text{Beginning Backlog} + \text{New Orders} - \text{Shipments} = \text{Ending Backlog}$$

Figure 7.14 shows MGEC's backlog for three years.

	Historic		
$ in 000s	Year 1	Year 2	Year 3
Beginning Backlog	$200,000	$219,790	$169,670
Plus New Orders	165,000	105,000	35,000
Less Shipments (Sales)	–145,210	–155,120	–150,780
Equals Ending Backlog	$219,790	$169,670	$53,890

FIGURE 7.14 MGEC Corp Backlog

Based on GAAP accounting, as shown in Figure 7.15, MGEC had 6.8% and –2.8% sales growth in years 2 and 3, respectively.

	Historic		
$ in 000s	Year 1	Year 2	Year 3
Sales	$145,210	$155,120	$150,780
Sales Growth	NA	6.8%	–2.8%

FIGURE 7.15 MGEC Corp Sales Growth

However, this analysis is not complete without a mention of the disconnect between revenue and order growth. Orders have declined materially, and therefore sales growth does not tell the whole story, as shown in Figure 7.16.

	Historic		
$ in 000s	Year 1	Year 2	Year 3
Orders	$165,000	$105,000	$35,000
Orders Growth		–36.4%	–66.7%

FIGURE 7.16 MGEC Corp Order Growth

Using the information provided in the footnotes is critical to your analysis. Relying solely on the income statement would overlook the dramatic deterioration in the order book—which ultimately will translate into revenue deterioration.

Another way to incorporate orders into profitability analysis is to calculate the book-to-bill ratio. As shown in Figure 7.17, the book-to-bill ratio is the ratio of new orders to sales.

	Historic		
$ in 000s	Year 1	Year 2	Year 3
Orders	$165,000	$105,000	$35,000
Sales	145,210	155,120	150,780
Book-to-Bill Ratio	1.14x	0.68x	0.23x

FIGURE 7.17 MGEC Corp Book-to-Bill Ratio

When this ratio is greater than 1, sales growth understates the true economic growth of the company, and the reverse is true as well: a ratio below 1 means sales growth overstates the true economic growth of the company. MGEC's year 2 and 3 book-to-bill ratios of 0.7x and 0.2x are a leading indicator of revenue weakness; the rapid decline in backlog will result in a lagged decline in future sales.

Let's use a real-life example. Texas Instruments Incorporated (TI), a semiconductor manufacturer, reported sales growth of 1.7% for the quarter ending September 30, 2006. In contrast to the reported 1.7% revenue growth, the company's orders declined by 12.2%, resulting in a 0.91x book-to-bill ratio. This leading indicator signaled an approaching decline in sales—which is exactly what happened, as shown in Figure 7.18.

	Historic			
$ in millions	6/30/06	9/30/06	12/31/06	3/31/07
Orders	$3,908	$3,430	$3,072	$3,200
Orders Growth		−12.2%	−10.4%	4.2%
Sales	$3,697	$3,761	$3,463	$3,191
Sales Growth		1.7%	−7.9%	−7.9%
Book-to-Bill Ratio	1.06x	0.91x	0.89x	1.00x

FIGURE 7.18 Summary of Orders, Sales, and Book-to-Bill Ratio for TI
Source: Adapted from TI financial statements, 2006–2007

Sales Red Flag #3: Impact of Foreign Exchange (FX) Rate

GAAP accounting requires a company to translate sales in foreign currencies into US dollars using the exchange rate prevalent when the revenues were recognized. Therefore, reported sales for multinational companies might be driven by foreign exchange movements rather than operations. You must determine what sales growth would have been if exchange rates did not change in the reporting period, referred to as constant currency sales, to understand a company's true growth rate. Figures 7.19 and 7.20 show the difference between reported sales and constant currency sales.

	Historic		
$ in 000s	Year 1	Year 2	Year 3
US Sales in $	$87,126	$93,105	$88,000
Foreign Sales in Euros	€56,392	€48,831	€43,297
FX Exchange Rate ($/Euros)	1.03	1.27	1.45
Foreign Sales in $	$58,084	$62,015	$62,780
Reported Sales on Income Statement	$145,210	$155,120	$150,780
Reported Growth		6.8%	−2.8%

FIGURE 7.19 MGEC Corp Sales by Region (US and Foreign)

	Historic		
$ in 000s	Year 1	Year 2	Year 3
US Sales in $	$87,126	$93,105	$88,000
Foreign Sales in Euros	€56,392	€48,831	€43,297
Constant Currency Exchange Rate ($/Euros)	1.03	1.03	1.03
Foreign Sales in $	$58,084	$50,296	$44,595
Sales in Constant Currency	$145,210	$143,401	$132,595
Sales Growth Based on Constant Currency		−1.2%	−7.5%

FIGURE 7.20 MGEC Corp Sales on a Constant Currency Basis

Again, relying solely on the income statement without reading the footnotes and MD&A would overlook the substantial, positive impact of the euro's appreciation relative to the dollar on the company's performance.

While sales on a constant currency basis are not disclosed on the income statement, most companies provide this information in their earnings press release, earnings conference call, and/or the MD&A section of the 10-Q and 10-K. For instance, in IBM's third quarter 2022 10-Q, it disclosed the following in the MD&A section:

> *Total revenue grew 6.5 percent as reported and 15 percent adjusted for currency compared to the prior-year period.*

Sales Red Flag #4: Impact of Acquisitions

A company that makes an acquisition has higher revenue growth than its peers. Since acquisitions can mask deterioration in a company's core business, you must disaggregate revenue growth into organic growth (i.e., growth in the core business excluding acquired revenue) and acquisition-related growth. Let's assume that in year 3 MGEC made an acquisition that contributed $25,000 to revenues that year. Figure 7.21 shows the impact.

	Historic		
$ in 000s	Year 1	Year 2	Year 3
Reported Sales	$145,210	$155,120	$150,780
Reported Sales Growth	NA	6.8%	–2.8%
Reported Sales	$145,210	$155,120	$150,780
Less Sales Related to Acquisitions	–0	–0	–25,000
Organic Sales	$145,210	$155,120	$125,780
Organic Sales Growth	NA	6.8%	–18.9%

FIGURE 7.21 MGEC Corp Organic Sales Growth

Relying solely on the income statement without reading the footnotes would overlook a massive decline in the company's performance. While reported sales declined 2.8%, once the positive impact of the acquisition is stripped out, the company's organic revenue declined by 18.9%.

While there is no standard of how the impact of an acquisition is reported and disclosed, if it is material, it should be included somewhere in the financial reports. For instance, Figure 7.22 is a disclosure from the MD&A section of Coca-Cola's third quarter 2022 10-Q.

	Percent Change 2022 versus 2021				
	Volume (+)	Price, Product & Geographic Mix	(+) Foreign Currency Fluctuations (+)	Acquisitions & Divestitures	(=) Total
Consolidated	6%	10%	(6)%	2%	12%

FIGURE 7.22 Coca-Cola Disclosure on Year-over-Year Changes in Revenue

This disclosure permits adjustments for FX movements (discussed in the prior section) and M&A activity. While reported sales grew 12%, organic growth, which eliminates the unfavorable effect of F/X movements and the revenues associated with M&A, was 16% (from a 6% volume increase and 10% pricing/mix shift).

Summary: Sales Red Flags

Figure 7.23 provides a summary of situations in which GAAP reported sales do not reflect economic reality.

Red Flag	Description
Dealer dumping	Sales are inflated as the company pushes inventory to its dealers.
Orders lagging shipments	The company's growth is overstated as its backlog is decreasing.
F/X rates	Sales are inflated as foreign currency has appreciated resulting in greater revenues based on US dollars.
M&A	Reported sales are overstated relative to true organic growth.

FIGURE 7.23 Summary of Sales Red Flags

PROFITABILITY SUB-STEP #3 CONTINUED—WHEN REPORTED EXPENSES ARE MISLEADING

Next, we will examine the expense line items: cost of goods sold (COGS) and selling, general, and administrative expenses (SG&A). As my friend Carla Cassella, a managing director in JP Morgan's leveraged credit research group, points out, companies might differ on cost allocation between COGS and SG&A. Carla made the following point while reviewing a draft of this section of the book.

> *When analysts perform peer comparisons of companies, they must pay particular attention to cost allocation, especially in COGS and SG&A. For instance, retailers can choose how to allocate rent expenses associated with their distribution centers and stores to COGS or SG&A. Arts and crafts retailers Michaels Stores and Jo-Ann stores take different approaches to this. Michaels includes all rent expenses in COGS, resulting in lower gross margin, while Jo-Ann allocates them to SG&A. The gross margin differential is as much as 20 points (i.e., Jo-Ann's gross margin is in the 50% range versus Michaels' which is in the 30% range), but EBITDA margins differ by less than five percentage points, with Michaels typically higher than Jo-Ann.*

Cost of Goods Sold Expense (COGS)

COGS refers to the direct costs of producing the good or service sold by a company. COGS includes materials and labor costs directly used to create the product. It excludes indirect expenses, such as distribution and sales force costs, that are included in SG&A expenses. However, as Carla mentioned, the footnotes must be read carefully to determine how certain expenses are allocated between SG&A and COGS.

Reported COGS might be artificially low, which overstates the company's gross margin and operating profit. This can take two forms:

1. Absorption costing (over-manufacturing to leverage fixed costs); and
2. Holding excess inventory on the balance sheet with either fad/fashion risk or obsolescence risk.

COGS Red Flag #1: Absorption Costing

Figure 7.24 compares the gross profit margins of three hypothetical jewelry companies. All incurred $250,000 in fixed costs to produce jewelry, with additional variable costs of $2/unit. The selling price is $10/unit.

		Company Comparison	
	Co #1	Co #2	Co #3
A Total Fixed Cost to Manufacture [Given]	250,000	250,000	250,000
B Divided by # of Units Produced [Given]	50,000	100,000	150,000
C = Fixed Cost per Unit Produced [A/B]	5.00	2.50	1.67
D Plus Variable Cost per Unit [Given]	2.00	2.00	2.00
E = Total Cost per Unit [C + D]	$7.00	$4.50	$3.67
F Sales Price [Given]	$10.00	$10.00	$10.00
G Less Cost per Unit [E]	7.00	4.50	3.67
H Profit per Unit [F – G]	$3.00	$5.50	$6.33
I Profit Margin [H/F]	30.0%	55.0%	63.3%

FIGURE 7.24 Gross Profit Margins for Three Hypothetical Jewelers

Most students believe Company #3 is the most profitable, because its superior fixed cost leverage results in the lowest cost per unit and the highest margin. However, this is only true if the company can sell the additional units it produces. In our hypothetical, let's assume the three companies have identical demand for their products—45,000 units. Companies #2 and #3 show higher profit margins than company #1 because they are overproducing, which leaves them with excess inventory. Company #3 produced 150,000 units but will only end up selling 45,000, resulting in an increase in inventory of 105,000 units, or 2.3 years of supply.

To identify potential absorption costing issues for a manufacturer, monitor the trend in inventory days and compare to the peer group. Inventory days is a measure of how long, on average, it takes a company to sell its inventory. If a company is overproducing, inventory days will increase year-over-year and exceed peers'. The calculation of inventory days is 365 × (average inventory/COGS).

Cisco Systems was one of the most valuable companies in the world with a market cap of $550 billion in March 2000. As the largest global supplier of networking equipment, Cisco saw its sales grow from $4.1 billion in 1996 to $19 billion in 2000. However, the company became a victim of its own success and significantly overproduced in 2001, resulting in a $2.4 billion inventory write-down in the fiscal third quarter of 2001. As shown in Figure 7.25, the red flag was the meaningful upward trend in days inventory from the low 40s in early 2000 to 78 in the quarter ended January 27, 2001.

	Historic Quarters								
Quarter Ended	1/29/00	4/29/00	7/29/00	10/28/00	1/27/01	4/28/01	7/28/01	10/27/01	1/26/02
Inventory Days	39	40	46	60	78	91	89	66	42

FIGURE 7.25 Cisco Inventory Days
Source: Adapted from Capital IQ

Selling, General and Administrative Expenses (SG&A)

SG&A expenses include the day-to-day operating costs of running a business not directly related to producing a good or service. SG&A includes a wide range of expenses, such as some types of rent expense (as discussed by Carla above), advertising and marketing, and management and administrative staff salaries. Since there are so many separate expenses lumped into SG&A, it is always a good idea to read all footnotes and break out the expenses in as much detail as possible.

There are three expenses I always try to isolate. The first two are research and development (R&D) and advertising. These two expenses are relatively easy to cut to make short-term financial targets, but such cuts can have long-term negative consequences. For example, a technology company having a tough year can cut R&D by 20% without hurting that year's sales. However, it will have a hard time keeping up with its peers in developing cutting-edge products in the long run. Similarly, a consumer brand company can cut advertising to meet short-term financial goals—but over the long run, decreased advertising impacts brand recognition, which is generally the most significant value driver of the business.

Interstate Baking Corporation (Hostess) provides an example of the impact of cutting R&D and advertising to boost short-term profitability and cash flow. Hostess, the owner of iconic brands such as Wonder Bread and Twinkies, was a highly levered company with a largely fixed cost structure driven by a 92 percent unionized workforce. Profitability and cash flow started to decline as consumers shifted away from white bread and snack cakes to focus on low-carb diets and healthier products. Management decided to cut the "easy" costs of R&D and advertising to bolster margin and cash flow. While this helped the situation in the short run, it compounded Hostess's issues in the long run. Without R&D to support product development to meet changing consumer tastes and advertising to support existing and new products, sales and profitability declined. After several years of deterioration, Hostess filed for bankruptcy protection in 2004 and again in 2012, as it never fully regained its market dominance.[vi] Its equity value was wiped out, and its debt traded at a significant discount to par. The earliest signals of Hostess's eventual demise were the cuts to advertising and R&D.

The third expense buried in SG&A that deserves scrutiny is bad debt expense. Companies must evaluate the collectability of their receivables, i.e., the likelihood that customers to whom they extended credit will pay them back. Each year a company books some amount of bad debt expense, reflecting its estimate of receivables that will not be collected. This expense decreases the carrying value of the receivable through an account called allowance for doubtful accounts (ADA), which is the company's estimate of receivables that will never be collected. Accounts receivable in the current assets section of the balance sheet is shown *net* of this allowance.

Bad debt expense is only an estimate, based on management's best information at the time of the financial report. If uncollectable receivables are underestimated, earnings are correspondingly overstated. Once it becomes apparent a receivable will not be repaid, for example in a scenario in which a customer files for bankruptcy, the company must book a catch-up charge, and future profits will be lower than expected.

To identify bad debt expense red flags, use the footnotes to:

1. Track the ratio of allowance for doubtful accounts to gross receivables.
2. Monitor the creditworthiness of any large customers (5%+ of revenue) or customer segments (e.g., oil and gas). If the customer or industry segment has financial problems, the company should increase its ADA and book higher bad debt expense.
3. Ask for the aging of accounts if there are any red flags.

Finally, a rule of thumb: if a company is intentionally understating its bad debt expense, it could be playing other games with its financial statements. Vitesse Semiconductor is an example of this. In his book *Financial Shenanigans,* Howard Schilit discusses how Vitesse significantly cut bad debt expense in 2003 to bolster earnings—but this turned out to be the tip of the iceberg. Schilit also discovered the company was under-reporting inventory obsolescence and sales returns. In April 2006, Vitesse's board of directors completed an internal investigation of its accounting practices. The board issued a press release stating that serious accounting issues in the company's financial statements for the three years ended September 30, 2005, had been identified, and cautioned that earlier periods should not be relied upon.[vii] The company's shares traded down 27% on the news.

Improperly Capitalizing Operating Expenses

Finally, a company can mislead investors by improperly capitalizing operating expenses, in other words, classifying a routine operating expense as capex. WorldCom's investors were shocked in 2002 when the company admitted to doing this. The second largest long-distance telecommunication company announced that it had overstated earnings in the first quarter of 2002 by more than $3.8 billion by classifying line cost (an operating expense) as capex. World Com's short-dated bonds traded down 50 points on the news, and the company filed for Chapter 11 bankruptcy protection in July 2022. The warning sign was the massive 32% increase in capex in 2000 when the fraud began.

PROFITABILITY SUB-STEP #3 CONTINUED—SUMMARY

Although I've provided several examples of sales and expense red flags, financial statements are usually a reasonable representation of a company's economic reality. However, a paranoid mindset will occasionally be rewarded. Spotting these issues before the market will allow you to sell out of or avoid a bad investment. Furthermore, if you get conviction that a company's accounting is misleading, you can short the company's debt directly or synthetically using credit default swaps (CDS), discussed in Chapter 18.

Figure 7.26 summarizes the questions that you must ask and answer to evaluate a company's earnings quality.

- Are there any red flags that make you question the GAAP income statement?
- Is the reported income statement a good reflection of economic reality, or is it potentially misleading?

FIGURE 7.26 Earnings Quality Questions

PROFITABILITY SUB-STEP #4

In this sub-step, you perform sub-steps 1–3 for the company's competitors to compare the company to its most direct peer group. The need for so-called comp analysis shows why developing an industry expertise as an analyst can give you a leg up.

PROFITABILITY SUB-STEP #5

Now it's time to write up your conclusions. This write-up should address the questions summarized in Figure 7.27.

- Did the company meet, beat, or miss expectations (yours and the market's)?
- How did the company perform relative to its peer group?
- What are the critical drivers of performance?
- If accounting concerns are identified in sub-step #3, they should be discussed here, and any follow-up due diligence will be listed in sub-step #6.

FIGURE 7.27 Profitability-Related Questions

PROFITABILITY SUB-STEP #6

Make a list of follow-up questions for management and other due diligence.

- Put the list in priority order of importance for making an investment recommendation.
- Work on getting answers to your follow-up questions.

END OF CHAPTER: PROFITABILITY ANALYSIS OF JCPENNEY[1]

I recommend downloading JCPenney's 2012 10-K[2] and attempting the complete analysis outlined above independently. After that, compare your work and conclusions to the analysis below.

[2]Download JCPenney's 2012 10-K (fiscal year ended February 2, 2013) at the SEC Edgar website for public company filings, https://www.sec.gov/edgar/searchedgar/companysearch, using the search term "Old Copper Company." The company's search term on Edgar is Old Copper Company, Inc., not JCPenney.

Sub-Step #1: Calculate the company's adjusted income (using data from the income statement along with management's commentary) for nonrecurring gains and losses. These adjustments will be an exhibit to your investment memo. As discussed earlier, use judgment to determine what to include as nonrecurring items. Figures 7.28, 7.29, and 7.30 show adjustments that the analyst felt were reasonable. You might decide not to include some or add others as you review JCP's 10-K.

In the management discussion and analysis (MD&A) section of the 10-K, the company discloses multiple reasons for the gross margin deterioration. The analyst decided only to add back the impact of the inventory write-down.

	Historic		
$ in millions	**2010**	**2011**	**2012**
Reported Gross Profit	$6,960	$6,218	$4,066
Adjustment for Excess Inventory Write-Down	0	0	91
Adjusted Gross Profit	$6,960	$6,218	$4,157

FIGURE 7.28 Gross Profit Adjustments for JCPenney

	Historic		
$ in millions	**2010**	**2011**	**2012**
Reported SG&A Expense[a]	$6,124	$5,748	$5,402
Adjust for Pension Settlement Chrg	0	0	(148)
Adjusted SG&A	$6,124	$5,748	$5,254

[a]Includes D&A and pension expense

FIGURE 7.29 SG&A Adjustments for JCPenney

	Historic		
$ in millions	**2010**	**2011**	**2012**
Reported Operating Income	$832	$(2)	$(1,310)
Excess Inventory Write-Down	0	0	91
One Time Pension Chrg	0	0	148
Net Gain on Sale of Non-Op Assets	0	0	(397)
Net Gain from Sale of Op Assets	(8)	(6)	0
Store Impairments	3	58	26
Operating Asset Impairments	0	0	60
Restructuring and Mgmt Transitions	32	451	298
Adjusted Operating Income	859	501	(1,084)
Plus Depreciation and Amortization	511	518	543
Adjusted EBITDA	$1,370	$1,019	$(541)

FIGURE 7.30 EBITDA Adjustments for JCPenney

Sub-Step #2: Create a summary adjusted historical income statement.

As shown in Figure 7.31, the analyst looked at a time period long enough to incorporate a full economic cycle.

	Historic						
$ in millions	**2006**	**2007**	**2008**	**2009**	**2010**	**2011**	**2012**
Sales	$19,903	$19,860	$18,486	$17,556	$17,759	$17,260	$12,985
Sales Growth	6.0%	(0.2%)	(6.9%)	(5.0%)	1.2%	(2.8%)	(24.8%)
Same Store Sales Growth[a]	4.9%	0.0%	(8.5)	(6.3%)	2.5%	0.2%	(25.1%)
Adj EBITDA	$2,312	$2,305	$1,615	$1,175	$1,370	$1,019	$(541)
Margin	11.6%	11.6%	8.7%	6.7%	7.7%	5.9%	(4.2%)

[a] Same-store sales growth is a metric used by retail companies that measures the growth in revenue from store locations that have been in operation for at least one year. Sometimes called comparable store sales, it's an important metric to gauge organic growth from existing stores versus growth through store expansion.

FIGURE 7.31 JCPenney Historical Income Statement

Sub-Step #3: Analyze earnings quality. Are there any red flags that make you question the GAAP income statement?

Other than the modest increase in inventory days, no significant red flags were identified. The company did not decrease inventory levels in proportion to the massive sales decline. Therefore, there is a heightened risk of future inventory write-downs.

Sub-Step #4: Create summary adjusted income statements for the company's most direct peer group (i.e., competitors). Figure 7.32 shows comps for JCP.

	Company Comparison					
$ in millions	JCP	Macy's	Kohl's	Dillard's	Bonton	Peer Avg
2010 Sales	$17,759	$25,003	$18,391	$6,258	$3,046	$13,175
2011 Sales	17,260	26,405	18,804	6,405	2,953	13,642
2012 Sales	12,985	27,686	19,279	6,751	2,978	14,174
2010 Sales Growth	1.2%	6.4%	7.1%	0.5%	0.4%	3.6%
2011 Sales Growth	(2.8%)	5.6%	2.2%	2.3%	(3.1%)	1.8%
2012 Sales Growth	(24.8%)	4.9%	2.5%	5.4%	0.8%	3.4%
2010 Same Store Sales Growth	2.5%	4.6%	4.4%	3.0%	0.9%	2.8%
2011 Same Store Sales Growth	0.2%	5.3%	0.5%	4.0%	(2.8%)	1.8%
2012 Same Store Sales Growth	(25.1%)	3.7%	0.3%	4.0%	0.5%	2.1%
2010 Gross Profit Margin	39.2%	40.7%	38.2%	36.4%	38.9%	38.6%
2011 Gross Profit Margin	36.0%	40.4%	38.2%	36.8%	37.5%	38.2%
2012 Gross Profit Margin	32.0%	40.3%	36.3%	37.1%	37.1%	37.7%
2010 SG&A/Sales	34.5%	33.0%	22.8%	26.8%	30.9%	32.5%
2011 SG&A/Sales	33.3%	31.4%	22.6%	26.2%	31.7%	27.9%
2012 SG&A/Sales	40.5%	30.6%	22.1%	25.3%	31.4%	27.3%
2010 EBITDA Margin	7.7%	12.3%	15.5%	9.3%	8.0%	11.3%
2011 EBITDA Margin	5.9%	13.1%	15.6%	10.6%	5.8%	11.3%
2012 EBITDA Margin	-4.2%	13.4%	14.1%	11.8%	5.9%	11.3%

FIGURE 7.32 JCPenney Peer Group/Comp Analysis
Source: Adapted from Capital IQ

Sub-Step #5: Draw conclusions.

As shown in Figure 7.33, JCP reported a massive decline in its 2012 profitability, driven by self-inflicted wounds. Sales fell by approximately 25%, and EBITDA went from over $1 billion to negative $541 million. In the same period, the company's peer group saw an average sales increase of 3.4% (see Figure 7.32, peer group analysis, above).

$ in millions		Historic	
Fiscal Year End	**1/29/11**	**1/28/12**	**2/2/13**
Calendar Year	**2010**	**2011**	**2012**
Sales	$17,759	$17,260	$12,985
Sales Growth	1.2%	–2.8%	–24.8%
Same Store Sales Growth	2.5%	0.2%	–25.2%
Gross Profit	$6,960	$6,218	$4,157
Gross Profit Margin	39.2%	36.0%	32.0%
Adjusted SG&A Expense[a]	$6,124	$5,748	$5,254
Adjusted SG&A/Sales	34.5%	33.3%	40.5%
Adjusted EBITDA	$1,370	$1,019	$(541)
Adjusted EBITDA Margin	7.7%	5.9%	–4.2%

[a]Includes D&A and pension expense

FIGURE 7.33 Summary Adjusted Income Statement for JCPenney

A major shift in strategy created these problems. In late 2010, activist hedge fund Pershing Square acquired a 17.8% stake in JCP for approximately $900 million, alongside Vornado Realty Trust (a publicly traded REIT) with a 9.39% stake. Each investor received a seat on JCP's 11-person board of directors and immediately began a campaign to shift the company's strategy.

The first step in their attempt to transform JCP was firing long-time CEO Mike Ullman and replacing him with Ron Johnson from Apple at the end of 2011. Johnson was a pioneer in the retail world, having created and launched the Apple store and Genius Bar concepts. He also oversaw a successful rebranding of Target Corp. After joining JCP, Johnson replaced many of its management team with his own hires, including his new COO, Michael Kramer, who followed him from Apple.

Johnson had based his decisions on instinct rather than data and ignored one crucial difference between this role and his prior one: customers went to Apple stores because they wanted Apple products—an advantage lacking in JCP's undifferentiated apparel aisles. Rather than testing the strategy in a small group of pilot stores, Johnson rolled out the new promotional plan across all stores simultaneously.

Before the strategy change, JCP's performance was fine from a credit perspective, generating north of $1 billion in EBITDA every year, even during the 2008 GFC. However, the company's performance could have been more inspiring from an equity perspective, with sales and EBITDA declining five out of six years from 2007 through 2012. *(This highlights one difference between an equity and a debt mindset. While executed recklessly, the potential upside from the change in strategy made sense for shareholders, who might see substantial appreciation in the stock price if it worked. However, since the company was generating sufficient cash to service its existing debt, which was trading at par, there was no upside for creditors—but substantial downside if it failed.)*

Sub-Step #6: Make a list of follow-up questions for management and other due diligence.

- What initiatives are in place to turn around the business?
- How has EBITDA been tracking since year end?
- Inventory days are above peers and have trended higher. Are you concerned that your inventory has markdown risk, resulting in lower gross profit and EBITDA margins?
- What is your guidance for sales and EBITDA?

We will continue to build on these due diligence questions, adding more after we cover liquidity and capital structure analysis.

CHAPTER CONCLUSION

This chapter provided an exhaustive tour of the income statement and various parts of the financial reports (MD&A, footnotes). But our deep dive into the income statement is only the first step in analyzing financial statements. The next chapter combines our profitability analysis with the statement of cash flows, to flesh out the picture of a company's cash generation potential and liquidity position—a critical component of credit analysis.

NOTES

i. Buffett, Mary, and David Clark. (2008). *Warren Buffett and the Interpretation of Financial Statements*. New York: Scribner.

ii. Reuters staff. "Coca-Cola Agrees to $137.5 mln Settlement in Case." Reuters.com (July 6, 2008).

iii. "The Coca-Cola Company Settles Anti-Fraud and Periodic Reporting Charges Relating to Its Failure to Disclose Japanese Gallon Pushing." US Securities and Exchange Commission (accessed August 17, 2023). https://www.sec.gov/news/press/2005-58.htm.

iv. Martinez, Barbara. (August 5, 2005). "Bristol-Myers to Pay $150 Million to End SEC's Audit-Fraud Case." *Wall Street Journal*.

v. Ibid.

vi. Adams, Susan. (November 21, 2012). "Why Hostess Had to Die." *Forbes*.

vii. Forelle, Charles. (April 27, 2006). "Vitesse Internal Probe Finds Accounting Concerns." *Wall Street Journal*.

CHAPTER 8

Step 3(b) of the Credit Analysis Process: Financial Statement Analysis—Cash Flow and Liquidity

In the previous chapter, you learned how to analyze a company's profitability rigorously and thoroughly using the financial statements and management's notes and commentary. Our next step, highlighted in Figure 8.1, is liquidity analysis, which evaluates a company's ability to pay its obligations in the short run.

Step 1	Sources and Uses (only applicable to originations) (a) Why is the company seeking financing? (b) What are the proposed sources of capital to fund the financing need?
Step 2	Qualitative Analysis (a) Industry analysis (b) Business strategy (c) Management assessment (d) ESG concerns
Step 3	**Financial Statement Analysis** **(a) Profitability** **(b) Cash flow and liquidity** **(c) Capital structure**
Step 4	Forecasting (d) Identification of key business drivers and assumptions (e) Development of base, upside, and downside cases
Step 5	Corporate Valuation (a) Comparable company analysis (b) Precedent transactions (M&A comps) (c) Discounted cash flow analysis (d) Liquidation analysis
Step 6	Structuring and Documentation (a) Economic points (b) Structure and collateral (c) Covenants
Step 7	Preparing an Investment Recommendation and Credit Committee Memo (a) Investment thesis and recommendation (b) Risks and mitigants (c) Relative value analysis

FIGURE 8.1 The Seven-Step Process of Evaluating a Debt Instrument

At the risk of stating the obvious, liquidity analysis is particularly relevant to highly levered companies and is not routinely performed by equity analysts (sometimes to a fault). For example, at the end of 2022, Meta had a very high investment grade credit rating of A1/AA– and a cash balance in excess of its debt (a position referred to as "net cash"). Meta also generates roughly $20 billion in free cash flow annually. It would be borderline ridiculous, and certainly not time well spent, to analyze its liquidity. But the further you go down the credit rating spectrum, the more important this analysis becomes.

As shown in Figure 8.1, analyzing cash flow and liquidity is the second step in financial statement analysis.

Before I teach my students how to analyze a company's liquidity, I ask how they've been trained to do this. Virtually every student brings up the current ratio (current assets / current liabilities). It's not their fault; if you google "how do you measure a company's liquidity," most search results include the current ratio. Most accounting textbooks and many professors discuss the current ratio as a measure of liquidity.

Many analysts are taught that a current ratio below 1.00 signals a potential liquidity issue. In contrast, a ratio over 1.5 generally indicates ample liquidity.

To quote fifth-grade teacher and author Katie Ganshert, "Just because a lot of people believe something doesn't make it true." The current ratio is my version of "fake news." It is meaningless with respect to a company's liquidity. In twenty-five years of investing, I have never relied on the current ratio to flag liquidity issues. Not one leveraged finance professional I've asked uses this ratio.

Walmart's current ratio is consistently below 1.00, and it has excellent liquidity and an AA credit rating. Contrast that with Radio Shack; its current ratio in 2013 was 2.28, and it was in bankruptcy less than two years later. Or take Cumulus Media, the owner-operator of 8,200 broadcast radio stations. In 2016, Cumulus reported $440 million in current assets and only $101 million in current liabilities for a current ratio of 4.35, which, based on my expertise in mathematics, is much higher than the 1.50 rule of thumb for healthy liquidity. However, Cumulus filed for bankruptcy within a year of reporting these numbers.

After that overview of my disdain for the current ratio, you may be wondering what to use instead. The steps summarized in Figure 8.2 are a guide to liquidity analysis. After we review them, we will practice each one on JCP.

1. Perform a static analysis
2. Input the debt maturity schedule for the next five years
3. Calculate free cash flow (FCF)
4. Analyze the cash cycle and liquidity implications of future changes in working capital
5. Assess the company's ability to raise additional capital and refinance debt as it comes due
6. Analyze trade creditor relationships
7. Determine the company's ability to conserve cash by managing capex
8. Note other levers to improve liquidity
9. Draw conclusions from your work
10. Make a list of questions for management and other due diligence follow-ups

FIGURE 8.2 Sub-Steps to Analyzing Cash Flow and Liquidity

1. Perform a static analysis (Figure 8.3), which measures a company's immediately available sources of cash.

	Current Liquidity
Excess Cash on Balance Sheet	
Plus Availability Under Any Committed Revolving Credit Agreement[a]	
Total Immediate Liquidity	

[a]The analyst should note all relevant terms of the revolving credit agreement including maturity dates, borrowing base constraints, financial covenants, etc.

FIGURE 8.3 Static Analysis

2. Input the debt maturity schedule for the next five years (Figure 8.4). This can be found in the debt footnote in the company's 10-K.

	$ Debt Maturing
Current Year	
Second Year	
Third Year	
Fourth Year	
Fifth Year	

FIGURE 8.4 Debt Maturity Schedule

3. Calculate free cash flow (FCF), the formula for which is shown in Figure 8.5.

	Most Recent or Projected Free Cash Flow
Adjusted EBITDA	
Less Capex	
EBITDA Less Capex (EBITDAX)	
Less Cash Interest	
Less Cash Taxes	
FCF b/f Changes in WC	
+/– Changes in WC	
Free Cash Flow (FCF)	

FIGURE 8.5 Free Cash Flow Calculation[1]

[1]The free cash flow calculation for liquidity purposes differs from that used for valuation purposes. We include the cash impact of leverage (interest) for liquidity analysis. However, when valuing a company using the DCF method (see Chapter 11), the calculation assumes an unlevered balance sheet and does not subtract interest expense. Furthermore, when doing a DCF analysis, tax expense is before the benefit of any deductible interest.

4. Analyze the cash cycle and liquidity implications of future changes in working capital (Figure 8.6).

	Historic		
	Year 1	Year 2	YoY Change
Inventory Days			
+ Receivable Days			
Subtotal			
Less Payable Days			
Cash Cycle			

FIGURE 8.6 Cash Cycle and Changes in Working Capital

5. Assess the company's ability to raise additional capital and refinance debt as it comes due.
   - Analysis of recent debt and/or equity raises;
   - Conversations with the capital market desks of investment banks;
   - Analysis of unencumbered assets and ability to borrow against these assets;
   - Credit ratings (current and forecast);
   - Market trading levels of the company's debt and equity.
6. Analyze trade creditor relationships.
   - How likely is it that the trade will tighten terms?
   - What would be the impact? (In Step 4, forecasting, the impact of trade tightening will drive a downside case forecast.)
7. Determine the company's ability to conserve cash by managing capex.
   - How much of the budgeted capex is needed to maintain current operations?
   - How easy is it to cut or defer growth capex?
8. Note other levers to improve liquidity.
   - Sale of non-core assets;
   - Securitization of accounts receivables;
   - Increase in ABL's borrowing base or addition of a first-in, last-out (FILO) tranche to the ABL facility;
   - Sale of a division;
   - Other.
9. Draw conclusions from your work.
   - Is the company in danger of running out of liquidity and defaulting on its debt?
   - How long does it have to turn around its operations before it is in danger of running out of liquidity?
10. Make a list of questions for management and other due diligence follow-ups.
    - Put the list in priority order of importance for making an investment recommendation;
    - Pursue various avenues for getting answers to your follow-up questions.

END-OF-CHAPTER CASH FLOW AND LIQUIDITY ANALYSIS FOR JCPENNEY

The goal of a liquidity analysis is to determine your level of comfort with a company's ability to pay its obligations over the next three to five years.

As discussed in prior chapters, before beginning this chapter, I recommend you download JCP's 2012 10-K[2] and attempt the complete analysis, comparing your work and conclusions to the analysis below.

1) Sub-step #1: Figure 8.7 shows the static analysis for JCP

$ in millions	Most Recent
Excess Cash and Cash Equivalents on Balance Sheet	$930
Plus Availability under Any Committed Revolving Credit Agreement	1,241
Total Immediate Liquidity	$2,171

FIGURE 8.7 Static Analysis

Static analysis measures the cash available to pay debt as it comes due, fund any cash burn, and meet any other cash needs. It includes availability under all committed revolving credit agreements. As discussed in Chapter 5, a revolving credit facility is like your personal credit card; it can be repaid when the company has excess cash and (re)borrowed when the company needs cash.

Footnote #10 of JCP's 10-K describes its revolving credit facility. Below is the most critical information in this footnote.

(i) Paragraph 1 provides the maturity date.
   - *"The 2012 Credit Facility matures on April 29, 2016."*

   The further off the maturity date is, the better for the company's liquidity position. Since most credit facilities have a five-year maturity at inception, the fact that JCP's facility matures more than three years in the future is positive for its liquidity position.

(ii) Paragraphs 2 and 3 describe the type of facility.
   - *"The 2012 Credit Facility is an asset-based revolving credit facility and is secured by a perfected first-priority security interest in substantially all of our eligible credit card receivables, accounts receivable and inventory."*
   - *"Availability under the 2012 Credit Facility is limited to a borrowing base which allows us to borrow up to 85% of eligible accounts receivable, plus 90% of eligible credit card receivables, plus 85% of the liquidation value of our inventory, net of certain reserves."*

   This revolver is an asset-backed loan (ABL). It is the lowest-risk debt instrument because the amount available for the company to borrow is limited by a formula based on the liquidation value of inventory and receivables. Even if

[2]Download JCP's 2012 10-K using the free Edgar search at https://www.sec.gov/Archives/edgar/data/1166126/000116612613000016/jcp-20130202x10k.htm. The company's search term on Edgar is Old Copper Company, Inc., not JCPenney.

JCP files for bankruptcy and eventually liquidates, the ABL lenders can expect to get 100 cents on the dollar—a full recovery—through the liquidation of their collateral.

(iii) Paragraph 4 tells you how much of the revolver is available to borrow.

- *"For the fiscal year ended 2012, we had $1,241 million available for borrowing under the 2012 Credit Facility."*

Revolver availability is critical to the analysis of a company's liquidity. You cannot calculate this number yourself, since you don't have all the inputs needed for the borrowing base formula. And keep in mind that the availability provided in a financial statement disclosure is as of one moment in time (in this case, JCP's fiscal year end of February 2). In practice, it's common for highly levered companies to provide an update on their revolver availability subsequent to the date of the financial statement, since weeks or months elapse between the end of the reporting period and the filing of the report. It would be unusual *not* to disclose this material fact on the earnings call. In contrast, since higher quality and investment grade companies are unlikely to draw on their bank facilities, availability is unlikely to come up during the earnings call. However, revolver terms are a standard disclosure even for companies without liquidity challenges.

2) Sub-step #2: Figure 8.8 outlines JCP's debt maturities

	Debt Maturity Schedule		
$ in millions	$ Maturing	Cumulative	% of Total
2013	$0	$0	0%
2014	0	0	0%
2015	200	200	7%
2016	200	400	14%
2017	285	685	24%
Thereafter	2,183	2,868	100%
Total	$2,868		

FIGURE 8.8 Debt Maturity Schedule

Footnote 11 of JCP's 10-K describes all the company's outstanding debt, including its maturity schedule. As shown above, JCP has no obligations coming due in the next two years (very good for liquidity), and in aggregate, only $685MM or (24%) of its total debt comes due in the next five years. In sub-step #1, we determined that JCP has $2,171MM of cash plus availability under its revolving credit facility—clearly adequate to deal with the next five years of debt maturities. So far, JCP's liquidity looks good. However, we are not done with our analysis.

3) Sub-step #3: Free Cash Flow for JCP

Thus far we've focused on balance sheet items—cash and debt balances. But even more important for companies entering a distress spiral is operational analysis. A company struggling with its operations might be burning cash—and the liquidity identified in sub-step #1 might be required to fund this. Free cash flow analysis focuses on how much cash the company generates or burns before borrowing or paying down debt. Figure 8.9 shows the massive cash burn JCP is experiencing.

$ in millions	FCF	Notes
Adjusted EBITDA	-541	From profitability analysis
Less Capex	-810	See note (i) below
EBITDA Less Capex (EBITDAX)	-1,351	
Less Interest Expense	-226	From JCP income statement
Less Cash Taxes	0	See note (ii) below
FCF before Chg in Operating Working Capital	-1,577	
+/- Chg in Operating Working Capital	631	See note (iii) below
Free Cash Flow (FCF)[3]	-946	

FIGURE 8.9 FCF Calculation

(i) *Capex:*

The capital expenditure (capex) line item is found in the "Cash Flows from Investing" section of the cash flow statement (below the operating cash flow section). For now, we have included the capex as reported. However, in sub-step #7, we will estimate how much capex is needed to maintain the business versus grow it. If the company encounters liquidity problems, it should defer or eliminate spending on growth initiatives.

(ii) *Tax assumption:*

JCP received a tax refund in 2012. Since it no longer has any tax carrybacks, it is not entitled to any future tax refunds. But since it has a significant tax carryforward from its massive 2012 loss, even if it becomes profitable, it will not be a taxpayer in the near term. (This disclosure can be found in Note 18: Income Taxes.) Therefore, we are ignoring taxes for JCP's FCF analysis. It is common for liquidity-challenged companies not to pay taxes, as they are typically operating in a net loss position.

(iii) *Changes in operating working capital:*

Changes in operating working capital can impact operating cash flow meaningfully—in either direction. Understanding historical working capital trends and forecasting working capital changes are critical to predicting cash flow for companies in working capital–intensive industries, including retail.

The bottom part of the operating section of the cash flow statement provides the cash flow impacts of the changes in the operating working capital components. As shown in Figure 8.10, changes in working capital were a positive contributor to JCP's cash flow in 2012.

[3]JCP's actual 2012 FCF was better than the above calculation because the analyst ignored its tax refund, as he doesn't believe they will receive any further refunds. In addition, a few other items impacted 2012 cash flows, but the analyst does not expect them to influence future cash flows.

$ in millions	Historic Working Capital & Notes	
Changes in Cash From:	**2012**	**Notes**
Inventory	575	
Prepaid Expenses and Other Assets	- 5	
Merchandise Accounts Payable	140	
Current Income Taxes	0	See note (ii) above
Accrued Expenses and Other	- 79	
Total Cash Flow Impact	631	

FIGURE 8.10 Impact of Changes in Operating Working Capital on Cash Flow

This might seem counterintuitive; why would a company in distress *generate* cash from working capital? We will discuss this in more detail in sub-step #4; for now, hold the thought that working capital can be a life preserver for distressed companies.

The free cash flow analysis above shows that JCP is burning $946 million of cash flow annually. At this burn rate, its static liquidity of $2,171 will be depleted in approximately two years. Note also that the calculation of cash burn includes a positive impact of $631MM from changes in working capital, which are typically nonrecurring. Using a normalized cash burn of $1,577 (free cash flow before the positive impact of operating working capital changes), JCP will run out of liquidity in just over a year without a significant turnaround or substantial cuts in capex.

4) Sub-step #4: Analyze changes in the cash cycle and the liquidity implications of future changes in working capital

The cash cycle, depicted in Figure 8.11, is a measure of the time to convert inventory into cash less the time to pay vendors for this inventory. Companies typically pay their vendors for inventory before they sell it and collect cash from their customers, which gives rise to the cash cycle. The analysis below draws on information from the income statement and the balance sheet.

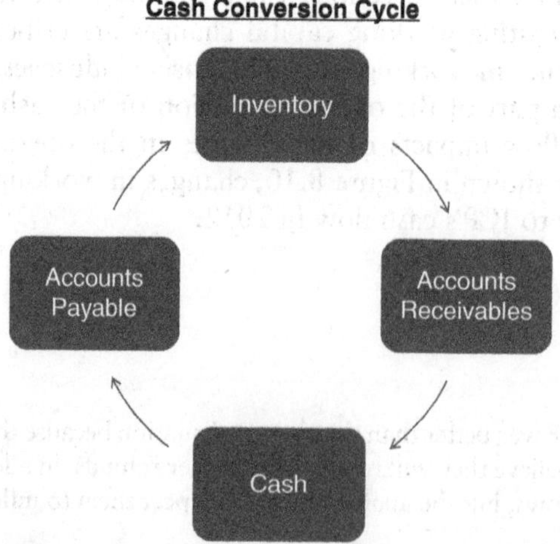

FIGURE 8.11 Cash Conversion Cycle

Figure 8.12 shows the components of the cash cycle, while Figures 8.13, 8.14, and 8.15 show the calculation of each component for JCP.

	Calculation Description
Inventory Days	Average number of days it takes to sell inventory
Plus Receivable Days	(+) Average number of days it takes to collect cash from customers after the sale is made
Subtotal	Average number of days it takes to convert inventory into cash
Less Payable Days	(−) Average number of days until the company pays its vendors for the inventory
Cash Cycle in Days	Average days to convert inventory into cash less time to pay vendors

FIGURE 8.12 Components of Cash Cycle

Inventory days are the average number of days a company holds inventory before selling it. The lower this ratio is, the better for liquidity. The formula to calculate inventory days is:

Inventory days = 365 × (Average inventory from the B/S) / (COGS from the I/S)

2012 JCP Inventory days = 365 × ($2,629/$8,919) = 107.6 days

To calculate average inventory:[4]

(Last year ending inventory + Current year ending inventory)/2

2012 JCP Average inventory = ($2,916 + $2,341)/2

	2011	2012	Change
Inventory Days	101.3	107.6	6.3

FIGURE 8.13 Calculation of JCP's Inventory Days

Receivable days are the average number of days it takes a company to collect cash from its customers after a sale was made. The lower this ratio is, the better for liquidity. The formula to calculate receivable days is:

Receivable Days = 365 × (Average receivables from the B/S) / (Sales from the I/S)

JCP's 2012 balance sheet does not include a line item for accounts receivable. Retail customers either pay cash or with a credit card, and the credit card companies pay the retailer in one to two days.[5] Therefore, the amount of JCP's accounts receivable is immaterial and "buried" in other assets.

[4]I used year-end numbers to calculate average inventory, receivables, and payables for teaching purposes, so only one financial statement (the 10-K) is required. However, given the seasonality of the business, it is advisable to use all four quarters (and corresponding 10-Q filings) to calculate the averages.

[5]Before the turn of the century, it was typical for retailers to keep their receivables on balance sheet by issuing proprietary credit cards. Virtually all retailers now contract with a bank to manage and administer their private label credit cards—so even if you have a Macy's card, Macy's has outsourced that business to a financial institution and thus kept the associated receivables off its balance sheet.

	2011	2012	Change
Receivable Days	0	0	0

FIGURE 8.14 Calculation of JCP's Receivable Days

Payable days are the average number of days it takes the company to pay its vendors for inventory. The higher this ratio is, the better for liquidity, as long as that number is sustainable.

If a company's payable days increase from 30 to 100 because vendors extended better terms, that is good for liquidity. However, if the company is "stretching" payables, meaning paying its vendors late, then the company is at risk of losing vendor support (referred to as the vendors "pulling support"). Pulling support means the vendor will no longer accept payment terms, instead demanding payment in advance of shipping. A decrease in trade/vendor support can be a disaster for a retailer's liquidity, and even rumors of this can send its bonds down sharply.

The formula to calculate payable days is:

Payable days = 365 × (Average account payables from the B/S) / (Cost of goods sold from the I/S)[6]

2012 JCP payable days = 365 × ($1,092/$8,919) = 44.7 days

To calculate average accounts payable[7] = (Last year ending accounts payable + Current year ending accounts payable) / 2

2012 JCP average accounts payable = ($1,022 + $1,162)/2

	2011	2012	Change
Payable Days	35.6	44.7	9.1

FIGURE 8.15 Calculation of JCP's Payable Days

Observations and Conclusions Related to JCP's Cash Cycle To draw conclusions, we need to compare each component of the cash cycle to competitors' and analyze the trend (year-over-year changes) in each component. Figure 8.16 shows the cash cycle for JCP and competitor Kohl's.

[6] Some analysts calculate payable days using inventory purchases instead of COGS. Since inventory purchased during the year is not a required disclosure, the analyst must estimate it by using the formula: Inventory purchases = ending inventory – beginning inventory + COGS for the period.

[7] I used year-end numbers to calculate average inventory, receivables, and payables for teaching purposes, so the reader only needs to look at one 10-K. However, given the seasonality of the business, it is advisable to use all four quarters to calculate the averages.

	JCP Cash Cycle in Days			Kohl's Cash Cycle in Days		
	2011	2012	Change	2011	2012	Change
Inventory Days	101.3	107.6	6.3	101.0	103.4	2.4
+ Receivable Days	0.0	0.0	0.0	0.0	0.0	0.0
Subtotal	101.3	107.6	6.3	101.0	103.4	2.4
-Payable Days	35.6	44.7	9.1	38.7	37.7	-1.0
Cash Cycle	65.7	62.9	-2.8	62.3	65.7	3.4

FIGURE 8.16 Comparison of JCP and Kohl's Cash Cycles

To identify red flags, you need both the ratios above and the numbers from sub-step #3 (free cash flow calculation, working capital line items).

1. *Inventory Days*: In 2012 JCP had a slight increase in inventory days but no significant red flags. The company brought inventory levels down, though not exactly in line with the material underperformance of sales. Since retailers typically pay their vendors before they monetize merchandise in their stores, inventory is a cash drain for a growing retailer and a cash contributor for a shrinking one. JCP saw a $575 million inflow from inventory in 2012 (see cash impact of changes in working from sub-step #3 above). In other words, sales declined enough for the company to cut back purchasing meaningfully while at the same time monetizing the inventory that had already been paid for. However, we should not expect JCP to get this benefit next year, especially if sales stabilize or increase.
2. *Receivable Days*: There are no red flags for JCP, given it has no material receivables (as discussed above).
3. *Payable Days*: Accounts payable and vendor terms are among the most challenging and critical cash flow items to interpret and forecast. As discussed above, a sustainable increase in payable days is good for liquidity. However, a company in distress might "stretch" its payables to preserve cash, that is, take longer to pay its suppliers. If a company pays its vendors late, the positive effect on liquidity is likely temporary. It might even hurt liquidity in the long term as late payments could make vendors more nervous about a customer's financial health, leading to tighter terms and a resultant cash outflow / liquidity drain.

   In 2012 JCP's payable days increased by 26 percent to 45 days, contributing to the $140 million inflow from payables (from sub-step #3). While the increase in payable days was good for 2012's cash flow, it's questionable whether 45 days payable is sustainable for JCP, particularly since higher-quality peer Kohl's has a lower number (38). Since JCP's profitability declined meaningfully in 2012, a reasonable conclusion is that JCP tried to conserve liquidity by paying its vendors late. If this persists, suppliers could tighten terms (e.g., demand payment in 30 rather than 45 days), or even demand payment in advance of shipping. This would be a disaster for JCP's liquidity; think of this as a liability of roughly

$1.162 billion (that is, the accounts payable balance) coming due immediately. JCP felt the need to discuss this risk in its 10-K.

Substantially all of our merchandise suppliers and vendors sell to us on open account purchase terms. There is a risk that our suppliers and vendors could respond to any actual or apparent decrease in or any concern with our financial results or liquidity by requiring or conditioning their sale of merchandise to us on more stringent payment terms. [. . .] There can be no assurance that one or more of our suppliers may not slow or cease merchandise shipments or require or condition their sale or shipment of merchandise on more stringent payment terms. If any of the above circumstances were to occur, our need for additional liquidity in the near term could significantly increase.

---

5) Sub-step #5: Analyze JCP's ability to raise additional capital in the debt and equity markets

A company can improve its liquidity by issuing new debt or equity. To assess a company's access to the capital markets, you must look at the trading levels of the company's securities. Based on observable trading levels, JCP has limited ability to access either the credit or equity market.

- After releasing its dismal 2012 earnings report, the company's long-dated unsecured bonds traded down to $70 (versus close to par when Pershing Square first got involved in late 2010). Investors evaluating JCP would not underwrite a bond at par if they could buy its existing debt at such a large discount to par without a significant increase in coupon and structure. Conversations with investment banks confirm that JCP could not access the unsecured debt market.
- JCP's equity is trading at an all-time low. Its market cap troughed around $1.5 billion in 2013 on the heels of its disastrous performance in 2012. While an equity raise is possible, it will be punitively dilutive if management believes the current stock price does not reflect the true value of the business.
- This leaves new secured debt as the company's most realistic option. All current assets (primarily inventory) are already pledged to the revolving credit facility. The company has unencumbered real estate, so it might be able to borrow using the real estate as collateral. However, JCP discloses in its 10-K that it has a $255 million bond with a covenant that restricts incremental debt issuance in certain circumstances:

We have an indenture covering approximately $255 million of long-term debt that contains a financial covenant requiring us to have a minimum of 200% net tangible assets to senior funded indebtedness (as defined in the indenture). This indenture permits our Company to issue additional long-term debt if we are in compliance with the covenant. At year-end 2012, our percentage of net tangible assets to senior funded indebtedness was 304%.

What does this mean in plain English? You'd have to pull the indenture for the referenced bond for more detail, including definitions of the terms "senior funded indebtedness" and "net tangible assets." However, you can infer from the 10-K language above that the holders of the $255MM bond enjoy a protective covenant that restricts the company from issuing debt above a certain ceiling amount. Using the numbers provided in JCP's 10-K, you can back into the amount of incremental debt permitted by this covenant by calculating the denominator of the calculation ("senior funded indebtedness") if the ratio falls to 200%. The other consideration is that the numerator, "net tangible assets," could fall if the company has to write down its tangible assets. Asset write-downs are typical on the heels of a huge loss like that experienced in 2012. The conclusion is that, despite the presence of unencumbered assets that could be pledged to new secured debt issues, new debt issuance would be contingent upon either paying back that $255MM bond or convincing the holders of the $255 million bond to waive the restriction. Incidentally, this is a very unusual covenant that was only found in one of JCP's dozen or so bonds outstanding at the time. We will return to this situation and discuss covenants in general in later chapters.

6) Sub-step #6: Analysis of JCP's trade support

I have broken out sub-step #6 because trade support is such a critical component of a company's liquidity. The work needed to draw conclusions about trade support was already done in sub-step #4 above, so this is intentionally repetitive. If you evaluated trade support adequately in the cash cycle analysis, you can skip this sub-step.

Trade payables generally come due every 30 to 60 days. A company is continuously buying new inventory on the same terms in the ordinary course of business, which means its trade partners effectively refinance themselves. However, if vendors get concerned about the company's viability, they might tighten terms or, in the most extreme case, demand cash in advance of shipment. This has a material impact on liquidity.

As discussed above in sub-step #4, deterioration in trade support is a material risk. With approximately $1.2B of accounts payable outstanding, it would be devastating to liquidity if the trade pulled.

7) Sub-step #7: Determine JCP's ability to conserve cash by managing capex

In a liquidity crisis, companies attempt to conserve cash wherever possible. As discussed in sub-step #3, capex is a significant cash outflow for virtually all companies. To assess how much capex is easy to cut or defer, you must estimate how much of it is required to maintain the business (maintenance capex) versus what portion is to grow the business (growth capex). In a liquidity crisis, a company is likely to cut growth capex proactively. However, there may be some lead time to cut capex, since budgets for larger projects are set years in advance and might entail non-cancelable contracts.

Some companies disclose information that helps quantify the amount of maintenance versus growth capex. For instance, Figure 8.17 is a disclosure from Walmart's 2012 10-K.

$ in millions	Allocation of Capital Expenditures Fiscal Years Ending January 31,	
Capital Expenditures	**2013**	**2012**
New stores and clubs	$4,340	$3,735
Information systems, distribution, e-commerce, and other	2,922	2,852
Remodels	995	1,648
Total US	8,257	8,235
Walmart International	4,641	5,275
Total capital expenditures	**$12,898**	**$13,510**

FIGURE 8.17 Walmart's 10-K Capex Disclosure

Based on this disclosure, we know that at least $4.3B (roughly a third) of the company's capex is growth related (new stores and clubs). Your follow-up diligence questions would include one related to how much of the international capex is growth versus maintenance.

Unfortunately, the table so helpfully provided by Walmart is not a required disclosure. JCP provides no details other than the amount spent each year. In the absence of a similar disclosure, some analysts estimate growth capex as total capex less depreciation expense, which assumes that depreciation is equal to maintenance capex. This methodology has significant flaws, including the use of different depreciation methods (straight line, accelerated, etc.). Depreciation is purely an accounting methodology to estimate the amount of fixed assets "used up" during a year. It does not necessarily represent what the company must spend annually to maintain its operations.

JCP's 10-K discloses the number of new stores but not the amount spent on them. From the cash flow statement, we know that JCP increased capex significantly in 2011 and 2012 despite opening very few new stores. So what was that spending for? As part of Bill Ackman's new strategy, JCP embarked on a massive capex program to change its store layouts. 2010's capex of $499MM (before the store layout expenditures began) is a reasonable estimate of maintenance capex, since JCP only opened two new stores that year.

Figure 8.18 shows historical capex and stores for JCP. If JCP's liquidity position continues to deteriorate, it can likely cut capex from 2012's $810 million level to approximately $500 million, saving $310 million.

	Historical				
$ in millions	2008	2009	2010	2011	2012
Total Capex	969	600	499	634	810
Number of New Stores	35	17	2	3	9

FIGURE 8.18 Information on Capex Disclosed in JCP's 10-K

8) Sub-step #8: Other levers to improve liquidity

- As discussed in Chapter 5, ABLs are extremely low risk as the borrowing base formula effectively limits the amount outstanding to an amount covered even in a worst-case liquidation scenario. Given the low-risk nature of the ABL facility, it is possible in a liquidity crunch that JCP could negotiate to increase the advance rates in exchange for a fee or increase in coupon. It might also be possible to bring in a new lender willing to take a second lien on the ABL's collateral, a structure referred to as a first-in, last-out (FILO) loan. Since the FILO is junior to the revolver, it would have a significantly higher coupon.
- No meaningful other liquidity levers exist. JCP's 10-K discloses it owns approximately 15% of Martha Stewart Living Omnimedia purchased in 2012 for $39 million. However, even if JCP monetized this ownership interest, its small size means it would not materially enhance liquidity.

9) Sub-step #9: Draw conclusions from your work

You've done most of the hard work for liquidity analysis. To finish, incorporate all the outputs of the prior sub-steps to formulate and state your view on the company's liquidity position.

JCP's liquidity situation is very concerning.

- JCP is burning $1.6B of FCF annually before the impact of working capital changes. At this rate, the company has one to two years before it burns through its cash and availability on its revolving credit facility.
- There is also risk that the liquidity situation deteriorates much more quickly if vendors tighten terms, or even pull support entirely on the $1.2 billion accounts payable balance.
- JCP does not appear to have access to the debt capital markets since its unsecured debt is trading well below par, and one of its bonds restricts raising much new debt.

10) Sub-step #10: Make a list of questions for management and other due diligence follow-ups. Put the list in priority order of importance for making an investment recommendation

The questions below are a wish list. The company may not be able to respond to some questions, particularly those with specific quantitative answers, if doing so would disclose material, nonpublic information.

Business turnaround:

- What initiatives are in place to turn around the business?
- How has EBITDA been tracking since year end?
- Inventory days are above peers' and have trended higher. Are you concerned that your inventory has markdown risk, resulting in lower gross and EBITDA margins?
- What is your guidance for sales and EBITDA?

Vendor support:

- Has any vendor changed terms?
- In 2012, payable days increased. Are you stretching payables? How many of your payables are past due? *(It's also important to call large vendors directly rather than relying entirely on management's responses.)*

Revolving credit facility:

- Your revolver availability is determined by a borrowing base tied to receivables and the liquidation value of your inventories. Would your revolving credit lenders consider increasing the facility's availability? How much? Have you considered bringing in a FILO lender?
- At year end, you reported a cash balance of $930MM and availability on your revolving credit facility of $1,241. What are those levels today?
- How much cash do you expect to use for the remainder of this year and next? How much do you anticipate drawing on your revolving credit facility (peak and average)?

Capex:

- How much of your historic capex was maintenance versus growth?
- How much capex are you budgeting for this year and next?
- What is the lowest amount you can spend on capex, and how long can this bare-bones level be maintained without permanent damage to your franchise?

Other liquidity enhancements:

- Do you have plans to raise additional unsecured debt or equity? Are the capital markets open to you?
- Do you have unencumbered real estate or other assets to pledge as collateral for incremental secured debt?
- Your 10-K disclosed that a $255 million bond has a restrictive covenant that might prevent you from raising more debt. How do you plan to address that? Have you or your advisors had conversations with bondholders on amending that restriction? What has been their response?
- Are there any other levers you can pull to improve your liquidity position?

CHAPTER CONCLUSION: LAST WORD ON LIQUIDITY

Based on the above analysis, it is unambiguous that JCP has liquidity issues. In contrast, Walmart, a competing retailer, has excellent liquidity as of its fiscal 2012 year end. Walmart has $26 billion of cash and availability on its revolving credit facility, and it generates $12 billion of free cash flow annually versus $6 billion of debt coming due in 2013, meaning the company can pay down maturing debt with free cash flow rather using its cash or drawing on its revolver. Walmart also has access to the capital markets, as evidenced by the low yields on its AA-rated bonds and large equity market capitalization and can easily tap the debt and equity markets as needed.

Let's end the chapter by looking at the ratio we started with, the current ratio. Based on Figure 8.19, which company, JCP or Walmart, has more liquidity?

	Company Comparison	
$ in millions	**JCP**	**WMT**
Current Assets (CA)	3,683	59,940
Current Liabilities (CL)	2,583	71,818
Current Ratio (CA/CL)	1.43	0.83

FIGURE 8.19 2012 Current Ratio for Walmart and JCPenney

JCP's current ratio is almost double that of Walmart. What would you think of a credit analyst who concluded that JCP has better liquidity than Walmart based on this metric? You would think he is not very good at his job!

CHAPTER 9

Step 3(c) of the Credit Analysis Process: Financial Statement Analysis—Capital Structure

Understanding capital structure is one of the most critical components of credit analysis. Put simply, "capital structure" refers to the mix of various debt instruments and equity used to finance the company. As highlighted in Figure 9.1, to recommend a credit investment, you must develop a view on whether a company's capital structure is appropriate for its underlying business and how it is likely to evolve in the forecast period.

Step 1	Sources and Uses (only applicable to originations) (a) Why is the company seeking financing? (b) What are the proposed sources of capital to fund the financing need?
Step 2	Qualitative Analysis (a) Industry analysis (b) Business strategy (c) Management assessment (d) ESG concerns
Step 3	**Financial Statement Analysis** **(a) Profitability** **(b) Cash flow and liquidity** **(c) Capital structure**
Step 4	Forecasting (a) Identification of key business drivers and assumptions (b) Development of base, upside, and downside cases
Step 5	Corporate Valuation (a) Comparable company analysis (b) Precedent transactions (M&A comps) (c) Discounted cash flow analysis (d) Liquidation analysis
Step 6	Structuring and Documentation (a) Economic points (b) Structure and collateral (c) Covenants
Step 7	Preparing an Investment Recommendation and Credit Committee Memo (a) Investment thesis and recommendation (b) Risks and mitigants (c) Relative value analysis

FIGURE 9.1 The Seven-Step Process of Evaluating a Debt Instrument

WHICH COMPANY IS MORE PROFITABLE?

To start this chapter, let's do a brief review of what you might have learned from a "Finance 101" textbook, beginning with a simple question: Which company in Figure 9.2 is more profitable?

	Company Comparison	
Income Statement	**Co #1**	**Co #2**
Sales	$2,000	$2,000
Cost of Goods Sold	800	800
Gross Profit	1,200	1,200
Selling, General & Administrative Expenses	625	625
Operating Profit	575	575
Interest Expense	0	210
Pretax Profit	575	365
Tax Expense at a 21% rate	121	77
Net Income	454	288
Balance Sheet Summary:	**Co #1**	**Co #2**
Current Assets	200	200
Property Plant and Equipment, net	4,800	4,800
Total Assets	5,000	5,000
Current Liabilities	100	100
Long Term Debt	0	3,500
Owner's Equity	4,900	1,400
Total Liabilities and Owners' Equity	5,000	5,000

FIGURE 9.2 Profitability Analysis for Two Hypothetical Companies

While Company #1 has higher net income (both dollars and margin), this is only part of the story. In an operational sense, their profitability is the same—that is, they generate the same operating profit with the same dollar amount of assets. However, if we look beyond operating profitability and take a shareholder's point of view, Company #2 is significantly more profitable because, as shown in Figure 9.3, its return on equity (ROE) is higher.

	Company Comparison	
Income Statement	**Co #1**	**Co #2**
Net Income	454	288
Divided by Owners' Equity	4,900	1,400
Return on Equity Investment (Net Income / Owners' Equity)	**9.3%**	**20.6%**

FIGURE 9.3 ROE for Two Hypothetical Companies

The difference in profitability springs from the difference in the approach to capital structure. Company #1 has only equity, whereas Company #2 has a combination of debt and equity. As the example above illustrates, using leverage can improve ("juice") shareholder returns as long as the company's return on assets (ROA) is higher than its after-tax cost of debt.

Why wouldn't every company maximize its debt if it improves ROE? There are two answers to this.

- First, the cost of debt increases with its proportion of the capital structure, all else equal. A company that finances its business using 90% debt and 10% equity has a higher cost of debt than if it had 60% debt and 40% equity.
- Second, debt increases the chance of financial distress. There are no contractual cash flows associated with equity because it is permanent capital. Although many companies choose to pay dividends and buy back stock, these are discretionary payments. On the other hand, debt requires cash coupon/interest payments, and unlike equity it has a contractual maturity date. Failure to service debt (i.e., make required interest and principal payments) leads to financial distress and, potentially, bankruptcy.

Determining the right mix of debt and equity is a balancing act. A higher proportion of debt *should* increase shareholder returns, but too much debt increases the risk of financial distress and a complete wipeout of equity in bankruptcy. Therefore, as depicted in Figure 9.4, companies with very low operational risk (i.e., stable, predictable cash flow) can and should have more debt than companies with higher

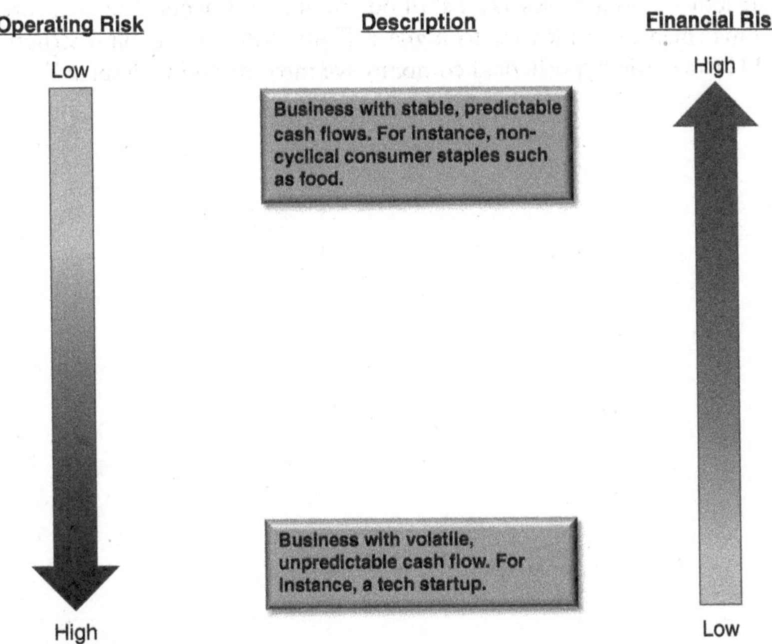

FIGURE 9.4 Operating and Financial Risk Considerations

operational risk (i.e., volatile, unpredictable cash flow). In the example in Figure 9.4, higher financial risk means a higher proportion of debt in the capital structure, and vice versa.

CAPITAL STRUCTURE ANALYSIS

In the following sections we will walk through six sub-steps to analyze a company's capital structure, as outlined in Figure 9.5.

1. Lay out the company's capital structure table
2. Calculate credit ratios
3. Adjust for or note off–balance sheet and debt-like obligations
4. Understand the company's credit ratings (current, historical, trajectory)
5. Draw conclusions on capital structure
6. Make a list of follow-up questions for management and other due diligence follow-ups.

FIGURE 9.5 Sub-steps to Analyze a Company's Capital Structure

SUB-STEP #1: CAPITAL STRUCTURE ANALYSIS—CAPITAL STRUCTURE TABLE

Your first step is to create a table that includes every instrument (loans, bonds, equity) used to finance the company. This table has several functions: it calculates ratios (discussed in sub-step #2), it shows real-time valuations of each portion of the capital structure, and it serves as a list of potential investments. The list is ordered by risk of impairment, from lowest to highest. Figure 9.6 is the capital structure table for MGEC Corp, the hypothetical company we introduced in Chapter 7.

MGEC Capital Structure Table

	Amount	Coupon	Maturity	Price[a]	Yield-to-Maturity[b]	Ratings S&P & Moody's[c]	Leverage as a Multiple of LTM EBITDA ($48.04MM) Face	Market	Loan-to-Value Face	Market
ABL Revolver	30,000	SOFR+2.25%	2 years	100.0%	3.25%	BB-/ /Ba3				
1st Lien Term Loan	100,000	SOFR+2.75%	2 years	100.0%	3.75%	BB-/ /Ba3				
Capital Leases	8,000	Various	Various	100.0%	N/A	N/A				
Total 1st Lien Debt	**138,000**						2.87x	2.87x	43.0%	43.0%
2nd Lien Term Loan	30,000	SOFR+4.5%	3 years	90.5%	9.27%	B+/ B1				
Total Secured Debt	**168,000**						3.50x	3.44x	52.3%	51.4%
Senior Unsecured Bond #1	45,000	7.000%	7 years	79.0%	11.53%	B/ B2				
Senior Unsecured Bond #2	2,000	7.125%	7 years	79.5%	11.55%	B/ B2				
Total Senior Debt	**215,000**						4.48x	4.27x	67.0%	63.9%
Subordinated Debt	15,000	8.000%	10 years	68.0%	14.18%	B-/ B3				
Total Debt	**230,000**						4.79x	4.69x	71.7%	70.2%
Less: Cash	(4,000)									
Net Debt	**226,000**						4.70x	4.60x	70.4%	68.9%
Equity Market Cap.	95,000									
Total Enterprise Value	**321,000**						6.68x	6.68x[d]	100.0%	100.0%

[a] Price. This is the price at which you can buy each debt instrument. The company's 10-K does not disclose the trading price of its debt issues. Debt pricing is not ascertainable without access to Bloomberg, a credit trader, or sell-side research.
[b] Yield to maturity (YTM). The return on your investment if you buy the debt at the quoted price and the company pays all coupons and repays the debt at maturity. See Chapter 3 for a primer on yields. For the purposes of this example, SOFR is assumed to be 1%.
[c] Ratings. In sub-step #4 we discuss the role of credit ratings in capital structure analysis.
[d] Face and market leverage and LTV metrics are identical at the total enterprise value level, even though some of the debt trades below par, because each layer of the capital structure is calculated as if all layers above it are priced at par/100%. This concept is explained in detail later in the chapter.

FIGURE 9.6 Capital Structure Table – MGEC Corp

SUB-STEP #2: CAPITAL STRUCTURE ANALYSIS—RATIOS

There are three key ratios used to analyze a company's capital structure. Two appear in the right-hand columns of Figure 9.6.

1. Leverage ratio = debt / adjusted EBITDA
2. Loan-to-value ratio = debt / enterprise value

Note that these are calculated in two ways: "face" and "market." Face value refers to the actual amount of debt outstanding, while market value takes into consideration the trading prices of the debt (more on this below).

The third ratio is:

3. Coverage ratio = (adjusted EBITDA - capex) / interest expense

To practice calculating each of the ratios and discuss how we use them, let's return to MGEC Corp. Its LTM adjusted EBITDA, interest expense, and capex are $48,044, $11,602, and $27,900, respectively.

Debt is analyzed by its ranking or priority. If a company cannot meet its debt obligations and files for bankruptcy, then debt repayment from the value of the company's assets follows a "waterfall" based on the priority/seniority of the debt. This waterfall doesn't matter unless a company gets into trouble—but, in that case, it matters a lot. No value is allocated to the shareholders of a bankrupt company unless all creditors can be paid off in full.

A simplified order of priority is shown in Figure 9.7. We will expand on this in Section III on distressed debt investing.

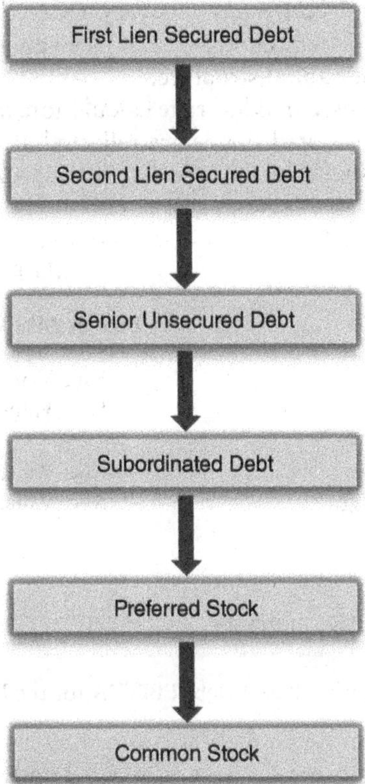

FIGURE 9.7 Order of Priority

Leverage based on face value of debt

The most common metric to measure a company's leverage is debt / adjusted EBITDA. The first lien loan is first in line to get paid. For this reason, it is sometimes referred to as "dollar one risk." For the first lien loan to avoid impairment in bankruptcy, that is, get one hundred cents on the dollar, or "par," MGEC's total enterprise value must be at least 2.87x EBITDA (First lien debt of 138,000 / adjusted EBITDA of 48,044).

Leverage based on market value of debt

In non-distressed situations, it is adequate to use the par value of a company's debt instruments to analyze its capital structure. However, if a company has financial problems and its debt is trading at a significant discount to par, it's also necessary to look at the market value of the debt. This is sometimes referred to as the "creation multiple," meaning the valuation at which you could "create" the company by buying the debt at current trading levels and then converting the debt into equity through the bankruptcy process. Part III discusses the bankruptcy process and distressed debt analysis in detail.

These calculations use a combination of market and face values based on the seniority of each instrument. At each level of priority, the analyst uses the face value of all debt senior to that level because those instruments must be repaid at par before the lower-priority debt can receive any recovery. Once the calculation reaches the level of debt being analyzed, market rather than face value is used to incorporate the discount at that level of the capital structure.

For the MGEC Corp unsecured leverage calculation, all secured debt is included at face value, while the unsecured bonds are reflected at market value, resulting in market-based leverage through the unsecured bonds of 4.27x (Figure 9.8).

	Market-Based Calculation	
	Face or Mkt Value	**Debt Amount Used**
1st Lien Debt	Face Value	138,000
2nd Lien Debt	Face Value	30,000
Total Debt with Higher Priority		168,000
Unsecured Bonds #1 (@79%)	Mkt Value	35,550
Unsecured Bonds #2 (@79.5%)	Mkt Value	1,590
Debt through Unsecured		205,140
EBITDA		48,044
Debt through Unsecured (market) / EBITDA		4.27x

FIGURE 9.8 Calculation of Market-Based Debt/EBITDA for the Unsecured Bonds

The leverage calculation for the subordinated bonds is similar but values the more senior unsecured bonds at par (as well as the secured debt) rather than market to reflect the need to pay out all senior layers before the subordinated debt is eligible for any recovery. As shown in Figure 9.9, this calculation results in market-based leverage through the subordinated debt of 4.69x.

	Market-Based Calculation	
	Face or Mkt Value	**Debt Amount Used**
1st Lien Debt	Face Value	138,000
2nd Lien Debt	Face Value	30,000
Unsecured Bonds #1	Face Value	45,000
Unsecured Bonds #2	Face Value	2,000
Total Debt with Higher Priority		215,000
Subordinated Debt (@68%)	Mkt Value	10,200
Debt through Subordinated		225,200
EBITDA		48,044
Debt through Subordinated (market) / EBITDA		4.69x

FIGURE 9.9 Calculation of Market-Based Debt/EBITDA for the Subordinated Debt

We will spend more time on the relevance of market and creation value in the distressed debt section. For now, the goal is to provide you with the formulas and calculations for concepts that will come into play when you evaluate distressed opportunities.

Loan-to-value (LTV)

The value of a business is equal to net debt (debt less cash) plus the market value of equity (for a publicly traded company). This is commonly referred to as total enterprise value (TEV). In Chapter 11, "Step 5 of the Credit Analysis Process: Corporate Valuation," we will discuss different ways to value a company in detail. LTV is debt divided by the value of the company. This is conceptually similar to the LTV calculation a mortgage lender performs when you borrow money to buy a home; the amount you put down is the analog to the equity discussed here, and since appreciation in the price of your home accrues to the "V" of the equation, LTV decreases as your house goes up in value. The lower the ratio, the lower the risk of the debt. A 90% LTV means that the business valuation (TEV) can only decline by 10% before creditors are impaired.

We'll use a similar approach to the leverage calculations above, looking at the LTV of each layer of the capital structure. MGEC's TEV based on the publicly traded market price of the equity is $321,000, which means the LTV through the first lien debt is equal to 43.0% (first lien debt of 138,000 divided by total enterprise value of $321,500). At the subordinated debt level, LTV increases to 71.7% (total debt of 230,000 divided by total enterprise value of $321,500).

In distressed scenarios, companies frequently have market LTVs over 100%, suggesting that some portion of the capital structure is impaired—but it's important to remember that impairment is only realized if a company crystallizes that valuation. Let's return to the mortgage analogy. If your house declines in value below the loan you've taken out, its LTV is over 100%, and if you default on your mortgage, the bank that lent you money will take a hit. However, you might choose to continue making your mortgage payments for various reasons (you like your home, you are still able to afford the payments and don't want the stain on your credit, you think the decrease in value is temporary, etc.). Similarly, while your analysis might temporarily show an LTV over 100%, that does not necessarily mean a company will default on its debt obligations or that your debt will be impaired.

Coverage ratio

The coverage ratio measures a company's ability to service its debt. There are multiple ways to measure coverage; I typically use (adjusted EBITDA – capex) / interest expense. A coverage ratio of at least two times is generally viewed as healthy, although less-levered companies might have double-digit coverage ratios reflecting a very small interest burden. On the other hand, a coverage ratio below one means that a company cannot service its debt with internally generated funds—a potential sign of distress.

Based on MGEC Corp's EBITDA, interest expense, and capex of $48,044, $11,602, and $27,900, respectively, its coverage ratio is 1.7x. The company's EBITDA can decline by approximately 18% before its EBITDA won't cover capex and interest. A critical due diligence point is to understand the proportion of growth versus maintenance capex. If a significant amount of the capex is growth related (and thus theoretically discretionary), the cushion (i.e., the amount by which EBITDA can fall) is even more significant for two reasons. First, the growth capex should lead to higher EBITDA, so the ratio will improve. Second, if the company is having trouble servicing its debt, it can likely cut capex to a maintenance level to free up cash for interest payments.

SUB-STEP #3: CAPITAL STRUCTURE ANALYSIS—OFF-BALANCE SHEET OR DEBT-LIKE INSTRUMENTS

Finding the debt disclosure in the 10-K is straightforward. But there are other obligations that, while not categorized as debt in the financial statements, give rise to future cash outlays that are sometimes just as obligatory as debt repayment—yet are not reflected as such on the balance sheet. Not only are these obligations important to consider in the context of the ratios discussed above, they also will come into play if a company goes bankrupt. Some of the non-debt creditors discussed below will be sitting beside bond and loan holders in the Chapter 11 process and will have a say in its outcome.

There are three important categories of non-debt obligations that should be considered in your capital structure analysis.

1. Leases;
2. Pensions; and
3. Other contingent liabilities.

1) Leases

Leases are contracts in which a company pays a fee to use PP&E for a contractual period of time. GAAP categorizes leases as either capital leases (sometimes referred to as finance leases) or operating leases. Details on leases can be found in a separate footnote called "Leases" in the company's 10-K.

Capital leases (also referred to as "finance leases") A lease is treated as a capital lease if it satisfies any of the criteria outlined in Figure 9.10.

1. The lease transfers ownership of the PP&E by the end of the lease period.
2. The present value of the lease payments is greater than 90% of the asset's fair market value.
3. The lease term is equal to at least 75% of the economic life of the property.
4. The lease contains a bargain purchase option for a price less than the asset's fair market value.

FIGURE 9.10 Criteria for Capital Leases

If any of these criteria are met, in effect, the company owns the PP&E. Therefore, when creating a capital structure table, you should treat the capital lease liability as secured debt. When a company enters a capital lease, it increases PP&E (in assets) and capital leases (in liabilities) on the balance sheet by the same amount.

A capital lease results in two income statement effects: interest expense (associated with the lease liability) and depreciation expense (associated with the asset financed with the capital lease).

Operating leases Before 2018, all leases deemed operating leases were off–balance sheet. This means that upon entering the lease, the company did **not** put the asset or the related lease liability on the balance sheet. Instead, the company recognized lease or rent expense on its income statement (either in COGS or SG&A, depending on the accounting practice, as discussed in Chapter 7).

New accounting treatment went into effect at the end of 2018, requiring that operating leases with a term over 12 months be reflected as both an asset, called "Right of Use or Operating Leases," and a liability, called "Operating Lease Liability," on the balance sheet. Bizarrely, it makes no changes to the income statement, which still includes rent expense associated with the operating leases in either COGS or SG&A rather than allocating it to interest and depreciation expense (as is the case for capital/finance leases). In effect, the new accounting only went halfway; it adjusted the balance sheet to be consistent with capital lease accounting but did not make a comparable change to the income statement.

Adjusting leverage ratios for operating leases (pre-2018 change in accounting) Prior to 2018, companies could use operating lease accounting to hide assets and debt from investors. As a result, it was common practice for analysts to calculate two sets of leverage ratios: the first as described in sub-step #2, excluding any adjustments for operating leases, and the second to reflect off–balance sheet operating leases. This requires two steps to adjust the numerator (debt) and denominator (EBITDA):

(i) Increase the company's reported debt by the "hidden" operating lease debt. The most typical approach to this is to multiply annual lease or rent expense (disclosed in the lease footnote in the 10-K) by eight, in line with the approach established by the rating agency Standard & Poor's. This amount is added to the debt balance.

(ii) Add the most recent year's rent expense back to EBITDA to calculate "EBITDAR"—earnings before interest, taxes, depreciation & amortization, and rent expense.

Calculation of leverage

1. Leverage calculation ignoring operating leases = debt / adjusted EBITDA
2. Leverage calculation including operating leases = (debt + 8 × rent expense)/ (adjusted EBITDA + 1 × rent expense)

Example of Operating Lease Adjustment (pre-2018 change in accounting)—Safeway Safeway is a supermarket chain. In 2012, it had reported debt of $5,573.7 million and EBITDA of $2,238.4 million. Its leverage before considering off–balance sheet operating leases was 2.49x (debt of $5,573.7 divided by EBITDA of $2,238.4).

Figure 9.11 from Safeway's operating lease footnote shows the composition of total rental expense for all operating leases (in millions). The disclosure indicates that Safeway's annual rent expense in 2012 was $481.2.

(Amounts in millions)	2012	2011	2010
Property leases:			
Minimum rentals	458.7	452.2	447.9
Contingent rentals	8.3	8.1	8.8
Less rentals from subleases	(10.5)	(9.0)	(8.7)
	456.5	451.3	448.0
Equipment leases	24.7	24.4	26.5
Total Rent Expense	481.2	475.7	474.5

FIGURE 9.11 Safeway Lease Disclosure
Source: Adapted from Safeway 2012 10-K

Using the 8x times rule, debt must be increased by $3,849.6 million (8 × rent), and EBITDA by $481.2 million (1 × rent). As shown in Figure 9.12, its leverage when operating leases are included as debt is 3.46x—almost an entire turn higher than the un-lease adjusted leverage calculation, illustrating the substantial impact of bringing operating leases on balance sheet.

	Lease Adjusted Leverage Ratio		
$ in millions	Reported	Operating Lease Adjustment	Including Op Leases
Debt	5,573.7	8 × $481.2 of rent = 3,849.6	9,423.3
EBITDA	2,238.4	1 × $481.2 of rent = 481.2	2,719.6
Debt / EBITDA	2.49x		3.46x

FIGURE 9.12 Calculation of Safeway Leverage Ratio (with/without lease adjustment)

Example of Operating Lease Adjustment (post-2018 change in accounting)—Target As discussed above, since the 2018 accounting change only went halfway (by bringing operating lease obligations on–balance sheet without a corresponding change to the income statement), some analysts continue to perform the same adjustment outlined above. Another approach is to add the new balance sheet entry ("Operating Lease Liability") to debt and add annual lease expense to EBITDA to arrive at EBITDAR.

Target is a discount retailer. In 2018 it reported debt excluding operating leases of $11,275 million and EBITDA of $6,584 million. Its leverage before considering operating leases was 1.71x (debt of $11,275 divided by EBITDA of $6,584). Target's lease footnote disclosure is shown in Figure 9.13.

Liabilities ($MM)			
Current		*2018*	*2017*
Operating	Accrued and Other Liab	$166	$148
Finance	Current Portion of Long-Term Debt & Other Borrowings	53	80
Noncurrent			
Operating	Noncurrent Operating Lease Liab	2,004	1,924
Finance	Long-Term Debt and Other	968	885
Total lease liabilities		$3,191	$3,037

Lease Cost ($MM)			
Classification		*2018*	*2017*
Operating lease cost	SG&A Expenses	$251	$221
Finance lease cost			
Amort Exp	Depreciation & Amortization	65	63
Interest	Net Interest Expense	42	42
Sublease Income	Other Revenue	(11)	(9)
Net Lease Cost		$347	$317

FIGURE 9.13 Target Lease Footnote
Source: Adapted from Target 2018 10-K

The footnote combines operating leases and capital leases (referred to as "finance leases" by Target). Based on this footnote, the liability associated with operating leases is $2,170 million ($166 million current portion of operating leases + $2,004 million noncurrent operating lease liabilities). The operating rent expense is $251 million. Figures 9.14 and 9.15 show the two different methodologies to calculate Target's 2018 Debt/EBITDA to include operating leases.

	Lease Adjusted Leverage Ratio		
$ in millions	**Reported**	**Operating Lease Adjustment**	**Including Op Leases**
Debt	11,275	8 x $251 of rent = 2,008	13,283
EBITDA	6,584	1 x $251 of rent = 251	6,835
Debt / EBITDA	1.71x		1.94x

FIGURE 9.14 Target Leverage Calculation Using 8x Methodology

	Lease Adjusted Leverage Ratio		
$ in millions	**Reported**	**Operating Lease Adjustment**	**Including Op Leases**
Debt	11,275	2,170 op lease liability	13,445
EBITDA	6,584	1 x $251 of rent = 251	6,835
Debt / EBITDA	1.71x		1.97x

FIGURE 9.15 Target Leverage Calculation Using Operating Lease Liability

Option #1: Leverage calculation including operating leases = (Debt excluding operating leases + 8 × last year's rent expense)/(adjusted EBITDA + 1 × last year's rent expense).

Option #2: Leverage calculation including operating leases = (Debt + operating lease liability as disclosed)/(Adjusted EBITDA + 1 × last year rent expense).

In Target's case, there is minimal difference in the outputs of the two approaches (0.03x). In cases where the leverage ratios diverge meaningfully, I believe option #2 is the better way to adjust for operating leases because it considers the remaining term of the leases.

2) Pensions

There are two types of pension plans offered to employees:

(a) *Defined Contribution (DC) Plans, such as 401(k)s.* The employee contributes pretax dollars to a retirement plan. Some companies match a portion of the employee's contribution. The contributions are invested in individual accounts for each participating employee. These plans create no liability for the company and therefore do not impact capital structure analysis.

(b) *Defined Benefit (DB) Plans.* A defined benefit plan (also known as a pension) promises a specified monthly benefit at retirement. The plan may state this promised benefit as an exact dollar amount, such as $100 per month at retirement. More commonly, it uses a plan formula calculation that considers such factors as salary and service. For example, a company might pay 1.5% of the average salary for the last five years of employment for every year of service with an employer. An employee with 20 years of service would thus retire with an annual pension payment of 30% of average compensation in the last five years of employment. Given DB plans are legal obligations, they should be treated as debt when analyzing a company's capital structure.

While many companies have replaced defined benefits with defined contributions over the last few decades, some still have significant pension liabilities. The US Bureau of Labor Statistics estimated that in 2020 15% of private-sector workers have some component of their retirement savings through defined benefit plans. That number increases to 64% for unionized workers.[i]

Defined Benefit Pension Footnote Disclosure If a company has a defined benefit plan, a footnote disclosure is required in its 10-K. The accounting for pensions is complex, and the footnote can be intimidating to the non-accountant. However, only four numbers are relevant to our analysis:

(i) *Projected Benefit Obligation (PBO):* The PBO is the estimate of the present value of pension liability.

(ii) *Fair Market Value of Plan Assets (FMV):* The FMV is the value of assets (typically invested in a combination of stocks and bonds) set aside to satisfy the pension liabilities as they come due.

(iii) *PBO – FMV = the net pension liability:* This is the amount by which the pension plan is underfunded. If the FMV is greater than the PBO, then the plan is fully funded, and there is no adjustment needed.
(iv) *Pension expense:* Any company with a pension plan has related pension expense that flows through the income statement as an operating expense, lumped in either with COGS or SG&A, which is a required disclosure in the footnote.

Adjusting Leverage for Pensions As with leases, you will calculate leverage without pensions (sub-step #2) and with pension liabilities included. To do this, add the underfunded amount (PBO – FMV) to the debt, and adjust EBITDA by adding back the pension expense.[1] The rationale is similar to that of the operating lease addback: since the pension is debt-like, the associated expense should not be included in the income statement as an operating expense but rather, as debt expense.

1. Leverage calculation ignoring pensions = debt / adjusted EBITDA.
2. Leverage calculation including pensions = (debt + PBO – FMV) / (adjusted EBITDA + pension expense).

In the US, pensions are generally unsecured liabilities. The Pension Benefit Guaranty Corporation (PBGC) receives an unsecured claim in the event of a bankruptcy filing, and this claim becomes part of the unsecured creditor pool.

Example of Pension Adjustment—Safeway Safeway is a supermarket chain. In 2012, it reported debt of $5,573.7 million and EBITDA of $2,238.4 million. Its leverage before considering underfunded pensions was 2.49x (debt of $5,573.7 divided by EBITDA of $2,238.4). Safeway's footnote disclosure in Figure 9.16 indicates that its pension plan is underfunded by $789.7 million (PBO of $2,635.4 less FMV of $1,845.7). For 2012, the company recorded $141.8 million in pension expense.

[1]There is an argument to add back pension expense excluding the service cost component, since the service component is part of compensation expense, not related to the unfunded status of the plan. While this is technically correct, most analysts add the entire pension expense back to EBITDA. As long as you are only adjusting for companies with materially underfunded plans and are consistent in the analysis, it is acceptable to add back the entire pension expense.

	Pension	
	2012	2011
Change in projected benefit obligation:		
Beginning balance	$2,424.5	$2,257.2
Service cost	42.5	39.6
Interest cost	113.9	122.9
Plan amendments	0.4	1.0
Actuarial loss (gain)	203.4	149.0
Plan participant contributions	-	-
Benefit payments	(158.8)	(136.2)
Currency translation adjustment	9.5	(9.0)
Ending balance	$2,635.4	$2,424.5
Change in fair value of plan assets:		
Beginning balance	$1,641.4	$1,652.2
Actual return on plan assets	204.6	(37.9)
Employer contributions	152.1	169.0
Plan participant contributions	-	-
Benefit payments	(158.8)	(136.2)
Currency translation adjustment	6.4	(5.7)
Ending balance	$1,845.7	$1,641.4
Funded Status	$(789.7)	$(783.1)

Pension Footnote Continued:

	Pension		
	2012	2011	2010
Components of net expense:			
Estimated return on plan assets	$ (123.8)	$ (139.5)	$ (124.5)
Service cost	42.5	39.6	36.1
Interest cost	113.9	122.9	125.8
Settlement loss	5.9	1.1	-
Curtailment loss	1.8	-	-
Amortization of prior service cost (credit)	13.9	15.8	17.3
Amortization of net actuarial loss	87.6	64.30	58.60
Net expense	$141.8	$104.2	$113.3

Source: Adapted from Safeway 2012 10-K

FIGURE 9.16 Safeway Pension Footnote ($000,000)

Adjusting for pension obligations increases Safeway's leverage from 2.49x to 2.67x as shown in Figure 9.17.

Pension Adjusted Leverage Ratio			
	Reported	Pension Adjustment	Including Pensions
Debt	5,573.7	789.7	6,363.4
EBITDA	2,238.4	141.8	2,380.2
Debt / EBITDA	2.49x		2.67x

FIGURE 9.17 Safeway Leverage Calculation (with/without pension adjustment)

3) Contingent Liabilities

A long tail of contingent liabilities may appear in the financial statement footnotes—and might pose significant risk. A contingent liability is a *potential* liability that may or may not become an *actual* liability and that does not typically show up on the balance sheet. There are two requirements for a liability to be included on the balance sheet: the company must believe it has more than a 50% chance of being realized, and the company must be able to estimate its size. Given that both criteria must be met and substantial management discretion is involved in determining this, it is relatively easy for a company to keep contingent liabilities off balance sheet. However, the company must disclose all material contingent liabilities in its footnotes. Examples of contingent liabilities are pending litigation, product warranties, self-insurance, and guarantees of another company's liability.

Credit analysts must identify all contingent liabilities and ensure that any material risk is clearly highlighted as an investment risk. If the amounts are potentially material, further due diligence is needed to formulate a view on the likelihood of the liability's materializing and the potential impact on leverage.

Example of Contingent Liabilities: Krispy Kreme Doughnuts Krispy Kreme is a leading retailer of premium doughnuts, known for its "Hot Doughnuts Now" neon sign informing customers when freshly baked doughnuts are available. In its early days, the chain had a cult-like following, and it would not be unusual for customers to camp out all night when a new store opened. The company was also a darling of Wall Street after its 2000 IPO. *Fortune* called the company "the hottest brand in America."[ii] However, in 2005 Silver Point got a call from the company's financial advisor. Krispy Kreme had liquidity issues, was in breach of its bank loan financial covenants, and was looking for a new lender to provide emergency financing to help it avoid bankruptcy.

Many investors were caught off guard, but analysts who read all the footnotes to Krispy Kreme's financial statements and included off–balance sheet contingent liabilities in their leverage ratio calculations were not. A significant amount of the company's growth came from expanding its franchisee base, which paid Krispy Kreme for the rights to operate stores under the Krispy Kreme banner.

Krispy Kreme profited from these franchisee contracts in two ways. First, franchisees paid an up-front fee and royalties as a percentage of revenue. Second, they purchased equipment and supplies at a markup. Krispy Kreme's profits depended in part on the high markups that it charged franchisees. However, the markups became so aggressive that the franchisees had trouble paying their fees to Krispy Kreme.

To keep the "gravy train" going, Krispy Kreme facilitated relationships between banks and the weaker franchisees—and although banks wouldn't lend to them on a stand-alone basis, they would lend if Krispy Kreme guaranteed the loans. In other words, if franchisees could not pay back their loans, the banks could then collect from Krispy Kreme, resulting in a contingent liability (i.e., the amount of all the franchisee loan guarantees) of $25MM.

> Krispy Kreme did not include the guarantees as debt on the balance sheet but was required to disclose them in the footnote below.
>
> *Krispy Kreme footnote disclosure on Other Contingencies and Commitments*
>
> *The Company has guaranteed certain leases and loans from third-party financial institutions on behalf of franchisees, primarily to assist the franchisees in obtaining third-party financing. The loans are also collateralized by certain assets of the franchisee, generally the Krispy Kreme store and related equipment. The terms of the guarantees range from 2 to 20 years. The Company's contingent liability related to these guarantees was approximately $25,060,000 at January 30, 2005.*
>
> *Source:* Krispy Kreme 2004 10-K

Due diligence on these contingent liabilities was a critical piece of our analysis. We required financial statements from all franchisees whose debt Krispy Kreme had guaranteed, and included the guarantee liability as debt since most franchisees were having problems (which is why the banks required the guarantee in the first place). In addition, we worked with management to adjust pricing to improve franchisee viability. Our due diligence gave us the confidence to extend a highly structured loan to Krispy Kreme with a much higher coupon than its existing loan. While costly, this financing gave the company the liquidity it needed as it changed its franchisee pricing strategy.

By focusing on the guarantees, we made a more informed investment decision and priced the loan appropriately, whereas investors who ignored this critical footnote were taken by surprise when Krispy Kreme experienced liquidity issues due to the guarantee liability.

SUB-STEP #4: CAPITAL STRUCTURE ANALYSIS—UNDERSTAND THE COMPANY'S CREDIT RATING

As discussed in Chapter 1, a corporate credit rating is the opinion of an independent agency regarding the creditworthiness of a company and the risk of its various debt obligations. The rating agencies consider both the probability of default and the expected loss in the event of default (also referred to as "LGD," loss given default). For example, a company's secured debt would have a higher credit rating than its unsecured debt because, in the event of default, a secured lender would lose less money than an unsecured lender.

To refresh from Chapter 1, Figure 9.18 summarizes the major agencies' rating scales.

Bond Rating Scale

	MOODY'S	STANDARDS & POOR'S	FITCH
Investment Grade	Aaa	AAA	AAA
	Aa1	AA+	AA+
	Aa2	AA	AA
	Aa3	AA-	AA-
	A1	A+	A+
	A2	A	A
	A3	A-	A-
	Baa1	BBB+	BBB+
	Baa2	BBB	BBB
	Baa3	BBB-	BBB-
Non-Investment Grade	Ba1	BB+	BB+
	Ba2	BB	BB
	Ba3	BB-	BB-
	B1	B+	B+
	B2	B	B
	B3	B-	B-
	Caa	CCC	CCC
	Ca	CC	CC
	C	C	C
		D	D

FIGURE 9.18 Corporate Debt Rating Scale

In capital structure analysis, we use the company's credit ratings as an input into determining its financial health. Figure 9.19 provides perspective on the predictive value of credit ratings. One year after being rated, virtually no investment grade companies defaulted, 0.83% had defaulted five years from the initial rating, and 1.81% had defaulted 10 years from the initial rating. In contrast, 3.60% of speculative grade/high yield companies defaulted within the first year of being rated, 14.16% defaulted within five years, and 20.04% defaulted within 10 years.

	Percent of Credits That Defaulted									
(%)	Time Horizon (Years)									
Rating	1	2	3	4	5	6	7	8	9	10
Investment-Grade	0.08	0.23	0.40	0.61	0.83	1.05	1.26	1.45	1.63	1.81
Speculative-Grade	3.60	6.97	9.86	12.23	14.16	15.75	17.06	18.16	19.14	20.04
All rated	1.50	2.93	4.17	5.22	6.10	6.83	7.45	7.97	8.43	8.86

FIGURE 9.19 Global Corporate Average Cumulative Default Rates (1981–2021)
Sources: S&P Global Ratings Research and S&P Global Market Intelligence's CreditPro®

With two or three independent opinions available for any rated issuer—the vast majority of companies with loans and bonds outstanding—why do firms need credit analysts at all? Credit ratings are an input into credit research, but they do not substitute for the analytical approach outlined in this textbook. Many investors believe credit ratings are backward-looking, and in fact rating downgrades tend to lag price declines in companies' debt instruments. Generally, the market looks through credit ratings if a company has a strongly positive or negative trajectory; there are examples of BB-rated debt trading at CCC levels, and vice versa. And rising stars (companies transitioning from high yield to investment grade ratings) often trade at BBB valuations for months before attaining investment grade ratings.

Additionally, the credit rating agencies have an implicit conflict of interest because they are paid by the companies they rate rather than by the investors who use their ratings. Before the 1970s, investors paid for credit ratings; however, during the 1970s, companies began paying for their own ratings.[iii] Once the payer for the service changed from the investor to the debt issuer, the rating agencies lost their impartiality. Those critical of the rating agencies point to high-profile blunders, such as Enron, which was rated investment grade by the agencies weeks before filing for bankruptcy. Further, some investors took massive losses in investment grade–rated tranches of the mortgage-backed securities that were catalysts for the GFC. Since some of these securities were rated AAA by the rating agencies, many holders believed they were at no risk of impairment.

Even if you discount the information content of a credit rating, there may be rating limits and restrictions in some or all of the portfolios that make use of your analysis. Many funds and separately managed accounts (SMAs) have ratings-based restrictions; for example, some investment grade funds must have at least 90% of the portfolio in investment grade–rated securities (BBB-/Baa3 or better), and no more than 20% below single-A. Some CLO structures (discussed in Chapter 1) limit the amount of CCC exposure to 7%. During challenging economic periods, when there are increased downgrades, these rules-based funds can become forced sellers—which creates fantastic opportunities for investors without ratings-based limitations. Those with the credit skills to analyze downgraded bonds and the "patient" or "sticky" capital to buy when most investors are selling can make highly profitable investments.

Credit ratings strive to offer a common framework for comparing investments across industries, although investors sometimes price the same rating differently across industries. Ratings are also helpful in originating new bonds and loans by suggesting "comps" (i.e., comparably rated debt in the secondary market) as pricing touchpoints.

SUB-STEP #5: CAPITAL STRUCTURE ANALYSIS—DRAW CONCLUSIONS

Let's return to the example at the beginning of the chapter, which demonstrates that increased leverage improves shareholder returns but also increases the risk of financial distress. The leverage of a company should be dictated by how risky the business is. Companies with low operating risk can take more financial risk, and companies with high operational risk should have lower leverage. As with all steps of financial statement analysis, a peer group analysis is required to understand the company's risk profile relative to its competitors.

As a general frame of reference, in my experience investing in the leveraged loan and high-yield bond markets, most companies have leverage ranging from 2.0x to 7.0x. Due to regulatory constraints and internal policies, most banks will not lend beyond 6.0x EBITDA,[iv] leaving the most highly leveraged transactions to non-bank entities such as dedicated institutional loan and high yield bond strategies and hedge funds. Figure 9.20 shows the range of leverage ratios.

Leverage (Debt / EBITDA)	General Qualitative Assessment[a]
2.0x–3.0x	Low to moderate leverage
3.0x–5.0x	Moderate to high leverage
5.0x–7.0x	High leverage

[a] As discussed earlier in the chapter, what constitutes low/moderate/high leverage depends on the operational risk of the industry. While Figure 9.20 a starting point, it might not hold for all sectors.

FIGURE 9.20 Range of Leverage Ratios

END-OF-CHAPTER CAPITAL STRUCTURE ANALYSIS OF JCPENNEY[2]

Figure 9.21 shows JCP's capital structure, sourced primarily from the "Long Term Debt" footnote #11 in its 2012 10-K (more detail on this below). Since JCP's 2012 adjusted EBITDA was negative, the current leverage ratio (debt / adjusted EBITDA) is meaningless; however, rather than inputting not meaningful ("NM"), we will use our base case forecast EBITDA of $1,000 million to calculate leverage. We will go into more detail later in the book; to simplify, the EBITDA used to calculate the leverage ratio for a company experiencing distress is the base case ("normalized") level you'll come up with in step four, forecasting.

[2]Download JCPenney's 2012 10-K (fiscal year ended February 2, 2013) at the SEC Edgar website for public company filings, https://www.sec.gov/edgar/searchedgar/companysearch, using the search term "Old Copper Company." The company's search term on Edgar is Old Copper Company, Inc., not JCPenney.

JCPenney Capital Structure Table

$ in millions							Leverage as a Multiple of EBITDA		Loan-to-Value	
2/2/2013	**Outstanding**	**Coupon**	**Maturity**	**Price**	**Yield-to-Maturity**	**Ratings S&P & Moody's**	**Face**	**Market**	**Face**	**Market**
$1.75B ABL Revolver	0	L + 3%	4/29/2016	100.0%						
Secured Term Loan	0	NA	NA							
Capital Leases & other	114									
Total Secured Debt	**114**						0.1x	0.1x	2.1%	2.1%
Senior Unsecured Bonds	200	6.875%	10/15/15	93.0%	9.9%	CCC+ / Caa1				
Senior Unsecured Bonds	200	7.65%	8/15/16	94.5%	9.5%	CCC+ / Caa1				
Senior Unsecured Bonds	285	7.95%	4/1/17	92.5%	10.2%	CCC+ / Caa1				
Senior Unsecured Bonds	300	5.75%	2/15/18	88.0%	8.7%	CCC+ / Caa1				
Senior Unsecured Bonds	400	5.65%	6/1/20	81.0%	9.3%	CCC+ / Caa1				
Senior Unsecured Bonds	255	7.125%	11/15/23	86.0%	9.2%	CCC+ / Caa1				
Senior Unsecured Bonds	2	6.9%	8/15/26	84.0%	9.0%	CCC+ / Caa1				
Senior Unsecured Bonds	400	6.375%	10/15/36	71.0%	9.5%	CCC+ / Caa1				
Senior Unsecured Bonds	326	7.4%	4/1/37	70.0%	11.0%	CCC+ / Caa1				
Senior Unsecured Bonds	500	7.625%	3/1/97	66.8%	11.4%	CCC+ / Caa1				
Total Senior Debt	**2,982**						3.0x	2.4x	55.2%	44.6%
Subordinated Debt	0									
Total Debt	**2,982**						3.0x	2.4x	55.2%	44.6%
Less: Cash	–930									
Net Debt	**2,052**						2.1x	1.5x	38.0%	27.4%
Equity Mkt. Cap.	3,347									
Total Enterprise Value	**5,399**						5.4x	5.4x	100.0%	100.0%

FIGURE 9.21 JCPenney's 2012 Capital Structure Table
Sources: JCP 2012 10-K; trading levels from Bloomberg

Notes on where to find debt instruments outstanding, coupon, and maturity

1. **ABL revolving credit facility.** Information comes from footnote #10 of JCP's 10-K, "Credit Facility." The 10-K does not disclose the coupon; however, the loan agreement, which is publicly available, has the coupon as LIBOR + 3.0%.
2. **Secured term loan.** At year-end 2012, JCP did not have a secured term loan.
3. **Capital leases and other.** From JCP's balance sheet: "Current portion of capital leases and note payables" of $26 million plus "Long-term capital leases and note payables" of $88 million. JCP does not disclose details on maturity and coupon. Capital leases are secured debt.
4. **Senior unsecured bonds.** Information comes from footnote 11, "Long-Term Debt." The 10-K provides only the year (not the actual date) each bond matures. Bloomberg brings up all bond issues, including maturity, coupon, and type (secured/unsecured, etc.) when you type JCP Corp <Go>.
5. **Subordinated debt.** JCP does not have any subordinated debt.
6. **Cash.** From JCP's balance sheet.
7. **Equity Market Capitalization.** This is the public market value of the company's equity (i.e., its market cap) calculated by multiplying the price per share by the shares outstanding. Note that this is different from the book value of the company's equity, which can be much lower or higher than the market cap.
8. **Total Enterprise Value (TEV).** TEV is the total value of the business = total debt minus cash plus equity market cap. Chapter 11 will discuss TEV in more detail.

Other Analysis of JCP's Capital Structure

1. Coverage ratio = (adjusted EBITDA – capex)/interest expense:
   - Given JCP's negative EBITDA, its coverage ratio is meaningless. As shown in Figure 9.22, even using our base case forecast "normalized" EBITDA of $1,000 million (see Chapter 10, "Step 4 of the Credit Analysis Process: Forecasting"), JCP's coverage ratio is less than 1x, meaning that after capex, the company does not generate enough cash to pay its interest expense. However, if JCP can achieve our normalized EBITDA and cuts capex to a maintenance level (see Chapter 8), it would achieve a respectable 2.2x coverage ratio.

	JCP Coverage Ratio	
$ in millions	**2012 Capex**	**Maint Capex**
Normalized EBITDA	1,000	1,000
Less Capex	–810	–500
Normalized EBITDA – Capex	190	500
2012 Interest Expense	226	226
Coverage Ratio (Normalized EBITDA – Capex)/Interest	.84x	2.2x

FIGURE 9.22 JCP Coverage Ratio

2. Operating leases:
   - Footnote #14 discloses 2012 rent expense of $294MM. As shown in Figure 9.23, capitalizing the leases as described above would increase debt by $2.4 billion and increase debt to normalized EBITDA by 1.1 turns.

	Lease Adjusted Leverage Ratio		
$ in millions	Reported	Operating Lease Adjustment	Including Op Leases
Debt	2,982	8 × $294 of rent = 2,352	5,334
Normalized EBITDA	1,000	1 × $294 of rent = 294	1,294
Debt / EBITDA	3.0x		4.1x

FIGURE 9.23 JCP Lease Adjustment

3. Pension plans (defined benefit):
   - Footnote #15 discloses that JCP's main defined benefit plan is nearly fully funded ($5,035 million of assets / $5,042 of PBO liability = 99.9% funded). In addition, there is a small supplemental plan for senior-level executives (SERP) that in 2012 was underfunded by $303 million and had an annual cost of $38 million. Given the small size, as shown in Figure 9.24, the SERP did not materially impact leverage.

	Pension Adjusted Leverage Ratio		
$ in millions	Reported	Pension Adjustment	Including Pensions
Debt	2,982	+303 underfunded	3,285
Normalized EBITDA	1,000	+38 annual expense	1,038
Debt / EBITDA	3.0x		3.2x

FIGURE 9.24 JCP Pension Adjustment

4. Other contingent liabilities:
   - Nothing material. Footnote #20 discloses a $20 million maximum guarantee related to an insurance reserve of a former subsidiary, a $20 million maximum on 10 assigned leases, and several other immaterial potential liabilities.
5. Credit ratings:
   - JCP's disastrous 2012 performance led both credit rating agencies to downgrade its unsecured debt to the low end of non-investment grade (CCC+/Caa1), with further downgrades expected if the company cannot turn around its operations in 2013.
6. Peer group analysis:
   - Figure 9.25 shows JCP's ratings and leverage ratios relative to peers. As shown, even using normalized EBITDA, its leverage is elevated relative to all peers other than Bon-Ton, which was also experiencing distress at the time of this analysis.

	JCP Peer Group Analysis				
	JCP	Macy's	Kohl's	Dillard's	BonTon
S&P Rating	CCC-	BBB	BBB+	BB+	B-
Moody's Rating	Caa2	Baa3	Baa1	Ba3	Caa1
Debt / EBITDA[a]	NM	1.9x	1.7x	0.8x	5.4x

[a] Using $1 billion normalized EBITDA, JCP's Debt/EBITDA would be 3.0x.

FIGURE 9.25 JCP Peer Group Analysis
Source: Bloomberg; ratings as of May 2013; debt/EBITDA as of FYE 2012 (Jan 31st)

JCP Capital Structure Conclusions

JCPenney's capital structure is only sustainable if the company can quickly turn around its operations and move from negative EBITDA to our normalized level. Based on the liquidity analysis performed in Chapter 8, it only has one or two years to achieve this before it runs out of availability on its revolving credit facility and must file for bankruptcy.

CHAPTER CONCLUSION

This chapter completes the initial phases of our work. Now that you have performed qualitative and historical financial statement analysis, you are ready to embark on forecasting. Since a company repays a loan with future, not historical, cash flow, producing and sensitizing a forecast model are critical next steps. As a debt investor, your focus will be on modeling downside events to assess the ability of the company to service its debt not only during good times but also in adverse scenarios.

NOTES

i. US Bureau of Labor Statistics. "The Economic Daily." March 1, 2021. https://www.bls.gov/opub/ted/2021/67-percent-of-private-industry-workers-had-access-to-retirement-plans-in-2020.htm#:~:text=Source%3A%20U.S.%20Bureau%20of%20Labor%20Statistics.%20Among%20union,to%20have%20access%20to%20defined%20benefit%20retirement%20plans.

ii. Serwer, Andy. (June 14, 2004). "A Hole in Krispy Kreme's Story." CNN Money. https://money.cnn.com/magazines/fortune/fortune_archive/2004/06/14/372629/index.htm.

iii. Rivlin, Alice, and John B. Soroushian. (March 6, 2017). "Credit Rating Agency Reform Is Incomplete." Brookings Institute. https://www.brookings.edu/research/credit-rating-agency-reform-is-incomplete/.

iv. Benhart, Darrin. (March 22, 2013). "Leveraged Lending: Guidance on Leveraged Lending." OCC Bulletin 2013-9. https://www.occ.gov/news-issuances/bulletins/2013/bulletin-2013-9.html.

CHAPTER 10

Step 4 of the Credit Analysis Process: Forecasting

In the words of physicist Niels Bohr, "It's very hard to make predictions, especially about the future."[i] He's right, but there are other reasons for forecasting besides pinpointing an accurate number in the future. As my favorite statistician, George Box, says, "All models are wrong, but some are useful."[ii] A company will never perform exactly as modeled; however, a useful forecast lays out a reasonable range of outcomes that will help analyze default probability and the severity of loss in the event of a default. This chapter introduces you to forecasting, step four of the credit analysis process outlined in Figure 10.1.

Step 1	Sources and Uses (only applicable to originations)
	(a) Why is the company seeking financing?
	(b) What are the proposed sources of capital to fund the financing need?
Step 2	Qualitative Analysis
	(a) Industry analysis
	(b) Business strategy
	(c) Management assessment
	(d) ESG concerns
Step 3	Financial Statement Analysis
	(a) Profitability
	(b) Cash flow and liquidity
	(c) Capital structure
Step 4	**Forecasting**
	(a) Identification of key business drivers and assumptions
	(b) Development of base, upside, and downside cases
Step 5	Corporate Valuation
	(a) Comparable company analysis
	(b) Precedent transactions (M&A comps)
	(c) Discounted cash flow analysis
	(d) Liquidation analysis
Step 6	Structuring and Documentation
	(a) Economic points
	(b) Structure and collateral
	(c) Covenants
Step 7	Preparing an Investment Recommendation and Credit Committee Memo
	(a) Investment thesis and recommendation
	(b) Risks and mitigants
	(c) Relative value analysis

FIGURE 10.1 The Seven-Step Process of Evaluating a Debt Instrument

FORECASTING

A credit investment recommendation typically includes at least three forecasts:

1. Management or consensus case;
2. Base case; and
3. Downside case or cases.

If you are evaluating a new loan origination, you will generally have the benefit of a detailed three-to-five-year forecast provided by the company, which is your "management case." If you are analyzing a new high yield bond or broadly syndicated loan origination, or a secondary trade, it's unlikely you'll have this level of detail. Instead, you will build your management case based on the company's guidance on public calls supplemented by your work and sell-side analysts' estimates.

Your base case removes the typical optimism that management (and, often, sell-side consensus) reflects in its model. You've achieved a reasonable base case if it's a coin toss as to whether the company is more likely to do better or worse than your forecast. Some base cases are too conservative; while this may sound like the right approach in credit analysis, given the inherent riskiness of investing in leveraged credit, being too conservative is almost as bad as being too aggressive. If your base case errs on the side of conservatism, you might miss a good investment that more pragmatic analysts will be willing to make and find yourself scrambling to buy the debt at a higher price later.

For credit investing, the downside scenarios are critical. The risks identified in your qualitative analysis from Chapter 6 need to be incorporated into your downside scenarios. For instance, any cyclical company forecast requires a downside case reflecting a recession. If customer concentration is a significant risk, you must model a downside case that incorporates losing that customer.

PREPARING A FORECAST

Forecasting can range from back-of-the-envelope forecasts, in which three to five key variables are sensitized, to a full-blown Excel model that sensitizes every income statement, balance sheet, and cash flow statement assumption. I warn my students that the first rule of fight club is you do not talk about fight club.[1] However, that is not relevant to modeling. What is relevant is the first rule of modeling: "Garbage in, garbage out." The key is how thoughtful you are in determining the key drivers of your forecasts and making logical assumptions.

We'll approach forecasting from two perspectives:

(i) A new loan origination, Taylor M Corp (TM Corp),[2] for which you have been provided with the company's model and access to management to answer your questions.

[1] If you don't understand this reference, stream the movie *Fight Club* starring Edward Norton and Brad Pitt.

[2] TM Corp is based on an actual company. The name of the company and certain financial information have been altered.

(ii) A secondary trade opportunity in JCPenney, a public company for which you only have access to publicly available financial statements.

The sub-steps to preparing a forecast are summarized in Figure 10.2.

---

1. Input historical financial statements (the process outlined in Chapter 7).
2. Set up an assumption page detailing the drivers and the cells of the model that are sensitized to run cases.
3. Forecast the income statement.
4. Forecast the balance sheet excluding cash and debt, as both depend on cash flow.
5. Forecast the cash flow statement and link it to the balance sheet to determine the amount of cash and debt iteratively.
6. Perform sensitivity analysis by changing assumptions to run different cases.
7. Analyze and summarize the outputs of the model on a summary page that includes the key financial ratios discussed in previous chapters.
8. When appropriate, assign probabilities to all cases.

FIGURE 10.2 Sub-Steps to Preparing a Forecast

If this sounds complex and challenging—it is! But this book is here to walk you through each of these steps in detail. As you read this section, I recommend that you build an Excel model and forecast for TM Corp using the financial statements provided step by step.

Your Excel model will link the projection periods to calculations driven by an assumption page. This allows you (or anyone using your model) to change the assumptions, which will recalculate the projected income statement, balance sheet, cash flow statement, and summary financial ratios. There should be no hard-coded numbers in the projection period on the income statement, balance sheet, and cash flow statement. Every cell should be a formula referencing either earlier periods or the assumption page. For example, sales for the projection period will be a formula equal to last year's sales × (1+ growth rate from the assumption page).

PREPARING A FORECAST—STEP ONE

Input (or download) TM Corp's Income Statement, Balance Sheet, and Cash Flow Statements

A quick note on downloading versus inputting numbers from financial statements. Various subscription programs, such as Factset and Capital IQ, allow you to download numbers directly rather than inputting them. I am not opposed to starting with a download of the numbers rather than a manual build—as long as you still read the notes to the financial statements. The numbers themselves are only the beginning of the story; as discussed in Chapter 7, you have to dig into the narrative of the financial statements for relevant information on many components of your model.

Refer back to Chapter 7 if you need a refresher on this step. As shown in Figure 10.3, we've gone back three years as a starting point—which is a typical historical time period, since a 10-K captures three years of historical income and cash flow statements (although only two years of balance sheet data). However, recall from Chapter 7 that you might need to go back further in time depending on the nature of the last three years. For a cyclical company such as TM Corp, be sure to analyze how the company performed during recessions; you will need this information to build your downside case. For a company in the commodity sector, this would involve looking at a peak-to-trough cycle for the commodity in question. For a sector with a cost structure that includes a substantial commodity component (e.g., airlines), ditto. This doesn't necessarily mean you have to build out all three financial statements for all trough periods in the industry but rather that you determine how the company performed during the downturns and incorporate that knowledge into your downside case.

Income Statement: Base Case

	Historic			Projections				
$ in 000s	Year 1	Year 2	Year 3	Year 1	Year 2	Year 3	Year 4	Year 5
Sales	168,790	172,503	175,091					
COGS	92,835	94,014	95,074					
Gross Profit	75,955	78,489	80,017					
SG&A	47,500	47,975	49,135					
Operating Profit	28,455	30,514	30,882					
Interest Expense	11,500	11,170	11,038					
Pretax Profits	16,955	19,344	19,844					
Tax Expense	6,443	7,389	7,422					
Net Income	10,512	11,955	12,422					

Balance Sheet: Base Case

	Historic			Projections				
$ in 000s	Year 1	Year 2	Year 3	Year 1	Year 2	Year 3	Year 4	Year 5
Cash	3,400	2,420	9,143					
A/R	25,000	25,400	25,189					
Inventory	24,000	26,785	24,000					
Total C.A.	52,400	54,605	58,332					
PP&E, net	184,600	187,650	189,050					
Total Assets	237,000	242,255	247,382					
Revolver Drawn	-	-	-					
A/P	22,000	22,800	23,005					
CPTL[a]	7,500	7,500	7,500					
Total C.L.	29,500	30,300	30,505					
Term Loan	75,000	67,500	60,000					
Unsecured Bonds	100,000	100,000	100,000					
Total Liabilities	204,500	197,800	190,505					
O/E	32,500	44,455	56,877					
Liab. + O/E	237,000	242,255	247,382					
Check	-	-	-	-	-	-	-	-

Cash Flows: Base Case

	Historic			Projections				
$ in 000s	Year 1	Year 2	Year 3	Year 1	Year 2	Year 3	Year 4	Year 5
Operating Profit	28,455	30,514	30,882					
Plus D&A	14,400	14,450	14,800					
Adjusted EBITDA	42,855	44,964	45,682					
Less Capex	(15,000)	(17,500)	(16,200)					
EBITDAX	27,855	27,464	29,482					
Interest Expense	(11,500)	(11,170)	(11,038)					
Taxes	(6,443)	(7,389)	(7,422)					
FCF b/f chg WC	9,912	8,905	11,022					
Chg Rec	(700)	(400)	211					
Chg Inven	800	(2,785)	2,785					
Chg Payables	100	800	205					
FCF #1[b]	10,112	6,520	14,223					
Debt Pymts	(7,500)	(7,500)	(7,500)					
FCF #2[c]	2,612	(980)	6,723					
RC Draws / Repymt	-	-	-					
Change in Cash	2,612	(980)	6,723					

[a] CPTL stands for current portion of term loan
[b] FCF #1 is before any debt repayment
[c] FCF #2 is before RC Draws / (Repayment)

FIGURE 10.3 TM Corp Summary Historical Financial Statements

PREPARING A FORECAST—STEP TWO

Create an assumption section that ties to the projected financial statements. In your investment memo, you will include an exhibit that explains your rationale for each assumption.

Thoughtful assumptions require incorporating and quantifying the most important conclusions from your qualitative and financial statement analyses. The key findings on TM Corp are:

- The company designs and manufactures consumer products.
- The industry is mature but cyclical (grows with the economy).
- Revenue growth has been 1%–3% yearly, except during recessions. During the 2008–2009 recession, the company's sales decreased by 20% in 2008 and 10% in 2009 and recovered to pre-recession levels in 2010.
- Competitive dynamics are good and have been stable. The industry is an oligopoly, with three companies making up 85% of the market. The number one player has a 33% market share; TM Corp is number two with a 30% market share; the third largest player has a 22% share.

- None of the competitors has a cost advantage, and all have similar EBITDA margins. In addition, they have been price-rational; that is, they have not historically engaged in price wars to increase market share.
- The other 15% of the market is made up of mom-and-pop businesses with cost structures that aren't competitive with the top three players. They focus on smaller, regional customers that the big three don't service.
- Your firm engaged a consultant to analyze the probability of changes in the healthy competitive dynamic. The consultant did not identify any threats from new entrants, substitutes, or disruptive technology.
- The company's customer base is extremely diverse, including over 15,000 customers, with no customer accounting for more than 1.5% of its sales. Customers generally have three- to five-year contracts.
- The company's contracts allow pass-through of commodity price increases.
- The company has a largely fixed cost structure. Based on conversations with the management team and our consultants, we believe:
  - $37 million, or approximately 40% of the company's COGS, is fixed, and the rest is variable.
  - $29 million, or approximately 60% of the company's SG&A, is fixed, and the rest is variable.
- The company has a $30MM revolver, priced at SOFR + 1.75%. The revolver is undrawn and fully available.
- In addition to the revolver, the company has $167.5 million of debt made up of:
  - A $67.5 million secured term loan priced at SOFR + 3.25% with amortization of $7.5 million per year and a maturity date of seven years from today.
  - A $100 million unsecured bond with a fixed rate coupon of 7.25% and a maturity date 10 years from today.
- Management expects capex to be between $16 million and $20 million annually over the next three years. Since the company is not growing, we believe most of this is for maintaining operations. According to management, the company could cut capex to $15 million annually if needed.

PREPARING A FORECAST—STEP THREE

Forecast the income statement.

The next step is to quantify and explain the rationale for our base case assumptions. One of the most important parts of modeling is determining which inputs of your model to forecast and include on your assumptions tab versus which ones to keep constant. Generally speaking, your revenue and margin forecasts will be the most important assumptions to get right. Once your assumptions have been determined, tie these to the income statement to generate a forecast as shown in Figure 10.4.

Assumptions Income Statement: Base Case

	Historic			Projections				
$ in 000s	Year 1	Year 2	Year 3	Year 1	Year 2	Year 3	Year 4	Year 5
Sales Growth	NA	2.2%	1.5%	1.5%	1.5%	1.5%	1.5%	1.5%
Fixed $ COGS	37,000	37,000	37,000	37,000	37,000	37,000	37,000	37,000
Var % of Sales	33.1%	33.1%	33.2%	33.1%	33.1%	33.1%	33.1%	33.1%
Fixed $ SG&A	29,000	29,000	29,000	29,000	29,000	29,000	29,000	29,000
Var % of Sales	11.0%	11.0%	11.5%	11.2%	11.2%	11.2%	11.2%	11.2%
SOFR – Index Rate	1.75%	1.65%	1.80%	1.80%	1.82%	1.85%	1.85%	1.88%
RC SOFR + 1.75%	3.5%	3.4%	3.6%	3.55%	3.57%	3.60%	3.60%	3.63%
TL SOFR + 3.25%	5.0%	4.9%	5.1%	5.05%	5.07%	5.10%	5.10%	5.13%
Bond Interest Rate	7.25%	7.25%	7.25%	7.25%	7.25%	7.25%	7.25%	7.25%
Tax Rate	38.0%	38.2%	37.4%	38.0%	38.0%	38.0%	38.0%	38.0%

Assumptions Balance Sheet: Base Case

	Historic			Projections				
$ in 000s	Year 1	Year 2	Year 3	Year 1	Year 2	Year 3	Year 4	Year 5
Cash Cycle:								
Receivable Days	NA	53.3	52.7	53.0	53.0	53.0	53.0	53.0
Inventory Days	NA	98.6	97.5	98.0	98.0	98.0	98.0	98.0
Payable Days	NA	87.0	87.9	87.4	87.4	87.4	87.4	87.4
PP&E Worksheet:								
PP&E, beg	184,000	184,600	187,650	189,050	192,304	195,304	198,071	200,621
Plus Capex	15,000	17,500	16,200	18,000	18,000	18,000	18,000	18,000
Minus Depr Exp	(14,400)	(14,450)	(14,800)	(14,746)	(15,000)	(15,234)	(15,450)	(15,648)
Equals PP&E, end	184,600	187,650	189,050	192,304	195,304	198,071	200,621	202,973
Depr Exp / PP&E[a]	7.8%	7.8%	7.9%	7.8%	7.8%	7.8%	7.8%	7.8%
Debt Maturity Schedule:								
Term Loan	7,500	7,500	7,500	7,500	7,500	7,500	7,500	7,500
Bonds	-	-	-	-	-	-	-	-

[a] Depreciation expense is represented as a percent of beginning PP & E

FIGURE 10.4 Base Case Assumptions

Rationale for Base Case Assumptions (Figures 10.5–10.14)

1. *Sales.* The company is in a mature industry and has experienced 1%–3% annual revenue growth in non-recessionary periods, so a base case annual growth rate of 1.5% is reasonable. (We will run a recession case as our downside case.)

	Historic			Projections				
$ in 000s	Year 1	Year 2	Year 3	Year 1	Year 2	Year 3	Year 4	Year 5
Sales	168,790	172,503	175,091	177,717	180,383	183,089	185,835	188,623
Sales Growth	NA	2.2%	1.5%	1.5%	1.5%	1.5%	1.5%	1.5%

FIGURE 10.5 Base Case Sales Assumptions for TM Corp

2. *COGS.* A simple way to forecast COGS is as a percent of sales, since COGS is typically viewed as a variable cost. Over the last three years, COGS/sales has averaged 54.6%, and some analysts might keep this stable in their forecasts.

	Historic			Projections				
$ in 000s	Year 1	Year 2	Year 3	Year 1	Year 2	Year 3	Year 4	Year 5
COGS	92,835	94,014	95,074	97,034	98,489	99,966	101,466	102,988
COGS/Sales	55.0%	54.5%	54.3%	54.6%	54.6%	54.6%	54.6%	54.6%

FIGURE 10.6 Historical and Projected COGS for TM Corp (constant percent of sales)

However, it's preferable to break COGS into fixed and variable components and forecast each separately. Based on discussions with management and outside consultants, approximately $37 million of the company's COGS is fixed, and the rest is variable. Over the last three years, the variable component of COGS has averaged 33.1% of sales.

	Historic		
$ in 000s	Year 1	Year 2	Year 3
Total COGS	92,835	94,014	95,074
Less Fixed Component	(37,000)	(37,000)	(37,000)
= Variable Component	55,835	57,014	58,074
Var COGS/Sales	33.1%	33.1%	33.2%

FIGURE 10.7 Fixed versus Variable Component of COGS for TM Corp

We can now forecast COGS by assuming the fixed component stays at $37 million per year, and the variable part stays at 33.1% of sales.

Based on the second methodology, the company's total COGS as a percent of revenue will decline gradually over the forecast period due to the operating leverage related to the fixed cost component of COGS. This is called "fixed cost leveraging" or "absorption costing" and can be a powerful margin enhancement for companies that manage to keep their dollars of fixed costs stable as revenues increase. While we have modeled this here, in practice, it is often challenging for higher-growth companies to keep fixed costs stable; when sales are growing, there is less focus on cost control. Mature companies such as TM Corp typically have more discipline in keeping fixed costs stable.

	Projections				
$ in 000s	**Year 1**	**Year 2**	**Year 3**	**Year 4**	**Year 5**
Sales	177,717	180,383	183,089	185,835	188,623
x Variable COGS as a % of Sales	33.1%	33.1%	33.1%	33.1%	33.1%
= Variable COGS	58,824	59,707	60,602	61,511	62,434
Plus Fixed Component of COGS	37,000	37,000	37,000	37,000	37,000
= Total COGS	95,824	96,707	97,602	98,511	99,434
Total COGS as a % of Sales	53.9%	53.6%	53.3%	53.0%	52.7%

FIGURE 10.8 Base Case Fixed and Variable COGS Projections for TM Corp

3. *SG&A*. We will also forecast the fixed and variable costs in SG&A separately. Based on discussions with management and outside consultants, $29 million of the company's SG&A is fixed, and the rest is variable. Figure 10.9 shows that the variable component of SG&A has averaged 11.2% of sales over the last three years.

	Historic		
$ in 000s	**Year 1**	**Year 2**	**Year 3**
Total SG&A	47,500	47,975	49,135
Less Fixed Component	(29,000)	(29,000)	(29,000)
= Variable Component	18,500	18,975	20,135
Var SG&A/Sales	11.0%	11.0%	11.5%

FIGURE 10.9 Fixed versus Variable Component of SG&A for TM Corp

We assume the fixed component of SG&A remains at $29 million per year, and the variable component stays at the three-year average of 11.2% of sales. Similar to our discussion above about fixed cost trajectories in high growth versus mature companies, if the company is in growth mode, you would likely grow this dollar amount as some function of revenue growth. Figure 10.10 shows projections for TM Corp's SG&A.

	Projections				
$ in 000s	Year 1	Year 2	Year 3	Year 4	Year 5
Sales	177,717	180,383	183,089	185,835	188,623
x Variable SG&A as a % of Sales	11.2%	11.2%	11.2%	11.2%	11.2%
= Variable SG&A	19,904	20,203	20,506	20,814	21,126
Plus Fixed Component of SG&A	29,000	29,000	29,000	29,000	29,000
= Total SG&A	48,904	49,203	49,506	49,814	50,126
Total SG&A as a % of Sales	27.5%	27.3%	27.0%	26.8%	26.6%

FIGURE 10.10 Base Case Fixed and Variable SG&A Projections for TM Corp

4. *Interest Expense.* Forecasting interest expense relies on several inputs that vary depending on the liquidity needs of the company. Two changes in interest expense must be forecasted:
   i. *Interest associated with revolving credit facility (RCF) borrowings:* This component of interest expense is an output of your cash flow forecast, which assumes that negative cash flow will be offset by drawing on the revolver, and positive cash flow will be deployed to pay off the revolver (referred to as a cash flow sweep).
   ii. *Changes in interest resulting from refinancing debt maturities:* As you forecast the balance sheet (below), you will make two assumptions about debt maturities in the forecast period:
      (a) Will the debt be paid off at maturity or refinanced? If the debt is not refinanced but paid off, interest expense will decrease by the amount of the interest associated with the maturing debt.
      (b) If maturing debt is refinanced, what is the likely interest rate on the new debt? In year one, you can obtain "comps" (trading levels of peer companies) to estimate the likely coupon on new debt issued. In years two and onward, you can either keep the year one rate constant, or make assumptions about likely changes in the company's financing cost. For example, you might forecast a lower coupon on new issues as the company delevers and investors become more comfortable with its credit profile.

   For the sake of simplicity, the forecast below estimates annual interest expense based on the debt balance at the beginning of the forecast year. However, Excel allows a more accurate forecast based on the average debt outstanding. To avoid a circular reference error in your model, you must turn on the iteration calculation function in Excel.[3]

   The revolving credit facility and the term loan have floating rate coupons benchmarked to SOFR. Since this component of interest expense changes with SOFR, we need to input the SOFR forward curve, which can be found on Bloomberg, and add the facility spread to forecasted SOFR to project the dollar amount of interest expense associated with TM Corp's floating rate debt. As shown in Figure 10.11, with a term loan coupon of SOFR + 3.25% and the market's SOFR projection of 1.8% in year one, the coupon for that year is 1.8% SOFR + 3.25% spread or 5.05%.

[3] To enable iterative calculations in Excel, select File/Options/Formulas, and click "Enable iterative calculation" on the upper right-hand side.

	Projections				
	Year 1	Year 2	Year 3	Year 4	Year 5
Market Expectation of Future SOFR	1.80%	1.82%	1.85%	1.85%	1.88%
Revolver Spread over SOFR	1.75%	1.75%	1.75%	1.75%	1.75%
Revolver Coupon Rate	3.55%	3.57%	3.60%	3.60%	3.63%
Market Expectation of Future SOFR	1.80%	1.82%	1.85%	1.85%	1.88%
Term Loan Spread over SOFR	3.25%	3.25%	3.25%	3.25%	3.25%
Term Loan Coupon Rate	5.05%	5.07%	5.10%	5.10%	5.13%
Bond's Fixed Rate Coupon	7.25%	7.25%	7.25%	7.25%	7.25%

FIGURE 10.11 Base Case Interest Projections for TM Corp

5. *Taxes.* Based on the historical period and conversations with management, TM Corp's tax rate is forecast at 38% of pretax earnings.[4]

PREPARING A FORECAST—STEP FOUR

Forecast the balance sheet.

1. *Cash.* Cash is driven by projected cash flow, so this balance sheet component will be an output of your model.
2. *Inventory, Accounts Receivable, and Accounts Payable.* Chapter 8 discussed the cash cycle, shown in Figure 10.12, which is calculated as the time it takes a company to convert its inventory into cash less the time it takes to pay its vendors for those inventories. Another common approach is to grow all working capital accounts at the same rate as the forecasted sales growth.

	Calculation Description
Inventory Days	Average number of days it takes to sell inventory
Plus Receivable Days	(+) Average number of days it takes to collect cash from customers after a sale is made
Subtotal	Average number of days it takes to convert inventory into cash
Less Payable Days	(–) Average number of days until the company pays its vendors for the inventory
Cash Cycle in Days	Average days to convert inventory into cash less time to pay vendors

FIGURE 10.12 The Cash Cycle

Formulas to calculate the cash cycle:

- Receivable days = 365 × (Average accounts receivable / sales)
- Inventory days = 365 × (Average inventory / COGS)
- Payable days = 365 × (Average accounts payable / COGS)

For our base case, it is reasonable to use the historical average, as shown in Figure 10.13.

[4]At the time of this transaction the corporate tax rate was 35%, plus an additional 3% tax from state and local taxes.

	Historic			Projections				
	Year 1	Year 2	Year 3	Year 1	Year 2	Year 3	Year 4	Year 5
Receivable Days	NA	53.3	52.7	53.0	53.0	53.0	53.0	53.0
Inventory Days	NA	98.6	97.5	98.0	98.0	98.0	98.0	98.0
Payable Days	NA	87.0	87.9	87.4	87.4	87.4	87.4	87.4

FIGURE 10.13 Historical and Projected Base Case Cash Cycle for TM Corp

Once we have projections for receivable, inventory, and payable days, we can easily calculate the amount outstanding. For year one, we project receivable days of 53. We have already forecasted sales in year one of $177,717, so we can solve for receivables as follows. The same math works to calculate inventory and payables, except for replacing sales with COGS.

Forecast of year one receivables:

- Receivable days = 365 × (Average receivables / sales)
- 53 days = 365 × (Average receivables / $177,717.3)
- 53 days × $177,717.3 / 365 = Average receivables
- Average receivables = $25,806
- Average receivables = (Prior year receivables + year one projected receivables)/2
- $25,806 = ($25,189 + 2023 Projected receivables)/2
- Year one projected receivables = ($25,806 × 2) – $25,189
- Year one projected receivables = $26,422

3. *Property, Plant, and Equipment (PP&E) Net of Accumulated Depreciation.* Each year PP&E increases by the amount of capex and decreases by that year's depreciation expense. Therefore, the PP&E forecast relies on our assumptions for capex and depreciation. The company plans to spend between $16 and $20 million of capex annually, so it is reasonable to use the average ($18 million). Over the last three years, depreciation as a percent of PP&E at the beginning of the year has been 7.8%, a reasonable assumption for the projection period. Figure 10.14 shows historical and projected PP&E for TM Corp.

	Historic			Projections				
$ in 000s	Year 1	Year 2	Year 3	Year 1	Year 2	Year 3	Year 4	Year 5
PP&E, beg	184,000	184,600	187,650	189,050	192,304	195,304	198,071	200,621
Plus Capex	15,000	17,500	16,200	18,000	18,000	18,000	18,000	18,000
- Depr Exp	(14,400)	(14,450)	(14,800)	(14,746)	(15,000)	(15,234)	(15,450)	(15,648)
= PP&E, end	184,600	187,650	189,050	192,304	195,304	198,071	200,621	202,973
Depr Exp[a]	7.8%	7.8%	7.9%	7.8%	7.8%	7.8%	7.8%	7.8%

[a] Depreciation expense as a % of PPE, beg

FIGURE 10.14 Historical and Projected Base Case PP&E for TM Corp

4. *Revolving Credit Facility Balance.* Like cash, the RCF balance is driven by projected cash flow, so this balance sheet component will be calculated last.

5. *Current Portion of Long-Term Debt.* This will be based on the maturity and amortization schedule of the debt. The only mandatory payment on the debt over the projection period is the annual amortization of $7.5 million on the term loan.

6. *Owners' Equity.* Each year, owners' equity increases by the amount of net income or decreases by the amount of net loss and is also reduced by dividends and/or share buybacks.

   Using our base case assumptions, we can construct the first projection year's income statement as shown in Figure 10.15. However, we can only create part of the company's balance sheet as the cash flow statement forecast is required to calculate the amount of cash and revolver outstanding.

Income Statement

	Historic			Projections
$ in 000s	**Year 1**	**Year 2**	**Year 3**	**Year 1**
Sales	168,790	172,503	175,091	177,717
COGS	92,835	94,014	95,074	95,824
Gross Profit	75,955	78,489	80,017	81,893
SG&A	47,500	47,975	49,135	48,904
Operating Profit	28,455	30,514	30,882	32,989
Interest Expense	11,500	11,170	11,038	10,659
Pretax Profits	16,955	19,344	19,844	22,330
Tax Expense	6,443	7,389	7,422	8,485
Net Income	10,512	11,955	12,422	13,844

Balance Sheet

	Historic			Projections
$ in 000s	**Year 1**	**Year 2**	**Year 3**	**Year 1**
Cash	3,400	2,420	9,143	NA[a]
A/R	25,000	25,400	25,189	26,422
Inventory	24,000	26,785	24,000	27,456
Total Current Assets	52,400	54,605	58,332	53,878
PP&E, Net	184,600	187,650	189,050	192,304
Total Assets	237,000	242,255	247,382	246,183
Revolver Drawn	-	-	-	NA[a]
A/P	22,000	22,800	23,005	22,886
Current Portion of TL	7,500	7,500	7,500	7,500
Total Current Liabilities	29,500	30,300	30,505	30,386
Term Loan	75,000	67,500	60,000	52,500
Unsecured Bonds	100,000	100,000	100,000	100,000
Total Liabilities	204,500	197,800	190,505	182,886
O/E	32,500	44,455	56,877	70,721
Total Liabilities + O/E	237,000	242,255	247,382	253,607
Check	-	-	-	*(7,425)*

[a] Need to complete cash flow statement.

FIGURE 10.15 Base Case I/S and B/S Forecast for TM Corp

PREPARING A FORECAST—STEP FIVE

Forecast the cash flow statement.

Now let's calculate the company's cash flow for year one of the projection period, as shown in Figure 10.16. (For a refresher on calculating free cash flow, refer back to Chapter 8.)

Cash Flows

	Historic			Projections
$ in 000s	Year 1	Year 2	Year 3	Year 1
Operating Profit	28,455	30,514	30,882	32,989
Plus D&A	14,400	14,450	14,800	14,746
Adjusted EBITDA	42,855	44,964	45,682	47,734
Less Capex	(15,000)	(17,500)	(16,200)	(18,000)
EBITDAX	27,855	27,464	29,482	29,734
Interest Expense	(11,500)	(11,170)	(11,038)	(10,659)
Taxes	(6,443)	(7,389)	(7,422)	(8,485)
FCF b/f chg WC	9,912	8,905	11,022	10,590
Cash Impact chg Rec	(700)	(400)	211	(1,233)
Cash Impact chg Inven	800	(2,785)	2,785	(3,456)
Cash Impact chg Payables	100	800	205	(119)
FCF b/f Repayment	10,112	6,520	14,223	5,782
Repayment of Debt	(7,500)	(7,500)	(7,500)	(7,500)
Actual FCF b/f RC Draws	2,612	(980)	6,723	(1,718)
RC Draws/(Repayment)	-	-	-	-
Change in Cash Levels	2,612	(980)	6,723	(1,718)

FIGURE 10.16 Base Case Cash Flow Forecast for TM Corp (year one)

The "RC draws/(repayment)" line is the tricky part of modeling the cash flow statement, and this aspect of your forecast relies on a revolver draw worksheet.

The Excel formula is written such that if "Actual FCF b/f RC draws" is positive, the revolver is repaid by the amount of cash flow until the RC is zero. In other words, the model assumes that the first use of cash flow is paying down the revolver, and the remainder increases cash on the balance sheet. If "Actual FCF b/f RC draws" is negative, the model calculation should draw down excess cash on the balance sheet to a minimum needed to run the business and then show a draw on the revolver by the amount of the cash deficit. In other words, the model assumes that the revolver covers any cash flow shortfall/burn.

Now we can complete the balance sheet by linking it to the cash flow statement.

Congratulations! If you've been following along step by step with your own Excel spreadsheet, you have now built a three-statement forecast. Our base case five-year forecast is shown Figure 10.17.

Income Statement: Base Case

	Historic			Projections				
$ in 000s	Year 1	Year 2	Year 3	Year 1	Year 2	Year 3	Year 4	Year 5
Sales	168,790	172,503	175,091	177,717	180,383	183,089	185,835	188,623
COGS	92,835	94,014	95,074	95,824	96,707	97,602	98,511	99,434
Gross Profit	75,955	78,489	80,017	81,893	83,676	85,486	87,324	89,189
SG&A	47,500	47,975	49,135	48,904	49,203	49,506	49,814	50,126
Operating Profit	28,455	30,514	30,882	32,989	34,473	35,981	37,510	39,063
Interest Expense	11,500	11,170	11,038	10,659	10,292	9,928	9,545	9,174
Pretax Profits	16,955	19,344	19,844	22,330	24,181	26,053	27,965	29,889
Tax Expense	6,443	7,389	7,422	8,485	9,189	9,900	10,627	11,358
Net Income	10,512	11,955	12,422	13,844	14,992	16,153	17,338	18,531

Balance Sheet: Base Case

	Historic			Projections				
$ in 000s	Year 1	Year 2	Year 3	Year 1	Year 2	Year 3	Year 4	Year 5
Cash	3,400	2,420	9,143	7,425	15,900	16,966	28,224	32,070
A/R	25,000	25,400	25,189	26,422	25,963	27,208	26,761	28,017
Inventory	24,000	26,785	24,000	27,456	24,474	27,937	24,962	28,433
Total C.A.	52,400	54,605	58,332	61,303	66,337	72,111	79,947	88,520
PP&E, net	184,600	187,650	189,050	192,304	195,304	198,071	200,621	202,973
Total Assets	237,000	242,255	247,382	253,607	261,642	270,181	280,568	291,493
Revolver drawn	-	-	-	-	-	-	-	-
A/P	22,000	22,800	23,005	22,886	23,428	23,315	23,863	23,757
CPTL	7,500	7,500	7,500	7,500	7,500	7,500	7,500	7,500
Total C.L.	29,500	30,300	30,505	30,386	30,928	30,815	31,363	31,257
Term Loan	75,000	67,500	60,000	52,500	45,000	37,500	30,000	22,500
Unsecured Bonds	100,000	100,000	100,000	100,000	100,000	100,000	100,000	100,000
Total Liabilities	204,500	197,800	190,505	182,886	175,928	168,315	161,363	153,757
O/E	32,500	44,455	56,877	70,721	85,714	101,867	119,205	137,736
Liab. + O/E	237,000	242,255	247,382	253,607	261,642	270,181	280,568	291,493
Check	-	-	-	-	-	-	-	-

(Continued)

CONTINUED

Cash Flows: Base Case

	Historic			Projections				
$ in 000s	Year 1	Year 2	Year 3	Year 1	Year 2	Year 3	Year 4	Year 5
Operating Profit	28,455	30,514	30,882	32,989	34,473	35,981	37,510	39,063
Plus D&A	14,400	14,450	14,800	14,746	15,000	15,234	15,450	15,648
Adj. EBITDA	42,855	44,964	45,682	47,734	49,473	51,214	52,960	54,711
Less Capex	(15,000)	(17,500)	(16,200)	(18,000)	(18,000)	(18,000)	(18,000)	(18,000)
EBITDAX	27,855	27,464	29,4812	29,734	31,473	33,214	34,960	36,711
Interest Expense	(11,500)	(11,170)	(11,038)	(10,659)	(10,292)	(9,928)	(9,545)	(9,174)
Taxes	(6,443)	(7,389)	(7,422)	(8,485)	(9,189)	(9,900)	(10,627)	(11,358)
FCF b/f chg WC	9,912	8,905	11,022	10,590	11,992	13,387	14,788	16,180
Chg Rec	(700)	(400)	211	(1,233)	459	(1,245)	447	(1,257)
Chg Inven	800	(2,785)	2,785	(3,456)	2,983	(3,464)	2,975	(3,471)
Chg Payables	100	800	205	(119)	542	(113)	548	(106)
FCF #1[a]	10,112	6,520	14,223	5,782	15,975	8,565	18,759	11,346
Debt Pymts	(7,500)	(7,500)	(7,500)	(7,500)	(7,500)	(7,500)	(7,500)	(7,500)
FCF #2[b]	2,612	(980)	6,723	(1,718)	8,476	1,065	11,259	3,846
RC Draws/Repymt	-	-	-	-	-	-	-	-
Change in Cash	2,612	(980)	6,723	(1,718)	8,476	1,065	11,259	3,846

[a] FCF #1 is before any debt repayment
[b] FCF #2 is before RC Draws / (Repayment)

FIGURE 10.17 Base Case Forecast for TM Corp

PREPARING A FORECAST—STEP SIX

Perform sensitivity/scenario analysis.

Now that we have a working model with base case assumptions, we can run downside scenarios. If you've built your model correctly, the assumption page is the only part you will change.

But how do you choose which line items to vary in your scenarios? Since the major risk identified in our qualitative analysis of TM Corp is the cyclicality and macroeconomic sensitivity of its business, we model a recession as the downside case. Only assumptions most relevant to the particular case are modeled and varied.

Figure 10.18 compares our base case assumptions to our recession downside case. Pay particular attention to the key drivers that vary between the base and downside cases. Most recession cases include a downturn with a return to pre-recessionary levels of revenue and margin within the five-year forecast horizon. Often, multiple downside cases are required. For example, you might model moderate and extreme downside cases, which vary the severity of the downturn and the timing and strength of the subsequent recovery.

	Projections				
$ in 000s	Year 1	Year 2	Year 3	Year 4	Year 5
Sales Growth: Base	1.5%	1.5%	1.5%	1.5%	1.5%
Sales Growth: Downside	-20.0%	-10.0%	15.0%	15.0%	1.5%
Var COGS: Base	33.1%	33.1%	33.1%	33.1%	33.1%
Var COGS: Downside	33.1%	34.0%	34.0%	33.1%	33.1%
Inventory Days: Base	98.0	98.0	98.0	98.0	98.0
Inventory Days: Downside	108.0	108.0	98.0	98.0	98.0
Payable Days: Base	87.4	87.4	87.4	87.4	87.4
Payable Days: Downside	87.4	75.0	75.0	87.4	87.4
Capex: Base	$18,000	$18,000	$18,000	$18,000	$18,000
Capex: Downside	$18,000	$15,000	$15,000	$21,000	$20,000

FIGURE 10.18 Base versus Downside Case Assumptions for TM Corp

Rationale for downside case assumptions:

1. Sales growth: We modeled an immediate recession comparable to the company's performance in the 2008 recession.
2. COGS: Based on discussions with management and our consultant, we believe that in a downside, the variable component of COGS would increase from 33.1% to 34.0% of sales for years 2 and 3.
3. SG&A: We made no changes to the assumptions. However, margin declines due to the absorption of the fixed component of SG&A over a lower sales base.
4. Interest rate and taxes: We made no changes to the assumptions. This is conservative because in a recession it is likely that SOFR will decrease. The assumption that a company's interest expense will decline in a downturn only applies to floating rate debt; if a company has only fixed rate debt in its capital structure, it won't benefit from a decrease in the risk-free rate.
5. Receivable days: We made no changes to our base case, although an increase in receivable days in the downside case might be reasonable, as customers take longer to pay.
6. Inventory days: These increase in the downside case by 10 days in years one and two, as the company is likely to carry excess inventory until demand returns to prior levels.
7. Payable days: Our downside case assumes that some vendors might get nervous and tighten terms (i.e., demand quicker payment) until sales start to rebound.
8. Capex: We assumed that after the recession's first year, the company would cut capex to a maintenance level and increase it coming out of the recession to a level higher than the base case as the company catches up on investments deferred during the downturn.

For the investment committee memo, include a summary of your cases and conclusions in the body of the memo and your model and accompanying assumptions rationale as an exhibit.

PREPARING A FORECAST—STEP SIX CONTINUED: BASE CASE SUMMARY AND CONCLUSIONS

In the base case, as shown in Figure 10.19, TM Corp should have no issues servicing its debt. It generates significant cash flow during the projection period, resulting in deleveraging from 3.5x to 1.8x Net Debt[5] / EBITDA, and does not need to access its $30 million revolver.

Summary Stats: Base Case

	Historic			Projections				
$ in 000s	Year 1	Year 2	Year 3	Year 1	Year 2	Year 3	Year 4	Year 5
Sales	168,790	172,503	175,091	177,717	180,383	183,089	185,835	188,623
Sales Growth	NA	2.2%	1.5%	1.5%	1.5%	1.5%	1.5%	1.5%
Gross Profit	75,955	78,489	80,017	81,893	83,676	85,486	87,324	89,189
Gross Profit %	45.0%	45.5%	45.7%	46.1%	46.4%	46.7%	47.0%	47.3%
SG&A	47,500	47,975	49,135	48,904	49,203	49,506	49,814	50,126
SG&A/Sales	28.1%	27.8%	28.1%	27.5%	27.3%	27.0%	26.8%	26.6%
EBITDA	42,855	44,964	45,681	47,734	49,473	51,214	52,960	54,711
EBITDA Margin	25.4%	26.1%	26.1%	26.9%	27.4%	28.0%	28.5%	29.0%
RC Commit	30,000	30,000	30,000	30,000	30,000	30,000	30,000	30,000
Less RC Drawn	-	-	-	-	-	-	-	-
RC Avail	30,000	30,000	30,000	30,000	30,000	30,000	30,000	30,000
Plus Cash	3,400	2,420	9,143	7,425	15,900	16,965	28,224	32,070
Liquidity	33,400	32,420	39,143	37,425	45,900	46,965	58,224	62,070
FCF #1[a]	10,112	6,520	14,223	5,782	15,975	8,565	18,759	11,346
FCF #2[b]	2,612	(980)	6,723	(1,718)	8,475	1,065	11,259	3,846
Inven Days	NA	98.6	97.5	98.0	98.0	98.0	98.0	98.0
Receivable Days	NA	53.3	52.7	53.0	53.0	53.0	53.0	53.0
Sub-Total	NA	151.9	150.2	151.0	151.0	151.0	151.0	151.0
Payable Days	NA	(87.0)	(87.9)	(87.4)	(87.4)	(87.4)	(87.4)	(87.4)
Cash Cycle	NA	64.9	62.3	63.6	63.6	63.6	63.6	63.6
Debt / EBITDA	4.3x	3.9x	3.7x	3.4x	3.1x	2.8x	2.6x	2.4x
Net Leverage[c]	4.2x	3.8x	3.5x	3.2x	2.8x	2.5x	2.1x	1.8x
Coverage Ratio[d]	2.4x	2.5x	2.7x	2.8x	3.1x	3.3x	3.7x	4.0x

[a] FCF #1 is Free cash flow before any mandatory debt repayments
[b] FCF #2 is Free cash flow after any mandatory debt repayments
[c] Net leverage is (Debt - Cash) / EBITDA
[d] Coverage ratio is (EBITDA - Capex) / Interest

FIGURE 10.19 Projected Ratios for TM Corp (Base Case)

[5] Net Debt = Debt less cash.

PREPARING A FORECAST—STEP SIX CONTINUED: DOWNSIDE SUMMARY AND CONCLUSIONS

As shown in Figure 10.20, even in the downside case, which is conservatively based on a severe recession, the company can service its debt. However, it burns $7.8MM in cash in the first two years before paying its required term loan amortization. The company can only make required amortization payments in years one to four by drawing on its revolver. In year five, it starts to generate enough cash flow to make those payments without using the RCF. TM Corp uses all cash on its balance sheet

Summary Stats: Downside Case

	Historic			Projections				
$ in 000s	Year 1	Year 2	Year 3	Year 1	Year 2	Year 3	Year 4	Year 5
Sales	168,790	172,503	175,091	140,073	126,066	144,975	166,722	169,222
Sales Growth	NA	2.2%	1.5%	-20.0%	-10.0%	15.0%	15.0%	1.5%
Gross Profit	75,955	78,489	80,017	56,709	46,203	58,684	74,537	76,210
Gross Profit %	45.0%	45.5%	45.7%	40.5%	36.7%	40.5%	44.7%	45.0%
SG&A	47,500	47,975	49,135	44,688	43,119	45,237	47,673	47,953
SG&A/Sales	28.1%	27.8%	28.1%	31.9%	34.2%	31.2%	28.6%	28.3%
EBITDA	42,855	44,964	45,682	26,766	18,084	28,446	41,864	43,725
EBITDA Margin	25.4%	26.1%	26.1%	19.1%	14.3%	19.6%	25.1%	25.8%
RC Commit	30,000	30,000	30,000	30,000	30,000	30,000	30,000	30,000
Less RC Drawn	-	-	-	-	(13,699)	(18,007)	(23,283)	(22,670)
RC Avail	30,000	30,000	30,000	30,000	16,301	11,993	6,718	7,330
Plus Cash	3,400	2,420	9,143	1,513	-	-	-	-
Liquidity	33,400	32,420	39,143	31,513	16,301	11,993	6,717	7,330
FCF #1[a]	10,112	6,520	14,223	(130)	(7,712)	3,192	2,224	8,112
FCF #2[b]	2,612	(980)	6,723	(7,630)	(15,212)	(4,308)	(5,276)	612
Inven Days	NA	98.6	97.5	108.0	108.0	98.0	98.0	98.0
Receivable Days	NA	53.3	52.7	53.0	53.0	53.0	53.0	53.0
Subtotal	NA	151.9	150.2	161.0	161.0	151.0	151.0	151.0
Payable Days	NA	(87.0)	(87.9)	(87.4)	(75.0)	(75.0)	(87.4)	(87.4)
Cash Cycle	NA	64.9	62.3	73.6	86.0	76.0	63.6	63.6
Debt / EBITDA	4.3x	3.9x	3.7x	6.0x	9.2x	5.7x	3.8x	3.5x
Net Leverage[c]	4.2x	3.8x	3.5x	5.9x	9.2x	5.7x	3.8x	3.5x
Coverage Ratio[d]	2.4x	2.5x	2.7x	0.8x	0.3x	1.3x	2.0x	2.4x

[a] FCF #1 is free cash flow before any mandatory debt repayments
[b] FCF #2 is free cash flow after any mandatory debt repayments
[c] Net leverage is (Debt - Cash) / EBITDA
[d] Coverage ratio is (EBITDA - Capex) / Interest

FIGURE 10.20 Projected Ratios for TM Corp (Downside Case)

and must draw on its RCF in the downside case.[6] Its leverage peaks at 9.2x Net Debt / EBITDA in year two and then begins to decline coming out of the recession. Starting liquidity (availability on the revolving credit facility plus cash) goes from $39MM to a low point of $6.7MM in year four and then starts to grow. At the end of the projection period, leverage has returned to a reasonable level of 3.5x.

PREPARING A FORECASTING—STEP SEVEN

Assign probabilities to your cases.

Once your cases are done, you will assign probabilities to each scenario. This might sound like an exercise in false precision if not futility. What does it matter if your downside case has a 10% versus a 15% probability? Don't let the perfect be the enemy of the good. If your downside case seems likely, rerun it as your base case; if your base case seems draconian and unlikely, rerun it as your downside case. Your probability assessment is an educated guess that you will present to some combination of your boss and an investment committee, who will debate and refine the assumptions and probabilities.

For example, let's consider a company whose largest customer makes up 25% of sales. You run a downside scenario that incorporates the loss of this customer, and your analysis predicts that you will lose 15%–20% of your investment if that happens. No doubt your boss or the credit committee will ask, "How likely do you think it is that the customer will defect?" Examples of responses (taken from actual credit memos) could be:

- We believe less than 5%. The company is a critical software provider, and its products are integrated within its client's operations; therefore, the switching cost would be tremendous for the client. While the client makes up 25% of the company's revenue, 10 different software products are sold to this client, and no single product makes up more than 5% of its sales. Finally, the client is an investment grade-rated company.
- We believe there is a 50% chance of losing the key customer. The company offers a commodity-like product with many other suppliers. There are no long-term contracts and no significant switching costs. Furthermore, the company used to be the sole source provider, but the customer has announced plans to diversify its supply base in the future. Finally, the company's margins are significantly below some of its competitors, so if a competitor wants to compete on price, the company is at a significant disadvantage. Over the term of our loan, we think it is more likely than not that the company will see a continued erosion of its "share of wallet," and it would not be surprising if it lost the entire customer relationship over time.

You might recommend the first investment, given that the probability of the downside case is less than 5%, and pass on the second since you think it is 50%, even though they have the same loss potential if the downside materializes. The big difference is the probability assessment.

---

[6] Some models build in the concept of minimum cash. In these models, the cash is always at least the minimum needed to run the business. The only difference is that the revolver will be drawn earlier.

END-OF-CHAPTER FORECAST FOR JCP[7]

Unlike TM Corp, where we have the luxury of detailed projections and access to the management team, we have none for JCP and will thus perform a back-of-the-envelope forecast.

JCP Base Case Model

Our investment thesis is that once the company reintroduces promotions and coupons, its customers will return, and EBITDA will stabilize at approximately $1 billion a year (its lowest EBITDA over the last 10 years before the impact of the change in strategy). Figure 10.21 shows the base case cash flow forecast, and Figure 10.22 shows the related revolver draw forecast.

	Actual			Forecast Period			
$ in millions	**2010**	**2011**	**2012**	**2013**	**2014**	**2015**	**2016**
Sales	17,759	17,260	12,985	12,985	13,634	14,657	14,803
Sales Growth	*1.2%*	*-2.8%*	*-24.8%*	*0.0%*	*5.0%*	*7.5%*	*1.0%*
EBITDA	1,370	1,019	(541)	114	409	879	1,000
EBITDA Margin	7.7%	5.9%	-4.2%	0.88%	3.00%	6.00%	6.75%
EBITDA	1,370	1,090	(541)	114	409	879	1,000
Less Capex	(499)	(334)	(810)	(800)	(400)	(400)	(400)
EBITDAX	871	685	(1,351)	(686)	9	479	600
Less Interest Expense	(231)	(227)	(226)	(226)	(246)	(272)	(264)
FCF b/f chg in WC	640	458	(1,668)	(912)	(237)	207	336
+/- Chg in WC	(336)	156	631	0	(65)	(102)	(15)
FCF b/f Nonrecurring[a]	304	614	(946)	(912)	(302)	105	322
Nonrecurring[a]	NM	NM	NM	(50)	(25)	0	0
Free Cash Flow	304	614	(946)	(962)	(327)	105	322

[a] Nonrecurring are cash restructuring charges

FIGURE 10.21 JCP Base Case Cash Flow Forecast

[7] Download JCPenney's 2012 10-K (fiscal year ended February 2, 2013) at the SEC Edgar website for public company filings, https://www.sec.gov/edgar/searchedgar/companysearch, using the search term "Old Copper Company." The company's search term on Edgar is Old Copper Company, Inc., not JCPenney.

	Forecast Period			
$ in millions	2013	2014	2015	2016
Beginning Cash	930	100	100	100
Less Minimum Cash Needed to Run the Business	(100)	(100)	(100)	(100)
Cash Available to Fund Cash Burn	830	-	-	-
Free Cash Flow (from Figure 10.21)	(962)	(327)	105	322
Revolver Draws or Repayments [A]	(132)	(327)	105	322
Debt Outstanding at the Beginning of the Year	2,982	3,114	3,441	3,336
Revolver Draws or Repayments [A]	132	327	(105)	(322)
Debt Outstanding at Year End	3,114	3,441	3,336	3,014
Debt / EBITDA	NM	8.4x	3.8x	3.0x

FIGURE 10.22 JCP Base Case Revolver Draw Forecast

Rationale for JCP Base Case Assumptions

1. Sales: The company reintroduces couponing that drives traffic, and sales stabilize at approximately 85% of the 2011 level (the year before the change in strategy).
2. EBITDA margin: As sales increase, EBITDA margin increases as the company works through old inventory and leverages its fixed costs. EBITDA margin stabilizes at 6.75% (average margin of 2010 and 2011). JCP's margin still lags behind that of top competitors (Macy's 13.4%, Kohl's 14.1%, and Dillard's 11.8%).
3. Capex: The company completes its existing capex program and then spends only maintenance capex. Based on management's guidance, capex can be decreased to $400 million, $100 million lower than estimated in Chapter 8.
4. Interest expense: Beginning debt outstanding × average interest rate.
5. Taxes: No cash taxes, as the company has NOLs to offset future earnings.
6. Changes in working capital: Working capital growth follows the historic cash cycle, increasing by 10% of the change in sales. This ratio is the two-year average of (inventory less payables)/sales. The trade continues to support the business in the base case.
7. Nonrecurring cash charges: The forecast incorporates a modest amount of cushion for unforeseen adverse events as the company attempts its turnaround.

JCP Downside Case Model

In our downside case model, shown in Figure 10.23, the company does not win back customers quickly, EBITDA stays negative, and the trade vendors start to tighten terms in 2014. In this case, as shown in Figure 10.24, JCP burns through its liquidity (see Chapter 8 for JCP's liquidity analysis) over the next two years and will be forced to file for bankruptcy sometime in 2014 or early 2015.

Rationale for JCP Downside Case Assumptions

1. Sales: It takes longer than expected to recapture lost customers, and sales continue to decline in 2013, albeit at a slower rate, and then stabilize at 2013's depressed level in 2014.

2. EBITDA margin: In 2013 and 2014 margins improve due to cost cutting; however, EBITDA remains negative.
3. Capex: JCP completes its existing capex program and then spends only maintenance capex. Based on management's guidance, capex can be decreased to $400 million, $100 million lower than estimated in Chapter 8.
4. Interest expense: Beginning debt outstanding × average interest rate.
5. Taxes: No cash taxes, as the company has NOLs to offset future earnings.

	Actual			Forecast Period			
$ in millions	2010	2011	2012	2013	2014	2015	2016
Sales	17,759	17,260	12,985	12,336	12,336	NM	NM
Sales Growth	*1.2%*	*-2.8%*	*-24.8%*	*-5.0%*	*0.0%*	*NM*	*NM*
EBITDA	1,370	1,019	(541)	(496)	(300)	NM	NM
EBITDA Margin	7.7%	5.9%	-4.2%	-4.0%	-2.4%	NM	NM
EBITDA	1,370	1,090	(541)	(496)	(300)	NM	NM
Less Capex	(499)	(334)	(810)	(800)	(400)	NM	NM
EBITDAX	871	685	(1,351)	(1,296)	(700)	NM	NM
Less Interest Expense	(231)	(227)	(226)	(226)	(289)	NM	NM
FCF b/f Chg in WC	640	458	(1,668)	(1,522)	(989)	NM	NM
+/- Chg in WC	(336)	156	631	65	(500)	NM	NM
FCF b/f Nonrecurring[a]	304	614	(946)	(1,457)	(1,489)	NM	NM
Nonrecurring Cash Charges	NM	NM	NM	(50)	(25)	NM	NM
Free Cash Flow	304	614	(946)	(1,507)	(1,514)	NM	NM

[a] FCF b/f Nonrecurring is FCF before cash restructuring charges

FIGURE 10.23 JCP Downside Case Cash Flow Forecast

	Forecast Period			
$ in millions	2013	2014	2015	2016
Beginning Cash	930	100	NM	NM
Less Minimum Cash Needed to Run the Business	(100)	(100)	NM	NM
Cash Available to Fund Cash Burn	830	-	NM	NM
Free Cash Flow	(1,507)	(1,514)	NM	NM
Revolver Draws or Repayments [A]	(677)	(1,514)	NM	NM
Debt Outstanding at Beginning of the Year	2,982	3,659	NM	NM
Revolver Draws or Repayments [A]	677	1,514	NM	NM
Debt Outstanding at Year End	3,659	5,173	NM	NM
Debt / EBITDA	NM	NM	NM	NM

FIGURE 10.24 JCP Downside Case Revolver Draw Forecast

6. Changes in working capital: In 2013, working capital follows the historic cash cycle, increasing by 10% of the change in sales. This ratio is the two-year average of (inventory less payables)/sales. However, in 2014, the trade begins to pull, resulting in a $500 million cash drain from working capital.
7. Nonrecurring cash charges: The forecast incorporates a modest amount of cushion for unforeseen adverse events as the company attempts its turnaround.

CHAPTER CONCLUSION

Investing in a company requires formulating a view of its future profitability and cash flow. Forecasting allows analysts to use their historical financial and qualitative analysis of the industry, business, and management to present a range of likely outcomes. The assumptions that drive the models should be debated by the firm's investment committee (or equivalent) to ensure they are as realistic and helpful as possible.

In Chapter 13, "Step 7 of the Credit Analysis Process: Preparing an Investment Recommendation and Credit Committee Memo," you will see how forecasts are used in evaluating a loan origination and a high yield bond transaction. And in Chapter 19, "Making Money in Distressed Situations," we will use the JCP analysis and forecast from this chapter to recommend trades.

NOTES

i. Dickstein, Daniel P. (December 28, 2020). "It's Difficult to Make Predictions, Especially about the Future." *Journal of the American Academy of Child and Adolescent Psychiatry*. https://pubmed.ncbi.nlm.nih.gov/33383160/.
ii. Wasserstein, Ron. (September 2010). "George Box: A Model Statistician." *Significance*. https://academic.oup.com/jrssig/article/7/3/134/7029882.

CHAPTER 11

Step 5 of the Credit Analysis Process: Corporate Valuation

In steps one through four, you've identified business and industry risks, analyzed financial performance, and built a model for the potential investment, then performed scenario analysis to get comfortable with the company's trajectory and range of outcomes. As shown in Figure 11.1, the next step is developing a view of what the company is worth—that is, its valuation. This chapter provides an overview of corporate valuation methods. For a much more in-depth treatment of valuation, I recommend *Investment Banking: Valuation, Leveraged Buyouts, and Mergers & Acquisitions* by Joshua Rosenbaum and Joshua Pearl.

Step 1	Sources and Uses (only applicable to originations) (a) Why is the company seeking financing? (b) What are the proposed sources of capital to fund the financing need?
Step 2	Qualitative Analysis (a) Industry analysis (b) Business strategy (c) Management assessment (d) ESG concerns
Step 3	Financial Statement Analysis (a) Profitability (b) Cash flow and liquidity (c) Capital structure
Step 4	Forecasting (a) Identification of key business drivers and assumptions (b) Development of base, upside, and downside cases
Step 5	**Corporate Valuation** **(a) Comparable company analysis** **(b) Precedent transactions (M&A comps)** **(c) Discounted cash flow analysis** **(d) Liquidation analysis**
Step 6	Structuring and Documentation (a) Economic points (b) Structure and collateral (c) Covenants
Step 7	Preparing an Investment Recommendation and Credit Committee Memo (a) Investment thesis and recommendation (b) Risks and mitigants (c) Relative value analysis

FIGURE 11.1 The Seven-Step Process of Evaluating a Debt Instrument

Before we dive into corporate valuation, an important note on terminology. Debt investors use the term "valuation" to refer to several different metrics. This chapter addresses corporate valuation, which uses Total Enterprise Value (TEV) as a measure of the value of a company's operations. This value is shared among all the company's investors, both debt and equity. This meaning is not to be confused with the term "valuation" in the context of the trading levels and yields/spreads of bonds and loans discussed in Chapter 3. For example, an analyst might describe the valuation of an individual bond as cheap or rich. A "cheap" bond has a yield that provides more than adequate compensation compared to the yields of other companies' bonds or relative to other bonds and loans in the company's own capital structure. The yield of a "rich" bond does not provide adequate compensation for the underlying risk of the company and/or relative to other investment opportunities. This concept will be more fully addressed in Chapter 13 when I discuss relative value and risk-adjusted return analysis.

This chapter focuses on corporate valuation (TEV). Calculating TEV serves two purposes in credit research. First, calculating a range of TEVs for an investment opportunity shows the potential for impairment in different forecast scenarios. And second, formulating a differentiated view of a company's worth can help identify mispricing and subsequent investment opportunities—either long or short.

CALCULATING TEV

If a company has publicly traded equity, the observable TEV is equal to the calculation in Figure 11.2.

TEV Calculation Inputs
Debt Outstanding
Less: Cash and Cash Equivalents
Plus: The Equity Market Capitalization of the Company (stock price × shares outstanding)
Equals Total Enterprise Value

FIGURE 11.2 TEV Calculation

But that's just what the market thinks a company is worth. The more important question is: What do *you* think the company is worth? Investing requires a contrarian view to that of the market. If your estimate of TEV is higher, you "go long" (invest); if it's lower, you "short." This can apply to a company's stock, bonds, or some combination of securities across the capital structure, depending on the various prices of each layer. Even if you're considering investing in the debt of a performing company, you need to formulate a view on its TEV to quantify how much "cushion" you have before the debt you hold is at risk of impairment.

To determine TEV, we'll discuss four standard valuation techniques.

1. Comparable company analysis (market multiples);
2. Precedent transactions (M&A comps);
3. Discounted cash flow analysis (DCF); and
4. Liquidation analysis (asset valuations).

You will likely use more than one of these techniques to arrive at a reasonable TEV or range of corporate valuations. Each of the above approaches has pros and cons and might be more relevant for a specific point in a company's lifecycle. For example, liquidation analysis is mostly used for deeply distressed companies with value only in their remaining assets (as opposed to franchise value). In this chapter, we will use these methodologies to value VCC Company.[1] VCC is a leading global provider of flow control products (e.g., regulators and valves). Sixty percent of its revenue comes from selling valves used in propane tanks (heating and cooking). In 2019 the company sought a $200 million loan to refinance its existing credit facility. Potential lenders had to perform their own valuation analysis as there was no public equity since the company was taken private in an LBO in 2013. The original LBO valuation is not a meaningful reference point, as the industry and company's performance have been very different in the seven years since being acquired.

VALUATION TECHNIQUE #1: COMPARABLE COMPANY ANALYSIS

This is the most common method used by both debt and equity investors. A publicly traded group of similar companies (referred to as "comps") is used to come up with the right multiple for valuing the potential investment. The most common multiples are summarized in Figure 11.3.

1. TEV/EBITDA (most commonly used)
2. TEV/Sales (more common for high-growth companies without positive EBITDA)
3. TEV/(EBITDA – capex) (sometimes used in addition to an EBITDA multiple to account for different capex requirements)

FIGURE 11.3 Multiples Used for Comp Analysis

Steps to perform comparable company analysis:

(i) Select "comps," publicly traded companies in the same or similar industries that are most comparable to the company being valued. Financial considerations can include size, geographies, growth prospects, etc. No comp is perfect, and judgment is required to determine the most relevant peer group. Industry-focused investment bankers are a great resource when selecting comps.

(ii) Fill out a comp table, as shown in Figure 11.4.

[1]VCC is based on a company acquired in an LBO. The name of the company and certain financial information have been altered.

	Total Enterprise Value				Operating Metrics					Trading Multiples		
Company	Equity Mkt Cap	Plus Debt	Minus Cash	Equals TEV	Sales	Sales Growth[a]	EBITDA	EBITDA Margin	EBITDAX	Sales	EBITDA	EBITDAX
Co A												
Co B												
Co C												
Co D												
Co E												
Co F												
Median												
Mean												

[a] For VCC analysis, the analyst used the most recent year's growth rate. However, some analysts prefer to use a 3-to-5-year average growth rate.

FIGURE 11.4 Comp Table

(iii) Comment on each comp versus the company you are valuing.
- Do you think the comp is better or worse?
- Should the target company trade at a higher or lower multiple?

Figure 11.5 summarizes the pros and cons of using comparable company analysis to value a company.

Pros:
- It is easy to perform as long as there are good publicly traded comps representative of the firm being valued (e.g., similar growth rates, margins, etc.).
- There is no need to build a long-term forecast and make growth rate assumptions (versus the discounted cash flow method, which relies heavily on out-year growth forecasts).
- It is designed to reflect valuation based on current market conditions and sentiment.

Cons:
- Comp analysis is only as good as the comps selected. Choosing the right universe of comps requires judgment and at times in-depth industry knowledge/expertise.
- Valuation might be overly influenced by market sentiment. If you're valuing a company during a period of "irrational exuberance," either for the industry or the market as a whole, all valuations will skew high.
- It does not incorporate a control premium or the value of synergies to a strategic buyer.

FIGURE 11.5 Pros and Cons of Comparable Company Analysis

EXAMPLE OF COMPARABLE COMPANY ANALYSIS—VCC

In consultation with industry experts, the analyst identified three public comps:

1. *Flowserve:* One of the world's largest manufacturers of flow control products (~$3.8B sales) with a portfolio of more than 50 brands.
2. *Watts Water:* Designer and manufacturer of residential and commercial flow control products for plumbing and HVAC applications.
3. *CIRCOR Intl:* Manufacturer of specialized flow and motion control products.

As shown in Figure 11.6, two of the three comps trade in a range of 9.0x–9.7x EBITDA, with the third at 15.6x. The analyst believes VCC's business is better than the comps in three respects:

1. Less cyclical due to a higher proportion of recurring revenues;
2. Higher EBITDA margin; and
3. Lower capex needs.

However, these positives are offset by the following:

1. The comps are significantly larger and more diversified, with revenues ranging from $1 to $4 billion versus $160 million for VCC.
2. VCC has experienced a slower rate of sales growth.
3. VCC has an extremely leveraged balance sheet (7.3x).

The analyst disregards the outlier and believes VCC should trade at a 1 to 1.5x discount to the other comps, mainly to reflect its smaller size. He uses 7.5x–8.5x EBITDA for a valuation of $262.5 to $297.5 million.

	Total Enterprise Value				Operating Metrics				Leverage	Trading Multiples		
Company	Equity Mkt Cap	Plus Debt	Minus Cash	Equals TEV	Sales	Sales Growth	EBITDA	EBITDA Margin	Net Debt/ EBITDA	Sales	EBITDA	EBITDAX
VCC	NA	NA	NA	NA	162	−0.9%	35[a]	21.6%	7.30x	NA	NA	NA
FLS	4,927	1,483	620	5,790	3,836	4.8%	372	9.7%	2.32x	1.51x	15.56x	17.01x
WTS	2,188	353	204	2,337	1,565	7.4%	240	15.4%	0.62x	1.49x	9.73x	10.90x
CIR	428	786	69	1,145	1,013	NM[b]	127	12.5%	5.65x	1.13x	9.02x	10.72x
Median	2,188	786	204	2,337	1,565	NM	240	12.5%	2.32x	1.49x	9.73x	10.90x
Mean[c]	2,514	874	298	3,091	2,138	6.1%	246	12.5%	2.86x	1.38x	11.43x	12.88x

[a] VCC's EBITDA is based on the 2017/2018 two-year average. See Chapter 13 VCC memo for rationale.
[b] Growth rate "NM" due to the impact of an acquisition.
[c] Mean EBITDA margin, leverage, and multiples are not size-weighted.

FIGURE 11.6 Comp Table for VCC
Source: Capital IQ

VALUATION TECHNIQUE #2: PRECEDENT TRANSACTION ANALYSIS

This methodology uses previously completed mergers and acquisitions (M&A) to value a company. It is similar to the analysis above in that it relies on multiples to value the business. Here, the implied multiple based on the acquisition price is used.

Valuations using M&A comps tend to be higher than comparable company analysis for two reasons:

1. *Control premium:* In most M&A, the buyer must pay a higher price than the stock's current trading level. This premium is referred to as a control premium.
2. *Synergies:* If the company is being acquired by a strategic buyer (i.e., another company in the same line of business), certain costs will be easy for the acquirer to reduce. Costs that can be easily cut result in what are commonly referred to as synergies. For example, the company only needs one CEO and CFO. Given these synergies, the acquirer uses a higher EBITDA, which includes anticipated synergies, as the basis of its bid.

Steps to perform precedent transaction analysis:

1. Select a universe of precedent transactions.
2. Fill out precedent transaction table, shown in Figure 11.8.
3. Comment on each M&A comp versus the company you are valuing.
   - Do you think the comp is better or worse?
   - Should the target company trade at a higher or lower multiple?

Figure 11.7 summarizes the pros and cons of using precedent transactions analysis to value a company.

<u>Pros:</u>
- If the company you are valuing might be a future M&A target, this approach incorporates the control premium and potential value of synergies.

<u>Cons:</u>
- Data might be unavailable if there haven't been recent, publicly disclosed M&A transactions in the industry.
- Like the prior method, this one is only as good as the precedent transactions selected. The valuation might not reflect current market conditions if time has elapsed since the transaction.
- The control premium and synergies are embedded in the valuation and multiple. These are unique to each transaction and thus might not apply to the company being analyzed.

FIGURE 11.7 Pros and Cons of Precedent Transaction Analysis

Transaction Details				Operating Metrics					Acquisition Multiples		
Target	Acquirer	Date	Purchase TEV	Sales	Sales Growth	EBITDA	EBITDA Margin	EBITDAX	Sales	EBITDA	EBITDAX
Co A											
Co B											
Co C											
Co D											
Co E											
Co F											
Median											
Mean											

FIGURE 11.8 Precedent Transaction Table

EXAMPLE OF PRECEDENT TRANSACTION ANALYSIS—VCC

In consultation with industry investment bankers, the analyst identified two relevant M&A transactions. As shown in Figure 11.9, these precedent transactions trade in a tight range of 8.6x–9.6x EBITDA.

- *GESTRA:* Designs and manufactures valves and control systems for heat and process fluid control applications.
- *Critical Flow Solutions:* Manufactures high-technology valves for refining operations.

$ in millions	Relevant Precedent Transaction[a]						
Target	Acquirer	Date	Purchase Price	Sales	EBITDA	EBITDA Margin	EBITDA Multiple
GESTRA	Spirax-Sarco	May 2017	$159.2	$92.5	$16.6	17.9%	9.6x
Critical Flow Sys	CIRCOR	Oct 2016	214.0	122.0	25.0	20.5%	8.6x
Average[b]			$186.6	$107.3	$20.8	19.2%	9.1x

[a] Due to limited information on the acquired company, the analyst did not include every component of the precedent transaction table in Figure 11.8.
[b] Average EBITDA margin and multiple are not size-weighted.

FIGURE 11.9 Precedent Transactions for VCC

The analyst believes both transactions are representative of what VCC would be worth in an M&A context. He uses 8.5x–9.5x, approximately one turn greater than the comparable company multiple arrived at in the prior approach, to reflect the potential control premium and synergies, resulting in a valuation of $298 to $333 million.

VALUATION TECHNIQUE #3: DISCOUNTED CASH FLOW (DCF) ANALYSIS

The DCF valuation technique requires the analyst to project the company's cash flow (similar to our process in the prior chapter) and identify an appropriate discount rate to calculate present value (PV). Entire courses are taught on DCF analysis; this is a brief overview.

There are four sub-steps:

1. Forecast unlevered cash flow during the period.
2. Determine the appropriate discount rate, which corresponds to the company's weighted average cost of capital (WACC).
3. Translate the unlevered cash flow calculated above into today's dollars using the WACC as the discount rate, i.e., calculate the PV of the forecast period cash flow.
4. Calculate the PV terminal value, that is, the value of the cash flows after the projection period.

1) Forecast unlevered cash flow during the period

Figure 11.10 shows the template for forecasting cash flow. Note that this is a summary version of the forecasts created for TM Corp and JCP in the prior chapter; the supporting analysis and calculations are similar.

	Projections				
	Year 1	Year 2	Year 3	Year 4	Year 5
EBITDA					
Less Capex					
+/– Changes in Working Capital					
Less Taxes[a]					
Unlevered Free Cash Flow (FCF)					

[a]The estimate of taxes is before the benefit of any deductible interest (i.e., assume an unlevered company)

FIGURE 11.10 Cash Flow Forecast Template

2) Determine the appropriate discount rate—that is, the company's weighted average cost of capital (WACC)

WACC Calculation Inputs
After-tax Cost of Debt × Percent of Debt in Capital Structure
Plus Cost of Equity × Percent of Equity in Capital Structure
Equals the Company's WACC

FIGURE 11.11 WACC Calculation

After-tax cost of debt:

- Average market yield of company's debt × (1 – company's tax rate)[2]

Cost of equity:

- Since equity is riskier than debt, the cost of equity is always higher than the cost of debt for an individual company.
- Unlike the cost of debt (weighted average market yield of all debt instruments), the cost of equity is not directly observable.
- One method of calculating the cost of equity is the capital asset pricing model (CAPM).

Calculating the cost of equity using CAPM:

- Cost of equity = the risk-free rate + the company's equity risk premium

[2] In 2017, the Tax Cuts and Jobs Act (the Act) reduced some of the tax benefits of debt financing. Before the Act, companies were unrestricted in the amount of interest they could deduct. After the Act, companies were limited to deducting up to 30% of their most recent 12-month EBITDA. After 2021, the cap became 30% of EBIT. As a result, interest above the 30% EBIT cap should not be tax-adjusted, which increases the after-tax cost of debt.

Input #1 for CAPM – the risk-free rate:

- The 10-year Treasury yield is usually used for the risk-free rate

Input #2 for CAPM – the company's equity risk premium:

- A company's equity risk premium is a function of the volatility of its stock relative to the general equity market, a concept referred to as beta. A beta of one means the company's stock volatility is equal to that of the market. If the equity market goes down 10%, we would expect the company's stock to decline by 10%. A beta greater than one means the company is more volatile than the market. If a company's beta is 1.5 and the market goes down by 10%, we would expect the company's stock to go down by 15% (the beta of 1.5 multiplied by the 10% market decline). A beta below one means the company's stock is less volatile than the market.
- The company's equity risk premium equals the company's beta multiplied by the market risk premium, which is generally accepted as the long-term outperformance of the S&P 500 index versus Treasury bonds. As of 2022, the number commonly used is 5.5%. Beta is a statistical measurement of volatility and can be obtained through Bloomberg, Factset, Capital IQ, or other financial data services.

Weakness of CAPM:

- Many professional investors (including me) believe estimating the cost of equity using CAPM is largely an academic exercise rather than a meaningful input into valuation because an investor's required return to invest in the company is based on opportunity cost. In their fantastic book *Pitch the Perfect Investment*, Paul Sonkin and Paul Johnson make this point by quoting an exchange between legendary investors Warren Buffett and Charlie Munger during the Berkshire Hathaway 2003 annual meeting. I recommend this book for those interested in a career in equity investing.

  Buffett: "Charlie and I don't know our cost of capital. It's taught in business schools, but we're skeptical. We just look to do the most intelligent thing we can with the capital that we have. We measure everything against our alternatives. I've never seen a cost of capital calculation that made sense to me. Have you, Charlie?"

  Munger: "Never. If you take the best text in economics by Mankiw, he says intelligent people make decisions based on opportunity cost—in other words, it's your alternatives that matter."[i]
- If you use CAPM to estimate the equity cost, double-check the output with your PM (portfolio manager) to ensure it reflects what investors would require to make the investment.

3) Translate the unlevered cash flow calculated above into today's dollars using the WACC as the discount rate, i.e., calculate the present value (PV) (Figure 11.12)

$$\text{Present Value} = \frac{FCF_1}{(1+r)^1} + \frac{FCF_2}{(1+r)^2} + \frac{FCF_3}{(1+r)^3} + \frac{FCF_4}{(1+r)^4} + \frac{FCF_5}{(1+r)^5} + \frac{FCF_n}{(1+r)^n}$$

FIGURE 11.12 Present Value Calculation

PV is equal to the FCF in each year (Year 1, Year 2, Year 3, etc.), divided by a discount factor of 1 + the discount rate, which is WACC, taken to the nth power, where "n" is the number of years into the future that the cash flow is occurring. If you model these numbers out manually year by year, you'll notice that the "out year" numbers are smaller than the nearer years. This is because cash flows are worth less the further away they occur (a basic tenet of financial theory).

4) Calculate the terminal value (the value of the cash flows after the projection period).

The DCF valuation method includes the present value of *all* future cash flows, not just those within the forecast window. Since it is impossible to forecast with any certainty beyond a five-year projection period, the DCF must address cash flows beyond the projection period. The value of the business derived from cash flows beyond the projection period is generally referred to as the company's terminal value.

There are two methods to compute a company's terminal value:

(a) *Exit multiple method:* This technique uses the comparable company method outlined above by multiplying the final projected year's EBITDA by the EBITDA multiple derived from the comparable company analysis. This number is discounted into today's dollars using the company's WACC for the number of years in the projection period.

(b) *Perpetuity method:* This method assumes that the cash flow of the business grows in perpetuity at a given rate using the following formula:

$$\text{PV of the terminal value} = \text{Last projected year FCF}$$
$$\times(1+\text{assumed growth rate})/(\text{WACC}-\text{assumed growth rate})$$

The DCF valuation of the business is the sum of the PV of the projected cash flows and the PV of the terminal value.

Figure 11.13 summarizes the pros and cons of using DCF analysis to value a company.

Pros:

- Most theoretically "correct" valuation method; a company's intrinsic value is definitionally a function of the present value of its future cash flows
- Less influenced by current market conditions than the comparable company or precedent transaction methodologies
- Not dependent on identifying a "perfect" peer group

Cons:

- Viewed by some investment professionals as academic and theoretical with unreliable outcomes driven by the difficulty in forecasting cash flow beyond five years
- Highly sensitive to the discount rate, which is challenging to estimate

FIGURE 11.13 Pros and Cons of DCF Analysis

EXAMPLE OF DCF ANALYSIS—VCC

The analyst ran a DCF model using his downside, base, and management/sponsor forecast cases. The DCF analysis produced the following valuation range:

$ in millions	Downside	Base	Upside
Enterprise value based on DCF analysis	$228.9	$275.7	$399.4

FIGURE 11.14 VCC DCF Analysis

Figure 11.15 is the base case valuation model. (See VCC Credit Committee Memo in Chapter 13 for all three cases.)

	Projections				
$ in millions	**Year 1**	**Year 2**	**Year 3**	**Year 4**	**Year 5**
Unlevered Free Cash Flow					
Adjusted EBITDA	$37.5	$38.2	$39.0	$39.8	$40.5
Less Capex	(4.2)	(5.8)	(5.8)	(4.3)	(4.5)
+/– Change in WC	0.0	(1.6)	(1.7)	(1.7)	(1.7)
Less Unlevered Taxes (i)	(5.9)	(5.7)	(5.6)	(5.6)	(5.5)
Less Misc. Other Cash Flows	(1.5)	(1.5)	(1.5)	(1.5)	(1.5)
Unlevered Free Cash Flow (UFCF)	$25.9	$23.6	$24.4	$26.7	$27.3
Divide by Discount Factor (1+WACC)^ Years	1.1200	1.2544	1.4049	1.5735	1.7623
Present Value (UFCF/Disc factor)	$23.1	$18.8	$17.4	$17.0	$15.5
PV of FCF (sum of above PVs) [A]	**$91.8**				
Terminal Valuation Calculation					
Year 5 Forecasted EBITDA					$40.5
Mid-Point EBITDA Multiple from Comps					8.0x
Terminal Value at the End of Year 5					$324.0
Discount Factor (1+WACC)^ Years					1.7623
PV of Terminal Value [B]					**$183.9**
Enterprise Value Based on DCF Analysis:					
PV of FCF [A]	**$91.8**				
PV of Terminal Value [B]	**183.9**				
Enterprise Value	**$275.7**				

(i) Estimate of taxes is before the benefit of any deductible interest (i.e., assumes an unlevered company).

FIGURE 11.15 VCC Base Case Valuation Model

Notes on VCC DCF valuation:

1. Projection rationale: See VCC investment committee memo in Chapter 13.
2. WACC: 12% is based on guidance from the analyst's portfolio manager.

VALUATION TECHNIQUE #4: LIQUIDATION ANALYSIS (ASSET OR COLLATERAL VALUATION)

This methodology considers only the monetizable value of a company's assets rather than its franchise or "going concern" value. This valuation technique is usually reserved for the downside case in a very distressed scenario and uses the valuation approach of asset-backed lenders who rely solely on the value of collateral when they extend credit. As discussed in Chapter 5, the availability of an ABL facility is based on a borrowing base formula tied to the liquidation value of the company's working capital assets. In some instances, real estate and/or brand value may be included in the borrowing base.

Steps to perform liquidation analysis:

Identify all the company's assets and estimate recovery values, as shown in Figure 11.16. Chapter 19, "Making Money in Distressed Situations," will perform a step-by-step liquidation valuation of a company.

	Liquidation Analysis		
	Book Value	Expected Recovery %	Expected Recovery Value $
Excess Cash			
Accounts Receivables			
Inventory			
Owned Real Estate			
In the Money Leases			
Brand Value			
Other Assets			
Total Value			
Less Expenses to Liquidate			
Liquidation Value after Expenses			

FIGURE 11.16 Liquidation Analysis Template

Figure 11.17 summarizes the pros and cons of using liquidation analysis to value a company.

Pros:
- Provides a draconian downside scenario; assumes the business fails and is liquidated ("floor value")
- Extremely useful for asset-backed lenders relying on their collateral's value

Cons:
- In most instances, meaningfully undervalues the company because it does not consider franchise value

FIGURE 11.17 Pros and Cons of Liquidation Analysis

EXAMPLE OF LIQUIDATION ANALYSIS—VCC

While the analyst ran a liquidation analysis, he did not place much value on it. Given the company's market share, he was doubtful the company would ever liquidate. The analyst viewed the liquidation value of the hard collateral of $102 to $124 million shown in Figure 11.18 as a draconian valuation, especially as his analysis assigned zero value to the brand.

		Recovery Rates (%)			$ Recovery		
$ in millions	Amount	Low	Mid	High	Low	Mid	High
Minimum Cash on Balance Sheet	$5.0	100%	100%	100%	$5.0	$5.0	$5.0
Accounts Receivable	35.0	85%	90%	95%	29.8	31.5	33.3
Inventories	55.0	60%	68%	75%	33.0	37.4	41.3
Value of Owned RE	60.0	70%	75%	80%	42.0	45.0	48.0
Machinery and Other Assets	25.0	10%	15%	20%	2.5	3.8	5.0
Other	20.0	0%	10%	15%	0.0	2.0	3.0
Total	$200.0				$112.3	$124.7	$135.6
Less Liquidation Expenses (5%)					(5.6)	(6.2)	(6.8)
Less Other Wind-Down Expenses/Cushion					(5.0)	(5.0)	(5.0)
Liquidation Value to Secured Lenders					$101.7	$113.5	$123.8

FIGURE 11.18 VCC Liquidation Analysis

SUMMARY OF VCC VALUATION ANALYSIS

It is common to summarize the range of values calculated using different methodologies in a "football field chart," as illustrated in Figure 11.19. The analyst did not include the liquidation analysis below because he felt it was irrelevant to this company.

Based on this work, the analyst concluded the LTV of VCC's new financing is 67%, using the mid-point valuation of $300 million. The loan is still covered even using the lowest valuation, which results in an LTV of 87%.

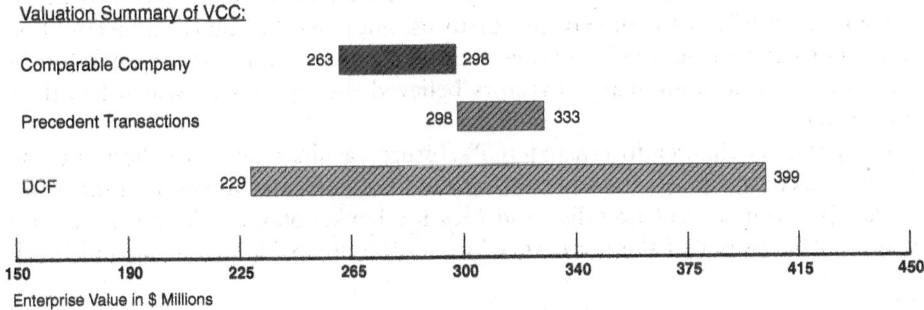

FIGURE 11.19 Valuation Summary of VCC

END-OF-CHAPTER VALUATION ANALYSIS FOR JCPENNEY[3]

JCP has publicly traded equity. Based on its trading level, the company's observable enterprise value is $5.4 billion as shown in Figure 11.20.

		TEV Calculation
$ in millions		Outstanding
	Maturity	2/2/2013
$1.75B ABL Revolver	4/29/2016	0
Capital Leases & other		114
Total Secured Debt		**114**
6.875% Senior Unsecured Bonds	10/15/15	200
7.65% Senior Unsecured Bonds	8/15/16	200
7.95% Senior Unsecured Bonds	4/1/17	285
5.75% Senior Unsecured Bonds	2/15/18	300
5.65% Senior Unsecured Bonds	6/1/20	400
7.125% Senior Unsecured Bonds	11/15/23	255
6.9% Senior Unsecured Bonds	8/15/26	2
6.375% Senior Unsecured Bonds	10/15/36	400
7.4% Senior Unsecured Bonds	4/1/37	326
7.625% Senior Unsecured Bonds	3/1/97	500
Total Unsecured Debt		**2,868**
Subordinated Debt		0
Total Debt		**2,982**
Less: Cash		-930
Net Debt		**2,052**
Equity Market Cap.		3,347
Total Enterprise Value		**5,399**

FIGURE 11.20 JCP Observable Enterprise Value

However, many analysts did not believe that JCP's market-based TEV accurately reflected the company's value. Its long-dated unsecured debt traded at an average price of $70 at the time of this analysis, implying the equity value could be inflated. Furthermore, its stock had one of the highest short interests of any publicly traded company, meaning many investors believed the equity was worth less than market value.

The previous chapter forecasted JCP's future earnings and cash flow. In one scenario, the company successfully turns around the business; however, in the other scenario, JCP runs out of liquidity and files for bankruptcy, rendering the equity worthless. The output of the forecast, which in the downside case is at odds with

[3] Download JCPenney's 2012 10-K (fiscal year ended February 2, 2013) at the SEC Edgar website for public company filings, https://www.sec.gov/edgar/searchedgar/companysearch, using the search term "Old Copper Company." The company's search term on Edgar is Old Copper Company, Inc., not JCPenney.

any equity value, means that you must perform your own valuation analysis for JCP rather than relying on the public market. Figure 11.21 shows a range of valuations for the forecast scenarios developed in the prior chapter.

	Valuation Scenarios		
$ in millions	Downside	Base	Upside
Projected Stabilized EBITDA	$800	$1,000	$1,200
EBITDA Multiples	5.25x	5.50x	5.75x
Enterprise Value at the End of Projection Period (future value)	$4,200	$5,500	$6,900
Required Return to Invest in JCP (WACC)	15.0%	15.0%	15.0%
Discount Factor to PV (1+WACC)^ 4 Years to Stabilize	1.7490	1.7490	1.7490
Discount Factor to PV (1+WACC)^ 3 Years to Stabilize	1.5209	1.5209	1.5209
Discount Factor to PV (1+WACC)^ 2 Years to Stabilize	1.3225	1.3225	1.3225
PV of Enterprise Value if Turnaround Takes 4 Years (FV /disc factor)	$2,401	$3,145	$3,945
PV of Enterprise Value if Turnaround Takes 3 Years (FV /disc factor)	$2,762	$3,616	$4,537
PV of Enterprise Value if Turnaround Takes 2 Years (FV /disc factor)	$3,176	$4,159	$5,217

FIGURE 11.21 JCP Valuation for Various Turnaround Scenarios

Notes on assumptions driving "successful turnaround" valuations:

1. *Projected stabilized EBITDA:* In the base case, EBITDA approaches JCP's 2011 EBITDA (the level the year before the disastrous change in strategy). The analyst ran the downside and upside cases at a 20% variance to the base case.
2. *EBITDA multiples:* The analyst's multiples were based on the comp analysis shown in Figure 11.22.

Comparable Company Analysis							
In $MM	Equity Mkt Cap	Plus Debt	Less Cash	Equals TEV	EBITDA	EBITDA Margin	EBITDA Multiple
Macy's	15,791	6,930	1,836	20,885	3,717	13.4%	5.62x
Kohl's	10,470	4,553	537	14,486	2,723	14.1%	5.32x
Dillard's	3,994	824	124	4,694	798	11.8%	5.88x
Average						13.1%	**5.61x**

FIGURE 11.22 Comp Analysis for JCP
Source: Adapted from Capital IQ

3. *Required return to invest in JCP (WACC):* Based on trading levels of the company's debt, the analyst believes the cost of debt is approximately 9%. Since the

company is not currently paying taxes due to net operating losses (NOLs), there is no tax advantage to debt. Given the business's turnaround nature, she thinks the equity cost should be 20%. She also assumed a logical capital structure would be 60% debt and 40% equity and concluded that a 15% WACC was reasonable for valuation purposes. The WACC calculation is shown in Figure 11.23.

WACC Calculation			
	Cost	**Weight**	**WACC**
Debt	9.0%	40%	3.6%
Equity	20.0%	60%	12.0%
			15.6%

FIGURE 11.23 WACC Calculation for JCP

The analyst rounded the WACC to 15%.

4. *Years to stabilize:* The analyst ran turnaround scenarios ranging from two to four years.

However, the turnaround is not a certainty. The downside model (as forecasted in Chapter 10) predicts the company will run out of liquidity over the next two years. For the draconian downside valuation, the analyst must perform a liquidation analysis. In Chapter 19, "Making Money in Distressed Situations," we will perform a full liquidation analysis for a retailer.

CHAPTER CONCLUSION

Valuation is an art, not a science, and the goal of the exercise is not an exact number, which would provide only a false sense of precision. Instead, your analysis should include some combination of the above approaches to assess a range of potential values. As shown in the VCC and JCP examples, a range of outcomes emerges from rigorous valuation analysis. As you develop your investment recommendation, a refined valuation estimate is a critical input to quantifying the company's LTV and gaining comfort with the "cushion" of subordinated debt and/or equity below the layer of debt you are evaluating.

NOTE

i. Tilson, Whitney. "Notes from the 2003 Berkshire Hathaway Annual meeting." Annual Meetings of the Shareholders of Berkshire Hathaway Inc., Omaha, Nebraska, May 3, 2003.

CHAPTER 12

Step 6 of the Credit Analysis Process: Structuring and Documentation

As shown in Figure 12.1, one critical piece of credit analysis remains. Before making an investment recommendation for a bond or loan, you need to understand the structure, terms, and specific nuances of each debt instrument. If you're originating a private, direct loan, your firm will negotiate terms directly with the borrower. If you're evaluating a new issue, the terms will be a work in progress that may change as the deal is being negotiated—and if you work for a large firm, you might have a say in these changes. If you're looking at an investment in the secondary market, you can find the terms in the indenture (if bond) or the credit agreement (if loan).

Step 1	Sources and Uses (only applicable to originations) (a) Why is the company seeking financing? (b) What are the proposed sources of capital to fund the financing need?
Step 2	Qualitative Analysis (a) Industry analysis (b) Business strategy (c) Management assessment (d) ESG concerns
Step 3	Financial Statement Analysis (a) Profitability (b) Cash flow and liquidity (c) Capital structure
Step 4	Forecasting (a) Identification of key business drivers and assumptions (b) Development of base, upside, and downside cases
Step 5	Corporate Valuation (a) Comparable company analysis (b) Precedent transactions (M&A comps) (c) Discounted cash flow analysis (d) Liquidation analysis
Step 6	**Structuring and Documentation** **(a) Economic points** **(b) Structure and collateral** **(c) Covenants**
Step 7	Preparing an Investment Recommendation and Credit Committee Memo (a) Investment thesis and recommendation (b) Risks and mitigants (c) Relative value analysis

FIGURE 12.1 The Seven-Step Process of Evaluating a Debt Instrument

This chapter covers the basic, standard terms found in most bond and loan documentation. Chapters 17 and 18 tackle more advanced topics such as structural subordination, asset stripping provisions, and non-pro rata repayments. And Chapter 19 includes some trade ideas that rely upon important structural features of individual debt issues that give them a different risk-reward profile than other debt instruments in the same capital structure.

As you read through the structural features below, you might reach the conclusion that more creditor protections are always better. But this perspective ignores the tension between pricing and structure that exists in new issue negotiations. Some investors will happily accept lower protections in exchange for a higher coupon, particularly for a higher-quality company, which is unlikely to become distressed.

STRUCTURE AND DOCUMENTATION—GENERAL TERMS

Figure 12.2 is a comprehensive list of the general terms that might be found in documentation for credit instruments. Not all of these will apply to every bond or loan issue.

1. Amount of bond or loan outstanding (face value or principal amount)
2. Debt type
3. Maturity date
4. Required amortization and excess cash flow (ECF) sweep
5. Coupon
6. Up-front fees or original issue discount (OID)
7. Prepayment penalties/call protection
8. Change of control put
9. Contractual and structural subordination (will be covered in Chapter 17)
10. Collateral
11. Covenants
12. Amendments

FIGURE 12.2 General Terms of Credit Instruments

Amount of bond or loan outstanding

This refers to the amount of the individual debt instrument (also referred to as the face value or principal amount) that is outstanding at the time of the analysis. This information is usually available in the debt note in the 10-K, as well as on Bloomberg. If you are evaluating a secondary investment, the amount of debt might differ from the original issuance amount if there has been partial repayment.

Debt type

Debt instruments vary in seniority and security. Figure 12.3 shows the most common debt instruments in order of safety/priority from most to least (see Chapters 5 and 9 for a more detailed discussion).

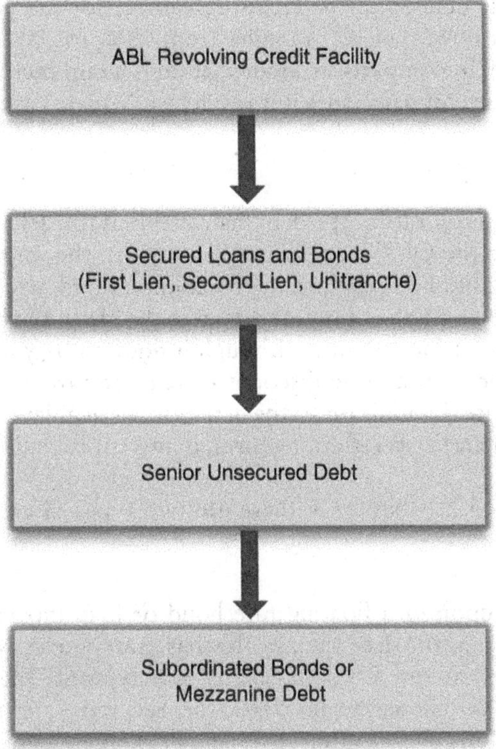

FIGURE 12.3 Types of Debt by Seniority

Maturity

The maturity (also referred to as tenor or term) is the date on which the debt must be repaid (i.e., due date).

Required amortization and excess cash flow (ECF) sweep

Amortization refers to any required repayment prior to maturity. For secured bank debt, it is common for a portion of the debt to be repaid during the life of the loan (e.g., repayment of 1% to 10% of the loan per year). On the other hand, bonds usually have a bullet maturity, meaning there is no required repayment during the bond's life, and 100% of the principal must be repaid on the maturity date.

For the avoidance of doubt, the term amortization has two unrelated meanings:

1. The expense related to the depletion of intangible assets, i.e., the noncash expense that, along with depreciation, is added back to operating profit to calculate EBITDA.
2. The required repayment of debt discussed above.

Some loan agreements include a provision for an excess cash flow (ECF) sweep. The ECF provision is more flexible than amortization. If the company produces positive cash flow as defined in the credit agreement for the period, it must use a portion of this cash flow, typically ranging from 25% to 75%, to sweep—that is, pay down—the loan. In comparison, amortization is a contractual obligation to pay down debt even if the company does not produce adequate cash flow to do so.

Coupon

The coupon is the interest rate of the debt instrument. If the debt instrument is issued at a discount to par (or OID, original issue discount), the imputed interest rate is greater than the coupon. For example, a zero-coupon bond, which is issued at a low dollar price to reflect an implicit interest rate over the life of the bond, does not actually have a zero percent interest rate, although it does not pay a cash coupon. Since debt issues, which price at a large discount to par, are rare, most investors equate coupon to interest rate. In addition to the actual numerical level of the coupon, you must identify idiosyncratic structural features, if any, for each debt instrument in the capital structure.

First, as discussed in Chapter 3, there are two types of coupons: floating rate and fixed rate.

Floating rate The coupon of a floating rate bond or loan moves ("floats") at a set spread to an underlying risk-free rate; as this base rate moves, so does the coupon. Historically, the base rate for US dollar loans[1] was typically the London Interbank Offered Rate (LIBOR); however, in 2020, the Secured Overnight Funding Rate (SOFR) replaced LIBOR. For example, if a bank debt coupon is SOFR + 500 (or 5%) and SOFR is 2%, then the coupon is 7% (the 2% SOFR rate plus the 5% agreed spread). If SOFR increases to 3%, then the coupon increases to 8% (the 3% SOFR rate plus the 5% agreed spread). Most leveraged loans are floating rate.

It is common for loans to have a SOFR floor. If a loan has a SOFR floor, the company won't enjoy savings in its coupon payments if SOFR falls below the floor. For instance, if you invest in a loan with a SOFR + 500 coupon and 1% floor, the coupon will adjust to changes in SOFR; however, it will never go below 6% (1% SOFR floor + the 500 bps spread).

Fixed rate The vast majority of high yield bonds are fixed-rate debt instruments, meaning the coupon does not change with the underlying risk-free rate.

There are several other coupon features that might exist in a debt instrument that are important to quantify and understand.

Coupon pricing grids Some leveraged loans have coupon step-ups and step-downs reflected on a pricing grid in the credit agreement. If a deal has a pricing grid, the spread over the base rate is determined by credit ratings, the leverage ratio, or another metric of the borrower determined at origination.

[1] For non-dollar loans, the base rate is typically Euribor (Euro Interbank Offered Rate), which was not affected by the LIBOR phase-out.

Coupon step-up provision While less common than pricing grids in loans, depending on market conditions at issuance, low-BBB investment grade bonds might include a coupon step-up feature if investors are concerned about the risk of a downgrade to high yield when the bond is issued.

For example, in 2021, Boeing (rated BBB-/Baa2) issued $9.8 billion of bonds. At the time of the issuance, the market had a heightened concern of a downgrade due to the company's 2020 $12 billion net loss, as the company faced COVID-19 headwinds for new aircraft orders and services and a grounding of its 737 MAX line. These bonds included a coupon step-up provision that provides for increases of 25 basis points to the coupon rates per each notch of downgrade below BBB-/Baa3, with those increases capped at 200 basis points. The provision falls away in the event ratings rise to BBB+/Baa1.

Payment in Kind Interest (PIK) Some debt allows the borrower to issue new debt in lieu of cash coupon payments, typically with a small (50–100 basis point) step-up in the underlying rate. If the company has the right to pay the coupon either in cash or in kind, then the debt is called PIK toggle debt. This was a common feature in many LBOs leading up to the GFC. For example, as you will see in Chapter 13, HCA included a second lien PIK toggle bond as part of its 2006 LBO financing. The coupon of the bond was 9.625%, with a 75 basis point increase to 10.375% if the company elected to PIK. As you might expect, HCA exercised this PIK option at the worst possible time for the holders of its bonds, which were trading at $80 when HCA PIK'd. While the coupon increased, this was more than offset by what was effectively a 20% discount on the interest payment, since it came in the form of debt trading at 80 cents on the dollar.

Timing of coupon Leveraged loan interest payments generally take place monthly or quarterly. Bonds pay interest semiannually (every six months).

Up-front fees or original issue discount (OID)

When a company issues a new loan, it is common for the investor to get an up-front fee for making the loan, typically 2%, which translates into an effective purchase price of $98. New bond issues don't include up-front fees, but it is common for a new issue to price at a slight discount (less than a point) to par. That discount to par is the original issue discount (OID), which is effectively the same as an up-front fee.

Prepayment penalties/call protection

Since many of our examples have involved JCP bonds trading at a substantial discount to par, you might wonder why the early repayment of debt would be an issue. Isn't it good news if you get your money back early? But most companies' debt trades as a going concern; you invest in bonds or loans because you have a favorable view of the issuer, and you'd like to receive your coupons through the contractual maturity date. If the borrower repays your loan or bond early, you must reinvest those proceeds since your clients are not paying you to hold cash. If interest rates and/or credit spreads have gone down, you will not be able to replicate the yield of your original investment.

If there is no penalty for early repayment, a creditor takes on *asymmetric* risk when buying a bond or loan. The debt instrument can never trade above par, but it can trade below par. If the company's credit profile improves, its debt is less risky—but without prepayment penalties, you won't get the benefit of that improvement because the borrower will refinance its debt at a lower coupon. The same holds true for the level of risk-free rates; if Treasury rates go down, a borrower can refinance its fixed-rate debt with lower-coupon debt if there is no penalty for doing so.

There are several ways creditors can protect themselves against prepayment risk, listed in order of most to least investor-friendly in Figure 12.4.

1. Non-call provision
2. Hard call protection
3. Soft call protection
4. No call protection

FIGURE 12.4 Lender Protection against Prepayment Risk

1. ***Non-call provision:*** The borrower cannot prepay the debt without paying an expensive make-whole premium (so named because the price paid effectively makes the investor "whole"). Virtually all investment grade bonds are non-callable other than with a make-whole premium, while most high yield bonds are non-callable for the first half of their life. The required make-whole premium is easiest to calculate using Bloomberg. Conceptually, it is the price that reflects a lump sum payment of the remaining coupon, present valued at the treasury rate plus a spread (usually 50 basis points), plus the principal. Because they are very expensive, make-whole call options are rarely exercised.
2. ***Hard call protection:*** This feature allows the borrower to repay the debt prior to maturity at a premium to par. High yield bonds are typically callable halfway through the lifetime of the bond at par plus half the coupon. For example, a bond with an eight-year maturity and an 8% coupon would be non-call (other than with a make-whole premium) for the first four years of its life. After four years (half-way to maturity), the bond would become callable at par plus $4 (half of the 8% coupon), or $104, after which the call price typically steps down linearly to par at maturity. A typical call structure on a private loan would be $103/$102/$101, meaning that if the company prepaid $100 of debt in year one, it would pay $103, or a 3% premium. The premium would decrease to 2% and 1% in years two and three, respectively. After year three, the loan is repayable at par. Loans issued in the BSL market tend to have less call protection; it is common to have a $101 call option for the first year, after which the loan becomes callable at par.
3. ***Soft call protection:*** The company only pays a prepayment penalty if refinancing the debt. However, if the owners sell the company and repay the debt early, there would be no penalty.
4. ***No call protection***: The debt is repayable at any time with no penalty. Before it became more institutionalized, bank debt typically had no call protection, but examples of this are rare today.

Change of control (CoC) put

If the ownership of a company changes, generally bank debt must be repaid at par upon the consummation of the transaction. In the early days of the high yield bond market, bonds did not have this provision, so bonds "traveled" to the new owners. This was good news if the acquirer was a higher-rated company—but if the change of control was due to an LBO, this was usually very bad news for the bonds. As discussed in Chapter 4, LBOs involve a substantial increase in leverage as debt is issued to finance the transaction. Holders of bonds issued without a change of control provision have a coupon that reflects the risk when those bonds were issued, and the legacy bonds of an LBO'd company typically trade down in price to reflect this increased risk.

A change of control provision, or put, protects the bondholder by mandating that the company tender for its bonds at a price of $101 in the event a change of control takes place. Change of control provisions have several defined terms in the indenture that must be understood to ensure that you are truly protected as a holder, including carve-outs for "permitted holders" to whom the CoC does not apply. And the CoC itself might be defined differently from one issuer to another.

STRUCTURE AND DOCUMENTATION—COLLATERAL

As discussed in Chapter 9, collateral is an extremely important consideration when evaluating a credit instrument. Debt can be secured or unsecured—but there are lots of different kinds of security/collateral packages and various priority positions (e.g., first lien versus second lien). To simplify, debt that is secured has specific collateral pledged against it, which means that holders of secured debt are first in line for recovery in a bankruptcy proceeding with respect to that collateral. There is an exception to this—if the lien is junior to another debt instrument (e.g., a second lien), the priority position is behind the more senior (first) lien. If the collateral value is not adequate to repay the secured claim at par, then what remains is called a deficiency claim, which is pari passu with other unsecured debt. As previously explained, pari passu is a Latin term meaning without partiality or at an equal rate or pace, in this context meaning that claims are treated equally. There are exceptions to this; occasionally the documentation specifies that the loan is non-recourse other than to the extent of the value of its collateral. In that case, the loan will not be allowed a deficiency claim.

If a loan is secured by all the company's assets, the secured lenders must receive par for their claims before the company can allocate any value to unsecured creditors in bankruptcy.

While collateral packages vary, a common structure is:

- Asset-based lending facilities/revolvers (ABLs) are generally secured by a first lien on the most liquid assets of the company, i.e., the working capital assets (inventory and receivables). They might also enjoy a second lien on the other assets of the company. ABL revolvers generally have the lowest risk of impairment of any debt instrument given that they are secured by the company's working capital assets (i.e., assets that can be monetized very quickly, easily, and cheaply).

- Term loans are generally secured by a first lien on the non-current assets of the company, such as PP&E, as well as the intellectual property of the company. They might also enjoy a second lien on the working capital assets securing the ABL.
- Bonds are generally unsecured.

STRUCTURE AND DOCUMENTATION—COVENANTS

Covenants are legally binding rules documented in the credit agreement (for loans) or the indenture (for bonds) that the borrower has agreed to follow.

Figure 12.5 shows the most common covenants, which fall into three basic categories: affirmative, negative, and financial.

Type of Covenant	Description	Examples
Affirmative	- Documents what a borrower *must* do - Generally standard/ boilerplate	- Maintaining corporate existence and books and records - Maintaining adequate levels of insurance - Issuing annual and quarterly financial statements on a timely basis - Staying in compliance with applicable laws - Paying all business and employment-related taxes
Negative	- Documents what a borrower *cannot* do - Individually negotiated for each deal/less boilerplate than affirmative covenants	- Limitations on amount of debt/incremental debt issuance - Limitations on shareholder payouts such as dividends (also referred to as a restricted payment covenant) - Limitation on granting of additional liens on assets (also referred to as a negative pledge) - Limitations on asset sales - Limitations on acquisitions - Limitations on transactions with related parties

Financial	- Financial ratios the company must either maintain (maintenance covenants in loans) or meet to take specific actions (incurrence covenants in bonds)
	- Highly negotiated
		- Maximum leverage (Debt / EBITDA)
		- Minimum fixed charge coverage (FCC), variations include:
		  - EBITDA / Interest expense
		  - (EBITDA – Capex) / Interest expense
		  - (EBITDA – Capex – Cash taxes) / (Interest expense + Mandatory debt repayment)

FIGURE 12.5 Most Common Covenants

Explanation of maintenance versus incurrence covenants

- <u>*Maintenance*</u> covenants are tested regularly. For instance, a company might have a maximum leverage covenant tested every quarter. These are typically found in loans. While breach of a maintenance covenant allows the lender to accelerate the maturity (i.e., demand immediate repayment), as discussed below, in practice a waiver is typically negotiated.

- *Incurrence* covenants are only tested if the company wants to take a specific action. For example, the company might have a covenant that is tested only when the company intends to pay a dividend. If the company is not in compliance with this governing covenant, then the only implication is it cannot pay dividends to its shareholders.

Further detail on negative covenants

Many negative covenants are subject to certain exceptions, referred to as baskets or carve-outs. These are some of the most negotiated aspects of new loan and bond issues. While there are too many baskets/carve-outs to outline here, a good rule of thumb is to look for "permitted" exclusions in the definitions. For example, HCA's LBO bonds, which are analyzed in Chapter 13's investment memo, include carve-outs for "permitted investments" and "permitted liens" that take up several pages of the bond indenture.

Further detail on financial covenants

You likely won't have all the numbers required to calculate compliance with financial covenants, but companies sometimes disclose covenant calculations in their financial statements, particularly if they are close to a covenant violation. These ratio calculations are based on the definitions of EBITDA, debt, and fixed charges in the loan agreements and bond indentures.

Analyzing so-called "EBITDA add-backs" permitted by the documentation is critical. These run the gamut from standard (e.g., private equity sponsor management fees, noncash stock compensation paid to employees) to egregious (e.g., borderline fictitious projected cost savings). Often, the EBITDA definition includes more permissive EBITDA add-backs than you might feel is appropriate. For example, a covenant EBITDA definition might allow the company to add back expected synergies related to M&A activity or anticipated future cost savings without limitations, which gives the company flexibility in avoiding a covenant breach. Additionally, the calculation of debt seldom adjusts for off–balance sheet liabilities as we did in step three of the credit analysis process (Chapter 9), making the standard covenant definition of leverage much more permissive in industries such as retail that have substantial off-B/S liabilities.

Although your model and ratio calculations might suggest a covenant violation, the calculation of EBITDA and debt permitted by the covenants might permit the company to avoid a breach. Permissive EBITDA add-backs can be a lifeline for a company experiencing distress, as they show covenant compliance long past the economic reality of a breach. The poster child for this is Realogy, which used very permissive EBITDA add-backs (in particular, for projected cost savings) to skirt bankruptcy and demonstrate covenant compliance despite a massive deterioration in its real estate brokerage business during the housing crisis of 2008.

The takeaways here are:

- For originations/new issues, EBITDA add-backs must be negotiated to prevent the borrower from artificially inflating EBITDA to maintain covenant compliance if possible.
- For secondary trades, the analyst must understand the ways in which the credit agreement or indenture allows the borrower to inflate EBITDA to maintain covenant compliance using permitted add-backs.

Why are covenants important to the lender?

Covenants exist to protect creditors. While you might have read about "cov-lite" issues (deals with no financial covenants) becoming common after the GFC, the reality is that virtually all high yield bonds and loans have some form of covenant protection through nonfinancial affirmative and negative covenants. The strength and reliability of this protection depend primarily upon the prevailing market conditions at the time the issue is underwritten. In bull credit markets, companies can get away with very loose (or porous) covenants that provide little protection from transactions that disadvantage creditors, while in bear credit markets investors can obtain strong protection including tight financial covenants.

Generally, covenants protect creditors in two ways:

(i) Covenants can prevent the company from taking steps that negatively impact its creditworthiness. For instance, a large, debt-financed acquisition generally increases leverage and thus the risk of the issuer. If a negative covenant restricts M&A, the company must go to its lending syndicate for a covenant waiver. The lenders can assess the merits and risks of the proposed transaction and decide whether they want to waive the existing covenant in exchange for an amendment fee and/or better terms to permit the acquisition.

(ii) Financial covenants give lenders "a seat at the table" if there are financial problems. If the company violates a financial covenant, it constitutes a default. Upon a covenant default, lenders have the right to demand immediate repayment of the loan, commonly referred to as calling or accelerating the loan. However, this rarely happens immediately. Instead, once it becomes obvious that the company will breach its covenants, it will attempt to negotiate a waiver with its lenders and, when appropriate, obtain looser/more relaxed covenant levels for a period that allows it to return to financial health. The ability to accelerate repayment of the loan if a covenant is breached allows for renegotiation with more favorable terms for lenders, as well as a waiver fee. For this reason, it is common to refer to a financial covenant as getting the lender "a seat at the table" if the company materially misses projections.

Negotiating loan covenants in a loan deal

In any origination, one of the most critical negotiations involves setting financial covenants. The interests of the borrower and lender are at odds in this negotiation. The borrower wants as few covenants as possible (ideally "cov-lite," meaning no financial covenants) and/or the biggest cushion to the forecast model to create a lot of breathing room between the current financials and a covenant breach, while the lender wants the opposite, to keep a tight rein on the company.

When I teach covenants, I start by asking my students: When negotiating financial covenants, would you base your negotiations on management's forecast case, your base case, or your downside case? Most students say that they would start negotiations by offering a cushion to their base case, since this is their view of the most realistic scenario. But I suggest starting with the management case. Since lenders want covenants to be as restrictive/tight as possible, using the most optimistic case will lead to the most restrictive financial covenants. It also signals how confident management is in its own forecast, based on how much pushback occurs over covenant cushions to projections.

Lenders generally set financial covenants with a 15%–30% cushion to management's EBITDA projections. For instance, if a company has $100 million of debt and management forecasts $25 million of EBITDA, the expected Debt/EBITDA is 4x. At a 15% cushion, the company would have a maximum Debt/EBITDA covenant of 4.7x ($100 million of debt / 85% of the $25 million projected EBITDA).

As discussed above, the structural features of bank debt and bonds differ as summarized in Figure 12.6. Note that there are some exceptions to the rules of thumb below.

Structure	Bank Debt	High Yield Bonds
Seniority/ collateral	– Most senior part of the capital structure – Secured	– Junior to bank debt – Unsecured
Coupon	– Floating rate – Pricing grid common – Lower cost to the borrower	– Typically, fixed rate – Unusual to have pricing grid – Higher cost to the borrower
Tenor	– Shorter – Typically, 3–7 years	– Longer – Typically, 7–10 years

Call Protection	– Low:
	  – Typically, 101 in first year then par (BSL)
	  – Typically, 103/102/101 (private loan)
		– High
		– Non-call for the first half of maturity, then callable at par + 50% of coupon scaling down to par

Covenants	– Maintenance covenants common
	– Typically has financial covenants (some deals are cov-lite with no financial covenants)
	– Common financial covenants are:
	  – Max leverage
	  – Min fixed charge coverage
		– Only incurrence covenants (no maintenance/ financial covenant)

FIGURE 12.6 Comparison of Structural Features of Bank Debt and High Yield Bonds

STRUCTURE AND DOCUMENTATION—AMENDMENTS

Generally, a majority vote (based on par amount rather than number of holders) can amend the credit agreement and bond indentures, except for a small list of "sacred rights." Changes in sacred rights need 100% of lenders (or affected lenders) to agree. Sacred rights typically include:

(a) Maturity date;
(b) Amortization schedule;
(c) Interest rate/coupon;
(d) An increase in the lender's commitment amount;
(e) Release of all or substantially all of the lender's collateral;
(f) Change to the pro rata sharing of payments to lenders (each lender must receive their fair share of every distribution from the borrower); and
(g) Any change that disproportionally and adversely affects some lenders. For instance, 51% of the lenders cannot amend the loan documents to subordinate the other 49% without the adversely affected lenders' consent.

END-OF-CHAPTER STRUCTURE AND DOCUMENTATION ANALYSIS OF JCPENNEY[2]

Figure 12.7 provides an overview of the terms of each of JCP's debt instruments.

	Summary of JCPenney Debt Terms		
	Revolving Credit Facility	7.125% Bonds Due 2023	6.375% Bonds Due 2036
Commitment/ Outstanding	▪ $1,850 million commitment but subject to borrowing base ▪ Nothing drawn, and $281 million LCs ▪ Availability of $1,241 million (as of February 2013)	$255 million	$400 million
Debt Type	Asset-Based Revolving Credit Facility	Unsecured Bonds	Unsecured Bonds
Borrowing Base	▪ 85% of accounts eligible receivables, plus ▪ 90% of accounts credit card receivables, plus ▪ 85% of liquidation value of inventory.	N/A	N/A
Maturity Date	4/29/2016	11/15/23	10/15/36

[2]Download JCPenney's 2012 10-K (fiscal year ended February 2, 2013) at the SEC Edgar website for public company filings, https://www.sec.gov/edgar/searchedgar/companysearch, using the search term "Old Copper Company." The company's search term on Edgar is Old Copper Company, Inc., not JCPenney.

	Summary of JCPenney Debt Terms		
	Revolving Credit Facility	7.125% Bonds Due 2023	6.375% Bonds Due 2036
Required Amortization	None	None	None
Collateral	Receivables and Inventory	Unsecured	Unsecured
Coupon	*Pricing Grid based on Moody's and S&P ratings:* ■ L+1.50% if rated Baa2/BBB or better ■ L+1.75% if rated Baa3/BBB- ■ L+2.00% if rated Ba1/BB- ■ L+2.50% if rated Ba2/BB ■ L+3.00% if rated Ba3/BB- or worse	7.125% fixed rate	6.375% fixed rate
Call Protection	None	Non-call life[a]	Non-call life[a]
Financial Maintenance Covenants	If RC availability is less than the greater of (i) $125 million or (ii) 10% of the borrowing base, the company will be subject to a minimum fixed charge coverage of 1:1	None	None
Financial Incurrence Covenants—Ability to Issue New Debt	No limits except as related to the Borrowing Base collateral	Limitation on incremental debt issuance (200% net tangible assets/ debt test)	None
Change of Control	100% change of control provision	None	101% change of control provision

[a]The bonds were issued when JCP was investment grade; therefore, the bonds were non-callable, like most investment grade issues.

FIGURE 12.7 Summary of Key Terms of JCP Debt

The above table only summarizes two of the eleven JCP bonds outstanding in 2012. The remaining nine bonds were issued under the same indenture as the 6.375% 2036 maturity bond and are thus identical except for the coupon and maturity date. However, the 7.125% 2023 maturity bond was issued under a separate indenture, and this bond alone has one additional term that restricts the company from issuing incremental non-ABL debt if net tangible assets to senior funded indebtedness exceeds 200%. We will delve into the importance of this difference and discuss a related trading strategy in Chapter 19.

CHAPTER CONCLUSION

Analysis of the structural features of the loan or bond you are evaluating is the final step in your credit work. In certain circumstances, covenants and/or structural features can be the difference between a good and bad investment. Creditors rely on structure and covenants to protect them from a range of issuer behaviors, from adding debt to an overleveraged balance sheet to paying out massive dividends to shareholders. In turn, issuers push for the most flexible terms to preserve optionality that does not always work in creditors' favor.

Even a bond or loan with weak covenants and/or structure can be an interesting investment opportunity—if there is adequate compensation for the risk. Your job as an analyst is to understand the unique features of each issue and to be comfortable that you are getting paid for the actions permitted and prohibited by the indenture or credit agreement.

THE SEVEN-STEP PROCESS: SUMMARY OF STEPS TWO THROUGH SIX

We have now completed a full credit analysis of JCP.

- In Chapter 6, we performed a qualitative analysis (step two).
- In Chapter 7, we performed profitability analysis (step three-a).
- In Chapter 8, we performed cash flow and liquidity analysis (step three-b).
- In Chapter 9, we performed capital structure analysis (step three-c).
- In Chapter 10, we forecasted future performance (step four).
- In Chapter 11, we did valuation work (step five).
- And finally, in this chapter, we analyzed the terms and structure of JCP's debt (step six).

For step seven, Preparing an Investment Recommendation and Credit Committee Memo, we will leave JCP behind to evaluate two new issues: VCC (a private loan origination) and HCA (a public bond issue). We will return to JCP in Chapter 19, with secondary trade recommendations based on our analysis and provide a post-mortem for the success of each trade idea.

CHAPTER 13

Step 7 of the Credit Analysis Process: Preparing an Investment Recommendation and Credit Committee Memo

As shown in Figure 13.1, the final step in the seven-step process is to bring all of your work together in a concise memo that includes your investment recommendation.

Step 1	Sources and Uses (only applicable to originations) (a) Why is the company seeking financing? (b) What are the proposed sources of capital to fund the financing need?
Step 2	Qualitative Analysis (a) Industry analysis (b) Business strategy (c) Management assessment (d) ESG concerns
Step 3	Financial Statement Analysis (a) Profitability (b) Cash flow and liquidity (c) Capital structure
Step 4	Forecasting (a) Identification of key business drivers and assumptions (b) Development of base, upside, and downside cases
Step 5	Corporate Valuation (a) Comparable company analysis (b) Precedent transactions (M&A comps) (c) Discounted cash flow analysis (d) Liquidation analysis
Step 6	Structuring and Documentation (a) Economic points (b) Structure and collateral (c) Covenants
Step 7	**Preparing an Investment Recommendation and Credit Committee Memo** **(a) Investment thesis and recommendation** **(b) Risks and mitigants** **(c) Relative value analysis**

FIGURE 13.1 The Seven-Step Process of Evaluating a Debt Instrument

Most firms have an investment committee that approves new investment ideas or a meeting in which portfolio managers (PMs) review and debate the analysts' recommendations. Before meeting to discuss the merits of an idea, the investment committee members or PMs typically receive a memo that incorporates an in-depth description of the company, the risks involved in the potential investment, the analyst's investment thesis, and all supporting **relevant** analyses outlined in steps one through six. I bolded and underlined "relevant" because it can be tempting to show all of your work. However, the time of the committee members and PMs is precious. Further, distilling the analyses and due diligence into the most critical points can refine and enhance your reasoning.

You might think that this final step is a formality after all the analyses up to this point. Based on your work, shouldn't it be obvious whether the bond or loan is a good investment opportunity? An effective investment recommendation incorporates one final component: ***relative risk-adjusted return***. The investment committee members/PMs want the analyst to help them answer the question: "Is this a good investment relative to everything else our firm can invest in?" The response must consider both the expected return and the potential for loss. I always ask analysts to rank their investment ideas versus every other portfolio position and every deal in our pipeline. At times the question takes the form of: "What investment would you sell to make room for this one?" In addition, in the groups I run for Silver Point, at least quarterly we force-rank every investment in our portfolio with all the analysts in the room. While credit analysts are generally industry/sector-focused, I believe in training them early to think about relative value outside their industry coverage—in other words, getting them to think like investors by listening to different perspectives and critically reviewing each other's recommendations.

Most firms have their own credit memo templates. Some want detailed financial analysis, others a brief summary. While the seven steps of credit analysis reviewed in this book are required for an effective investment recommendation, not all the steps necessarily need to be included in the memo. The analyst's job is to determine the most pertinent analyses and information to share.

A good memo includes:

1. A clear, concise, up-front recommendation that incorporates relative value versus other investment opportunities;
2. A clearly articulated investment thesis;
3. The significant risks to the investment with potential mitigants; and
4. Enough qualitative and quantitative analyses to support the investment thesis and allow for a meaningful debate of the merits and risks of the investment opportunity.

The best way to learn how to incorporate your work into an investment committee memo is to read original deal write-ups for investments that made it into the portfolio. In that vein, I have included four sample memos based on two actual transactions. Each transaction includes two write-ups.

- The first is what we call a teaser or screening memo. This is a quick summary of the deal with enough information to decide whether we should devote resources to complete due diligence.

- The second is a credit committee memo, which is a comprehensive analysis of the investment opportunity.

The first transaction is the VCC refinancing discussed in Chapter 11, "Step 5 of the Credit Analysis Process: Corporate Valuation." Since VCC was a private loan origination, the analyst enjoyed substantial access to management and information and negotiated all terms directly with the borrower.

The second transaction is a public bond deal that was part of the financing for HCA's 2006 LBO, an iconic deal that was the largest LBO in history at the time it was done. HCA is an excellent case study for several reasons. First, it opened the floodgates for the "mega-LBOs" that occurred in the run-up to the Global Financial Crisis of 2008; as such, it provides a good example of the many LBO-related new issue opportunities in the high yield bond market. Its capital structure includes several investment opportunities (term loan A and B, second lien PIK and non-PIK bonds, and legacy unsecured bonds that "traveled" with the LBO financing), necessitating relative value analysis across the capital structure. This memo was written from the perspective of a high yield bond analyst limited to investing in the bonds. However, it's still important to evaluate pricing for all components of the capital structure, even if you are limited to investing in one particular portion (e.g., bank debt vs. bonds). Finally, HCA operates in an industry with a long history in the high yield market—and while the defensive nature of hospitals, and their attractiveness to high yield investors, seem obvious in retrospect, at the time of the deal some industry-specific challenges made the LBO more challenging than you might imagine.

You will notice that the format, content, and level of detail differ for the VCC and HCA memos. As explained above, each investment firm has its own template and expectations. Further, analyzing and investing in a public bond deal differs from originating a private loan in several ways:

- *The level of detail about the company:* In a new origination where your firm acts as the lead investor, you will have much greater access to management and, as a result, more information than would be the case for a public company.
- *The forecast:* The loan origination has management projections to accompany the analyst's base and downside case forecasts; the forecast for the new bond issue is typically based mainly on the analyst's estimates, although as you will see in the HCA memo, management had released forecasts as part of the shareholder vote process.
- *Structure:* In a private loan deal, you negotiate all aspects of the loan directly with the borrower. In a public bond deal, you analyze the terms of the issue, but you don't negotiate directly with the borrower. If you work for a large high yield fund, the company's investment banker might ask you for feedback on the terms before going to market.
- *Type of terms/covenants:* As discussed in Chapter 12, loans have maintenance covenants while bonds have incurrence covenants. Other terms will differ, such as amortization (which bonds do not have) and call protection (more significant in bonds than loans).

As you read the following investment memos and review the accompanying models, in addition to observing the choices made by each analyst, pay particular attention to what they included, what they left out, and the primary drivers of the recommendation. I would also suggest you put yourself in the shoes of a PM. What questions didn't get answered? What do you agree and disagree with in the analyses and forecasting? To write an excellent investment memo, you must think like a PM and anticipate the committee's questions and concerns.

Sample Teaser/Screening Memo #1
Private Loan Origination
Valves Controls Company, LLC

Teaser/Screening Memo: Private Loan Origination

Valves Controls Company, LLC ("VCC" or the "Company")[1]

DEAL SUMMARY

VCC is seeking a five-year, $220MM credit facility consisting of a $200MM senior secured term loan and a $20MM unfunded priority revolver to refinance the existing senior secured debt previously issued to finance the 2013 LBO. The company also has an existing tranche of mezzanine debt, which will not be refinanced, but the proposed facility will have a springing maturity six months inside of this loan. Proforma net leverage through the term loan and mezzanine debt is approximately 5.0x and 7.3x base case 2019 projected EBITDA, respectively.

DEAL TERMS

Proposed terms on the new credit facility include a LIBOR[2]+700 coupon (1.5% LIBOR floor), 2.25% OID, five-year maturity (with springer to mezzanine), 2.5% amortization/year, 50% ECF sweep, NC1/102/101 call protection and financial covenants (max capex, max leverage, and min fixed charge coverage).

COMPANY SUMMARY

VCC is a market-leading provider of flow control products used in the transportation, delivery, and storage of propane, industrial gases ("IG"), and liquefied natural gas ("LNG"). The company derives 71% of its revenue from the sale of valves and regulators used in propane tanks, while 29% is tied to IG/LNG end markets. Eighty percent of the company's revenue is based on the replacement cycle of tanks, providing a source of recurring demand for its products. VCC operates in an effective oligopoly, with three major players dominating an addressable market of ~$130MM. VCC is the industry leader based on superior quality, a strong safety track record, and reliability.

---

[1] VCC is based on a 2019 transaction. The name of the company and certain financial information have been altered.

[2] Since this transaction, loans have transitioned from using LIBOR to SOFR as the base rate.

INVESTMENT HIGHLIGHTS

- Market leader with 55% share, 2x+ greater than the closest competitor;
- Strong safety track record, small market size, and oligopolistic competitive landscape create substantial barriers to entry;
- Recurring business model driven by replacement of flow control products (~10–13-year replacement cycle);
- Limited cyclicality, as revenue declined only 4.6% during the GFC;
- Reasonable leverage profile based on LTV (through our secured facility) of 56%–71% (using an estimated valuation range of 7.5–9.5x EBITDA);
- Strong FCF generation given low capex / cash tax requirements;
- Low severity of loss given strategic buyer interest, supportive financial sponsor ($226MM of capital invested), FCF/amortization-based deleveraging, and asset coverage from the propane segment alone;
- Strong management team;
- Relatively tight contemplated financial covenants/documentation.

INVESTMENT RISKS

- High fixed cost business;
- Input costs exposed to commodity pricing (brass, copper, zinc);
- Maturity of mezz debt inside of contemplated credit facility;
- Modest decline in propane's share of the US heating market;
- Historical volatility in IG/LNG segments.

DEAL TEAM RECOMMENDATION

The deal team recommends proceeding with the investment on the terms outlined above. VCC benefits from a favorable industry backdrop, resilient demand, strong free cash flow conversion, and attractive enterprise value coverage. At the contemplated pricing, we estimate an IRR/MOIC of 10.2%/1.3x assuming a three-year takeout and 9.5%/1.4x assuming held to maturity. Not only is this return profile compelling on an absolute basis given the attractive credit characteristics, we are also earning a 50–100 bps yield premium to similarly rated credits.

Pro Forma Capital Structure

				Leverage		Loan-to-Value[a]		
	Amt Out	Coupon	Maturity	2018	2019 proj	7.5x	8.5x	9.5x
$20MM First Out Revolver	--	L + 450	Oct-24					
Secured Term Loan	200.0	L + 700	Oct-24					
Total Secured Debt	$200.0			6.6x	5.3x	71.1%	62.7%	56.1%
(–) Estimated Cash at Close	(12.1)							
Net Secured Debt	$187.9			6.2x	5.0x	66.8%	59.0%	52.7%
Existing Mezz Debt	85.7	14% PIK	Dec-22					
Total Debt	$273.6			9.0x	7.3x	97.3%	85.8%	76.8%
Sponsor's Equity[b]	226.4							
Total Capitalization	$500.0			16.5x	13.3x	177.8%	156.9%	140.4%

[a] LTV was calculated using a multiple of 2019 projected EBITDA. The Financial Statement Analysis section of the full memo explains why 2018 is not a good representation of the company's earnings power. See Appendix #3 of the full memo for valuation analysis.

[b] Sponsor's equity is the amount the PE fund has invested into VCC. Based on the analyst's valuation, the sponsor's equity is out-of-the-money, resulting in a "Total Capitalization LTV" above 100%.

Lender Base Case: Revenue and EBITDA Projections

	Historical			Lender Base Case Projections				
	2016	2017	2018	2019	2020	2021	2022	2023
Total Revenue	$154.7	$163.7	$162.2	$170.3	$173.7	$177.2	$180.7	$184.3
% YoY	*(12.6%)*	*5.8%*	*(0.9%)*	*5.0%*	*2.0%*	*2.0%*	*2.0%*	*2.0%*
Adjusted EBITDA	$30.6	$40.9	$30.3	$37.5	$38.2	$39.0	$39.8	$40.5
Adj EBITDA Margin	*19.8%*	*25.0%*	*18.7%*	*22.0%*	*22.0%*	*22.0%*	*22.0%*	*22.0%*

Lender Base Case: Cash Flow Projections

	Historical			Lender Base Case Projections				
	2016	2017	2018	2019	2020	2021	2022	2023
Adjusted EBITDA	$30.6	$40.9	$30.3	$37.5	$38.2	$39.0	$39.8	$40.5
(–) Capex	(2.0)	(2.8)	(3.1)	(4.2)	(5.8)	(5.8)	(4.3)	(4.5)
Adj. EBITDAX	**$28.6**	**$38.1**	**$27.2**	**$33.3**	**$32.4**	**$33.2**	**$35.5**	**$36.0**
(–) Cash interest				(17.0)	(16.2)	(15.7)	(15.3)	(14.9)
(–) Cash taxes				(2.3)	(2.3)	(2.3)	(2.4)	(2.4)
(–/+) Cash impact chg WC and other				(1.5)	(3.1)	(3.2)	(3.2)	(3.2)
Free cash available to pay down debt				$12.5	$10.8	$12.0	$14.6	$15.5
(–) Required amortization of secured term loan				(5.0)	(5.0)	(5.0)	(5.0)	(5.0)
Free Cash Flow				$7.5	$5.8	$7.0	$9.6	$10.5
Senior secured term loan, beginning				$200.0	$195.0	$190.0	$185.0	$180.0
Less required amortization				(5.0)	(5.0)	(5.0)	(5.0)	(5.0)
Senior secured term loan, ending			$200.0	$195.0	$190.0	$185.0	$180.0	$175.0
Cash on balance sheet			(12.1)	(19.6)	(25.4)	(32.4)	(42.0)	(52.5)
Senior secured term loan net of cash, ending			187.9	$175.4	$164.6	$152.6	$138.0	$122.5
Senior Secured Debt / EBITDA			6.6x	5.2x	5.0x	4.7x	4.5x	4.3x
Net Senior Secured Debt / EBITDA			6.2x	4.7x	4.3x	3.9x	3.5x	3.0x

Sample Full Credit Memo #1
Private Loan Origination
Valves Controls Company, LLC

Credit Committee Memo: Private Debt Deal

Valves Controls Company, LLC ("VCC" or the "Company")[1]

EXECUTIVE SUMMARY

VCC is a leading global provider of flow control products (e.g., regulators, valves) used in the transportation, delivery, and storage of:

1. Liquefied petroleum gas ("LPG" or "propane"): 71% of the company's revenues,
2. Industrial Gases ("IG"): 20% of the company's revenues, and
3. Liquefied natural gas ("LNG"): 9% of revenues.

The business is most heavily weighted to valves and regulators used in propane tanks (71% of sales). VCC commands ~55% share in this market and is the industry leader due to the superior quality and reliability of its products. We believe our loan is covered by the value of the LPG/propane business alone, which is the focus of our due diligence and recommendation.

VCC was LBO'd for $470MM (10x EBITDA) in 2013, followed by a subsequent $37MM add-on acquisition bringing the combined purchase price to over $500MM. Since the LBO, the company's core LPG business has been stable other than specific idiosyncratic issues discussed further in this memo. However, there has been more volatility in the non-core IG and LNG businesses, discussed in the Financial Statement Analysis section.

DIRECT PRIVATE LOAN ORIGINATION OPPORTUNITY

The company seeks to refinance the credit facility established at the time of the 2013 LBO with a new $200MM term loan (plus a $20MM unfunded priority revolver). Closing net leverage through the term loan and the mezzanine debt ("mezz") is approximately 5.0x and 7.3x our 2019 projected EBITDA, respectively.

[1]VCC is based on a 2019 transaction. The name of the company and certain financial information have been altered.

Key Terms and Structure of Proposed Financing: (see Appendix #1 for a detailed term sheet)	
Amount	$200MM
Facility Type	Secured Term Loan (secured by all assets and junior only to a $20MM undrawn revolving credit facility)
Maturity	5 years with a springing maturity to 6 months prior to mezz debt if the mezz debt is not refinanced by that time
Interest rate	LIBOR[a] + 700 (with a 1.5% LIBOR floor)
OID	2.25%
Amortization	2.5% per year
ECF sweep	50% of excess cash flow, with step-downs to be negotiated
Call protection	NC1 / 102 / 101
Financial Covenants	Max net total leverage, max net senior leverage, min fixed charge coverage (FCC), and max capex (levels to be negotiated)

Summary of Sources and Uses

Sources		Uses	
$20MM First Out Revolver	—	Refi Existing Secured Debt	$188.7
New First Lien Term Loan	200.0	Est. Lender Fees	5.0
		Transaction Fees & Expenses	4.5
		Cash to Balance Sheet	1.8
Total	**$200.0**	**Total**	**$200.0**

[a]While this loan was indexed to LIBOR, as discussed in Chapter 3, loans have transitioned to SOFR as the base rate.

Pro Forma Capital Structure

				Leverage		Loan-to-Value[c]		
	Amt Out	Coupon	Maturity	2018	2019 proj	7.5x	8.5x	9.5x
$20MM First Out Revolver	—	L + 450	Oct-24					
Secured Term Loan	200.0	L + 700	Oct-24					
Total Secured Debt[a]	**$200.0**			**6.6x**	**5.3x**	**71.1%**	**62.7%**	**56.1%**
(–) Estimated Cash at Close	(12.1)							
Net Secured Debt	**$187.9**			**6.2x**	**5.0x**	**66.8%**	**59.0%**	**52.7%**
Existing Mezz Debt[b]	85.7	14% PIK	Dec-22					
Total Debt	**$273.6**			**9.0x**	**7.3x**	**97.3%**	**85.8%**	**76.8%**
Sponsor's Equity[d]	226.4							
Total Capitalization	**$500.0**			**16.5x**	**13.3x**	**177.8%**	**156.9%**	**140.4%**

[a] New revolver and first lien term loan will be structured with a springing maturity inside mezz debt. Both facilities have a 1.5% LIBOR floor.
[b] 14% PIK in FY19 with annual 50bp step-ups thereafter.
[c] LTV was calculated using a multiple of 2019 projected EBITDA. The Financial Statement Analysis section explains why 2018 is not a good representation of the company's earnings power. See Appendix #3 for valuation analysis.
[d] Sponsor's equity is the amount the PE fund has invested into VCC. Based on the analyst's valuation, the sponsor's equity is out-of-the-money, resulting in a "Total Capitalization LTV" above 100%.

CREDIT INVESTMENT THESIS AND RECOMMENDATION

We recommend proceeding with the proposed transaction based on the following:

1. VCC is the dominant market leader with a highly defensible position:
   - 55% market share.
   - More than double the size of the next largest player.
   - Substantial barrier to entry created by customer demand for a proven safety track record.
2. VCC's core LPG business is a stable, recession-resistant business.
   - 80% of its revenue is recurring based on the limited useful life of propane tanks.
   - In the last recession, LPG revenue only declined ~4.6% from 2007 to 2009 and rebounded strongly in 2010.
   - Analyzing the full cycle from 2006 to 2010, LPG's compounded average growth rate (CAGR) was +3.7%.

	Pre-Financial Crisis		Financial Crisis		Post	CAGR
	2006	2007	2008	2009	2010	2006–2010
LPG sales	$84.6	$89.3	$88.2	$85.2	$97.7	NM
% change	11.0%	5.6%	(1.2%)	(3.4%)	14.7%	3.7%

3. Attractive free cash flow profile.
   - The business has high free cash flow conversion given that it is capex light and has a favorable cash tax profile (see Cash Flow and Liquidity Analysis section).
4. Reasonable leverage through the term loan.
   - Through the $200 million term loan, leverage is 5.3x adjusted 2019 projected EBITDA. We believe this business would trade conservatively at 7.5x to 9.5x EBITDA (see Valuation section). At these multiples, the loan-to-value of our debt is 56%–71%.
   - Furthermore, we believe several strategic buyers would be interested in the business. These strategics would likely pay above the high end of this range due to synergies and willingness to pay a premium for dominant market share.
5. Two layers of capital below the $200 million term loan ($85 million of mezz debt and over $200 million of equity invested by the sponsor) provide substantial cushion for the loan, and the private equity sponsor could potentially support the company if it has liquidity issues.
   - The sponsor has supported the business twice through new equity injections (aggregate of $28.5MM) since the close of the initial transaction.
   - The fund that made this investment has significant remaining capital and a follow-on investment period through March 2021.
6. Extremely low severity of loss even if the company needs to restructure.
   - In a sale scenario, there would likely be strategic buyers interested in the business given the leading market position of the brand and PE sponsors who would look at this through the same lens as the current sponsor did in 2013 (i.e., as a stable business with equity upside in LNG/IG segments).

- Even in a restructuring scenario, the debt should be worth par (see Valuation and Downside Forecast sections).
- Furthermore, our exposure decreases over the life of the loan by the amortization and ECF sweep (combined approximately 5% per year).

7. This deal's return profile and structure are good relative value compared to other debt investments with similar risk profiles.
   - At the contemplated pricing, we estimate an IRR/MOIC of 10.2%/1.3x assuming a 3-year takeout and 9.5%/1.4x assuming it is held to maturity.
   - The loan generates 50–100 bps excess return relative to the risk (see Relative Value Analysis section).
   - The debt will have a tight structure significantly better than most comps. We are still finalizing the docs, but expect tight financial covenants, which could bring us back to the table to improve pricing if the business underperforms.

INDUSTRY OVERVIEW

LPG market The design and manufacturing market for valves and regulators used in propane tanks is dominated by three players comprising approximately 90% of industry revenue. Propane is used for heating and powering certain appliances. Residential and commercial propane users are serviced by a base of propane marketers who lease equipment (including tanks), refuel tanks, and perform required maintenance.

	% of market
VCC	55%
Competitor #1	20%
Competitor #2	15%
Others	10%
Total	100%

The demand for valves and regulators for propane tanks has three primary drivers:

(i) The replacement cycle of existing tanks
- This is the most dependable and predictable source of demand.
- Approximately 7.5% to 10% of existing tanks need to be replaced annually, resulting in a built-in source of demand for new valves and regulators.

(ii) The impact of propane users switching providers (churn)
- When a company or an individual switches propane suppliers, the new supplier installs a new tank, creating demand for the valves and regulators.

(iii) Housing starts (albeit to a lesser extent)

IG market The IG market is relatively stable and is largely correlated with industrial production. IGs consist of a large number of gases such as oxygen and hydrogen. IGs are commonly used in manufacturing and have a wide range of applications from medical gas to chemical processes in paper industries.

LNG market While demand for valves and regulators used in the LPG and IG markets has been stable, the LNG market has been less consistent due to its dependence on China's volatile LNG trucking market, which is tied to oil and diesel prices. The Profitability section discusses the dynamics of this market and its impact on VCC's profitability. Since this segment comprises less than 10% of the company's revenue, it is not core to our investment thesis. LNG is natural gas that has been cooled to a liquid state and is primarily used for heating and generating electricity.

COMPANY OVERVIEW

VCC designs and manufactures a comprehensive range of flow control equipment used in the transportation, delivery, and storage of liquefied petroleum gas ("LPG"), liquefied natural gas ("LNG"), and industrial gases ("IG"). VCC's valves and regulators are mission-critical parts of a delivery system and manage the movement of gases and liquids under a wide variety of temperatures and pressure extremes. The company is primarily focused on the LPG market (~70% of sales), while IG (~20%) and LNG (~10%) account for smaller amounts of revenue. Below we lay out the revenues by product category for 2018, including regional breakdowns.

	LPG	%	IG	%	LNG	%	Total	%
North America	102.1	88.4%	26.8	82.5%	5.0	35.2%	133.9	82.6%
Europe	11.3	9.8%	2.0	6.2%	1.1	7.7%	14.4	8.9%
Asia Pacific	2.1	1.8%	3.7	11.4%	8.1	57.0%	13.9	8.6%
Total	**115.5**	**100.0%**	**32.5**	**100.0%**	**14.2**	**100.0%**	**162.2**	**100.0%**
% of Total	*71.2%*		*20.2%*		*8.7%*		*100.0%*	

LPG/propane valve and regulator business (71% of revenue) VCC is the LPG market leader. It has an estimated 55% share across the US addressable market. Our industry consultant framed out an addressable market in the US for VCC's core LPG products of approximately $185MM as of 2015, which makes this an unlikely market for non-propane players to enter other than through an acquisition. Furthermore, it would be challenging for a new entrant to break into the market given the need for deep industry relationships and a safety track record.

VCC's core LPG business is stable and recession-resistant, primarily driven by the existing US installed base of propane heating (~5.8MM homes). Revenue comes from a combination of replacement products in existing propane-heated homes based on the tanks' replacement cycle (10–13 years) and propane supplier churn, which typically replace the valves and regulators (and, in some cases, the tanks) when customers change providers. In the last recession, the LPG business only declined ~4.6% from 2007 to 2009 and rebounded strongly in 2010.

We estimate ~$70MM of recurring US LPG revenue based on VCC's installed base and the replacement cycle.

Non-propane business (29% of revenue) The IG and LNG segments have potential tailwinds including:

- A growing relationship with the largest original equipment manufacturer ("OEM") in the industry.
- Potential growth in the European LNG truck OEM market, where the company was an early entrant, and which appears to have good tailwinds.

However, these products have more risk and cyclicality and are less critical to our credit thesis, although they help with fixed cost absorption. We believe that our loan is fully covered by the value of the propane business alone.

Top LPG customers Below are the top customers for the LPG business, which are distributors and OEMs. The company has 20+ year relationships with each of its top 10 customers, which contributed ~57% of total LPG sales in 2018. VCC has exclusive agreements with its distributors that prevent them from selling competitors' products.

		2016		2017		2018	
Customer	**Type**	**$**	**%**	**$**	**%**	**$**	**%**
Customer 1[a]	Distributor	$14.2	*12.4%*	$16.1	*14.0%*	$13.7	*11.9%*
Customer 2	OEM	6.3	*5.5%*	5.8	*5.0%*	7.7	*6.7%*
Customer 3	Distributor	6.1	*5.3%*	6.8	*5.9%*	7.6	*6.6%*
Customer 4	OEM	5.2	*4.5%*	6.1	*5.3%*	7.0	*6.1%*
Customer 5	OEM	6.2	*5.4%*	6.5	*5.6%*	6.8	*5.9%*
Customer 6	Distributor	5.2	*4.5%*	5.1	*4.4%*	5.7	*4.9%*
Customer 7	Distributor	4.6	*4.0%*	4.9	*4.2%*	4.7	*4.1%*
Customer 8	Distributor	4.6	*4.0%*	3.2	*2.8%*	4.5	*3.9%*
Customer 9	Distributor	4.1	*3.6%*	3.4	*2.9%*	4.0	*3.5%*
Customer 10	OEM	2.9	*2.5%*	3.3	*2.9%*	3.6	*3.1%*
Total Top 10		$59.4	*51.8%*	$61.2	*53.1%*	$65.3	*56.5%*
Other		55.3	*48.2%*	54.1	*46.9%*	50.2	*43.5%*
Total		$114.7	*100.0%*	$115.3	*100.0%*	$115.5	*100.0%*

[a]The dip in sales to customer #1 in 2018 resulted from over-ordering by Customer #1 in past years, which was followed by a down year as the customer worked through excess inventory. We believe sales to that customer have normalized.

MANAGEMENT

The sponsor has revamped VCC's management team, adding a new CEO, COO, and CFO in 2017. Additionally, the sponsor's operating partner spends around a third of his time on VCC. The CEO was previously the CEO of a public company with a strong track record. As part of our diligence, we were able to have discussions with several senior executives who worked with the CEO and the COO at previous jobs, and their feedback was positive.

FINANCIAL STATEMENT ANALYSIS

1) Revenue and Profitability

	2014	2015	2016	2017	2018
LPG/Propane	$110.2	$130.4	$114.7	$115.3	$115.5
IG	36.3	33.2	29.3	30.8	32.5
LNG	28.9	13.4	10.7	17.6	14.2
Total Revenue	$175.4	$177.0	$154.7	$163.7	$162.2
LPG Growth	-0.8%	18.3%	-12.0%	0.5%	0.2%
IG Growth	-7.0%	-8.5%	-11.7%	5.1%	5.5%
LNG Growth	-19.4%	-53.6%	-20.1%	64.5%	-19.3%
Total Revenue Growth	-5.7%	0.9%	-12.6%	5.8%	-0.9%
Adjusted EBITDA	$41.2	$39.0	$30.6	$40.9	$30.3
Adjusted EBITDA Margins	23.5%	22.0%	19.8%	25.0%	18.7%

LPG Revenue

- The LPG business has been characterized by stable growth. Over the last 15 years, it had an average growth rate of 3.0%, with only three down years.
- During the GFC, sales decreased by 4.6%, but quickly rebounded.
- LPG segment sales spiked to $130MM in 2015 as VCC took advantage of production issues at a competitor. The following year (2016), there was a decrease in sales as that one-time order rolled off.

IG Revenue

- The decline in IG from 2014 to 2016 was driven mainly by the loss of one large customer, which was known at the time of the acquisition. Excluding this, sales grew by an average of 4.1% during those years.

LNG Revenue

- LNG revenue grew strongly leading up to the acquisition, but the segment experienced a pullback in demand and has since stabilized at a lower revenue level.
- Revenue is tied to the China LNG trucking market which is volatile because demand for LNG trucks is dependent on oil and diesel prices. When those decline, the value proposition for LNG-powered vehicles becomes less compelling.
- We ascribe no value to this business; any value is upside.

EBITDA margin

- The company's EBITDA margin averaged 21.9% from 2014 to 2018, with a peak in 2017 at 25%, followed by a trough of 18.7% in the following year.

- The 2017 peak margin was the result of ramping up production levels to improve fixed cost absorption. This resulted in gross margin improvement. However, the company was not able to sell through the excess inventory produced, which resulted in lower production the following year and a corresponding decrease in gross margin.
- In addition to the impact of this decreased production, the 2018 margin decline resulted from a higher mix of products sold to primary OEMs, which have a lower margin than inventory sold to distributors.

Profitability versus peer group

We cannot compare VCC to the two other players in this niche market because one is part of a large public company without segment breakouts and the other is a private company. However, we have identified three companies that, while not direct competitors, manufacture and supply flow control products for other verticals.

1. ***Flowserve:*** One of the world's largest manufacturers of flow control products (~$3.8bn sales) with a portfolio of more than 50 brands.
2. ***Watts Water:*** Residential and commercial flow control products for plumbing and HVAC applications.
3. ***CIRCOR Intl:*** Manufacturer of specialized flow and motion control products.

	Operating Metrics			
Company	**Sales**	**Sales Growth**	**EBITDA**	**EBITDA Margin**
VCC	162	-0.9%	30	18.7%
FLS	3,836	4.8%	372	9.7%
WTS	1,565	7.4%	240	15.4%
CIR	1,013	NM	127	12.5%
Median	1,565	NM	240	12.5%
Mean	2,138	6.1%	246	12.5%

Despite being significantly smaller than the other three companies, VCC has considerably higher margins, resulting from its less competitive market and its brand value. This supports our view that strategic buyer interest in a downside scenario would more than cover our loan (see Valuation section). Furthermore, as discussed above, VCC's 2018 EBITDA margin of 18.7% is understated. Using the more normalized 2017/2018 average margin of 22% makes VCC look even better than the peer group.

II) Cash Flow and Liquidity

The company is in danger of a liquidity crisis if it is not successful in refinancing or extending the maturity of its $85MM mezz debt by June 2022 (six months before its maturity).

Away from this mezz maturity, the company's liquidity is strong:

- The company will have day-one liquidity of $27MM ($7MM excess cash[2] and nothing drawn on its $20MM revolver). Even in our downside case, the company's revolver remains undrawn. (see Appendix #3, Forecasts).
- The business is capex-light and has a favorable cash tax profile, resulting in high cash flow conversion. In our base case, the company generates $40MM of cumulative free cash flow after cash interest payments and required amortization. Even in our downside case, the company produces $16MM of FCF. (see Appendix #3, Forecasts).
- VCC has a long cash cycle driven by holding five to seven months of inventory. The company believes it still has excess inventory related to 2017 overproduction and expects a cash working capital benefit in 2019 of $5MM–10MM, of which $5MM is included in managements' forecast model. The company has approximately 40-day payable terms, just ~$10MM of payables. Therefore, there is only very modest reliance on trade support.

	2016	2017	2018
Inventory Days	150	200	170
+ Receivables Days	80	78	79
Time to convert inventory to cash	230	278	249
– Payable Days	(37)	(35)	(36)
Cash Cycle	193	243	213

iii) Capital Structure Analysis

- See page 2 of this memo for the pro forma capital structure table.
- The company will be highly leveraged at 7.3x through the mezz debt. However, through our proposed term loan, net secured leverage is more reasonable at 5.0x.
- There is no leakage to the mezz as its interest is PIK until senior secured leverage is below 3.5x (see Appendix #1 for full term sheet).
- The company has no material off-balance sheet liabilities except contingent warranty liabilities (see Risks and Mitigants below).

KEY RISKS AND MITIGANTS

1. *Potential need for a balance sheet restructuring:* The company is highly leveraged through the mezz debt at 7.3x. Furthermore, if the company does not refinance the mezz six months before its maturity date of December 2022, our loan comes due, which could be the catalyst for a bankruptcy filing.
   - *Mitigant:* We believe the mezz would be the fulcrum security in the event of a restructuring. In a forced sale of the business, our term loan should be worth par. Even in our downside case, at the lowest EBITDA level, net secured leverage is only 5.8x through our loan, and quickly declines below 5.0x thereafter. Our analysis values the business at 7.5x–9.5x. In addition, given VCC's

[2] VCC's minimum cash to run its business is $5 million. To calculate its liquidity, we only included cash in excess of $5 million.

dominant market share and potential synergies, a strategic buyer might be willing to pay 10x+ to own the company.

2. *Fixed Cost Absorption:* The company's profitability depends on maintaining volumes, given its substantial fixed cost base. The 2017/2018 experience illustrates the impact of changing production levels on margins, when the company built/drew down inventories, respectively, resulting in material margin swings. The IG and LNG businesses are exposed to cyclical end markets and likely would decline in a recession, which could impair profitability.
   - *Mitigant:* The LPG business, which accounts for ~70% of total sales, is much more stable (~5% peak to trough decline 2007–2009).
3. *Raw Material Prices:* The company is susceptible to swings in raw material prices (brass, copper, zinc) and other input costs. Increases in raw material prices could impact profitability if they cannot be passed through to end customers.
   - *Mitigant:* Historically, the company has included surcharges to pass through raw material price increases to customers, and material costs have been relatively stable as a percentage of revenue. All the company's competitors would be susceptible to the same swings.
4. *Outlook for Propane Heating:* Propane share in the US heating market has been slowly deteriorating, declining 27 bps over the past eight years from 4.81% to 4.54%. During that time, electric heat has grown fastest (+320 bps), while natural gas accessibility has continued to improve. LPG is best positioned in rural markets, and trends toward urbanization could impair future growth. Over the medium to long term, efforts to limit dependence on fossil fuels could affect the positioning of propane heating both in the US and internationally. There is risk of incremental tax incentives to encourage switching, particularly in areas where fossil fuels are not the primary electricity source. Longer term, other new sources of heat/electricity (e.g., solar) could impact the market.
   - *Mitigant:* While the market share of propane has declined, the number of households using propane has been stable at approximately 5.8 million. There have been losses within the existing installed base as natural gas pipelines have expanded. However, new housing starts that use propane and some conversions from fuel oil to propane have largely replaced these losses. Over the medium term, given the outlook for low propane costs and relatively high switching costs, we would expect the installed base to remain stable. VCC's volume is mainly driven by the installed base rather than new homes, although new homes do have a positive impact.
   - *Mitigant:* Electric heat is the primary competitor to propane in the absence of natural gas. Based on our primary research, in most cases (absent the need to install a new furnace), a strong economic incentive is required to switch from propane to electric heat. Additionally, the cold winters in the Northeast and Midwest reduce the viability of electric heat.
5. *Product Liability:* A significant incident resulting from faulty equipment could damage the brand and lead to loss of market share.
   - *Mitigant:* VCC has a strong safety track record, and its current reputation with customers is solid. In our industry study, VCC outperformed its competitors in both quality and safety reputation. In a 2018 analysis that the company commissioned, it ranked top in product quality among its competitors.
   - *Mitigant:* We spoke to the company's insurance broker and came away with confidence in the policies that the company maintains. Furthermore, we

walked through the historical product liability claims with management, and they are immaterial.

6. *Risk of Customer Losses:* While VCC has a reasonably diversified customer base, there is customer concentration at the top, with ~45%–50% of sales from its top 10 customers, including 9%–10% from its largest distributor customer. Within the LPG distributor channel, nearly all US sales come from 13 customers, with three distributors accounting for more than 10% of distributor channel sales in 2018.
   - *Mitigant:* The company has longstanding relationships (20+ years) with most of its large customers and focuses on category exclusivity with them.
7. *Historical Numbers Heavily Adjusted:* Meaningful adjustments in several of the historical periods had to be made to arrive at management's adjusted EBITDA calculation.
   - *Mitigant:* We had a third party perform a quality of earnings report. Our model incorporates the adjusted EBITDA from that report, which is approximately 10% lower than management's EBITDA. (See Appendix #2.)
   - *Mitigant:* We have structured a relatively tight EBITDA definition, with a cap on add-backs related to non-recurring charges at 10% and a cap on cost savings add-backs at 10% (which must be achieved within 12 months).

Summary of Management, Base, and Downside Forecasts

	Projections				
	2019	2020	2021	2022	2023
Revenue Growth					
Management Case	10.0%	5.7%	6.7%	6.3%	6.2%
Lender Base Case	5.0%	2.0%	2.0%	2.0%	2.0%
Recession Downside Case	5.0%	0.0%	-5.0%	2.0%	2.0%
EBITDA Margin					
Management Case	21.2%	23.6%	24.1%	24.9%	25.7%
Lender Base Case	22.0%	22.0%	22.0%	22.0%	22.0%
Recession Downside Case	22.0%	20.0%	17.0%	17.0%	20.0%
FCF after Required Debt Amortization					
Management Case	13.5	14.8	19.1	25.5	30.5
Lender Base Case	7.5	5.8	7.0	9.6	10.5
Recession Downside Case	7.5	3.6	1.9	(1.2)	4.2
Net Senior Secured Debt / EBITDA					
Management Case	4.5x	3.4x	2.6x	1.8x	1.0x
Lender Base Case	4.7x	4.3x	3.9x	3.5x	3.0x
Recession Downside Case	4.7x	4.9x	5.8x	5.6x	4.4x
Liquidity (Excess Cash Plus Availability on RC)[a]					
Management Case	40.6	55.4	74.5	100.0	130.5
Lender Base Case	34.6	40.4	47.4	57.0	67.5
Recession Downside Case	34.6	38.2	40.1	38.8	43.0

[a]VCC's minimum cash needed to run its business is $5MM. For liquidity we only counted cash above the $5MM.

Key takeaways from our forecast model

- See Appendix #3 for a more detailed model and assumptions rationale.
- Our downside case is conservative.
  - Sales decline consistent with the GFC.
  - Margin deteriorates below the company's historic trough margin.
- Even with these conservative assumptions, the company's leverage through our debt peaks at 5.8x, well below our view of the business' valuation (see Valuation Analysis).
- Liquidity is more than adequate, even at its low point.

RELATIVE VALUE ANALYSIS

IRR and Multiple of Money based on year repaid:

	Return (L+700, 1.5% Floor, 2.25% OID)				
	Year 1	Year 2	Year 3	Year 4	Maturity
IRR	14.6%	11.7%	10.2%	9.7%	9.5%
MoM	1.14x	1.22x	1.28x	1.35x	1.43x

VCC's debt is not rated. However, based on the rating agencies' methodology and discussions with rating agency analysts, we believe the term loan would be rated B/B- and the corporate rating would be CCC+.

The VCC term loan offers a 50–100 bps spread premium to similarly rated credits. Furthermore, the VCC loan has a much tighter structure, as many comps are covenant-light.

APPENDIX #1: Credit Agreement Summary

Facility	$220MM Senior Secured Credit Facility ("Credit Facility") consisting of (i) a $20MM First Priority Revolver ("Revolver"), and (ii) a $200M Senior Secured Term Loan ("Term Loan")
Borrower	Valve Controls International, LLC ("VCC" or the "Borrower")
Collateral	Perfected first priority security interests in substantially all tangible and intangible assets
Maturity	Earlier of (i) 5 years, and (ii) 6 months prior to the earliest maturity of any material subordinated indebtedness, including the Mezz Debt
Interest Rate	Revolver: L+450bps (1.50% floor) Term Loan: L+700bps (1.50% floor)

OID	2.25%
Unused Line Fee	0.50% per annum on the unused amount of the Revolver
Amortization	2.50% per annum, payable in equal quarterly installments (commencing in the first full quarter post-close)
Call Protection	Non-call for 12 months, 102 for 12–24 months, 101 for 24–36 months and par thereafter
ECF Sweep	50% commencing in FY2020, with step-down to 25% if Senior Net Leverage is less than 3.5x
Payment Priority	Post-default waterfall shall provide for the first priority repayment of the Revolver and the second priority repayment of the Term Loan
Financial Covenants	Total Net Leverage: [TBD] Max Capex [TBD] Senior Net Leverage: [TBD] Min FCCR: 1.10x
Restricted Payments	<u>Mezz Debt Cash Interest Payment Conditions</u>: Cash interest can only be paid on the Mezzanine Facility subject to the following conditions: ■ Up to 50% of the total interest rate may be paid in cash provided that pro forma Senior Net Leverage < 3.0x ■ Up to 25% of the total interest rate may be paid in cash provided that pro forma Senior Net Leverage >3.0x and <3.5x ■ Pro forma total liquidity of $5MM with undrawn revolver ■ Customary provisions such as no event of default and pro forma covenant compliance
Financial Reporting	Monthly financials, quarterly financials and lender calls, annual financials, audit and budget (all financials to include MD&A)
EBITDA Definition	Includes add-backs for the following: ■ 20% aggregate cap for (i) integration costs for Permitted Acquisitions, (ii) run-rate cost savings and transaction synergies to be realized within the next 12 months, and (iii) other non-recurring items ■ Pro forma cost savings subject to 10% cap and non-recurring items subject to 10% cap

APPENDIX #2: EBITDA Adjustments

Reported EBITDA includes significant adjustments. We engaged a third-party firm to do a quality of earnings report. Based on that report and the deal team's judgment, we are comfortable making the adjustments outlined below.

(FYE 12/31 – in $MM)	2014	2015	2016	2017	2018
Reported EBITDA	$38.0	$33.5	$20.9	$39.8	$24.1
(+) Severance Payments	–	1.6	1.2	–	–
(+) One-Time Integration Costs	1.4	0.8	2.7	–	–
(±) Net FX (Gain) / Loss	(1.7)	0.3	1.8	(0.8)	1.1
(+) Plant Closure	2.6	0.7	–	–	–
(+) Relocation of Chinese Facility	–	2.1	–	–	–
(+) Transaction Fees & Expenses	0.8	–	–	–	–
(+) One-time Product Liab Reserve	–	–	2.0	–	–
(+) 3rd Party Consulting / Legal Exp	–	–	0.7	–	3.2
(+) Special Improvement Project	–	–	–	0.5	0.8
(+) Supply Chain Initiatives	–	–	–	0.1	0.4
(+) Engineering Design & Training	–	–	–	0.1	–
(+) One-time Recruitment	–	–	–	1.2	0.7
(+) Other	0.1	–	1.3	–	–
Total adjustments to reported EBITDA	3.2	5.5	9.7	1.1	6.2
Adj as a % of reported EBITDA	*8.4%*	*16.4%*	*46.4%*	*2.8%*	*25.7%*
Adjusted EBITDA	**$41.2**	**$39.0**	**$30.6**	**$40.9**	**$30.3**

APPENDIX #3: Forecasts

Management Projections ($MM)

- Management expects growth to be driven by continued steady improvement in the core LPG products, market share expansion, and industry tailwinds in IG/LNG.
- EBITDA margin improvements are driven by pricing actions, operating leverage, and production efficiencies. We note that management's forecast margin seems aggressive, as in the later years it is at or above elevated 2017 levels (which had the benefit of absorption costing).
- Capex is consistent with the historical average (most capex is maintenance).
- The company is forecasting a ~$5MM working capital inflow in 2019 as it continues to work down excess inventory levels. Management believes the $5MM is conservative (potential for $10MM+). The management forecast keeps working capital flat for the remainder of the projection period.

(FYE 12/31–in $mm)

Management Case: Revenue and EBITDA Projections

	Historical			Management Projections				
	2016	**2017**	**2018**	**2019**	**2020**	**2021**	**2022**	**2023**
Total Revenue	**$154.7**	**$163.7**	**$162.2**	**$178.5**	**$188.6**	**$201.3**	**$213.8**	**$227.1**
% YoY	*(12.6%)*	*5.8%*	*(0.9%)*	*10.0%*	*5.7%*	*6.7%*	*6.3%*	*6.2%*
Adjusted EBITDA	$30.6	$40.9	$30.3	$37.8	$44.5	$48.5	$53.3	$58.4
Adj EBITDA Margin	*19.8%*	*25.0%*	*18.7%*	*21.2%*	*23.6%*	*24.1%*	*24.9%*	*25.7%*

Management Case: Cash Flow Projections

	Historical			Management Projections				
	2016	2017	2018	2019	2020	2021	2022	2023
Adjusted EBITDA	$30.6	$40.9	$30.3	$37.8	$44.5	$48.5	$53.3	$58.4
(–) Capex - maintenance	(2.0)	(2.8)	(3.1)	(2.7)	(4.3)	(4.3)	(4.3)	(4.5)
(–) Capex - growth	–	–	–	(1.5)	(1.5)	(1.5)	–	–
Adj. EBITDAX	**$28.6**	**$38.1**	**$27.2**	**$33.6**	**$38.7**	**$42.7**	**$49.0**	**$53.9**
(–) Cash interest				(17.0)	(16.2)	(15.7)	(15.3)	(14.9)
(–) Cash taxes				(2.3)	(2.7)	(2.9)	(3.2)	(3.5)
(–/+) Cash impact chg WC				5.0	–	–	–	–
(–/+) Other				(0.8)	–	–	–	–
Free cash available to pay down debt				$18.5	$19.8	$24.1	$30.5	$35.5
(–) Required amortization of secured term loan				(5.0)	(5.0)	(5.0)	(5.0)	(5.0)
Free Cash Flow				$13.5	$14.8	$19.1	$25.5	$30.5
Senior secured term loan, beginning of year				$200.0	$195.0	$190.0	$185.0	$180.0
Less required amortization				(5.0)	(5.0)	(5.0)	(5.0)	(5.0)
Senior secured term loan, end of year			$200.0	$195.0	$190.0	$185.0	$180.0	$175.0
Cash on balance sheet			(12.1)	(25.6)	(40.4)	(59.5)	(85.0)	(115.5)
Senior secured term loan net of cash, end of yr			187.9	$169.4	$149.6	$125.5	$95.0	$59.5
Senior Secured Debt / EBITDA			6.6x	5.2x	4.3x	3.8x	3.4x	3.0x
Net Senior Secured Debt / EBITDA			6.2x	4.5x	3.4x	2.6x	1.8x	1.0x

Note the model does not incorporate the required FCF sweep.

Lender Base Case ($MM)

- Our base case projections assume that the LPG segment reverts to its long-term annualized growth rate of 2% (versus management's 6+% projection).
- We assumed an EBITDA margin of 22%, consistent with the five-year average. There is probably upside to our margin assumption as the company recently increased pricing, which should result in 100 bps of margin expansion. However, we are uncomfortable incorporating this margin improvement until we see if the price increase sticks. Additionally, we assumed no benefit of fixed cost absorption from volume growth—an assumption we believe is conservative.
- Capex is consistent with the management case.
- For the cash impact of changes in working capital:

    - In 2019 we assumed flat working capital vs management's expectation of $5–10MM positive from better inventory management.
    - For the projection period beyond 2019 we grew working capital with revenue growth, resulting in a slight drag on annual cash flow.

Lender Base Case: Revenue and EBITDA Projections

	Historical			Lender Base Case Projections				
$ in millions	2016	2017	2018	2019	2020	2021	2022	2023
Total Revenue	**$154.7**	**$163.7**	**$162.2**	**$170.3**	**$173.7**	**$177.2**	**$180.7**	**$184.3**
% YoY	*(12.6%)*	*5.8%*	*(0.9%)*	*5.0%*	*2.0%*	*2.0%*	*2.0%*	*2.0%*
Adjusted EBITDA	$30.6	$40.9	$30.3	$37.5	$38.2	$39.0	$39.8	$40.5
Adj EBITDA Margin	*19.8%*	*25.0%*	*18.7%*	*22.0%*	*22.0%*	*22.0%*	*22.0%*	*22.0%*

Lender Base Case: Cash Flow Projections

	Historical			Lender Base Case Projections				
$ in millions	**2016**	**2017**	**2018**	**2019**	**2020**	**2021**	**2022**	**2023**
Adjusted EBITDA	$30.6	$40.9	$30.3	$37.5	$38.2	$39.0	$39.8	$40.5
(–) Capex - maintenance	(2.0)	(2.8)	(3.1)	(2.7)	(4.3)	(4.3)	(4.3)	(4.5)
(–) Capex - growth	=	=	=	(1.5)	(1.5)	(1.5)	=	=
Adj. EBITDAX	**$28.6**	**$38.1**	**$27.2**	**$33.3**	**$32.4**	**$33.2**	**$35.5**	**$36.0**
(–) Cash interest				(17.0)	(16.2)	(15.7)	(15.3)	(14.9)
(–) Cash taxes				(2.3)	(2.3)	(2.3)	(2.4)	(2.4)
(–/+) Cash impact chg WC				–	(1.6)	(1.7)	(1.7)	(1.7)
(–/+) Other				(1.5)	(1.5)	(1.5)	(1.5)	(1.5)
Free cash available to pay down debt				$12.5	$10.8	$12.0	$14.6	$15.5
(–) Required amortization of secured term loan				(5.0)	(5.0)	(5.0)	(5.0)	(5.0)
Free Cash Flow				$7.5	$5.8	$7.0	$9.6	$10.5
Senior secured term loan, beginning of year				$200.0	$195.0	$190.0	$185.0	$180.0
Less required amortization				(5.0)	(5.0)	(5.0)	(5.0)	(5.0)
Senior secured term loan, end of year			$200.0	$195.0	$190.0	$185.0	$180.0	$175.0
Cash on balance sheet			(12.1)	(19.6)	(25.4)	(32.4)	(42.0)	(52.5)
Senior secured term loan net of cash, end of yr			187.9	$175.4	$164.6	$152.6	$138.0	$122.5
Senior Secured Debt / EBITDA			6.6x	5.2x	5.0x	4.7x	4.5x	4.3x
Net Senior Secured Debt / EBITDA			6.2x	4.7x	4.3x	3.9x	3.5x	3.0x

Note the model does not incorporate the required FCF sweep.

Downside Case ($MM)

- In our downside case, we show no growth in 2020 followed by a 5% decline (similar to the decline during the GFC) and a rebound thereafter to the historical growth rate of 2%, which we think is conservative as the company's LPG sales rebounded 15% following the 2008 recession.
- We modeled an EBITDA margin decline to 17% (for two years) which is 450 bps below the long-term average and 120 bps below the company's lowest historic margin rate. This is partially attributable to negative fixed cost absorption associated with the volumetric declines.
- Despite the decrease in sales, we used the same capex and working capital methodology as our base case.
- Despite the meaningful decline in profitability, the business has adequate liquidity, and the loan remains well covered with peak net leverage <6.0x .

Downside Recession Case: Revenue and EBITDA Projections

	Historical			Downside Recession Case				
$ in millions	2016	2017	2018	2019	2020	2021	2022	2023
Total Revenue	$154.7	$163.7	$162.2	$170.3	$170.3	$161.8	$165.0	$168.3
% YoY	*(12.6%)*	*5.8%*	*(0.9%)*	*5.0%*	*0.0%*	*(5.0%)*	*2.0%*	*2.0%*
Adjusted EBITDA	$30.6	$40.9	$30.3	$37.5	$34.1	$27.5	$28.1	$33.7
Adj EBITDA Margin	*19.8%*	*25.0%*	*18.7%*	*22.0%*	*20.0%*	*17.0%*	*17.0%*	*20.0%*

Downside Recession Case: Cash Flow Projections

	Historical			Downside Recession Case				
$ in millions	2016	2017	2018	2019	2020	2021	2022	2023
Adjusted EBITDA	$30.6	$40.9	$30.3	$37.5	$34.1	$27.5	$28.1	$33.7
(–) Capex - maintenance	(2.0)	(2.8)	(3.1)	(2.7)	(4.3)	(4.3)	(4.3)	(4.5)
(–) Capex - growth	–	–	–	(1.5)	(1.5)	(1.5)	–	–
Adj. EBITDAX	**$28.6**	**$38.1**	**$27.2**	**$33.3**	**$28.3**	**$21.7**	**$23.8**	**$29.2**
(–) Cash interest				(17.0)	(16.2)	(15.7)	(15.3)	(14.9)
(–) Cash taxes				(2.3)	(2.0)	(1.7)	(1.7)	(2.0)
(–/+) Cash impact chg WC				–	–	4.1	(1.5)	(1.6)
(–/+) Other				(1.5)	(1.5)	(1.5)	(1.5)	(1.5)
Free cash available to pay down debt				$12.5	$8.6	$6.9	$3.8	$9.2
(–) Required amortization of secured term loan				(5.0)	(5.0)	(5.0)	(5.0)	(5.0)
Free Cash Flow				$7.5	$3.6	$1.9	($1.2)	$4.2
Senior secured term loan, beginning of year				$200.0	$195.0	$190.0	$185.0	$180.0
Less required amortization				(5.0)	(5.0)	(5.0)	(5.0)	(5.0)
Senior secured term loan, end of year			$200.0	$195.0	$190.0	$185.0	$180.0	$175.0
Cash on balance sheet			(12.1)	(19.6)	(23.2)	(25.1)	(23.8)	(28.0)
Senior secured term loan net of cash, end of yr			187.9	$175.4	$166.8	$159.9	$156.2	$147.0
Senior Secured Debt / EBITDA			6.6x	5.2x	5.6x	6.7x	6.4x	5.2x
Net Senior Secured Debt / EBITDA			6.2x	4.7x	4.9x	5.8x	5.6x	4.4x

Note the model does not incorporate the required FCF sweep.

APPENDIX #4: Valuation Analysis

Comparable company analysis

In consultation with industry experts, we identified three public comps.

1. Flowserve: One of the world's largest manufacturers of flow control products (~$3.8bn sales) with a portfolio of more than 50 brands.
2. Watts Water: Designs and manufactures residential and commercial flow control products for plumbing and HVAC applications.
3. CIRCOR Intl: Manufacturer of specialized flow and motion control products.

Two of the three comps trade between 9x–9.7x EBITDA, with the third being an outlier trading at 15.6x. We believe VCC's business is better than the comps in three respects:

1. Less cyclical due to a higher proportion of recurring revenues
2. Higher EBITDA margin
3. Lower capex needs

However, these positives are offset by:

1. The comps are significantly larger and more diversified with revenues ranging from $1 to $4 billion versus $160 million for VCC.
2. Slower sales growth.
3. An extremely leveraged balance sheet (7.3x based on 2017/2018 average EBITDA).

Disregarding the outlier, we believe VCC should trade at a 1 to 1.5x discount multiple to the other comps, mainly to reflect its smaller size. We use 7.5x–8.5x EBITDA and EBITDA of $35 for a valuation of $262.5 to $297.5 million.

	Total Enterprise Value				Operating Metrics				Leverage	Trading Multiples		
Company	Equity Market Cap	Debt	Cash	TEV	Sales	Sales Growth	EBITDA	EBITDA Margin	Net Debt/ EBITDA	Sales	EBITDA	EBITDAX
VCC	NA	NA	NA	NA	162	−0.9%	35	21.6%[a]	7.30x	NA	NA	NA
FLS	4,927	1,483	620	5,790	3,836	4.8%	372	9.7%	2.32x	1.51x	15.56x	17.01x
WTS	2,188	353	204	2,337	1,565	7.4%	240	15.4%	0.62x	1.49x	9.73x	10.90x
CIR	428	786	69	1,146	1,013	NM[b]	127	12.5%	5.65x	1.13x	9.02x	10.72x
Median	2,188	786	204	2,337	1,565	NM	240	12.5%	2.32x	1.49x	9.73x	10.90x
Mean[c]	2,514	874	297	3,091	2,138	6.1%	246	12.5%	2.86x	1.38x	11.43x	12.87x

[a] For VCC we used the 2017/2018 average EBITDA margin of 21.6% as 2017 is overstated and 2018 is understated due to absorption costing issues. See financial statement analysis section.

[b] Growth rate "NM" due to the impact of an acquisition.

[c] Mean EBITDA margin, leverage, and multiples are not size-weighted.

Source: Capital IQ.

Precedent transaction analysis In consultation with industry investment bankers, we identified two relevant M&A transactions, which took place in a tight range of 8.6x–9.6x EBITDA.

Target	Acquirer	Date	Purchase Price	Sales	EBITDA	EBITDA Margin	EBITDA Multiple
GESTRA	Spirax-Sarco	2017	159.2	92.5	16.6	17.9%	9.6x
Flow Sys	CIRCOR	2016	214.0	122.0	25.0	20.5%	8.6x
Average			186.6	107.3	20.8	19.2%	9.1x

1. **GESTRA:** Designs and manufactures valves and control systems for heat and process fluid control applications.
2. **Critical Flow Solutions:** Manufactures high-technology valves for severe service refining operations.

We believe both transactions represent what VCC could be worth in an M&A context. We use 8.5–9.5x, approximately one turn greater than our comparable company multiples reflecting potential control premium and synergies, resulting in a valuation of $298 to $333 million.

DCF analysis We ran a DCF model using our downside, base, and management/sponsor forecast case. The DCF analysis produced the following valuations:

	Downside	Base	Upside
TEV based on DCF	228.9	275.7	399.4

Below is our base case valuation model.

	Yr. #1	Yr. #2	Yr. #3	Yr. #4	Yr. #5
Unlevered free cash flow	**2019**	**2020**	**2021**	**2022**	**2023**
Adjusted EBITDA	37.5	38.2	39.0	39.8	40.5
Less capex	(4.2)	(5.8)	(5.8)	(4.3)	(4.5)
+/– change in WC	(0.0)	(1.6)	(1.7)	(1.7)	(1.7)
Less unlevered taxes[a]	(5.9)	(5.7)	(5.6)	(5.6)	(5.5)
Less misc. other cash flows	(1.5)	(1.5)	(1.5)	(1.5)	(1.5)
Unlevered Free Cash Flow (UFCF)	25.9	23.6	24.4	26.7	27.3
Divide by discount factor (1+WACC)^ years	1.1200	1.2544	1.4049	1.5735	1.7623
Present Value (UFCF/Disc factor)	23.1	18.8	17.4	17.0	15.5
PV of FCF (sum of above PVs) [A]	91.8				
Terminal Value Calculation					
Year 5 forecasted EBITDA					40.5
Mid-point EBITDA multiple					8.0x
Terminal Value at the end of year 5					324.0
Discount factor (1+WACC)^ years					1.7623
PV of Terminal Value [B]					183.9
Enterprise Value based on DCF analysis:					
PV of FCF [A]	91.8				
PV of Terminal Value [B]	183.9				
Enterprise Value	275.7				

[a] Estimate of taxes is before the benefit of any deductible interest (i.e., assumes an unlevered company).

Notes on VCC DCF valuation:

1. Projection rationale: See Appendix #3.
2. WACC: We used a 12% WACC based on internal conversations.

The following is a postmortem on the VCC loan

- After the closing of the transaction, the business performed very well. By March 2021, LTM EBITDA had reached ~$43MM, with a clear path to continued improvement.
- As a result, the lenders agreed to upsize the loan by $70MM in April 2021 to pay down a portion of the mezzanine loan.
- Following the upsize, performance continued to improve. Ultimately the sponsor sold the business to a strategic for $631MM, and the loan was repaid early at the call price of $101. The IRR of the investment was ultimately 10.6%.[3] The implied valuation multiple was in the low-to-mid-teens (depending on the EBITDA figure being used), which significantly exceeded our base case valuation.

[3]The IRR includes the coupon, the up-front fees for the original TL, upsized TL, and RC, and 101% call price.

Sample Teaser/Screening Memo #2
Public Bond Deal
HCA Leveraged Buyout Financing

Teaser/Screening Memo: Public Bond Deal

HCA Inc. ("HCA" or the "Company")[1]

DEAL SUMMARY

HCA Inc. ("HCA" or the "Company") is seeking to issue new debt to finance its LBO by a consortium of buyers, including a $2.0 billion asset-backed loan facility, $2.75 billion term loan A, $8.8 billion term loan B, €1.0 billion term loan, $4.2 billion second lien cash-pay notes, and $1.5 billion second lien PIK toggle notes. Additionally, $7.5 billion of legacy unsecured notes will remain outstanding after the LBO. Closing leverage is 3.5x through the first lien, 4.8x through the second lien, and 6.5x through the total debt balance based on 2006 projected PF EBITDA of $4.3 billion. We recommend buying the Company's second lien cash-pay notes, which have a compelling risk-adjusted relative/absolute return profile in light of HCA's market-leading presence in the defensive healthcare industry.

DEAL TERMS

Proposed terms on the new $4.2 billion second lien cash-pay notes include a 9.125% coupon, eight-year maturity, and a non-call period through the first half of the maturity with a call option at par + 50% of the coupon starting halfway through the maturity and a stepdown to par at maturity. This security will be rated B2/BB-.

COMPANY SUMMARY

HCA is the largest for-profit hospital operator in the US, with 176 hospitals and 92 freestanding surgical centers across 22 states, England, and Switzerland. HCA enjoys the leading market position in 15 of the 20 fastest-growing markets and a #1/#2 inpatient market position with a 25%–40% share in most geographies in which it operates.

INVESTMENT HIGHLIGHTS

- Market leader with 2.5x+ greater share than its closest competitor (Tenet), creating scale advantage/leverage in negotiations with managed care providers and suppliers;

[1]Transaction closed in November 2006 to support the LBO of HCA Inc.

- Limited concentration, with no single facility constituting more than 2.3% of revenue, and no Metropolitan Statistical Area (MSA) representing more than 7.5%;
- Revenue poised to increase at a 3%–4% CAGR (in line with industry healthcare spending);
- Noncyclical end-market demand for its services;
- A strong liquidity profile out of the gate;
- Attractive LTV of 63% (based on an estimated 7.7x valuation) supported by $12B of junior capital cushion;
- Strong, reputable management team, which is rolling a significant portion of its equity;
- Low position on industry cost curve;
- Relatively tight contemplated documentation; and
- Attractive relative value.

INVESTMENT RISKS

- Margin pressures from increasing bad debt expense and wage inflation;
- 53% of revenue attributed to Medicare/Medicaid creates greater risk of reimbursement pressures than exists for comps;
- Minimal free cash flow generation out of the gate;
- Small equity contribution from the sponsors at 15% of capitalization implies high closing leverage; and
- Bond offering will represent a significant increase in supply for the HY market to absorb, potentially creating technical pressure.

DEAL TEAM RECOMMENDATION

The deal team recommends proceeding with the investment on the terms outlined above. HCA benefits from a favorable industry backdrop, leading market share, and noncyclical end-market exposure. At a yield-to-worse (YTW) of 9.125%, the Company's second lien 9.125% notes offer an attractive risk-adjusted return on both an absolute and relative value basis. This return profile offers an attractive spread pickup to the Barclays BB (200 bps), B (100 bps), and Healthcare (35 bps) indices.

PRO FORMA CAPITAL STRUCTURE

	Expected Outstanding at Closing	Coupon / Yield[a]	Maturity	Multiple of EBITDA[b]	Loan-to-Value (%)
$2 Billon ABL Facility	1,750	LIBOR + 175	6-year		
$2 Billon Revolving Credit Agreement	188	LIBOR + 250	6-year		
Senior Secured Term Loan A	2,750	LIBOR + 250	6-year		
Senior Secured Term Loan B	8,800	LIBOR + 275	7-year		
1 Billion Euro Term Loan	1,250	EURIBOR + 275	7-year		
Other Secured Debt	230				
Total 1st Lien Debt[c]	**14,968**			**3.47x**	**45.4%**
2nd Lien-Cash-Pay Notes	4,200	9.125%	8-years		
2nd Lien PIK Toggle Notes	1,500	9.625%	10-years		
Total Secured Debt	**20,668**			**4.79x**	**62.6%**
Unsecured Legacy Notes[d]	7,472	various	various		
Total Debt	**28,141**			**6.52x**	**85.3%**
Less Cash	-141				
Net Debt	**28,000**			**6.48x**	**84.9%**
Equity	5,000				
Total Enterprise Value	**33,000**			**7.64x**	**100.0%**

[a] Assumes new debt to fund the LBO is issued at par (yield = coupon).

[b] 2006 estimated EBITDA of $4.319 billion.

[c] In connection with the LBO the company plans to enter into:

(i) $2.000 billion senior secured asset-based revolving credit facility with a borrowing base of 85% of eligible accounts receivable, subject to customary reserves and eligibility criteria. The company does not expect any excess availability on day one of the LBO (i.e., the ABL will be drawn to fund the LBO).

(ii) New senior secured credit agreement, consisting of:

- $2.000 billion revolving credit facility with an estimated $1.8 billion available after giving effect to letters of credit;
- $2.750 billion term loan A;
- $8.800 billion term loan B;
- €1.0 billion term loan ($1.250 billion based on exchange rates of 1 EUR/1.25 USD) with one European subsidiary as borrower.

(iii) Since the time of this deal, loans have transitioned from LIBOR to SOFR as the base rate.

[d] The unsecured legacy notes were issued pre-LBO without a change of control provision. These bonds will roll over to the pro forma post-LBO capital structure.

Base Case: Revenue and EBITDA Forecast

$ in millions	2003A	2004A	2005A	2006Epf	2007E	2008E	2009E	2010E	2011E
Revenue	21,808	23,502	24,455	25,409	26,425	27,482	28,581	29,725	30,914
% Growth	*10.5%*	*7.8%*	*4.1%*	*3.9%*	*4.0%*	*4.0%*	*4.0%*	*4.0*	*4.0*
EBITDA	3,920	3,910	4,225	4,319	4,387	4,452	4,630	4,815	5,008
Margin	*18.0%*	*16.6%*	*17.3%*	*17.0%*	*16.6%*	*16.2%*	*16.2%*	*16.2*	*16.2*

Base Case: Recurring Free Cash Flow Forecast

	2003A	2004A	2005A	2006Epf	2007E	2008E	2009E	2010E	2011E
EBITDA	3,920	3,910	4,225	4,319	4,387	4,452	4,630	4,815	5,008
Capital Expenditures	(1,838)	(1,513)	(1,592)	(1,779)	(1,800)	(1,500)	(1,500)	(1,500)	(1,500)
EBITDAX	**2,082**	**2,397**	**2,633**	**2,540**	**2,587**	**2,952**	**3,130**	**3,315**	**3,508**
Interest Expense	(491)	(563)	(655)	(2,040)	(2,037)	(2,030)	(1,998)	(1,954)	(1,898)
Cash Taxes	(328)	(394)	(563)	(317)	(322)	(328)	(380)	(439)	(503)
FCF b/f chg WC and Other	**1,263**	**1,440**	**1,415**	**183**	**228**	**594**	**752**	**922**	**1,107**
Change in Working Capital	197	1	(80)	(84)	(90)	(94)	(97)	(101)	(105)
Other	93	(2)	(72)	(50)	(50)	(50)	(50)	(50)	(50)
Free Cash Flow	**1,553**	**1,439**	**1,263**	**49**	**88**	**451**	**605**	**771**	**952**

Base Case: Leverage Ratios

	2006Epf	2007E	2008E	2009E	2010E	2011E
Beginning Debt	28,141	28,092	28,004	27,554	26,949	26,178
Debt Paydown[a]	(49)	(88)	(451)	(605)	(771)	(952)
Ending Debt	28,092	28,004	27,554	26,949	26,178	25,226
Debt / EBITDA through 1st Lien Debt	3.5x	3.4x	3.2x	3.0x	2.7x	2.4x
Debt / EBITDA through 2nd Lien Debt	4.8x	4.7x	4.5x	4.2x	3.9x	3.5x
Debt / EBITDA through Total Debt	6.5x	6.4x	6.2x	5.8x	5.4x	5.0x

[a] Assumes company will use 100% of FCF to pay down first-lien debt even though ECF sweep requires only 50%.

Sample Full Credit Memo #2
Public Bond Deal
HCA Leveraged Buyout Financing

Credit Committee Memo: Public Bond Deal—Buy at Indicated Price Talk

HCA Inc. ("HCA" or the "Company")[1]

EXECUTIVE SUMMARY

HCA is the largest for-profit hospital operator in the US and is seeking to issue new debt to finance its LBO, including a $2.0 billion asset-backed loan facility, $2.75 billion term loan A, $8.8 billion term loan B, €1.0 billion term loan, $4.2 billion second lien cash-pay notes, and $1.5 billion second lien PIK toggle notes. Additionally, $7.5 billion of its legacy unsecured notes will remain outstanding after the LBO. Closing leverage is 3.5x through the first lien, 4.8x through the second lien, and 6.5x through the total debt balance based on 2006 projected PF EBITDA of $4.3 billion. We recommend buying the company's second lien cash-pay notes, which have a compelling risk-adjusted return profile in light of HCA's market-leading presence within the defensive healthcare industry.

Summary of Key Terms (see Structure and Documentation Analysis section below for further detail):

- Issuer: HCA Inc. (note: structurally senior to HCA Holdings, the issuer of the legacy bonds);
- Debt issue: Second lien cash-pay notes;
- Ratings: B2/BB-;
- Maturity: 8-year;
- Price talk: 9.125%;
- Call structure: Standard (non-call first half of maturity, with call option at par + ½ coupon starting midway through/stepping down to par at maturity);
- Change of Control (CoC): Standard put at $101.

[1]Transaction closed in November 2006 to support the LBO of HCA Inc.

PRO FORMA CAPITAL STRUCTURE

	Expected Outstanding at Closing	Coupon/ Yield[a]	Maturity	Multiple Of EBITDA[b]	Loan-to-Value (%)
$2 Billon ABL Facility	1,750	LIBOR + 175	6-year		
$2 Billon Revolving Credit Agreement	188	LIBOR + 250	6-year		
Senior Secured Term Loan A	2,750	LIBOR + 250	6-year		
Senior Secured Term Loan B	8,800	LIBOR + 275	7-year		
1 Billion Euro Term Loan	1,250	EURIBOR + 275	7-year		
Other Secured Debt	230				
Total 1st Lien Debt[c]	**14,968**			3.47x	45.4%
2nd Lien-Cash-Pay Notes	4,200	9.13%	8-years		
2nd Lien PIK Toggle Notes	1,500	9.63%	10-years		
Total Secured Debt	**20,668**			4.79x	62.6%
Unsecured Legacy Notes[d]	7,472	various	various		
Total Debt	**28,141**			6.52x	85.3%
Less Cash	−141				
Net Debt	**28,000**			6.48x	84.9%
Equity	5,000				
Total Enterprise Value	**33,000**			7.64x	100.0%

[a] Assumes new debt to fund the LBO is issued at par (yield = coupon).

[b] 2006 estimated EBITDA of $4.319 billion.

[c] In connection with the LBO the company plans to enter into:

(i) $2.0 billion senior secured asset-based revolving credit facility with a borrowing base of 85% of eligible accounts receivable, subject to customary reserves and eligibility criteria. The company does not expect any excess availability on day one of the LBO (i.e., the ABL will be drawn to fund the LBO).

(ii) New senior secured credit agreement, consisting of:

- $2.0 billion revolving credit facility with an estimated $1.75 billion available after giving effect to letters of credit;
- $2.75 billion term loan A;
- $8.8 billion term loan B;
- €1.0 billion term loan ($1.25 billion based on exchange rates of 1 EUR/1.25 USD) with one European subsidiary as borrower.

(iii) Since the time of this deal, loans have transitioned from LIBOR to SOFR as the base rate.

[d] The unsecured legacy notes were issued pre-LBO without a change of control provision. These bonds will roll over to the pro forma post-LBO capital structure.

CREDIT INVESTMENT THESIS AND RECOMMENDATION

HCA is the largest for-profit hospital company in the US. We recommend buying its new second lien cash-pay notes at price talk of 9.125% based on five key factors:

1. *Market leader:* HCA is 2.5x the size of the next largest competitor, has significant diversification with no facility exceeding 2.3% of revenues, no market exceeding 7.5% of revenues, and has best-in-class margins (despite some recent bad debt expense issues).
2. *Cash flow profile:* HCA generates stable, defensive cash flow with upside from better bad debt management. Free cash flow generation positions the company for modest but steady deleveraging, even in our downside case.
3. *Reasonably levered capital structure:* HCA's loan-to-value through the recommended second lien notes is a reasonable 63% (based on an estimated 7.7x valuation) with over $12 billion of junior capital cushion ($7.5 billion legacy unsecured notes and $5.0 billion of equity).
4. *Management:* HCA's highly respected management team is rolling over a substantial amount of equity and staying on after the LBO.
5. *Attractive relative value:* The return profile of the second lien notes is attractive relative to the BB and B indices, hospital comps, and within the HCA capital structure (see return profile/relative value analysis section).

INDUSTRY OVERVIEW

The US healthcare industry has grown from $254 billion (9.1% of GDP) in 1980 to $1.9 trillion (15.9% of GDP) in 2004. Hospitals account for 30% of healthcare spending. Industry experts project hospital revenue growth of 7% annually through 2015 due to the aging population. The industry is defensive (non-cyclical), as healthcare is consumed regardless of the macro environment, although some segments exhibit cyclicality (e.g., elective surgeries).

COMPANY OVERVIEW

HCA is a leading healthcare provider in the US, with 176 hospitals and 92 freestanding surgical centers in 22 states, England, and Switzerland. The Company is the industry leader with unmatched scale, geographic diversification, and strong growth prospects.

- HCA enjoys the leading market share in 15 of the 20 fastest-growing markets in the US.
- Its #1 or #2 inpatient market position with a 25%–40% market share in most geographies provides substantial negotiating leverage vis-à-vis suppliers and managed care providers.[2] HCA's geographic footprint is shown below.

[2]A managed care provider is an insurance company or third party that negotiates with healthcare providers to reduce costs and improve healthcare quality.

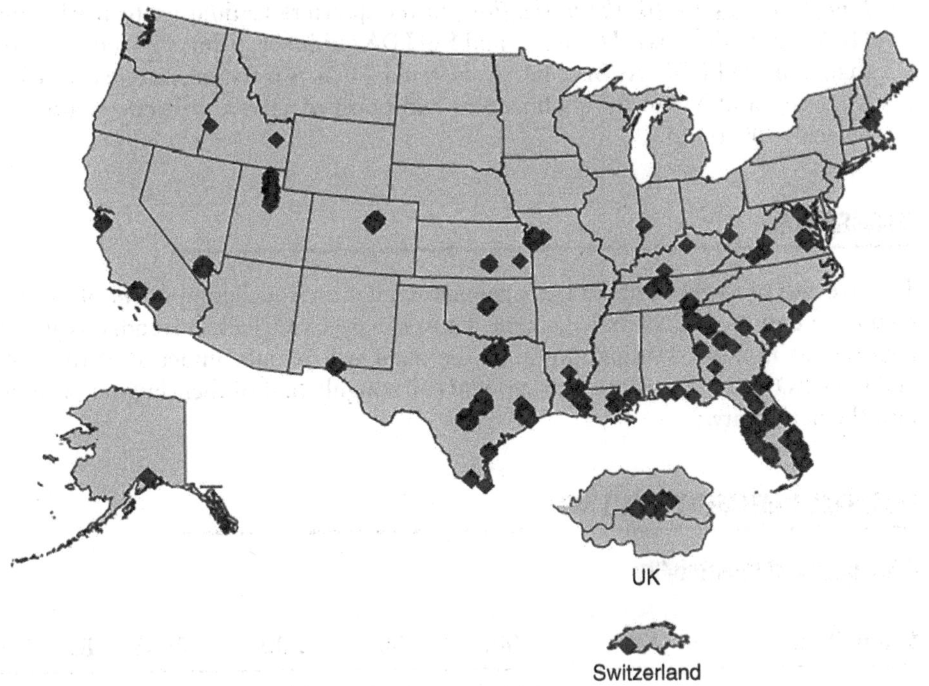

As the largest private hospital operator, HCA's business model has several creditor-friendly attributes:

- *Diversification across several metrics:* No single facility represents more than 2.3% of revenue, no MSA (metropolitan statistical area) represents more than 7.5%, and the payor base includes 2,600 managed care contracts.
- *Leading market positions:* HCA's hospitals are #1 or #2 in every MSA in which it operates, with market share ranging from 25% to 40%.
- *High-growth market presence:* Fast-growing Florida and Texas are large markets for HCA. Demographically, their population growth is set to exceed the US average.
- *Benefit of recent capital investment:* HCA has spent $8.5 billion on its facilities over the last five years, implying moderate maintenance capex over the life of the bond.
- *Outpatient segment:* Outpatient services are growing faster than hospital revenue as insurers increasingly divert non-acute patients to this lower-cost model. Thirty-six percent of HCA's sales come from this higher-growth segment.
- *Scale:* HCA's large footprint gives it improved negotiating leverage with managed care providers and efficiencies in billing, collection, etc.

HCA's post-LBO strategy is a continuation of initiatives already in place:

- *Physician relationships:* A critical element of successful hospital management is attracting physician talent. HCA is improving its pipeline of doctors by expanding specialty services and joint ventures (JVs) with existing physician practices for the outpatient business, developing medical office buildings, and enhancing IT.

- *Bad debt expense (BDE) mitigation:* In the quarters leading up to the buyout, HCA repeatedly missed earnings and EBITDA guidance, primarily due to higher-than-expected BDE. As BDE has accelerated, HCA is pursuing initiatives such as Medicare and Medicaid qualification and point-of-service collections aimed at reversing the trend.

MANAGEMENT

The strength of the incumbent management team is a critical component of our buy recommendation. HCA's management team, led by CEO Jack Bovender, is widely regarded as industry-leading. Notably, the team will remain intact after the LBO, and the CEO and COO (both staying) will roll roughly half of their buyout proceeds into the new entity.

FINANCIAL STATEMENT ANALYSIS

I) Revenue and Profitability

$ in millions	2002	2003	2004	2005	Est 2006
Revenues	19,729	21,808	23,502	24,455	25,409
Revenue growth	9.9%	10.5%	7.8%	4.1%	3.9%
Salaries and benefits expense	7,952	8,682	9,419	9,928	10,291
As a % of revenues	40.3%	39.8%	40.1%	40.6%	40.5%
Bad debt expense (BDE)	1,581	2,207	2,699	2,358	2,668
As a % of revenues	8.0%	10.1%	11.5%	9.6%	10.5%
Other operating expenses[a]	6,293	6,999	7,504	7,994	8,131
As a % of revenues	31.9%	32.1%	31.9%	32.7%	32.0%
EBITDA	3,903	3,920	3,910	4,225	4,319
EBITDA margin	19.8%	18.0%	16.6%	17.3%	17.0%

[a]Other operating expenses excludes D&A

HCA's five-year compound average growth rate (CAGR) of 8.0% is above the industry average of 7.0%. Furthermore, the company is the largest hospital chain in the industry, with more than 2.5x the revenue of the next largest player, Tenet Healthcare.

HCA has a highly diversified revenue base, with no single facility contributing more than 2.3% of revenues and no single market contributing more than 7.5%.

While EBITDA margin has decreased from 19.8% in 2002 to 17.0%, it remains well above the industry average of 12% (see Appendix #1: Summary Peer Group Analysis). The decline in margin is largely attributable to a 250 bps increase in bad debt expense as a percentage of revenues. The company believes these issues are behind it and expects EBITDA margin to stabilize above 17%. Note that we are using a 16%–17% margin in our base case projections and 15.5% in our downside case.

Even in our downside scenario, in which margin continues to decrease and stabilize at 15.5%, the company generates positive free cash flow after debt service (see Forecast section).

II) Cash Flow and Liquidity

HCA will have significant post-LBO excess liquidity, with approximately $1.8 billion available on its revolving credit facility. For the next five years, HCA will have virtually no debt maturities (other than standard 1%/year term loan amortization).

Furthermore, in our base case model, we project aggregate free cash flow of close to $3 billion for our six-year forecast period.

Even in our downside case, the company generates positive FCF every year.

Downside Case: Recurring Free Cash Flow Forecast

$ in millions	2006Epf	2007E	2008E	2009E	2010E	2011E
EBITDA	4,319	4,318	4,178	4,304	4,433	4,566
Capital Expenditures	(1,779)	(1,800)	(1,500)	(1,500)	(1,500)	(1,500)
EBITDAX	**2,540**	**2,518**	**2,678**	**2,804**	**2,933**	**3,066**
Interest Expense	(2,040)	(2,037)	(2,032)	(2,010)	(1,981)	(1,942)
Cash Taxes	(317)	(298)	(231)	(262)	(295)	(333)
FCF b/f Chg in WC & Other	183	183	415	532	657	791
Change in WC & Other	(134)	(117)	(119)	(122)	(124)	(126)
Free Cash Flow	49	66	296	410	533	665

There is little potential to lower capex as the forecast includes only a maintenance level of spending. However, if needed, the company can exercise its PIK option on the PIK toggle notes, eliminating another $144 million of cash outflow per year.

III) Capital Structure Analysis

See page 2 of this memo for the pro forma capital structure. HCA's debt load will almost triple after the LBO ($10.5 billion of pre-LBO debt outstanding versus $28.1 billion post-LBO). Furthermore, the sponsors are investing a relatively small amount of equity, only ~15% of the TEV, including management's rolled equity.

Despite the thin equity capital, the second lien notes benefit from over $12 billion of junior capital cushion ($7.5 billion unsecured notes plus $5.0 billion of equity), implying a loan-to-value through our investment of only 63% (based on the LBO purchase price).

The $7.5 billion of unsecured notes were issued primarily when HCA was investment grade–rated and thus do not enjoy a CoC provision. This legacy debt creates almost two turns' worth of cushion for the new second lien bonds. Since they do not have subsidiary guarantees, the legacy debt is structurally subordinated to the second lien notes.

KEY RISKS AND MITIGANTS

The primary risks to HCA are the continuation/acceleration of recent bad debt trends, regulatory changes that adversely impact for-profit hospital margins, and the relatively small amount of equity financing (15% of TEV).

1. *Bad debt expense escalation:* BDE has been a drag on margin for several years, increasing from 8.0% of revenue in 2002 to a forecasted 10.5% in 2006.
   - *Mitigant:* Management has implemented several initiatives to counteract this escalation, and our projections include ongoing BDE increases from LTM's elevated levels through 2008 in the base case and sharper deterioration in the downside case. In both cases, HCA continues to delever.
2. *Ongoing margin pressure from labor costs:* HCA's salaries/benefits have grown from 39.8% of revenue in 2003 to 40.6% in 2005.
   - *Mitigant:* Our forecasts incorporate continued escalation in labor costs from LTM's elevated level through 2008 in the base case and greater escalation in the downside case.
3. *Reliance on Medicare/Medicaid:* These two government programs account for 53% of revenue, implying significant exposure to regulatory changes.
   - *Mitigant:* There is a limit to how much reimbursement rates could be lowered without having a devasting impact on non-profit hospitals, which have significantly lower margins. Given the historical trend and political sensitivity to hurting the non-profit segment, we and our consultants believe that reimbursement rates will remain stable.
4. *High leverage and minimal cash flow out of the gates:* While HCA can support its post-LBO capital structure, it starts life as a private company with high leverage (6.5x) and only modest cash flow.
   - *Mitigant:* This risk is mitigated by the company's deleveraging potential in the projection period and the cushion of the legacy unsecured debt beneath the second lien bonds (almost 2x EBITDA). Additionally, the PIK feature provides ~$150MM/year in additional cash flow as an emergency lever (if necessary). Finally, HCA will have virtually no debt maturities (other than standard 1%/year term loan amortization) before 2010, as the LBO financing terms out all legacy debt maturities through 2009.
5. *Small equity component:* The equity invested into the deal, including management's rolled-over piece, is <20% of TEV.
   - *Mitigant:* Given the potential for BDE initiatives to grow EBITDA (as opposed to the continued deterioration modeled above), there should be substantial upside for the PE sponsors to exit even without multiple expansion. In other words, the sponsors will not have to extract value from creditors (e.g., by levering up for acquisitions or dividends using covenant loopholes/carve-outs). Additionally, the PE sponsors are not overpaying for HCA; 8x TEV/EBITDA is in line with public comps, below private transaction multiples, and on the low end of historic multiples, as the sector has been out of favor in the equity market for several years.

6. *Size:* HCA will represent a 2.5% position in the HY index and 40% of the HY healthcare sector, dwarfing the other healthcare issuers. While the HY market is only being asked to absorb ~$6 billion of the total $20 billion in debt, it is still a large deal and might trade down on the break if placed too aggressively by the underwriting syndicate.
   - *Mitigant:* Attractive pricing positions the cash-pay second lien notes to trade well versus competing fixed-income investments.

FORECAST

As part of the proxy materials for the shareholder vote, management released revenue, EBITDA, and capex forecasts through 2011. Management lowered EBITDA forecasts twice during the deal marketing, primarily related to escalating BDE. In addition to the company's internal model, we received an independent forecast from McKinsey, whose numbers were modestly below management's.

Since the business is noncyclical and government reimbursement rates are expected to be stable, revenues should grow 3%–4%, in line with healthcare spending. The model does not contemplate growth from new hospitals or acquisitions.

Our scenario analysis is driven primarily by margin. Our base case model assumes EBITDA margin stabilizes at 16.2%, driven by continued deterioration in bad debt expense and modest wage inflation. Our base case roughly aligns with McKinsey's forecast.

Our downside case assumes incremental margin pressure with a terminal EBITDA margin of 15.5% versus 2003's 18% margin level; this is a reasonably conservative/punitive forecast.

As shown below, assuming the company deploys FCF toward debt reduction, leverage will decline by ~1.5x over the projection period in the base case. Importantly, even in our conservative downside case, the company generates FCF every year and will delever by 0.8x.

Base Case Forecast ($MM)

- Assumes revenue growth of ~4.0% a year, which is in line with the industry growth rate.
- EBITDA margin declines, stabilizing at 16.2%.
- Capex is consistent with historical levels.
- Net working capital is a use of cash as the Company continues to grow.

Base Case: Revenue and EBITDA Forecast

	2003A	2004A	2005A	2006Epf	2007E	2008E	2009E	2010E	2011E
Revenue	21,808	23,502	24,455	25,409	26,425	27,482	28,581	29,725	30,914
% Growth	*10.5%*	*7.8%*	*4.1%*	*3.9%*	*4.0%*	*4.0%*	*4.0%*	*4.0%*	*4.0%*
EBITDA	3,920	3,910	4,225	4,319	4,387	4,452	4,630	4,815	5,008
Margin	*18.0%*	*16.6%*	*17.3%*	*17.0%*	*16.6%*	*16.2%*	*16.2%*	*16.2%*	*16.2%*

Base Case: Recurring Free Cash Flow Forecast

	2003A	2004A	2005A	2006Epf	2007E	2008E	2009E	2010E	2011E
EBITDA	3,920	3,910	4,225	4,319	4,387	4,452	4,630	4,815	5,008
Capital Expenditures	(1,838)	(1,513)	(1,592)	(1,779)	(1,800)	(1,500)	(1,500)	(1,500)	(1,500)
EBITDAX	**2,082**	**2,397**	**2,633**	**2,540**	**2,587**	**2,952**	**3,130**	**3,315**	**3,508**
Interest Expense	(491)	(563)	(655)	(2,040)	(2,037)	(2,030)	(1,998)	(1,954)	(1,898)
Cash Taxes	(328)	(394)	(563)	(317)	(322)	(328)	(380)	(439)	(503)
FCF b/f chg WC and Other	**1,263**	**1,440**	**1,415**	**183**	**228**	**594**	**752**	**922**	**1,107**
Change in Working Capital	197	1	(80)	(84)	(90)	(94)	(97)	(101)	(105)
Other	93	(2)	(72)	(50)	(50)	(50)	(50)	(50)	(50)
Free Cash Flow	**1,553**	**1,439**	**1,263**	**49**	**88**	**451**	**605**	**771**	**952**

Base Case: Leverage Ratios						
	2006Epf	2007E	2008E	2009E	2010E	2011E
Beginning Debt	28,141	28,092	28,004	27,554	26,949	26,178
Debt Paydown[a]	(49)	(88)	(451)	(605)	(771)	(952)
Ending Debt	28,092	28,004	27,554	26,949	26,178	25,226
Debt / EBITDA through 1st Lien Debt	3.5x	3.4x	3.2x	3.0x	2.7x	2.4x
Debt / EBITDA through 2nd Lien Debt	4.8x	4.7x	4.5x	4.2x	3.9x	3.5x
Debt / EBITDA through Total Debt	6.5x	6.4x	6.2x	5.8x	5.4x	5.0x
EBITDA / Interest	2.1x	2.2x	2.2x	2.3x	2.5x	2.6x
(EBITDA – Capex) / Interest	1.2x	1.3x	1.5x	1.6x	1.7x	1.8x

[a] Assumes company will use 100% of FCF to pay down first-lien debt even though ECF sweep requires only 50%.

Downside Case Forecast ($MM)

- Assumes revenue growth of ~3.0% a year, slightly below the industry growth rate.
- EBITDA margin declines, stabilizing at 15.5%.
- Capex is consistent with historical levels.
- Net working capital is a use of cash as the Company continues to grow.

Downside Case: Revenue and EBITDA Forecast

	2003A	2004A	2005A	2006Epf	2007E	2008E	2009E	2010E	2011E
Revenue	21,808	23,502	24,455	25,409	26,171	26,956	27,765	28,598	29,456
% Growth	*10.5%*	*7.8%*	*4.1%*	*3.9%*	*3.0%*	*3.0%*	*3.0%*	*3.0%*	*3.0%*
EBITDA	3,920	3,910	4,225	4,319	4,318	4,178	4,304	4,433	4,566
Margin	*18.0%*	*16.6%*	*17.3%*	*17.0%*	*16.5%*	*15.5%*	*15.5%*	*15.5%*	*15.5%*

Downside Case: Recurring Free Cash Flow Forecast

	2003A	2004A	2005A	2006Epf	2007E	2008E	2009E	2010E	2011E
EBITDA	3,920	3,910	4,225	4,319	4,318	4,178	4,304	4,433	4,566
Capital Expenditures	(1,838)	(1,513)	(1,592)	(1,779)	(1,800)	(1,500)	(1,500)	(1,500)	(1,500)
EBITDAX	**2,082**	**2,397**	**2,633**	**2,540**	**2,518**	**2,678**	**2,804**	**2,933**	**3,066**
Interest Expense	(491)	(563)	(655)	(2,040)	(2,037)	(2,032)	(2,010)	(1,981)	(1,942)
Cash Taxes	(328)	(394)	(563)	(317)	(298)	(231)	(262)	(295)	(333)
FCF b/f chg WC and Other	**1,263**	**1,440**	**1,415**	**183**	**183**	**415**	**532**	**657**	**791**
Change in Working Capital	197	1	(80)	(84)	(67)	(69)	(72)	(74)	(76)
Other	93	(2)	(72)	(50)	(50)	(50)	(50)	(50)	(50)
Free Cash Flow	**1,553**	**1,439**	**1,263**	**49**	**66**	**296**	**410**	**533**	**665**

Downside Case: Leverage Ratios

	2006Epf	2007E	2008E	2009E	2010E	2011E
Beginning Debt	28,141	28,092	28,026	27,730	27,320	26,787
Debt Paydown[a]	(49)	(66)	(296)	(410)	(533)	(665)
Ending Debt	28,092	28,026	27,730	27,320	26,787	26,123
Debt / EBITDA through 1st Lien Debt	3.5x	3.4x	3.5x	3.3x	3.1x	2.8x
Debt / EBITDA through 2nd Lien Debt	4.8x	4.8x	4.8x	4.6x	4.4x	4.1x
Debt / EBITDA through Total Debt	6.5x	6.5x	6.6x	6.3x	6.0x	5.7x
EBITDA / Interest	2.1x	2.1x	2.1x	2.1x	2.2x	2.4x
(EBITDA – Capex) / Interest	1.2x	1.2x	1.3x	1.4x	1.5x	1.6x

[a]Assumes company will use 100% of FCF to pay down first-lien debt even though ECF sweep requires only 50%.

STRUCTURE AND DOCUMENTATION ANALYSIS

The second lien bonds have guarantees from all the subsidiaries that guarantee the bank debt and a second lien (behind the term loans) on the capital stock of these subsidiaries. Furthermore, these bonds will have a second lien on any hospital not subject to the negative pledge language in the legacy bonds. Finally, they have a third lien on the ABL collateral.

The cash-pay bond's maturity is two years shorter than the PIK bond. We do not recommend the PIK bond, as we do not believe the modest (50 bp) pickup in yield adequately compensates us for the longer maturity and the company's option not to pay cash interest.

Review of covenants The covenant package is tight relative to other B2/BB- bonds. Key terms are summarized below.

- **Debt incurrence:** HCA can only raise incremental debt if the pro forma fixed charge coverage (FCC) ratio is at least 2.0x. This provision "falls away" if HCA is upgraded to investment grade ratings by Moody's and S&P. The indenture carves out the following debt raises (i.e., the debt funding below is not subject to the FCC incurrence test):
  - $16.5 billion in credit facilities (already incurred);
  - $2.0 billion debt incurred by restricted subs that are not guarantors;
  - Foreign subsidiary debt up to 7.5% of total foreign sub assets;
  - $200MM acquisition-related debt.
- **Restricted payments (RPs):** Dividends/stock buybacks are limited to 50% of net income. The RP covenant "falls away" if HCA is upgraded to investment grade ratings by both Moody's and S&P. Carve-outs include:
  - $75MM/year of stock buybacks from management (capped at $225MM);
  - After an initial public offering (IPO), HCA can pay a maximum 6% (of market cap) annual cash dividend.
- **Junior debt repurchases:** The company cannot buy back any legacy unsecured debt if secured leverage >5.25x and total leverage >7x.
- **Negative pledge:** The company cannot grant liens/collateral to other lenders, with a $100 million carve-out/basket.
- **Change of control (CoC):** Put at $101. The CoC provision "falls away" if HCA is upgraded to investment grade ratings by both Moody's and S&P.
- **EBITDA:** Addbacks for forecasted cost savings are capped at $150 million annually.

RETURN PROFILE / RELATIVE VALUE ANALYSIS

The risk-reward of the cash-pay second lien bond is attractive relative to the BB and B indices, hospital comps, and within the HCA capital structure as shown below:

	Yield-to-Worst YTW (%)	Spread	Leverage	Ratings
HCA 2nd lien cash pay due 2014 (recommend buy)	**9.125%**	**449**	**4.8x**	**B2/BB-**
Other HCA debt:				
HCA term loan B	7.650%	225	3.5x	Ba3/BB
HCA 2nd lien PIK due 2016	9.625%	499	4.8x	B2/BB-
HCA 6.5% unsecured bond due 2016	9.730%	509	6.5x	Caa1/B-
2nd largest hospital company				
Tenet Healthcare 9.875% unsecured bond due 2014	9.875%	524	6.9x	Caa1/ CCC+
Fixed-income indices:				
Barclay's BB index	7.030%	241	NA	BB
Barclay's B index	8.140%	353	NA	B
Barclay's healthcare index	8.820%	415	NA	NA

Source: Bloomberg/Trace.

COMMENTARY ON RELATIVE VALUE ANALYSIS

- Versus rating categories:
  - HCA's second lien cash-pay bond offers a higher yield than the single-B index, despite the defensiveness of the hospital sector and the second lien position (versus a largely unsecured index).
- Versus high yield healthcare comps:
  - HCA's second lien cash pay bond is a significantly better investment than Tenet Healthcare. Tenet's 9.875% bond only provides investors with 75 bps of incremental spread, which is not adequate incremental compensation for its lower credit rating, higher leverage, and lack of collateral.
- Versus the Barclays healthcare index:
  - Even though it is the largest hospital chain, HCA has a higher yield than the index. Many healthcare companies constitute the index, most of which do not enjoy HCA's leading market share. Furthermore, the index is predominantly comprised of unsecured bonds vs. the second lien priority of HCA's recommended bond.
- Versus other debt in the HCA capital structure:

- The second lien cash-pay bond offers a spread 224 bps wider than the Term Loan B, which is more than adequate compensation for only 1.3 turns of incremental leverage.
- The pari passu second lien PIK toggle bond coupon is 50 bps more than the cash pay bond. We do not believe the modest pickup in yield adequately compensates us for the longer maturity and the company's option not to pay cash interest.
- Finally, the legacy unsecured HCA bond spread is only 60 bps higher than the second lien cash-pay bond. We do not believe that 60 bps is adequate compensation for the lack of collateral and higher LTV (at 85%) versus our recommended bond at 63% LTV (based on the LBO purchase price).

APPENDIX 1: PEER GROUP ANALYSIS (2005)

$ in millions	HCA Inc.	Tenet Healthcare	Triad Hospitals	Universal Health Services	Community Health
Revenues	24,455	9,614	4,747	3,935	3,738
EBITDA	4,225	571	656	470	570
EBITDA margin	17.3%	5.9%	13.8%	11.9%	15.3%

Source: Companies' public 10-K filings.

THE FOLLOWING IS A POSTMORTEM ON THE HCA BOND DEAL

While the operational challenges (bad debt expense and other cost pressures) facing HCA were daunting at the time of the LBO, the company saw meaningfully better performance than expected. Although HCA's EBITDA margin contracted through 2008 (somewhat compounded by the GFC, as profitable elective surgeries saw a reduction in demand), by 2010, it had increased well above 2005's level (to 19.1%), as bad debt expense and labor costs moderated. Free cash flow also surpassed expectations, not only due to improved EBITDA but also lower-than-expected capex. By 2010, debt/EBITDA had declined to 4.8x versus our base case leverage of 5.4x.

So how did the bonds do? The 9.125% 2014 maturity cash-pay second lien was called at $104.56 in June 2011, which equates to an annualized return of 10% over the holding period. Over the same period, the Bloomberg Barclays high yield index returned 8.9%. Not only did this HCA bond outperform the benchmark by 110 bps/year, it also exhibited less volatility/lower risk. The bond troughed in March 2009 (the low point of the high yield bond market) at $77, while the high yield index troughed at $55.

After several dividends to its sponsors using cash raised in the high yield bond market, HCA ultimately IPO'd in 2011 at a lower TEV/EBITDA multiple (6.5x) than the take-private transaction. However, thanks to EBITDA growth and deleveraging, the sponsors ultimately realized an IRR of 26% on their investment (after a secondary stock offering in 2013).

HCA is an example of an LBO that worked out well for both creditors and shareholders.

As of the writing of this book in the spring of 2023, HCA is an investment grade–rated company (Baa3/BBB-) with a simple capital structure composed solely of unsecured bonds. Its leverage is below 4x debt/EBITDA, while its 9.4x TEV/EBITDA multiple suggests that the stock market holds hospitals in higher regard than at the time of the LBO (which took place at a multiple of 7.6x). But given its history of operating comfortably with high leverage, as well as the high yield bond and loan market's comfort with hospitals, a sell-off in its stock might stir interest in another leveraged buyout.

PART Three

Distressed Debt Investing

CHAPTER 14

Introduction to Distressed Debt Investing

In the prior section, you learned how to analyze a company from a credit perspective and how to identify attractive bond and loan investments in performing companies. As discussed in the introduction to this book, there are multiple career paths that make use of this skill set.

We are about to add another skill to your toolbox. So-called distressed debt investing involves analyzing companies heading toward, or already in, bankruptcy. For this type of investing, the seven-step process of credit analysis outlined in the prior section is necessary but not sufficient. What follows is a deep dive into the additional nuances, concepts, and analysis involved in successful distressed debt investing.

WHAT IS DISTRESSED DEBT INVESTING?

There is no single definition of what constitutes distressed debt. Many textbooks define any floating rate debt instrument trading below 85% of its face value or bond yielding more than 1,000 bps over Treasuries as distressed debt. I take an approach similar to that of former US Supreme Court Justice Potter Stewart, who in a 1964 case (Jacobellis v. Ohio)[i] famously stated that it was hard to define obscenity, but "I know it when I see it." If I believe a company is likely to restructure or experience a liquidity crisis, it falls into distressed debt investing.

HOW DO DISTRESSED DEBT INVESTORS DIFFER FROM PRIVATE EQUITY AND VALUE EQUITY INVESTORS?

When my students ask me this question, I answer with a story.

A company desperately needed access to liquidity. Three investors traveled to meet with management to consider an investment. The first investor worked for a private equity firm, the second at a value equity firm, and the last at a distressed debt firm.

On the way to meet with management, their car broke down. It was too late to get a mechanic, and there was no hotel in the area. However, there was a small farmhouse nearby, and they asked the farmer if they could stay there for the night. The farmer said he had room for two of them in the house but that one would have to sleep in the barn. The PE investor said he was fine sleeping in the barn, and everyone settled in for the night.

Two minutes later, there was a knock at the door. It was the PE investor. He said, "I was fine sleeping in the barn, but no one told me there was a cow in the barn.

I'm not going to sleep with a cow." The value equity investor called him a crybaby and volunteered to take his place.

Two minutes later, there was another knock on the door. It was the value equity investor. He said, "I was fine sleeping in the barn, I was fine sleeping with a cow, but no one told me there was a pig in the barn. I'm not going to sleep with a pig."

At this point, the distressed debt investor called them both crybabies and said he would sleep in the barn. Two minutes later, there was a knock on the door.

It was the cow and the pig.

The moral of this story is that distressed debt has the reputation of being an ugly asset class. Even the cow and the pig won't share a barn with the distressed investor. The popular press uses words like "vultures" or "grave dancers" in describing the asset class. I want to make it clear that it is not the *people* in the business who are ugly. That cannot be true. Just look at my book photo.

However, distressed debt investing does have an element of confrontation that some find unattractive. Such conflict is inevitable, as bankruptcy is usually a zero-sum game. Every class of creditors is fighting for their share of value from a company that tends to be worth less than the aggregate claims against it.

If you can get past its bad image, distressed debt is a great asset class. For instance, let's compare it to traditional private equity investing. Typically, the PE firm buys a company in an auction, usually in an all-or-nothing transaction. If another firm is willing to pay more, the losing PE firm has nothing to show for its work. Or suppose a strategic buyer (an existing company already in the business) shows up at the auction. In that case, it will be tough for the PE shop to compete because the strategic bidder can almost always pay more due to synergies (i.e., cost savings from combining the two businesses).

Now let's look at "distressed for control investing," where a distressed investor accumulates the company's debt at a significant discount to par, with the intent of converting this debt into equity through the bankruptcy process. Distressed for control investing has several advantages relative to gaining ownership through a traditional PE leveraged buyout:

- Unlike traditional PE, where the investment happens all at once, distressed investors build a position over time. If another investor starts to bid up the price, the distressed firm can sell out at a profit or hold as a minority owner. Distressed debt investors can profit from their work even if they get outbid, while the bidding process is all or nothing for traditional PE investors.
- Whereas a PE firm competes against strategic buyers, generally there is no competition from a strategic buyer in a distressed scenario. Strategic buyers don't have the trading capabilities to purchase distressed debt. Furthermore, it would be hard for management to convince the board to attempt an acquisition by buying the target's distressed debt. There would be too much uncertainty related to the bankruptcy process and the trading levels of the debt for the board to get comfortable with such a strategy. Additionally, certain loan documents prohibit the purchase of debt by a competitor. The lack of a strategic bid for distressed debt means fewer competitive bidders.
- Finally, in many distressed cases, the original investors are forced sellers, either because the company's credit ratings decline below a level permitted by the fund/account, or because the fund/account does not allow ownership of defaulted

debt. This forced selling dynamic creates a supply-demand imbalance and an attractive buying opportunity, in stark contrast to the aforementioned traditional private equity auction dynamic.

WHAT ARE OTHER DISTRESSED DEBT INVESTING STRATEGIES?

Although it's the best-known type of distressed debt investing, distressed for control is only one approach to investing in the asset class. In Chapter 19, "Making Money in Distressed Situations," we will discuss eight strategies employed by distressed debt investors (see Figure 14.1).

1) New financings for companies that can't access the traditional credit market
2) Spread-tightening trades
3) Distressed for control
4) Fundamental value plays
5) Capital structure arbitrage
6) Trade claims and vendor puts
7) Liquidations
8) Unique special situations trades

FIGURE 14.1 Distressed Debt Investing Strategies

Most, but not all, distressed investing takes place in the context of the underlying company's bankruptcy—either leading up to the filing, or during the bankruptcy proceeding. As a result, the next few chapters of the book will provide an overview of corporate bankruptcy from a credit investor's perspective. You don't need a law degree to invest in distressed debt, but you must be familiar with the way the bankruptcy process works, the types of conflicts that emerge, the manner in which value is distributed among creditors, and other aspects of a process that is not widely understood outside corporate law and distressed debt firms. If you end up working as a distressed debt investor and participating in a bankruptcy proceeding, it's likely you'll be sitting alongside one or more "par buyers," that is, investors who paid 100 cents on the dollar for bonds that your firm bought at steep discounts. These legacy holders are usually sticking with the investment because they believe their bonds are priced too low relative to the company's intrinsic valuation—but they are often not well-versed in the mechanics of bankruptcy, to their detriment.

As detailed in the following chapters, once a company enters bankruptcy, the allocation of value among various creditors is far from assured. A distressed debt investor must navigate this contentious process, recognizing that a good return is driven by both:

(i) The credit analysis discussed in the prior section; and
(ii) Successful legal arguments, astute assessment of other parties' motivations and limitations, and the ability to negotiate good deals with other creditors and creditor classes.

PART III—DISTRESSED DEBT INVESTING ROAD MAP

Figure 14.2 outlines the road map for Part III—Distressed Debt Investing.

Chapter 15	Bankruptcy 101 ■ An overview of the process of bankruptcy
Chapter 16	Bankruptcy Fights ■ A deep dive into the types of conflicts that arise in the bankruptcy process over valuation, avoidance actions, seniority/subordination, and other legal issues
Chapter 17	How Subordination Works in Bankruptcy ■ A primer on types of subordination (time, contractual, and structural) and how these play out in bankruptcy, including a discussion of substantive consolidation ("subcon")
Chapter 18	Liability Management and Creditor-on-Creditor Violence ■ A series of real-life case studies that illustrates the ways in which creditors disadvantage each other in their attempt to capture value
Chapter 19	Making Money in Distressed Situations ■ A discussion of strategies used by distressed investors to make money for their investors

FIGURE 14.2 Distressed Debt Investing Road Map

By the time you've finished this section, you will have a working knowledge of the bankruptcy process, associated conflicts, and ways in which your position in the capital structure can win or lose in court and outside of it. As an added bonus, the war stories will give you an inside view of the job of a distressed debt investor. And even if you are not planning on this career path, if you are a "par" buyer of credit, it is critical to understand what happens to the loans and bonds issued by healthy companies if they become distressed. Even par buyers end up with the occasional bankruptcy in their portfolios. Thinking like a distressed debt investor can help you navigate a challenged credit—and give you the tools you need to understand when you should sell, versus when the position justifies the long slog through bankruptcy outlined in the following chapters.

NOTE

i. Ward, Artemus. (2009) "Potter Stewart." The First Amendment Encyclopedia. mtsu.edu/first-amendment/article/1359/potter-stewart.

CHAPTER 15

Bankruptcy 101

Before you can make distressed debt investing recommendations, you must familiarize yourself with the corporate bankruptcy process and learn to identify situations in which retaining legal counsel is necessary. The bankruptcy code is extraordinarily complex, and this book focuses on the elements most relevant to an investor. This chapter provides a bankruptcy primer, and the following chapters will address more advanced issues. A couple of caveats to start: first, I have intentionally simplified some concepts. And second, bankruptcy judges are not obligated to follow a strict interpretation of the bankruptcy code because bankruptcy courts enjoy broad "equitable powers" to achieve a fair outcome. This dynamic means it is not always possible to predict the outcome of a bankruptcy proceeding, which incentivizes the various creditor classes to negotiate a resolution rather than leave it to a judge.

WHY DO COMPANIES FILE FOR BANKRUPTCY?

Corporations generally file for bankruptcy for one of three reasons, summarized in Figure 15.1.

1. A liquidity crisis
2. An unsustainable capital structure
3. The need to resolve litigation

FIGURE 15.1 Why Companies File for Bankruptcy

1. *A liquidity crisis:* A company might face a liquidity squeeze, such as an impending debt maturity that cannot be refinanced, or operational cash burn that exceeds liquidity sources. An example of this is Toys R Us, which was pushed into bankruptcy in the fall of 2017 when its vendors pulled support ahead of the holiday season.
2. *An unsustainable capital structure (i.e., too much debt):* This is sometimes referred to as a company's capital structure becoming "upside down"; its debt exceeds the value of the entire company. As discussed in Chapter 9, it is not unusual for a company's TEV to fall below the value of its debt for a period of time, for example during a cyclical downturn. In some cases, this situation resolves itself as the company returns to profitability. However, a bankruptcy filing may be necessary to resize the balance sheet for the underlying business. In addition to a sharp decline in profitability, triggers for an upside-down capital structure include overpaying for a debt-financed acquisition or an LBO undertaken in

peak-cycle conditions. Many of the pre-GFC LBOs that went bankrupt fall into this category, including TXU and Caesars.

3. *The need to resolve litigation:* Litigation can lead to large cash payments and liquidity issues. Legal claims can overwhelm a business due to the associated costs and required management attention, which is diverted from day-to-day operations. Bankruptcy provides an organized forum to settle or in some cases expunge legal claims, as well as structural features that make this easier than managing hundreds or thousands of separate litigations. For example, companies such as W.R. Grace and Owens Corning with massive asbestos claims and pharmaceutical companies such as Mallinckrodt that were mired in opioid-related claims used Chapter 11 to work through their legal issues.

WHAT ARE THE TYPES OF BANKRUPTCY FILINGS?

There are two types of bankruptcies in the US: Chapter 7 and Chapter 11 (see Figure 15.2). Chapter 7 is relatively straightforward; the court appoints a trustee to liquidate the company. There is no attempt to turn around the business and exit bankruptcy as a going concern. A Chapter 11 bankruptcy gives the company time and a process to exit bankruptcy with a viable business and capital structure.

Type	Description
Chapter 7	Liquidation of the business
Chapter 11	Reorganization of the business

FIGURE 15.2 Chapter 7 and 11 Comparison

This book will concentrate on the Chapter 11 process, as most large companies do not file for Chapter 7. Note that some companies file for Chapter 11 but fail to exit, at which point the case either converts to a Chapter 7 or the company effectively liquidates in Chapter 11.

WHAT IS THE CHAPTER 11 BANKRUPTCY PROCESS?

Chapter 11 is a unique structure created and perfected in the United States. While other restructuring/insolvency regimes can be navigated successfully by skillful practitioners, they tend to be less effective than the US at preserving businesses as going concerns, as Chapter 11 does. Many countries have adopted bankruptcy regimes similar to Chapter 11 in recent years, but Chapter 11 remains the bellwether bankruptcy regime. This book focuses on the US bankruptcy code.

Most Chapter 11 bankruptcy cases are voluntary, meaning the company chooses whether and when to file for bankruptcy. In rare cases, three or more creditors might attempt to place a company into bankruptcy through an involuntary petition with the courts. If the company believes these creditors will be successful, it will, in most instances, file itself to control the jurisdiction in which the case will be heard. While it might seem logical that a company would file in the district in which it's domiciled (e.g., a Nashville-based company would file in the Middle District of Tennessee), that is rarely the case for large bankruptcies. In practice, debtors file most often in one of three bankruptcy courts:

- Delaware;
- The Southern District of New York; and
- The Southern District of Texas.

Generally, these courts are more sophisticated (i.e., the judges are well versed in the corporate bankruptcy code) and predictable, and thus more expedient. The only requirement on filing jurisdiction is that at least one subsidiary or holding company has its incorporation, headquarters, or principal assets there. This flexibility permits forum shopping (i.e., filing in a court district that might lead to a better outcome for the debtor).

Once the company files, it is referred to as the "debtor" or "debtor in possession," and those with claims against the company are referred to as "creditors."

Chapter 11 is a debtor-in-possession regime, meaning that the existing board of directors and management team continue to run the day-to-day business. However, any action not undertaken in the ordinary course of business must be approved by the court, such as significant asset sales. A board of directors normally has a fiduciary duty to maximize the value of the company for the benefit of its shareholders. Once a company is insolvent (or in the zone of insolvency), the board still has a duty to maximize the value of the company, but with a focus on the impact of its actions on creditors without regard to shareholder benefit. The board's execution of its new fiduciary duty does not always happen smoothly; creditors frequently argue in court that the board is not prioritizing their interests. This is a common tension in LBO Chapter 11s, as LBO'd companies often appoint partners or employees of the PE sponsor to the company's board.

The three types of voluntary Chapter 11 filings are summarized in Figure 15.3.

Type	Description	Typical Time in Bankruptcy
Prepackaged	Fully negotiated pre-filing	Short (45–90 days)
Prearranged	Partially negotiated pre-filing	Modest (in between)
Traditional (freefall)	Nothing negotiated pre-filing	Long (1.5–3+ years)

FIGURE 15.3 Types of Chapter 11 Cases

In a prepackaged bankruptcy (or pre-pack), a deal has been negotiated with enough creditor votes in hand (the solicitation of which occurred prior to filing) to be approved by the court. This type of bankruptcy is structured to minimize the time in Chapter 11. A pre-pack does not usually address operational issues but rather is a relatively simple balance sheet restructuring that leaves nonfinancial creditors unimpaired (vendors, landlords, etc.).

A prearranged filing is similar to a pre-pack, with a deal in principle that has the support of some major creditors. The key difference is that the plan does not have enough votes to ensure approval. A prearranged filing requires solicitation of votes in bankruptcy, which results in a longer process, and at times renegotiation of some of the terms of the plan to get enough creditors on board. Over the last several years, prearranged bankruptcies have become more common, along with restructuring support agreements (RSAs). The RSA seeks to unite key creditor constituencies with the debtor around a proposed deal framework, thereby limiting the time spent in Chapter 11 negotiating with creditors. By reducing the time in Chapter 11, the debtor mitigates disruption to operations (e.g., loss of employees, customers, or suppliers), destruction of value, and high professional, legal, and advisory fees typically associated with lengthy cases.

This may make it sound like the choice to pursue a pre-pack or prearranged bankruptcy is an obvious one. However, these are still the exception, not the rule. Most bankruptcies are incredibly contentious, and there is no framework for how creditors will fare at the outset or road map for emergence. Traditional "freefall" bankruptcies take significantly more time; a large, complex Chapter 11 can easily take two to three years.

Figure 15.4 summarizes the typical steps in a traditional Chapter 11 bankruptcy.

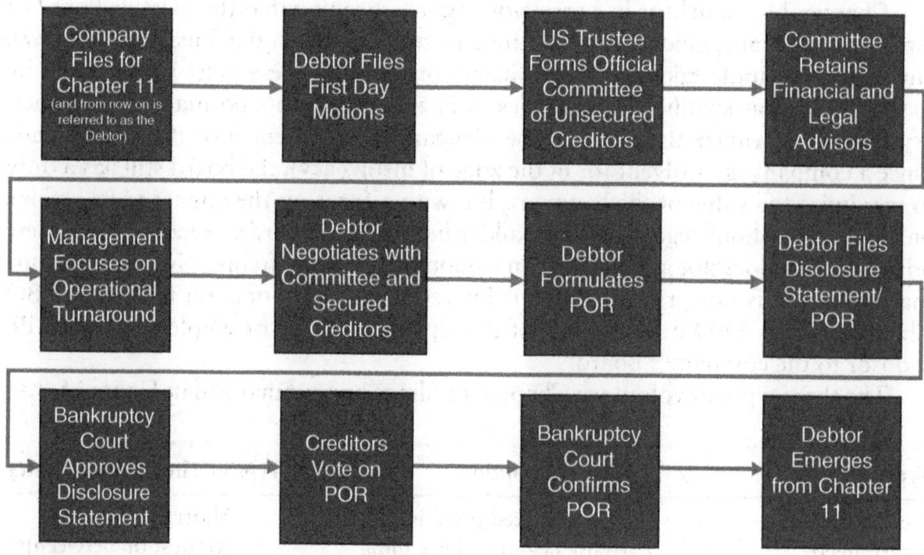

FIGURE 15.4 Chapter 11 Bankruptcy Steps

THE BANKRUPTCY PROCESS, DISTILLED

I will focus on several aspects of the bankruptcy process, summarized in Figure 15.5. These are not linear but rather take place on parallel paths.

1. First day motions
2. Formation of creditor committees
3. Operational improvements
4. Plan of reorganization (POR) formulation
5. Negotiations/vote on POR
6. Confirmation of POR
7. Emergence

FIGURE 15.5 Key Aspects of the Bankruptcy Process

FIRST DAY MOTIONS

The bankruptcy code provides for an "automatic stay," which is an injunction that stops lawsuits, foreclosures, garnishments, and all collection activity. This is basically a time-out that allows the debtor time to focus on fixing the problems that led to the filing so that it can put together a plan of reorganization (POR) and emerge from bankruptcy. The debtor enjoys the exclusive right to propose and file the POR within the first 120 days of the bankruptcy filing, a period routinely extended by the bankruptcy court, particularly for larger companies. The automatic stay and exclusivity give the company the opportunity to remain in control of its fate rather than forcing it to address competing plans put forward by creditors.

Upon filing, the debtor's counsel seeks several orders with the court to allow the company to operate with minimal disruption to its business. Figure 15.6 shows examples of first-day motions.

- Pay pre-petition (i.e., incurred before the company filed) employee wages.
- Retain bankruptcy professionals (lawyers and financial advisers).
- Use secured creditors' cash collateral (allows the company to use the cash in its bank accounts even if it is pledged to certain lenders).
- Seek debtor-in-possession (DIP) financing.

FIGURE 15.6 Examples of First-Day Motions

DIP financing

Depending on the company's cash needs, a hearing related to post-petition (i.e., after filing) financing will be heard on the first day or in the coming weeks. One of the most critical components of the first-day motions is approval of the company's DIP loan, a vital new source of liquidity that permits the company to operate in bankruptcy. To entice lenders to provide financing to a bankrupt company, DIPs are typically super senior secured claims, meaning that upon emergence from bankruptcy or liquidation they have the highest priority of repayment, even ahead of pre-petition secured lenders.

Because of their super-priority status, DIP facilities effectively "prime," that is, subordinate, pre-petition secured lenders. However, the bankruptcy code only allows a DIP loan to prime a pre-petition secured creditor if that secured creditor is over-collateralized (that is, the value of the collateral exceeds the value of the loan by at least the value of the DIP loan). The purpose of this rule is to protect the pre-petition secured creditors' right to their collateral. To avoid what is referred to as a "priming fight," it is common for pre-petition senior secured creditors to provide the DIP financing.

DIP lending usually provides a great risk-adjusted return, as the lender gets a premium yield on a loan with low risk of impairment, given its super-priority status, as compensation for dealing with the bankruptcy process.

FORMATION OF COMMITTEES

Shortly after the filing, various creditor committees are formed, including the Official Committee of Unsecured Creditors (UCC). The UCC is usually a diverse group including senior unsecured bondholders, financial institutions, vendors, and landlords, and, if the debtor has an underfunded pension, the Pension Benefit Guaranty Corp (PBGC). A creditor committee hires its own lawyers and financial advisors (FAs). During the bankruptcy proceeding, the committee is generally very involved in negotiating with the debtor and its counsel on the POR, with the goal of maximizing the consideration received by this class of creditors. The professional fees incurred by the UCC are reimbursed by the debtor, and its members have a fiduciary duty to maximize unsecured creditor recovery.

In complex bankruptcies, with multiple classes of unsecured creditors who have different types of claims and interests, the court could allow multiple committees. For example, there might be one official committee representing general unsecured creditors, and another representing subordinated bondholders.

In addition, ad hoc committees are frequently formed. These committees are not court-approved or court-appointed, and do not have the same duties as the formal UCC. In contrast to the UCC and other official committees, the ad hoc committee's fee reimbursement is not guaranteed, and its members have no fiduciary duty to the broader creditor class. Occasionally an ad hoc equity committee forms to argue that there is enough value for the pre-petition shareholders to receive some recovery in the plan. Very infrequently, there is enough enterprise value for the court to appoint an official shareholder committee. One example is the General Growth Properties (GGP) bankruptcy in 2009, which was triggered by the shutdown of the commercial mortgage-backed securities (CMBS) market during the GFC. When GGP could not roll over its CMBS maturities, the ensuing liquidity crisis pushed the company into default. However, its underlying operations were sound and rebounded quickly out of the depths of the GFC as customers returned to malls. The GGP shareholders received \$5.2 billion in equity, as the court acknowledged the company's fundamental solvency.[i]

FIXING OPERATIONAL PROBLEMS, INCLUDING COST-CUTTING

During the bankruptcy process, company management is working on two projects in addition to running the day-to-day business:

(i) Improving its operations, including cost-cutting; and
(ii) Formulating the POR to restructure the balance sheet.

It is much easier to fix the operational issues of a business in Chapter 11 because bankruptcy allows the debtor to reduce the payments associated with fixed contracts that cannot be discharged or renegotiated outside of bankruptcy. Two of the most commonly negotiated contracts are leases and union contracts.

For example, outside bankruptcy, a retailer cannot stop paying long-term leases, even if the underlying stores are not profitable, without negotiating with each landlord individually. However, Section 365 of the Bankruptcy Code gives the debtor 120 days to assume or reject commercial leases of real property. This assumption/rejection window can be extended 90 days by court order. If the debtor rejects a lease, section 502(b)(6) of the code limits the landlord's claim against the estate to the greater of one year's rent or 15 percent of the rent of the remaining term of the lease, not to exceed three years. Section 365 provides both a means for the debtor to extricate itself from an unprofitable lease at a significantly reduced claim and a "stick" (the threat of rejection) for use in negotiating better lease terms. For example, when Tops Markets, an upstate New York grocery chain, filed for bankruptcy in 2018, it closed 10 unprofitable stores[ii] and renegotiated its leases on significantly more, which improved profitability.

Furthermore, if any of the leases are "in the money," meaning the company's rent payment is below market for a particular store location, the company can monetize that value by assuming the lease and auctioning off the rights to another company. This would not be possible outside of bankruptcy, as most leases have a non-assignability clause.

Bankruptcy also makes it significantly easier for a company to renegotiate union contracts under Section 1113 of the code. During the GFC, auto manufacturers and suppliers relied on this provision to right-size their cost structures, which was critical to improved profitability upon emergence from bankruptcy.

FORMULATION OF A PLAN OF REORGANIZATION (POR)

The POR outlines how the debtor plans to restructure its business, including discharging debt. Its most critical output is the recovery allocated to each class of claims upon exit. The recovery can come in several forms, or a combination: cash, take-back debt, equity, warrants, or nothing.

Although exclusivity gives the debtor the right to put forward a POR, it does not formulate the plan in a vacuum; rather, it negotiates with secured creditors, the UCC, and the ad hoc committees before submitting a plan. In most cases, the debtor will be given extensions to its exclusivity period as long as the court believes the debtor is making a good faith effort to develop a plan. In the rare case in which a judge does not extend exclusivity, the UCC or individual creditors can submit their own competing POR.

NEGOTIATIONS/VOTE ON POR

Once the POR is formulated, it must be voted on by creditors. To hold a vote the plan proponent must draft a "disclosure statement," a legal document that provides adequate information to enable creditors to decide whether to approve or reject the plan. The disclosure statement must include a classification of claims and specify how each class of claims will be treated. The Bankruptcy Court must approve the disclosure statement before the debtor can begin to solicit the required votes to accept the plan.

The plan places each creditor into a voting class based on repayment priority. Generally, a POR has five broad categories of claims, some of which might have more than one voting class. For instance, secured creditors could have multiple classes based on differences in their underlying collateral, or the unsecured claim pool might have separate classes for subordinated debt or debt with different guarantors. Figure 15.7 summarizes the five claim categories in descending order of priority.

1. Administrative claims
2. Other priority claims
3. Secured claims
4. General unsecured claims (GUC)
5. Equity

FIGURE 15.7 Voting Classes in Order of Priority

1. **Administrative claims.** This class includes all post-petition claims arising after the company filed for bankruptcy, such as legal and other professional advisory fees and amounts owed to vendors that shipped products to the company after filing. For a company to exit bankruptcy, all administrative claims must be paid in full in cash. Pre-petition vendor or trade claims for products shipped before the filing are generally considered unsecured claims. However, vendors can petition the court to have any claims related to products shipped 20 or fewer days before the filing date to be classified as reclamation, that is, to treat their claims as if they originated during the insolvency period. If the court approves, these become administrative claims.
2. **Other priority claims.** This class includes wages, salaries, vacation pay, sick leave pay, commissions, and severance earned up to 180 days before or after the business closed or filed for bankruptcy and must also receive payment in full under the plan.
3. **Secured claims.** A secured creditor is entitled to a recovery of principal and pre- and post-petition accrued interest up to the value of its collateral before any recovery is allocated to constituents without a secured claim on this collateral. If a company pledged all its tangible and intangible assets to its secured lenders, and those lenders are impaired by even one penny, then all other claims would be entitled to nothing. If secured lenders are only collateralized by a portion of the assets, and their collateral value is insufficient to pay them in full, the remainder is called a deficiency claim, which is classified as a general unsecured claim. In some cases, secured debt is non-recourse, meaning its claim is limited to its collateral. This type of secured debt only receives recovery value from its collateral and is not allowed a deficiency claim.
4. **General unsecured claims.** This class includes all creditors except administrative, priority, and secured claims: pre-petition trade claims, accrued liabilities, underfunded pensions, and unsecured debt. Different seniorities of unsecured claims are separately classified; for example, subordinated unsecured debt is classified separately from senior unsecured debt.

Unlike secured debt, unsecured claims are generally not entitled to post-petition interest, with two exceptions:

- If the POR shows that the entity is solvent without impairment of any class of creditors, resulting in a recovery to the equity; or
- If post-petition interest is recovered through subordination turnover, covered in Chapter 17.

5. **Equity.** If value remains after full repayment of the unsecured claim pool, preferred stockholders are entitled to a recovery to the extent of their liquidation preference before any recovery to common equity. Common equity is entitled to the residual after payment of all other claims.

Any class not paid out in full (i.e., impaired) is entitled to vote on the POR. If a class is unimpaired, it does not vote. A creditor deemed unimpaired can receive new debt instruments as consideration instead of cash. However, disagreements about the value of the new debt and whether the claim is genuinely unimpaired are common. Compare a scenario in which a $100 million senior secured term loan is paid out in cash upon exit from bankruptcy versus receiving $100 million of new secured debt. If the terms of the new debt are below market, it would trade at a discount to par. For example, if the risk profile of the company after emergence implies a 10% market yield, but the proposed debt in the POR has a 7% coupon, the new debt would be marked down in price to yield 10%. (Refer back to Chapter 3 for a primer on yield and price.) The secured lenders would argue that their claim is impaired as the new debt is not worth par because of its below-market terms.

This is just one of many examples of bankruptcy fights that take place as the POR is being formulated. The debtor, its counsel, and its financial advisors may argue that a certain class of creditors, typically secured lenders, is unimpaired to prevent it from voting on the POR, while the senior secured lenders and their advisors argue the opposite. This is commonly referred to as the debtor trying to "cram up" the lenders. Most of the time, this will be a negotiation, and terms will be tweaked to get a consensual deal—but if an agreement cannot be reached, the judge settles it in court. The code says that reinstated debt must be the "indubitable equivalent"—a term subject to interpretation—to its secured claim. If the judge rules in favor of the debtor, the secured creditors are stuck with a below-market debt instrument.

Figure 15.8 summarizes the conditions under Section 1126(c) of the code in which a class of claims is deemed to accept a POR.

1. At least two-thirds in amount vote in favor; <u>and</u>
2. At least one-half in number (of those who vote) vote in favor.

FIGURE 15.8 Two Conditions for a Class of Creditors to Accept the POR

For instance, if the senior unsecured class has claims of $1 billion and there are 500 individual creditors, holders of at least $666.7 million of the claims <u>and</u> more than 250 creditors must accept the plan (assuming all 500 creditors vote). Otherwise, that class is a dissenting class.

If a class of creditors votes against the plan, the court can "cram it down," which means approving the plan despite a rejecting class. The ability of the court to support a plan despite a dissenting class is critical to the process. Otherwise, it would be nearly impossible for a company to exit bankruptcy, as any creditor class with a low or zero recovery would have tremendous hold-out power.

Enforcement of a cram-down must meet two conditions, outlined in Figure 15.9.

1. At least one impaired class has voted to accept the plan; and
2. The court finds that the plan does not "discriminate unfairly" and is "fair and equitable." This means the plan does not violate the "absolute priority" rule, which mandates that if a class is getting crammed down, no class beneath it can receive any recovery.

FIGURE 15.9 Two Conditions for a Class of Creditors to Accept the POR

In my experience, a junior claim legally entitled to zero recovery based on the absolute priority rule might receive a "tip" for voting for the plan, with cram-down as the threat if they don't come along. It is common for junior creditors to receive a fractional recovery (i.e., a few cents on the dollar) even when more senior creditors are impaired; the modest payout is a small price to eliminate their nuisance/hold-out value.

Not all Chapter 11 bankruptcies result in an approved POR. Two alternatives are:

- If the company cannot access liquidity to fund the administrative claims, such as bankruptcy lawyers and advisors, the case is usually converted to a Chapter 7 liquidation, in which a trustee is assigned to liquidate the assets. If the value of the assets is insufficient to pay all the post-petition expenses and liabilities incurred, the case is considered "administratively insolvent."
- In certain situations, the best way to maximize recoveries for all creditors is to sell the business rather than reorganize. A debtor can pursue a sale of the company under Section 363 of the bankruptcy code. Section 363 asset sales can be controversial, especially if the secured lenders are credit-bidding, as many argue the debtor is circumventing the standard creditor voting process. The next chapter, "Bankruptcy Fights," discusses 363 sales in more detail.

CONFIRMATION

The last step in the bankruptcy process is the bankruptcy court's approval of the plan, referred to as confirmation. If the plan is consensual, meaning all impaired classes voted in favor, then confirmation is just a logistical hurdle that satisfies the following confirmation standards:

- The court must establish "plan feasibility," i.e., that the debtor's business plan is credible and can reasonably support its post-bankruptcy capital structure.
- If any individual creditor objects to the plan, then the plan must also pass the "best interest of creditors test," which requires that dissenting creditors receive at least as much value (in present value terms) as if the business were liquidated. In practice this is relatively easy to demonstrate, as a going concern is typically worth substantially more than liquidation value, and a liquidation often triggers and crystallizes additional claims.

EMERGENCE

Once the court confirms the plan, it sets the plan effective date, on which the company exits bankruptcy as a new legal entity (commonly referred to as "NewCo").

While every plan is different, it is common for pre-petition equity to be wiped out, and some of the debt converted into NewCo equity, which permits the company to exit bankruptcy with a dramatically deleveraged balance sheet. The new equity is commonly referred to as "reorg equity," and the debt converted to equity is referred to as the fulcrum security. The way in which the value of the company is allocated among various classes of creditors and (in rare cases) pre-petition shareholders, along with valuation fights, will be discussed in more detail in the next chapter.

SUMMARY OF BENEFITS AND COSTS OF CHAPTER 11

Chapter 11 can be a very effective way for a business to turn around its operations and right-size and restructure its liabilities in an organized forum. Its key benefits are summarized in Figure 15.10.

1. The automatic stay gives the company time to address its operational and balance sheet issues.
2. Trade support is maintained, as after filing, any vendor payables receive administrative status.
3. New financing can be raised through a DIP facility.
4. Cessation of interest payments on unsecured debt moderates cash burn.
5. It is easier to cut costs as bankruptcy permits rejection of executory contracts and facilitates renegotiation of collective bargaining agreements.
6. The balance sheet can be right-sized by discharging debt.

FIGURE 15.10 Benefits of Chapter 11

However, there are costs to bankruptcy. The bankruptcy process and its associated fights and litigation involve business interruption, value destruction, and significant professional expenses. On balance, the benefits typically outweigh the costs for distressed debt investors who purchased debt at discounted prices, as long as they correctly accounted for the impact of these costs and fees on the total enterprise value of the company.

CHAPTER CONCLUSION

The bankruptcy process may sound straightforward based on the steps outlined above. In some cases, a POR is quickly and consensually obtained, driven by a valuation that makes sense to the majority of creditors. But this is by no means typical, as you will learn in the following chapters. The next chapter will introduce you to the most typical bankruptcy battles—along with the parties involved in fighting them.

NOTES

i. Jonas, Ilaina. (October 21, 2010). "General Growth Cleared to Exit Bankruptcy." Reuters. https://www.reuters.com/article/us-generalgrowth-idUSTRE69K41320101022.
ii. Gorbman, Randy. (November 8. 2018). "Bankruptcy Reorganization Approved for Tops Markets." WBFO-FM. https://www.wbfo.org/business-economy/2018-11-08/bankruptcy-reorganization-approved-for-tops-markets.

CHAPTER 16

Bankruptcy Fights

Distressed debt investing breeds conflict. In 2002, the *Wall Street Journal* published an article titled "Chaim Fortgang Defended Creditors, But Offended Many of His Colleagues," which highlights this unavoidable aspect of restructurings:

> *Bankruptcy lawyers are a notoriously combative bunch. But many in the profession say Chaim J. Fortgang is in a class all by himself. During his 30-year career as one of the nation's preeminent corporate bankruptcy attorneys, he has hurled food at adversaries. He has called the judgment of a federal bankruptcy trustee "moronic." He even once threatened to pull out a rival lawyer's tongue, that lawyer says.*[i]

Chaim Fortgang was already a legend when I started in the business. He was born in 1947 in a displaced persons camp in Bensheim, Germany. These camps were established after World War II, primarily for refugees from Eastern Europe and the former inmates of the Nazi concentration camps. His family immigrated to America when Chaim was five months old, where they settled in a working-class, Orthodox Jewish section of Brooklyn. Chaim thrived playing pick-up basketball despite being only 5 feet 8 inches tall. He went to Brooklyn College at night and graduated in just two and a half years. Chaim's raw intelligence, combined with street smarts honed in working-class Brooklyn, would become his competitive advantage in business.

Chaim graduated first in his New York University Law School class. He was recruited to work at the prestigious law firm Wachtell, Lipton, Rosen & Katz, and five years later, he became a partner at the age of 29. Chaim spent 30 years at Wachtell building and running the corporate bankruptcy practice. However, after a falling out with other partners over his aggressive style, Chaim left the firm. He did a temporary stint as a partner at the distressed debt hedge fund Fortress Capital and then, in 2005, put out his own shingle as an independent advisor. Silver Point immediately negotiated a retention agreement with Chaim that gave us 24/6 access to him. For several years he even shared office space with us, and we became his largest and most important client.

Over the next 20 years, I, or a member of my team, brainstormed with Chaim virtually every day on our restructuring cases. Chaim's best-in-class legal advice, coupled with our willingness to drive restructuring situations, positioned us for better outcomes.

Chaim was not only a brilliant attorney but also a real character. He wore expensive Brioni suits with $500 silk ties, but I often wondered why he bothered as his shirttails were always hanging out of the suit, which was so wrinkled that

I assumed he slept in it. His expensive suits were counter to how Chaim lived his life. He devoted an inordinate amount of his time and income to causes that he felt were important. He lived in a modest house in Brooklyn, which he bought when he was a young attorney, even though most of his peers were living in multimillion-dollar condos in New York City or mansions in Greenwich, Connecticut.

Chaim was always available except for the 24 hours between sunset on Fridays and Saturdays. An Orthodox Jew, he spent the Sabbath attending service and teaching at his temple. No matter what bankruptcy case he was involved in, he never violated the Sabbath. Many judges had to postpone emergency court hearings to accommodate Chaim's religious beliefs. He more than made up for those lost hours the other six days of the week; a chronic insomniac, Chaim often worked 16–20 hours daily. I found this out the hard way, when I sent Chaim a quick email at 2 a.m. on a Sunday after a late night out. The email, in reference to a motion we needed to file in the Delphi bankruptcy, ended with, "We can discuss on Monday morning." Seconds later, my phone rang, and Chaim jumped right in to give me his views. It was my mistake to send an email at that hour and subsequently answer my phone. I did, however, get off the phone several hours later with a better understanding of some of the complex issues we needed to address.

Chaim wasn't just an expert in every aspect of the bankruptcy code; he was witty, entertaining, and philosophical. When I saw him talking to himself and asked, "Chaim, who are you talking to?" he replied, without hesitation, "To the smartest person I know." Chaim liked to say that there are two kinds of people in this world (and only two kinds): (i) idiots who know they're idiots and (ii) idiots who don't know they're idiots. What he meant by this: type (i) understands his or her limitations and has the humility to be successful, while type (ii) is arrogant. Often, he would ask me which type of person someone was before meeting them. This could get awkward. Once, when we were sitting in bankruptcy court, the CFO of the bankrupt company walked in, and Chaim said in what he thought was a whisper but wasn't, "Does he know he's an idiot?"

Chaim was a tough guy who had no issues tearing an adversary apart and dropping the F-bomb. At the same time, he was incredibly respectful to young professionals early in their careers, and he did not tolerate bullying of younger employees. Once I asked, "Why are you so abrasive to everyone but junior lawyers and analysts?" He told me, "If I call you an idiot, it won't impact your self-esteem and confidence, and if you are getting too cocky, I'm doing you a favor. However, people early in their careers need nurturing." While my $500-hour shrink might disagree with this assessment of my resilience, I admired Chaim greatly. He didn't hesitate to put billionaire "masters of the universe" in their place and fight with the best legal minds in the world, but he never treated anyone more vulnerable than him in that manner.

Chaim loved mentoring and teaching young lawyers and restructuring professionals. He regularly participated in panel discussions for my Distressed Value Investing class at Columbia Business School. He could entertain my students for hours with war stories. One of his favorite deals was the 1996 Marvel Entertainment Bankruptcy. This case had a who's who of difficult personalities, including Ron Perelman (who owned the bankrupted Marvel), Carl Icahn (who then launched a hostile takeover of Marvel), Ike Perlmutter, and Avi Arad (two relatively unknown businesspeople who outsmarted them both). In the middle of all this was Chaim Fortgang, counsel to the senior unsecured creditor committee, playing one against the other to maximize value for creditors. For those interested in Marvel's bankruptcy and Chaim's role in this restructuring, a must-read is *Comic Wars: Marvel's Battle for Survival* by Dan Raviv.

Another of Chaim's favorite stories was about Trump's first casino restructuring in 1990. Trump showed up late to a meeting from a black-tie party and asked, "How we doing?" Chaim responded, "We are doing fine. You are the one who needs to be worrying." When asked about the incident by a *Wall Street Journal* reporter, Trump recalls that he told Chaim that he "doesn't worry about anything," adding that he found Chaim to be a "great guy."[ii] In another article published in *American Banker*, Trump is quoted as saying, "When he [Chaim] spoke, everyone listened."[iii] It was said that Chaim was the only person who could put Trump in his place.

It was a huge blow professionally and personally when Chaim confided in 2020 that he had been diagnosed with stage four cancer.

Over the next year and a half, Chaim was Chaim; he worked relentlessly for his clients and was available except for the Sabbath and chemotherapy treatments. The Friday before he died, we discussed the AeroMexico case on the phone. I asked him how he was doing, and he said, "Great, but the end is very near." His religious faith kept him strong, and he would go when God wanted him to go. Monday, October 11, 2021, Chaim's daughter called to tell us that he had passed away peacefully in his sleep and that Chaim wanted her to contact Silver Point immediately as he did not want anyone to think he was not returning their calls. I miss Chaim every day, not just for his unmatched legal analysis but as a friend and mentor.

I dedicate this chapter, "Bankruptcy Fights," to Chaim. If Chaim were still around for me to tell him that, he would respond, "F*** you, Michael. You should dedicate your entire book to me. No, you should dedicate your entire life to me." But that was just his tough guy act, and he would actually be saying, "I love you and my time working with the team at Silver Point." In tribute to Chaim and in honor of his many victories in bankruptcy court, let's discuss bankruptcy fights!

BANKRUPTCY FIGHTS

It is only a mild exaggeration to say that in Chapter 11 proceedings, everything is a fight. The sources of conflict can range from trivial (e.g., the time and location of the first creditors' meeting) to critical (e.g., determining the recoveries for each class of claims). Even hiring advisors and counsel can be an ordeal—every firm has its favorites. I will focus on the most substantial fights/negotiations outlined in Figure 16.1.

- Valuation fights
- Credit bids and 363 asset sale process
- Avoidance actions
  - Preferences
  - Fraudulent conveyances
- Equitable subordination
- Lender liability claims
- Substantive consolidation (addressed in Chapter 17)

FIGURE 16.1 Bankruptcy Fights

VALUATION FIGHTS

The intent of a bankruptcy proceeding is to determine the valuation of the company and allocate that value among the creditor classes (and, in rare circumstances, to the pre-petition equity owners), a process that takes place in court and outside of it (in negotiations among creditor classes). There is typically a wide range of valuation estimates going into bankruptcy, and the process narrows that range to one number upon emergence: the plan value, which is voted on by all creditors deemed impaired (i.e., not receiving 100% of their pre-bankruptcy claim). If any portion of their recovery comes in the form of equity in the post-emergence company, more senior creditors would like to strike as low a valuation as possible because this gives their class a larger portion of the company's total value. The most junior creditors (e.g., subordinated bondholders) will argue for as high a valuation as possible to ensure their class gets at least some recovery.

Let's use a hypothetical example to illustrate this. Pasta manufacturer David's Rigatoni Company is in bankruptcy. Creditor claims are listed in Figure 16.2.

	Creditor Claims ($MM)
DIP Financing and Other Administrative and Priority Claims	$50
First Lien Secured Debt	100
Total DIP / Admin Claims and First Lien Debt	150
Senior Unsecured Debt	200
Total DIP / Admin Claims / Senior Unsecured Debt	350
Subordinated Unsecured Claims	400
Total Claims	$750

FIGURE 16.2 Creditor Claims

On emergence from bankruptcy, the company has a commitment for $150MM of "exit financing," the proceeds of which will pay off the DIP, administrative claims, and the first lien term loan fully, in cash. "OldCo" equity will be wiped out, and creditor classes beneath the first lien will receive their recovery in equity in "NewCo." If the company's enterprise value is set by the bankruptcy court at $300MM, then the senior unsecured debt would be considered the fulcrum security. Think of the concept of a fulcrum, which is a pivot point; in bankruptcy, the fulcrum is the position in the capital structure where claims no longer receive 100% recovery. In other words, the fulcrum security is entitled to some recovery but not a full recovery—the value "runs out" before the fulcrum claim recovers par. In the above example, the senior unsecured debt is the fulcrum, receiving all of NewCo's equity. It is impaired with a recovery of 75% of the claim amount. Recoveries based on a $300MM enterprise value are shown in Figure 16.3.

	Recoveries ($MM)
David's Rigatoni Company's Enterprise Value	$300
Less Amount of Value Allocated to DIP/Admin/1st Lien	150
Remaining Value to be Distributed (deemed equity value of NewCo)	$150
x % of NewCo Equity Allocated to the Senior Unsecured Debt	100%
$ Value of Recovery to the Senior Unsecured Debt	$150
% Recovery to Senior Unsecured [$150 recovery / senior unsecured claim of $200MM]	75%

FIGURE 16.3 Recoveries Based on a $300MM Enterprise Value

Since value runs out before the senior unsecured debt is repaid in full, the court can cram down—that is, award zero recovery to—the subordinated unsecured claims. However, it would be unusual for these subordinated claims to go down without a fight. This class will argue the company's enterprise value is materially understated at $300 million. Given there are multiple valuation techniques, all requiring subjective judgment, it will not be hard for the sub debt holders to find an expert to testify in court that the EV should be $675 million, not $300 million.

If the EV of David's Rigatoni Co. is $675MM, the outcome for the creditor classes will be very different. Instead of getting 100% of NewCo equity, the senior unsecured debt will only be entitled to 38.1% because based on the higher plan value, 38.1% of the equity results in a par recovery, leaving the senior unsecured class unimpaired and, therefore, unable to vote. The remaining NewCo equity, 61.9% of the company's ownership, would be granted to the subordinated unsecured claims. Recoveries based on a $675MM enterprise value are shown in Figure 16.4.

	Recoveries ($MM)
David's Rigatoni Company's Enterprise Value	$675
Less Amount of Value Allocated to DIP/Admin/First Lien	150
Remaining Value to be Distributed (deemed equity value of NewCo)	$525
x % of NewCo Equity Allocated to Senior Unsecured Debt	38.1%
$ Value of Recovery to the Senior Unsecured Debt	$200
% Recovery to Senior Unsecured [$200 recovery / senior unsecured claim of $200MM]	100%
Remaining Value to be Distributed (deemed equity value of NewCo)	$525
x % of NewCo Equity Allocated to the Subordinated Claims	61.9%
$ Recovery to Subordinated Claims	$325
% Recovery to Subordinated [$325MM recovery / subordinated claims of $400MM]	81.3%

FIGURE 16.4 Recoveries Based on a $675MM Enterprise Value

The "plan value" is the enterprise value the debtor uses to determine recoveries in the plan of reorganization (POR). Plan value can be highly contested due to its impact on true economic recovery. For instance, in this example, let's assume $400MM is the most realistic valuation for the company. However, if the POR has a $300MM value, the senior unsecured debt will get a windfall at the expense of the subordinated debt. The senior unsecured class will receive 100% of NewCo equity worth $50 million more than the claim is entitled to, while the subordinated claims would get zero. Recoveries based on a $400MM enterprise value and a $300MM plan value are shown in Figure 16.5.

	Recoveries ($MM)
David's Rigatoni Company's "True Economic Value"	$400
Less Value Allocated to DIP/Admin/First Lien	150
"True" Value of NewCo Equity	$250
x % of "NewCo" Equity Allocated to the Senior Unsecured Debt	100%
"True" $ Recovery to Senior Unsecured Debt	$250
% Recovery to Senior Unsecured Claims [$250 "true" recovery / senior unsecured debt of $200MM]	125%

FIGURE 16.5 True Economic Recoveries at a $400MM TEV but a $300MM Plan Value

Now let's look at the impact of a plan value of $675MM when the "true economic value" is $400MM. In this case, the senior unsecured creditors will be harmed. They receive only 38.1% of NewCo equity. Since the plan value is indicated at $675MM, they are deemed unimpaired and, therefore, not entitled to vote. However, if the "true" EV is $400MM rather than the $675MM used to calculate recoveries, then their true economic recovery would be $95MM of reorg equity versus a claim of $200MM. In this case, the subordinated debt will receive 61.9% of NewCo equity, which represents a windfall relative to the value that should be allocated to the subs. Recoveries based on a $400MM enterprise value and a $675MM plan value are shown in Figure 16.6.

	Recoveries ($MM)
David's Rigatoni Company's "True Economic Value"	$400
Less Value Allocated to DIP/Admin/1st Lien	150
"True" Value of NewCo Equity	$250
x % of NewCo Equity Allocated to the Senior Unsecureds	38.1%
"True" $ Recovery to Senior Unsecured Debt	$95.25
% Recovery to Senior Unsecured [$95.25 "true" recovery / senior unsecured debt claim of $200MM]	47.6%
"True" Value of NewCo Equity	$250
x % of NewCo Equity Allocated to the Sub Debt	61.9%
"True" $ Recovery to the Subordinated Claims	$154.75
% Recovery to Subordinated Claims [$154.75 "true" recovery / subordinated claim of $400MM]	38.7%

FIGURE 16.6 True Economic Recoveries at a $400MM TEV but a $675MM Plan Value

Plan valuation is critical to determining recoveries. If the more senior parts of the capital structure are getting any portion of their recovery in NewCo equity, they want a lower valuation that makes their class the fulcrum entitled to all of the equity and its upside. The lower priority claims have the opposite incentive—they want a higher valuation, resulting in a "valuation fight." In the above example, the senior unsecured creditors' advisors will show an analysis that supports a $300MM plan value, while the subordinated debt advisors' work will support a $675MM valuation. The debtor and its advisors select a valuation and build the plan around it. Most often, a lot of posturing and negotiating leads to an agreed valuation. However, if a compromise is impossible, the court will be forced to decide.

The valuation fight regarding the hypothetical company David's Rigatoni illustrates the zero-sum game of many conflicts fought in bankruptcy. Figure 16.7 shows this—if one party is happy, the other is sad. If no one is happy after a negotiated settlement, the outcome is probably fair to both parties.

Scenario	Senior Unsecured Debt Holders	Subordinated Unsecured Debt Holders
Plan Value < "True Economic Value"		
Plan Value > "True Economic Value"		

FIGURE 16.7 Zero-Sum Game of Bankruptcy Fights

Broadcast radio giant Cumulus Media is an example of a court-settled valuation fight. Cumulus fell victim to negative secular trends as satellite radio and digital services such as Pandora and Spotify stole listeners, which resulted in a decline in advertising dollars. By early 2017, its leverage (debt/EBITDA) was over 10.0x, and S&P had downgraded its unsecured bonds to CCC. Its $1.8 billion first lien debt was trading at 70 cents on the dollar, while its $600 million unsecured bond was trading at 35 cents on the dollar. After a failed attempt at an out-of-court restructuring, the company filed for bankruptcy on November 29, 2017. Silver Point was one of the largest owners of the first lien debt, and we formed an ad hoc group to negotiate with the debtor and the unsecured creditors to restructure the company's balance sheet, with the goal of coming to bankruptcy court with an agreed, consensual POR. After multiple negotiations, it became clear that we could not come to a consensual deal with the unsecured debt because our valuations were too far apart; our valuation work showed our first lien position as impaired, whereas the unsecured class put forth a much higher (and in our view, inflated) valuation that showed it as the fulcrum security. We subsequently worked with the debtor to craft a fair reorganization plan. The secured lenders agreed to support a POR in which the $1.8 billion of secured term loan claims would receive

$1.3 billion of new first lien debt plus 83.5% of NewCo equity. The $600 million unsecured bonds would receive 16.5% of the equity.

For over a week, the court heard testimony from valuation experts about projections, discount rate, and every other input that goes into valuation. Holders of the unsecured debt objected that the plan put forth by the secured group undervalued Cumulus and resulted in a lower recovery for the unsecured debt than deserved. Based on their valuation, the secured creditors would be getting a package worth over $2 billion versus a claim of only $1.8 billion—that is, a recovery in excess of 100%.

I expected creditors would settle on the valuation on the courthouse steps (as is typical). However, since neither side would budge much from its valuation, the judge had to rule on the valuation issue. She ruled in favor of the debtor's valuation (which sided with the first lien debt), and our POR was eventually approved.

Who was right? At emergence from bankruptcy, based on the trading levels of NewCo equity, the secured creditors' recovery was around 92 percent of their original claim. These trading levels suggest that the deal was a fair and reasonable outcome for the unsecured claims, as they received a modest recovery despite a recovery below 100% for the secured creditors based on the market value of Cumulus upon emergence.

CREDIT BIDS AND 363 ASSET SALE PROCESS

Section 363 of the bankruptcy code allows for the sale of a bankrupt company with court approval. A 363 sale is an effective way to monetize the business as it enables the debtor to sell its operations and assets free and clear of all liens, claims, and encumbrances, removing the buyer's concerns about liabilities associated with the assets. Once the 363 sale is complete, the cash from the sale goes into the estate and is distributed to all creditors based on their ranking/priority.

These sales can be controversial as they tend to have a quick turnaround and do not require voting by creditors on a POR. For this reason, 363 deals are commonly described as "Sub Rosa Plans." *Sub rosa* is a Latin phrase indicating an unpleasant fragrance concealed "under the rose."[iv] The issues have some parallels to the valuation fights described above. Junior creditors argue that 363 sales do not maximize the estate's value because the sale process is rushed and happens before the company can stabilize its business.

The counter view is referred to as the "melting ice cube" argument: liquidity and company value are deteriorating so quickly that the only way to maintain value is to allow for a quick sale of the business without going through the process of getting a POR approved.

This gets more confrontational if the secured creditors are bidding for the company. Section 363(k) grants secured creditors the ability to "credit bid" (i.e., use the face value of their secured claim instead of cash). The secured creditors receive the full value of their claims (as part of the 363 sale price) regardless of trading levels.

For example, suppose a bankrupt company has the capital structure and trading levels outlined in Figure 16.8. In this case, distressed debt funds could buy the secured debt for $369 million, and get "bidding credit" for the total face value of $450 million in a credit bid.

	Capital Structure / Trading Levels		
	Amount Outstanding (in $MMs)	Trading Levels	Market Value
DIP and Other Administrative and Priority Claims	100	100.0%	100
Secured Debt	450	82.0%	369
General Unsecured Claims (GUCs)	300	45.0%	135

FIGURE 16.8 Capital Structure and Trading Levels

If distressed debt funds own the secured debt at a discount with the goal of owning the company through their debt investment, they will encourage the debtor to pursue a 363 sale. The ability to credit bid provides a tremendous leg up on competing bids, as $81 million of their $450 million bid is "funny money," the difference between the face value of the debt and what they paid for it. If no bidders are willing to pay more than $450 million, the general unsecured claims (GUCs) will receive a zero recovery.

If the bankruptcy court approves a 363 asset sale, the bid procedures become critical to ensure that the process is fair and competitive. While every process is different, a typical approach would be as follows. The debtor identifies and negotiates with a stalking horse bidder; generally, this happens before the debtor files a 363 motion with the court. It is common for the secured creditors to be the stalking horse, which serves as the floor price. The negative of being the stalking horse bidder is that the debtor will shop the deal, so the stalking horse bidder only wins if no one is willing to pay more. Furthermore, as there are very few outs, the stalking horse price cannot be adjusted if the company continues to deteriorate.

A stalking horse bidder gets the benefit of bid protections, typically in the form of a break-up fee if it is not the winner and expense reimbursement. Break-up fees are generally 2%–5% of the ultimate sale price. For someone to outbid the stalking horse, they must top its bid by this amount. Additionally, the stalking horse bid has more access and time to perform due diligence. While some 363 sales have no stalking horse bid, it is preferable for the estate not to go into an auction "naked."

Once the company has negotiated an asset purchase agreement (APA) with the stalking horse bidder that details all terms of the transaction, it must get court approval. A significant fight related to the bid procedures is the marketing period. While the stalking horse bidder prefers an expeditious marketing period, the GUCs want more time to allow competing bidders to complete the due diligence necessary. Before the marketing period expires, all bids are submitted to the court. If there are multiple bidders, an auction is held, and the court determines which bid is the highest and best. If no offer exceeds the stalking horse, the auction is canceled, and the stalking horse is declared the winner.

I asked my good friend Bruce Mendelsohn to give an example of a 363 sale process he ran. I started my career with Bruce on Goldman's distressed desk where he was one of my early mentors. His career has skyrocketed since then. Bruce sat on the Goldman distressed desk with me from 1998 to 2001. In 2001 he became global head of Goldman's special assets and bank debt portfolio groups, and served from 2006 to 2008 as chief underwriting officer for North America, where he was a member of Goldman's firm-wide Capital Committee and its Special Situations Specialty Lending Investment Committee. In 2008 Bruce was promoted to global head of Goldman's restructuring and distressed financing business and made partner in 2010. In 2015 he was recruited away from Goldman to run Perella Weinberg's restructuring advisory business. Bruce's 363 example, in his own words, is below.

Section 363 of the Bankruptcy Code offers debtors the ability to sell assets during a bankruptcy process. This can range from selling distinct assets owned by a company like a headquarters building or subsidiary, to selling the entire company. I have advised both buyers and sellers on many 363 sales. To some extent, the work my team and I do for a 363 sale is very similar to what an M&A investment banker does; however, since a 363 sale is part of a bankruptcy process, there is often a greater sense of urgency because time and liquidity may be running thin, there may be messy liabilities and legal claims, and emotions may be running high with distressed hedge funds and other creditors pressuring the process. My job when representing a debtor is to maximize the value of the estate and its assets under these extreme conditions. To illustrate what a 363 entails, I will briefly describe two deals, one which is ongoing, and the other which is fully resolved.

The first is FTX. In early 2022, FTX was the second-largest cryptocurrency exchange. Within one year, the company was in bankruptcy, and the founder and CEO, Sam Bankman-Fried, was arrested on fraud charges and replaced by John Ray, who in his first day affidavit described the situation as follows:

Never in my career have I seen such a complete failure of corporate controls and such a complete absence of trustworthy financial information as occurred here. From compromised systems integrity and faulty regulatory oversight abroad, to the concentration of control in the hands of a very small group of inexperienced, unsophisticated and potentially compromised individuals, this situation is unprecedented.

To put this in perspective, Mr. Ray made his name overseeing the liquidation of Enron, one of the largest and most complex frauds in US history.

Perella Weinberg Partners (PWP) represents the FTX debtors. FTX owns a large portfolio of distinct positions in various venture and crypto-type assets, limited partnerships, and numerous other assets. At the time of this writing, we have conducted sale processes for some of these assets, identified the highest bidders in each case, and filed several different bidding procedures motions to sell some of these assets. We designed the bidding procedures to give us the flexibility to designate a stalking horse for any single asset or combination of assets.

One thing which is interesting about 363 bankruptcy sales is that there is typically more than one auction process for each asset. The first auction *process is to determine which party, if any, should be designated the stalking horse, which provides that party various benefits like expense reimbursement, a break-up fee, and overbid protection (i.e., a higher bid must be at least $x greater). The second auction process is the actual 363 auction.*

Once a stalking horse is identified by the Debtor, the bankruptcy court must approve the bidding protections (i.e., break-up fee, expense reimbursement, and overbid protection). This typically takes at least 21 days from the time the Debtor files its motion for approval until the bidding protections are actually approved by the Court. During this time, it is possible a competing bidder can emerge to try to replace the stalking horse.

The actual 363 auction typically occurs in person at counsel's office, sometimes with multiple bidders in a single room in an auction type setting, sometimes with each bidder in a separate conference room while the Debtors' professionals shuttle between rooms to negotiate privately with each bidder. In the case of FTX, some of the auctions were done through live auctions as described above, while others were done through private sale motions where we first conducted a traditional M&A process, identified a winning bidder, and filed a motion with the court for approval of the sale pending the 21-day notice period during which time any competing party can propose a higher and better bid. The private sale process is most applicable when there are fewer bidders for an asset and an auction is less likely to be effective.

The second example of a 363 sale in which I was involved is Garrett Motion, Inc., an automotive supplier specializing in the design, manufacture, and sale of turbochargers, electric-boosting, and connected vehicle technologies for original equipment manufacturers (OEMs) and the automotive aftermarket. Garrett Motion was spun off from Honeywell International in October 2018 with $1.6 billion in debt and an indemnity agreement to reimburse Honeywell for the settlement of asbestos-related punitive damage claims arising from a non-Garrett, legacy Honeywell business unit. As a result, Garrett was on the hook for up to $5.25 billion in reimbursements over the 30-year life of the agreement.

Before filing for Chapter 11, the management team and board of Garrett Motion concluded that the company's high leverage and obligations to Honeywell undermined the ability of the company to compete. The Board of Directors concluded it was necessary to file a preemptive Chapter 11 to unshackle the company from these liabilities.

We concluded the best way to do this would be to conduct a pre-petition sale process followed by a Chapter 11 with a stalking horse 363 bidder. Following a multi-month pre-petition M&A process, the company reached an agreement to sell to a private equity firm, KPS Capital Partners, for $2.1 billion. We agreed to file Chapter 11 and name KPS as the stalking horse with a break-up fee of 3.0% ($63 million) and expense reimbursement of up to $21 million (both subject to court approval). This necessitated that a topping bid would likely have to be at least $84 million higher than the KPS purchase price (i.e., $63MM + $21MM). Garrett Motion filed for Chapter 11 on September 20, 2020, with the announcement of KPS' stalking horse bid of $2.1 billion.

While we were readying the bidding procedures to file with the court, two competing paths emerged. The first was with two investment funds, Centerbridge and Oaktree, who teamed up with Honeywell to put forward their own proposal. This group became known as the "COH" group (for Centerbridge, Oaktree, and Honeywell). The second was with a group of existing creditors led by hedge funds Owl Creek and Warlander who teamed up with Jefferies and became known as the "OWJ" group (for Owl Creek, Warlander and Jefferies). Both OWJ and COH preferred a plan of reorganization instead of a Section 363 sale and sought to be plan sponsors at higher valuations for their own plan of reorganization.

In response to this evolving competitive dynamic and in an effort to increase the likelihood the bidding procedures and KPS's break-up fee and expense reimbursement would be approved, we negotiated with KPS to increase its stalking horse bid from $2.1B to $2.6B. KPS agreed to do this because we made it clear that, given the increasingly competitive interest, if KPS did not increase their bid, it would be unlikely the court would approve them as the stalking horse, in which case they would not get the break-up fee and expense reimbursement. On October 23, 2020, the Court approved KPS' stalking horse bidding protections.

We used the next several months to conduct multiple rounds of bidding, naming each of OWJ, COH and KPS the leading bidder at various points in time as each party competed to put forward their most competitive terms. After many months and multiple bidding rounds, on January 11, 2021, we determined that the COH Group's bid was the winning one at the auction with a stand-alone restructuring plan valuing Garrett at $3.1 billion, a staggering 48% increase in value from the initial $2.1 billion opening bid. The COH plan provided that all of the company's creditors except Honeywell would be paid in full, the Honeywell claims were settled for a present value of $959MM to be paid over 10 years, and Centerbridge and Oaktree as plan sponsors backstopped a new preferred equity investment of $1.3 billion in the form of an 11% Series A convertible preferred stock.

You can imagine getting from start to finish was not an easy task. We had numerous rounds of bidding which lasted several months throughout the 2020 Christmas holiday, named each of KPS, OWJ and COH the "winning bidder" at various intervals, and ultimately used the process to extract the highest value to the estate through this incredibly competitive bidding process. KPS walked away with their $63MM breakup fee plus expense reimbursement, OWJ were paid in full for their credit claims, and COH, as of last report, were extremely happy with their investment.

AVOIDANCE ACTIONS

Frequently the debtor will file a lawsuit to recover money related to pre-bankruptcy transactions. These adversarial proceedings are referred to as avoidance actions. The two major avoidance actions are preferences and fraudulent conveyances.

Preferences

Section 547 of the code, commonly referred to as the preferential-payment rule, allows the debtor to recover payments made to creditors in the 90 days before filing. This period is extended to one year if an "insider" receives the payment. Insiders include the owners, officers, and directors of the company.

Fairness (equal treatment of all creditors) is the guiding principle of Section 547. Would it be fair if Toys R Us stopped paying small vendors right before filing but continued to make payments to Hasbro and Mattel? The debtor can "claw back," i.e., demand repayment of these preference payments to avoid violating Section 547. It is common practice for the debtor to send a "demand notice" requiring repayment by all creditors that received a payment during the preference period. However, there are several circumstances in which the money is not required to be returned. The burden of proof is on the creditor, not the debtor. The two most common affirmative defenses used by creditors to avoid this claw-back are summarized in Figure 16.9.

- *Ordinary course of business defense.* If a vendor had 60-day terms with the company and the only payments received were for payables that were due and consistent with the company's past practices, that vendor would argue it was an "ordinary course payment," not a preferential payment. Another example of an "ordinary course payment" is the payment of contractual interest on pre-petition debt.
- *New value defense.* This defense demonstrates that a payment was for a product or service rendered during the preference period, not related to an old obligation. Example: the payment related to products shipped on "cash on delivery" (COD) terms, and the cash did not relate to products shipped previously under credit terms.

FIGURE 16.9 Affirmative Defenses to Preference Claims

Fraudulent conveyances

Section 548 (fraudulent conveyance or transfer provision) of the code gives the company the ability to unwind a pre-bankruptcy transfer of assets if two criteria, outlined in Figure 16.10, are met.

- The company received less than reasonably equivalent (i.e., fair) value in exchange for the transferred assets; <u>and</u>
- The company was insolvent when the transfer was made or became insolvent due to the transaction.

FIGURE 16.10 Fraudulent Conveyance Criteria

Here's a hypothetical example. A private equity-owned company borrows $100 million to pay a dividend and goes bankrupt within a short period of time. After the company files for bankruptcy, it can attempt to recoup the dividend from the PE firm. This transaction unambiguously meets the first condition—the company got nothing in exchange for paying a dividend. The hurdle for the debtor to win the fraudulent transfer argument will be criterion (ii): it must prove that the company was either insolvent at the time or became insolvent by taking on debt to pay the dividend. This depends on the particular facts and circumstances of the case. If the company filed for bankruptcy soon (within a year) after paying the dividend, it would have a better case than if it filed for bankruptcy several years after the dividend.

Todd, an analyst at Silver Point, learned about fraudulent conveyance the hard way. Todd joined Silver Point in 2005 from the private equity firm Bain Capital. One of the deals he was able to coinvest in while at Bain was the $305 million LBO of KB Toys in 2000. In 2002, KB Toys paid a $120 million dividend to Bain funded by a new bank loan and cash on its balance sheet, a common transaction referred to as a dividend recap. KB Toys filed for bankruptcy less than two years later. The bankruptcy estate sued the shareholders under the fraudulent transfer provision and eventually settled with Bain Capital, which agreed to return part of the dividend.

The KB Toys case is small potatoes relative to the Caesars lawsuit. In January 2008, private equity firms Apollo and TPG closed their acquisition of casino giant Caesars Entertainment for $30.9 billion—the fourth largest LBO ever. The timing could not have been worse for a cyclical business with $25 billion of debt heading into the GFC. The most junior debt was trading below 20 cents on the dollar in early 2009. However, the company managed to stay out of bankruptcy through a combination of cost-cutting and financial engineering until 2014. Caesars was one of the most confrontational bankruptcies I have witnessed, driven by the complexity of the company's capital structure combined with aggressive maneuvers by the PE sponsors to preserve their equity value.

The most significant fight involved fraudulent conveyance. Secured lenders accused the company of transferring some of the collateral securing their debt at below-market prices from one legal entity to another, creating a "good Caesars" and a "bad Caesars." The inferior casinos remaining at "bad Caesars" secured the debt, which reduced the recovery value of the secured debt. Since Caesars' issuing subsidiary did not have an independent board of directors before filing, these transactions were easier to undertake than for a company with greater oversight.

One lawsuit claimed: "This is a case of unimaginably brazen corporate looting and abuse perpetrated by irreparably conflicted management . . . The fox has not only been put in charge of the hen house; it has barricaded the door and has even paid itself a salary."[v]

Caesars argued that neither condition of the test was met: all asset transfers were done at fair market value, and when the transactions took place the company was solvent, nor did the transactions cause the company to become insolvent.

In March 2015, the court authorized the appointment of an independent examiner, Richard Davis, a respected former partner at the law firm Weil, Gotshal, and Manges LLP. Davis was tasked with investigating over a dozen transactions over four years among different legal entities within Caesars and the LBO sponsors (Apollo and TPG) to determine if the fraudulent transfer claims were legitimate.

Davis received and reviewed more than 1.2 million documents consisting of 8.8 million pages. The documents included emails, board and committee presentations, transaction documents, fairness opinions, and valuation materials. From September 15, 2015, to February 25, 2016, Davis and his advisors interviewed 92 individuals.[vi]

On March 15, 2016, Davis filed his report,[vii] which concluded that potential damages to creditors ranged from $3.6 billion to $5.1 billion from specific claims considered "reasonable" or "strong" related to the transactions between the debtor and other entities controlled by its parent and the LBO sponsors. Given this damaging report, the sponsors agreed to forfeit most of their equity in exchange for a release from litigation related to the fraudulent transfers. Another motivation for the sponsors to settle was to avoid the judge's highly unusual subpoena of the personal financial statements of higher-ups at Apollo and TPG. A must-read for those interested in the Caesars saga is *The Caesars Palace Coup* by Max Frumes and Sujeet Indap.

EQUITABLE SUBORDINATION

Equitable subordination is a doctrine that allows the court to lower the priority of a claim. For equitable subordination to apply, three conditions must be met, summarized in Figure 16.11.

- The claimant must have engaged in inequitable conduct; and
- The misconduct must have injured other creditors or conferred an unfair advantage on the claimant; and
- Subordination of the claim must not yield a result that would conflict with other provisions of the Bankruptcy Code.[viii]

FIGURE 16.11 Conditions for Equitable Subordination

In my experience, courts are reluctant to challenge a claim's priority order. In practice, they will look for one of two situations to equitably subordinate a claim: the creditor is guilty of wrongful conduct (fraud or other illegalities), or the creditor exercised an unreasonable level of control over the debtor and its business. If your claim is subject to equitable subordination, it can be an unmitigated disaster. For example, if you are a senior secured creditor, you might expect par plus accrued interest as your recovery. However, if the judge deems your actions worthy of subordinating your claim, you might end up at the bottom of the debt stack, with minimal or even zero recovery.

Distressed debt investors are especially vulnerable to accusations that might lead to the subordination of their claims. It is not unusual in a debt restructuring for creditors to receive new debt plus NewCo equity as recovery consideration. If they also receive board rights and appoint members of their firm to the board, they become insiders. If the company subsequently becomes distressed again, every action taken by that particular creditor will be scrutinized. Other creditors or the debtor might argue that the distressed fund used its influence over the company to better its debt position and agenda versus other claims. This is sometimes referred to as an "alter ego" argument; the creditor acted more like equity so should be treated as such rather than enjoying the better recovery prospects of the secured creditor class.

For example, we owned the debt of a printing business that converted our holdings into 100 percent of its equity in bankruptcy. After emerging from bankruptcy, with our support and direction, the company merged with a competitor. After the merger, we owned a $210 million secured term loan junior to a $100 million ABL facility. We also owned 30 percent of the equity of the combined business, with the right to designate two of nine directors. The merger did not go well, and after a year, it was clear the company would break its financial covenants. We did not want to jeopardize the senior secured priority of the debt due to our equity position. To minimize the risk of equitable subordination, we gave up our board seats. The company filed for bankruptcy and was sold in a 363 process. The unsecured creditors threatened to pursue an equitable subordination claim, but we took care to protect ourselves as the company's performance deteriorated. We consulted various law firms and ensured our actions were consistent with a creditor rather than an equity owner, and we did not use any of our influence with the board to improve our position relative to other creditors.

In cases with the potential for litigation, you not only need to do everything right but also need to have a paper trail to prove it. An email taken out of context can be used as a "smoking gun" during litigation. In this case, we believed strongly that all accusations by the unsecured creditors were meritless. However, to ensure their agreement with the sale, the unsecured holders were given a small "tip" (i.e., recovery), and in return they agreed to support the deal and provide the senior secured debt holders with releases from future litigation.

Even a secured lender without board seats can be equitably subordinated, though this is rare. For example, if a company materially underperforms its budget, the lenders might push the company to hire a restructuring advisor as a condition of a covenant waiver. They are putting themselves at significant risk of an equitable subordination claim if they demand the company hire a specific advisor. The company and other creditors could argue that the secured lenders exercised undue influence by dictating that the company hire a particular advisor who would favor the interests of the secured lenders. The less risky approach is to present the company with a list of several well-known firms to interview and leave the ultimate decision to management.

LENDER LIABILITY

Lender liability is when the borrower sues the lender for breach of contract or other wrongful behavior in the lender/borrower relationship. The lender is then liable for "damages," which can be for an amount greater than their loan. To illustrate, I will give two examples: (1) when we threatened to sue a bank for breach of contract and (2) when we were threatened with a lender lawsuit.

Example #1

We owned the distressed debt of a branded consumer products company. In early 2008, a PE firm agreed to buy the company and had lined up $100 million of committed bank financing. The sponsor would inject significant equity into the business to provide liquidity for its operational turnaround. Our firm would receive reinstated debt with a lien junior to the bank financing and a little less than 50% of the equity. As 2008 progressed, the global economy went into recession. The banking system was fragile, and banks reduced originations as they dealt with their problems.

The underwriting bank had signed commitment papers subject only to the final documentation of the loan agreement. But the bank's actions suggested they were "slow playing" documentation negotiations and adding off-market terms that were not contemplated in the original commitment. Eventually, the debtor sent the bank a draft lender liability suit for $1 billion in damages, arguing that the bank was breaching its commitment by failing to negotiate in good faith. We had backup documentation of all our correspondence and the bank's turnaround time, along with all the provisions the bank was trying to slip into the loan agreement and expert testimony that these were not market standard. The suit was for $1 billion even though the loan commitment was only $100MM. The debtor showed its business plan and resulting valuation with the new liquidity and compared this to the valuation without it, estimating that the bank's breach would destroy $1 billion of value. After reviewing the letter and discussing it with counsel, the bank changed its tack, negotiated the document in good faith, and closed the deal before year end.

Example #2

We were the lender to a company that had broken a financial covenant by our calculation. We informed the company that it was in breach and that we planned to freeze its revolver (meaning we would no longer allow the company to make new draws on the facility). The company disagreed with our calculation of EBITDA; based on management's calculation, which added back items deemed nonrecurring, it was not in default. If we refused to fund the revolver, the company maintained that we were in breach of contract. The business would not be able to operate without access to the liquidity provided by our facility, and the borrower threatened to hold us accountable for the degradation in value, estimated at hundreds of millions of dollars.

While we knew our argument had greater merit, the risk of losing such a lawsuit was a strong incentive for us to come to a consensual deal. We agreed to reset covenant levels and tighten the definition of covenant EBITDA so that there would be less ambiguity in the future. In addition, we gave the company access to $15 of the $25 million committed, with the other $10 million available only if the sponsor injected $5 million more equity into the business.

CHAPTER CONCLUSION

Bankruptcy is a contentious process because it pits multiple constituencies against each other in the zero-sum game of carving up the debtor's value. This chapter has introduced you to a legend, Chaim Fortgang, who negotiated aggressively for his clients' best interests. While there will only ever be one Chaim, many other colorful characters in the world of distressed debt investing are just as aggressive. The war stories in this chapter might give you the impression that whoever yells the loudest wins. That is not always the case, but investors who rely purely on their credit analysis skills without an understanding or appreciation of the legal nuances and tactics of negotiations are likely to fall short in the distressed debt arena. Learning to navigate the conflicts and personalities of bankruptcy proceedings, both in court and outside of it, is essential to investing in this asset class.

But we have only just begun to examine outcomes in distressed debt investing as a company works its way through the bankruptcy process. In the following chapters, you'll learn about more complex and intricate nuances of corporate law that have been used by creditors to extract value from one another.

NOTES

i. Pacelle, Mitchell, and Richard B. Shmitt. (February 27, 2002). "Chaim Fortang Defended Creditors, but Offended Many of His Colleagues." *Wall Street Journal.* https://www.wsj.com/articles/SB1014760154784300400?mod=Searchresults_pos1&page=1.

ii. Ibid.

iii. "This Brooklyn Tale All Chapter 11." *American Banker* (April 20, 2001). https://www.americanbanker.com/news/this-brooklyn-tale-all-chapter-11.

iv. The Devil's Dictionary of Bankruptcy Terms. https://devilsdictionary.polsinelli.com/term/sub-rosa-plan/.

v. Mason, Jamie. (November 28, 2014). "Trustee Sues Caesars for 'Unimaginably Brazen Corporate Looting.'" TheStreet.com. https://www.thestreet.com/markets/mergers-and-acquisitions/trustee-sues-caesars-for-unimaginably-brazen-corporate-looting-12968885.

vi. https://www.wsj.com/public/resources/documents/CaesarsReport03-16-2016.pdf.

vii. Ibid.

viii. *New York Law Journal.* Corporate Update. Volume 244-NO.106. December 2, 2010.

CHAPTER 17

How Subordination Works in Bankruptcy

Chapter 9 laid out the basics of capital structure for leveraged companies. The level of security and seniority of each layer of the capital structure is relevant even for healthy companies, as debt investors price these differently to account for the greater risk associated with lower-priority positions. But the importance of priority level increases exponentially when a company becomes distressed or files for bankruptcy, as it dictates recoveries.

Thus far we have focused primarily on differences between secured and unsecured debt, which might lead you to believe that there is one big tent for unsecured lenders. But all unsecured liabilities are not created equal. We will consider three types of subordination summarized in Figure 17.1.

- Time subordination
- Contractual subordination
- Structural subordination

FIGURE 17.1 Types of Subordination

TIME SUBORDINATION

Once a company files for bankruptcy, all debt is considered "accelerated," and the maturity date of any individual debt issue becomes meaningless. Recovery is based only on collateral, guarantees, and seniority. However, if a company is distressed, but it is unclear whether it will file and in what timeframe, then maturity becomes critical. For instance, if a company has financial problems but believes it might be able to avoid bankruptcy, it could use up precious liquidity to repay debt with near-term maturities, regardless of its seniority, leaving the remaining debt in a worse position. It is common for a distressed debt investor to refer to the debt with longer maturities as "time subordinated" to debt with shorter maturities.

For this reason, most senior secured lenders to high-risk, low-credit-rated companies do not allow junior debt to have a maturity date before theirs. Since the typical maturity of a new senior secured issue is at least five years, when companies with nearer-term unsecured debt maturities seek new secured financing, this issue is addressed with contractual provisions that accelerate the maturity of the senior secured debt under certain conditions. For instance, we structured a secured loan to a company with a significant amount of mezz debt maturing in two years. The company requested a five-year maturity, with the expectation of refinancing the mezz debt closer to its maturity date. We agreed to a five-year maturity, with a "springing maturity" provision in the loan documentation. If the company could not refinance the junior debt at least six months prior to its maturity, our loan's maturity would move up to six months before that of the mezz debt.

CONTRACTUAL SUBORDINATION

Contractual subordination exists for unsecured bonds with a subordination clause included in the indenture. This clause requires holders of the bond to turn over any recovery they would receive in an insolvency, bankruptcy, or liquidation to senior debt, until the senior debt is paid in full.

Example: A company in bankruptcy is sold in a Section 363 auction for $275 million with the capital structure shown in Figure 17.2.

Type of Claim	Amount ($MM)
Secured Bank Debt	125
Administrative & Priority Claims	25
Total Secured and Administrative & Priority Claims	150
Senior Unsecured Bond #1	60
Senior Unsecured Bond #2	40
Unsecured Trade Claims and Other General Unsecured Claims	50
Subordinated Unsecured Bonds	75
Total Unsecured Claims	225
Total Claims	375

FIGURE 17.2 Hypothetical Post-Petition Capital Structure

After paying off the secured and administrative claims in full, there is $125 million of value remaining for the unsecured claims (enterprise value of $275 million less $150 million of secured and administrative and priority claims). The subordinated claims turn over their recovery to the contractually senior claims until those claims are paid in full. In most instances, subordinated bonds are only subordinated to other bonds and bank debt, not to other unsecured claims, such as what is owed to trade vendors. Figure 17.3 outlines the allocation of the remaining value after the secured debt and priority claims have been paid.

	Allocation of Value across Capital Structure				
(Monetary amounts in $MM)	Bond #1	Bond #2	Trade Claims	Sub Bonds	Total Unsecured Claims
Unsecured Claims	$60	$40	$50	$75	$225
% of Total Unsecured Claims (pro rata %)	26.7%	17.8%	22.2%	33.3%	100.0%
Value to Split Among Unsecured Claims	$125	$125	$125	$125	$125
(x) Pro Rata Share from Above	26.7%	17.8%	22.2%	33.3%	100.0%
$ Recovery before Sub Turnover	33.3	22.2	27.8	41.7	125.0
Less Sub Turnover	+25.0	+16.7	0.0	(41.7)	0.0
$ Recovery after Sub Turnover	$58.3	$38.9	$27.8	$0.0	$125.0
% Recovery ($ recovery / claim amount)	97.2%	97.2%	55.6%	0.0%	55.6%

FIGURE 17.3 Allocation of Value Among Claims (Scenario 1)

You must carefully read the bond indentures and subordination agreements to understand which claims are senior to subordinated debt. Sometimes you will discover unusual structural features overlooked by the market that can contribute meaningfully to recoveries. For example, I held a subordinated note through bankruptcy that was not subordinated to *all* bonds labeled as senior bonds. Per the indenture, one senior bond was not entitled to subordination turnover from this particular bond.

To illustrate the impact of this situation, let's go back to the previous example and assume only bond #1 is entitled to subordination turnover. The recoveries of bonds #1 and #2 are now materially different. Until the market figures this out, the two bonds would trade at similar prices since both are referred to in the 10-K as senior. A sophisticated fund could buy bond #1 and short bond #2 (known as a capital structure arbitrage trade). Since the subordinated bond only has to turn over enough to make bond #1 whole, this has recovery implications for all three bonds (bond #1 higher, bond #2 lower, and the subordinated bond higher) as shown in Figure 17.4. Note that this example ignores post-petition interest, which is discussed later in this chapter.

	Allocation of Value across Capital Structure				
(Monetary amounts in $MM)	**Bond #1**	**Bond #2**	**Trade Claims**	**Sub Bonds**	**Total Unsecured Claims**
Unsecured Claims	$60	$40	$50	$75	$225
% of Total Unsecured Claims (pro rata %)	26.7%	17.8%	22.2%	33.3%	100.0%
Value to Split Among Unsecured Claims	$125	$125	$125	$125	$125
x Pro Rata Share from Above	26.7%	17.8%	22.2%	33.3%	100.0%
$ Recovery before Sub Turnover	33.3	22.2	27.8	41.7	125.0
Less Sub Turnover	+26.7	0.0	0.0	(26.7)	0.0
$ Recovery after Sub Turnover	$60.0	$22.2	$27.8	$15.0	$125.0
% Recovery ($ recovery / claim amount)	100.0%	55.6%	55.6%	20.0%	55.6%

FIGURE 17.4 Allocation of Value Among Claims (Scenario 2)

Here's another example. When I was at Goldman Sachs, we extended credit insurance to a large vendor of Kmart, which gave the vendor the right to sell its Kmart receivables to Goldman for 90 cents on the dollar if Kmart filed for bankruptcy. When Kmart ultimately filed in 2002, we ended up owning $50 million of Kmart's unsecured trade claims. Upon filing, Kmart had approximately $7 billion in unsecured claims plus $890 million of "preferred securities," generally viewed as junior to all unsecured claims. This resulted in the unsecured trade claims trading at approximately the same price as the unsecured bonds. However, a close reading of the documents revealed that the preferred securities were not preferred stock, as some investors assumed. Rather, they were convertible preferred securities, and prior to conversion, they were only subordinated to the unsecured bank debt and bonds, not to the other unsecured claims, including the trade claims. We estimated that rather than trading "on top" of each other (i.e., at the same price), the trade claims were worth 5 to 10 points less than the bonds, as the bonds would benefit from subordination turnover from the preferred while the trade would not. As with most market inefficiencies, investors realized their mistake quickly; within a week, the pricing of the trade claims adjusted to reflect their lack of subordination turnover.

It may sound easy to figure out exactly where you stand in a subordination scenario, but bond indentures and loan agreements are complex, and wording can be tricky. At times, you will need to seek a legal opinion from expert counsel.

Subordination's impact on post-petition interest

Post-petition interest is interest accrued after the commencement of a bankruptcy case (i.e., earned after the date on which the company files for bankruptcy protection). As discussed in Chapter 15, a secured creditor is entitled to post-petition interest as long as the value of its collateral is enough to cover the principal, unpaid pre-petition interest, and any accrued post-petition interest. However, the bankruptcy code expressly states that unsecured creditors are not entitled to recover post-petition interest. There are two exceptions to this rule:

1. If the estate ends up solvent, meaning the equity is eligible for some recovery, then all claims (secured and unsecured) are entitled to post-petition interest. The appropriate rate of interest to accrue on unsecured claims in these situations is currently a subject of disagreement among the courts. Some award post-petition interest at the contractual rate (coupon) and others at another rate they consider more appropriate, such as the federal judgment rate (which is usually lower than the contractual rate).
2. If there is subordination turnover, senior bondholders may receive post-petition interest from subordinated holders, even though post-petition interest was not part of the senior bondholder's claim in the bankruptcy. [1]

In the example above, let's now assume that since filing bankruptcy, bond #1 had accrued $8 million of post-petition interest. In this case, the subordinated bonds would have to turn over another $8 million, resulting in bond #1 recovering $68 million, or 113.3% of its claim. (The convention is to quote recoveries as a percentage of the claim excluding post-petition interest.)

STRUCTURAL SUBORDINATION

A company's consolidated financial statements are presented as if the company is one legal entity. However, that is rarely the case. Most firms are structured with many legal entities. Typically, a holding company ("HoldCo" or "HC") owns numerous operating companies ("OpCos" or "OCs"), also referred to as operating subsidiaries. Each OpCo owns different assets, raises or creates various third-party liabilities, and lends/borrows from other subsidiaries in the same group (obligations known as "intercompany loans"). HoldCos and OpCos issue their own debt; debt at the HoldCo is

[1]The legal documents must explicitly state that subordination turnover includes post-petition interest, which it usually does.

structurally subordinated to OpCo debt because the HoldCo generally has no assets other than its equity stake in the OpCos. Claims at the OpCo are closer to the assets and generally receive full recovery before the HoldCo lenders receive anything.

Let's go through a simple example to illustrate how legal structures work and then build on this example. Ara Lovin Industries is structured as a HoldCo that owns one OpCo (Figure 17.5).

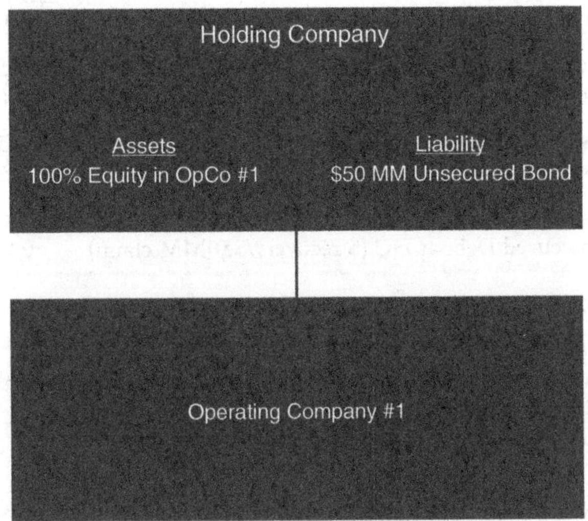

FIGURE 17.5 Ara Lovin Industries' Organizational Structure

- The HoldCo has a $50 million unsecured bond and no assets other than 100% of the operating company's equity.
- OpCo #1 has two liabilities: (1) a $15 million secured bank loan and (2) a $10 million unsecured bond.
- There are no bankruptcy-related administrative or priority claims.

We will consider recoveries in two scenarios: OpCo is sold in a 363 auction for (1) $20 million or (2) $40 million.

Because HoldCo only owns equity in OpCo, its recovery comes from the residual value, if any, after all claims at the OpCo are paid in full. Although both the $50 million HoldCo bond and the $10 million OpCo bond are unsecured, the HoldCo unsecured liabilities are structurally subordinated to the OpCo unsecured liabilities. The two recovery scenarios are outlined in Figure 17.6.

Monetary amounts in $MM	Recovery Scenarios	
	Scenario #1	Scenario #2
Enterprise Value of OpCo	$20	$40
Less OpCo Secured Debt	(15)	(15)
Remaining Value for OpCo Unsecured Claims	5	25
Unsecured Claims at OpCo	(10)	(10)
Equity Value Remaining (value to HC)	$0	$15
$ Recovery to Secured Debt at OpCo	$15	$15
% Recovery to Secured Debt ($ recovery /$15MM claim)	100%	100%
$ Recovery to Unsecured Debt at OpCo	$5	$10
% Recovery to Unsecured Debt ($ recovery /$10MM claim)	50%	100%
$ Recovery to Unsecured Debt at HC	$0	$15
% Recovery to Unsecured Debt at HC ($ recovery/$50MM claim)	0%	30%

FIGURE 17.6 Ara Lovin Industries Recovery Scenarios

The analysis above would be different if the OpCo guaranteed the HoldCo debt, which would eliminate structural subordination and effectively bring the HoldCo claim to the OpCo level. A guarantee from an OpCo to HoldCo debt is generally referred to as an upstream guarantee.

While a guarantee is an important aspect of HoldCo bond protection, it can be challenged in a bankruptcy proceeding. The debtor or other OpCo claims might argue the guarantee is invalid if the OpCo providing the guarantee received no consideration for providing the guarantee. There can also be a fraudulent conveyance argument (see Chapter 16).

In the Ara Lovin Industries example, if the $50 million HoldCo debt had a legally defensible OpCo guarantee, the HoldCo debt recovery would be the same as that of the OpCo unsecured debt. Figure 17.7 shows the difference in outcomes for two different enterprise values. In both cases, the HoldCo and OpCo receive the same recovery thanks to the upstream guarantee. The OpCo's recovery is meaningfully impaired by the guarantee, while the HoldCo's recovery increases substantially.

Monetary amounts in $MM	Recovery Scenarios	
	Scenario #1	Scenario #2
Enterprise Value of OpCo	$20	$40
Less OpCo Secured Debt	(15)	(15)
Remaining Value for OpCo Unsecured Claims	5	25
Unsecured Claims at OpCo[a]	(60)	(60)
Equity Value Remaining (value to HC)	$0	$0
$ Recovery to Secured Debt at OpCo	$15	$15
% Recovery to Secured Debt ($ recovery / $15MM claim)	100%	100%
$ Recovery to Unsecured Debt at OpCo and HC[b]	$5	$25
% Recovery to Unsecured Debt ($ recovery / ($10MM OpCo claim + $50MM guarantee claim)	8.3%	41.7%

[a] $10MM at OpCo and $50MM HC debt guaranteed by OpCo
[b] HC debt has valid OpCo guarantee

FIGURE 17.7 Ara Lovin Industries Recovery Scenarios with Upstream Guarantees

Now let's make the capital structure more complex. As shown in Figure 17.8, TA Wang Company has two operating subsidiaries.

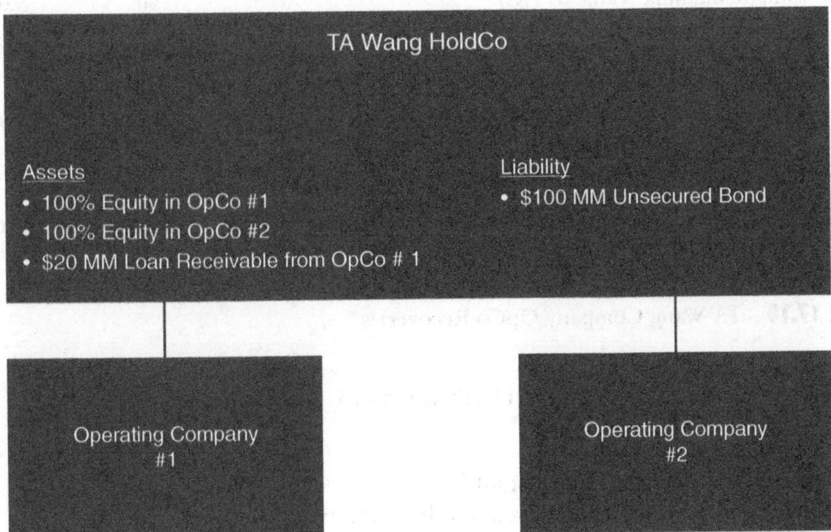

FIGURE 17.8 TA Wang Company's Organizational Structure

- TA Wang HoldCo has only three assets: (1) 100% of the equity of OpCo #1, (2) 100% of the equity of OpCo #2, and (3) a $20 million loan receivable from OpCo #1.
- TA Wang HoldCo issues a $100 million unsecured bond with no guarantees from either of the OpCos, which have the liabilities outlined in Figure 17.9.
- There are no bankruptcy-related administrative or priority claims.

OpCo #1 ($MM)		OpCo #2 ($MM)	
Claim	Amount	Claim	Amount
Secured Bank Debt	$25	Secured Bank Debt	$20
Unsecured Claims	10	Unsecured Claims	20
Unsecured Intercompany Loan	20	Total Claims Against OpCo #2	$40
Total Claims Against OpCo #1	$55		

FIGURE 17.9 TA Wang Company OpCo Liabilities

Figure 17.10 shows the recovery to OpCo claims if TA Wang Company files all entities for bankruptcy, OpCo #1 is sold for $50 million, and OpCo #2 is sold for $60 million.

	OpCo Recoveries	
Monetary amounts in $MM	OpCo #1	OpCo #2
Enterprise Value of OpCo	$50	$60
Less Secured Debt at the OpCo	(25)	(20)
Remaining Value for Unsecured Claims at OpCo	25	40
Unsecured Claims at OpCo[a]	(30)	(20)
Equity Value Remaining (value to HC)	$0	$20
$ Recovery to Secured Debt at OpCo	$25	$20
% Recovery to Secured Debt ($ recovery / secured claims)	100%	100%
$ Recovery to Unsecured Debt at OpCo (inc HC loan)	$25	$20
% Recovery to Unsecured Debt ($ recovery / unsecured claims, including HC loan)	83.3%	100%
$ Value of HoldCo's Equity Ownership of its Subsidiaries	$0	$20

[a] For OpCo #1 includes loan payable to HC

FIGURE 17.10 TA Wang Company OpCo Recoveries

Three sources of value to the HoldCo loan exist:

1. The equity value of OpCo #1;
2. The equity value of OpCo #2; and
3. The recovery value of the unsecured loan from HoldCo to OpCo.

Since the sale of OpCo #1 failed to cover the entity's debt and there is no upstream guarantee to the HoldCo, the HoldCo debt doesn't realize any recovery from its OpCo #1 equity ownership. It is, however, entitled to the residual equity value at OpCo #2, since OpCo #2's senior obligations are covered by the $60 million valuation.

The HoldCo's recovery is outlined in Figure 17.11.

Monetary amounts in $MM	HoldCo Recoveries
	HoldCo
Value of Equity Ownership of OpCo #1	$0.0
Value of Equity Ownership of OpCo #2	20.0
Value of Loan Made from HoldCo to OpCo #1[a]	16.7
Recovery to HoldCo Bond	$36.7
% Recovery to HoldCo Bond ($ recovery / $100MM HC bond)	36.7%

[a] $20MM loan x 83.3% recovery = $16.7

FIGURE 17.11 TA Wang Company HoldCo Recovery

Figure 17.12 is a summary of recoveries to TA Wang creditors.

	TA Wang Creditor Recoveries		
	Claim Amount ($MM)	Recovery $MM	%
Secured Debt at OpCo #1	$25.0	$25.0	100.0%
Secured Debt at OpCo #2	20.0	20.0	100.0%
Unsecured Claims at OpCo #1[a]	10.0	8.3	83.3%
Unsecured Claims at OpCo #2	20.0	20.0	100.0%
HoldCo Unsecured Bonds[b]	100.0	36.7	36.7%
Total 3rd-Party Claims against TA Wang Company	$175.0	$110.0	NM

[a] Excludes $10MM intercompany loan to HC
[b] See Figure 17.11 for the HoldCo recovery analysis

FIGURE 17.12 TA Wang Creditor Recoveries

SUBSTANTIVE CONSOLIDATION

Thus far, our examples have assumed that the OpCos and HoldCo at TA Wang are structurally separate, stand-alone legal entities. But what would happen to recoveries in TA Wang Company if the bankruptcy court does not recognize the different legal entities and elects to treat the company as if it were one entity? This is referred to as substantive consolidation, or "sub con." If a case is substantively consolidated, all intercompany claims are eliminated, and the claims of unsecured creditors no longer reside at separate legal entities but rather have pari passu claims against all the assets of the company.

If the TA Wang bankruptcy case is substantively consolidated, the recoveries to the HoldCo debt significantly improve while the recoveries to the OpCo unsecured debt are considerably worse, because the unsecured OpCo and HoldCo become pari passu, with identical recoveries, as outlined in Figure 17.13.

Monetary amounts in $MM	Sub Con Recoveries
	Substantive Consolidation
Enterprise Value of Entire Company	$110
Less Secured Debt	(45)
Remaining Value for Unsecured Claims	65
Unsecured Claims	(130)
Equity Value	$0
Recovery to Secured Debt at Operating Sub	$45
% Recovery to Secured Debt ($ recovery / secured claims)	100.0%
Recovery to Unsecured Debt	$65
% Recovery to Unsecured Debt ($ recovery / unsecured claim, incl HC loan)	50.0%

FIGURE 17.13 Substantive Consolidation Recoveries

Figure 17.14 compares the claims' recoveries for TA Wang if the legal structures are enforced by the courts versus if the courts substantively consolidate the company.

	Recovery Comparison	
	Legal Entities Hold	Legal Entities Sub Con
Secured Debt at OpCo #1	100.0%	100.0%
Secured Debt at OpCo #2	100.0%	100.0%
Unsecured 3rd-Party Claims at OpCo #1	83.3%	50.0%
Unsecured Claims at OpCo #2	100.0%	50.0%
HoldCo Unsecured Bond	36.7%	50.0%

FIGURE 17.14 TA Wang Company Recovery Comparison

Given the material recovery implications of substantive consolidation, it is another hard-fought bankruptcy fight. Its intensity is magnified since there is no bright line test for when a company's legal entities should be substantively consolidated. While the bankruptcy code does not have formal standards for this, sub con is generally deemed appropriate in the scenarios summarized in Figure 17.15.

1. Creditors dealt with the entities as a single economic unit and did not rely on their separate identity in extending credit; or
2. The affairs of the entities are so entangled that creating accurate, stand-alone financial statements for each entity would be impossible or prohibitively expensive and cumbersome, and consolidation would benefit all creditors.[i]

FIGURE 17.15 Sub Con Conditions

These conditions are sometimes referred to as the "scrambled egg" or "alter egos" rationale. Because the subsidiaries never operated as separate entities (did not keep individual financial records, commingled cash, etc.), the cost to unscramble the egg (if even possible) outweighs the benefits to any class of creditors. The separate legal entities operated as if they were one; they were alter egos of each other.

Threatening a sub con fight as a negotiating tactic is not uncommon, but actual sub con rulings in bankruptcy are rare, particularly absent outright fraud or systematic accounting irregularities. One landmark case, Owens Corning (OC), illustrates the stakes. Owens Corning is a manufacturer of glass fiber materials used in building products such as roofing and insulation. In 1997, Credit Suisse First Boston syndicated a $2 billion unsecured bank loan for OC to finance an acquisition. While the loan was unsecured, it did include a covenant that any domestic subsidiary with material assets must provide an unsecured guarantee to the loan. No other creditor enjoyed the benefit of this guarantee.

The company filed for bankruptcy in October 2000 in the face of higher-than-expected personal injury claims from consumers alleging wrongful death and disease due to asbestos inhalation from OC products. The asbestos liabilities related to old lines of business, as the company discontinued manufacturing asbestos-containing products in 1972 (well before the loan was underwritten). Prior to emerging from bankruptcy, OC had the capital structure outlined in Figure 17.16.

Type of Claim	Claims (in $MM)
Secured Claims	$12
Administrative and Priority Claims	766
Total	$778
Unsecured Bank Debt	$1,475
Unsecured Bonds	1,389
Other General Unsecured Claims (GUCs)	308
Estimate of Asbestos Claims	10,200
Total Unsecured Claims	$13,372
Total Claims	$14,150

FIGURE 17.16 Owens Corning Capital Structure

Since the bank loan was the only unsecured liability with a guarantee from the domestic operating subsidiaries, its recovery theoretically would be higher than that of the bonds. However, sub con would equalize bank and bond recoveries by refusing to honor the structural protection of the loan's guarantee. Therefore, bondholders fought vigorously to convince a judge to substantively consolidate, while bank debt holders did the opposite. The market was unsure who would win, as illustrated by the trading levels during the bankruptcy. As shown in Figure 17.17, except for three points in time, the bank debt always traded at a premium to the bonds to reflect the economic benefit of the operating subsidiary guarantee.

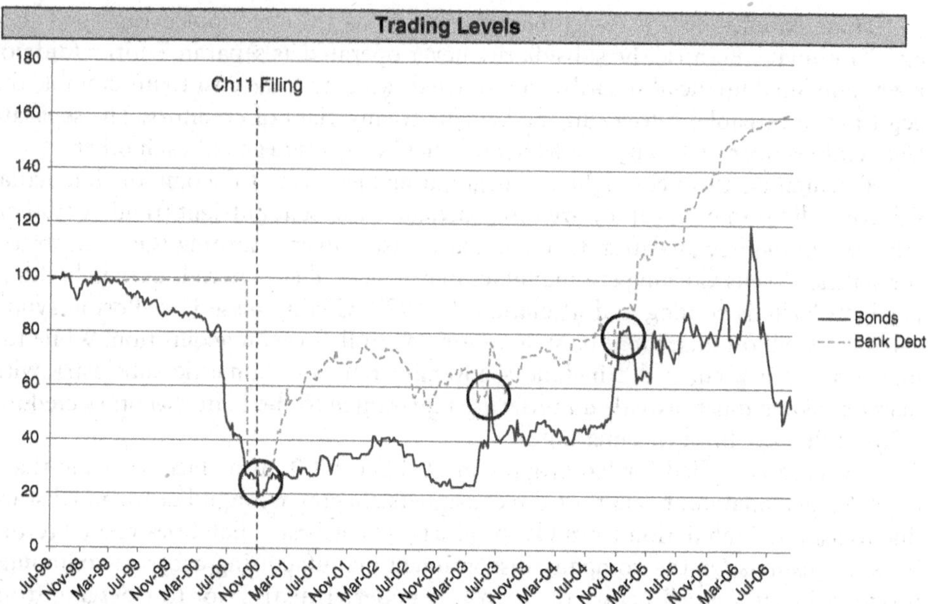

FIGURE 17.17 Owens Corning Debt Trading Levels

Point #1 (October 2000): When Owens filed, the bank debt and bonds were quoted on top of each other (that is, at the same price). Until more sophisticated investors read the underlying loan documents and bond indentures, the market treated both instruments the same, as they were both unsecured debt.

However, once the market appreciated that the bank debt had guarantees that were not extended to the bonds, the bank debt started to trade at a material premium.

Once investors became aware of the guarantee, they had to assess the probability of the court's substantively consolidating the cases and rendering the guarantees worthless. This was a multiyear legal battle with the bank debt holders' lawyers arguing that the legal entities must be maintained as a matter of law and all the other unsecured claims arguing that the entities were alter egos of each other and should be consolidated.

Points #2 and #3 (early 2003 and mid-2004): At various points in time, developments in the sub con fight led the market to believe that the entities would likely be consolidated. Ultimately the court did not consolidate, and the bank's recovery was significantly higher than that of the bonds.

What trade would you consider putting on when the bank debt and bonds were trading at the same level? Buy the bank debt and short the bonds. If the enterprise value is worth more than expected, you will break even by winning on your long bank debt position and losing an equal amount on your short bond position. If the enterprise value is worth less than expected, you will also break even since the loss on the long bank debt position offsets the gain on your short bond position. This is not a bet on valuation but solely on sub con. If the court respects the legal entities, you will make money since the bank debt (which you are long) will have a higher recovery than the bond (which you are short) due to the value of the guarantees. If the case is substantively consolidated, the bank debt and the bond will receive the same recovery, and you will break even.

In summary, you either make money (if legal entities are maintained) or break even (if the court sub cons the entities).[2] This is why prices only converged for very small periods of time; as long as there is any possibility the legal entities will be honored, the bank debt should always trade at a premium to the bonds.

DOUBLE DIP CLAIMS

Double dip claims defy logic for anyone not in the distressed debt or restructuring business. Let's go through an example using a hypothetical company, Teich Inc., with two legal entities: (1) Parent Co, which includes all the business operations, and (2) Finance Co, whose only purpose is to raise external debt. In our hypothetical (see Figure 17.18):

- Parent Co has $800 million of unsecured liabilities owed to non-related lenders (excludes the $500 million loan from Finance Co).
- Finance Co issues $500 million of bonds. Parent Co provides a guarantee.
- Finance Co lends the $500 million proceeds to Parent Co.
- Finance Co's only asset is the $500 million intercompany receivable from the parent (i.e., the loan it made to the parent).

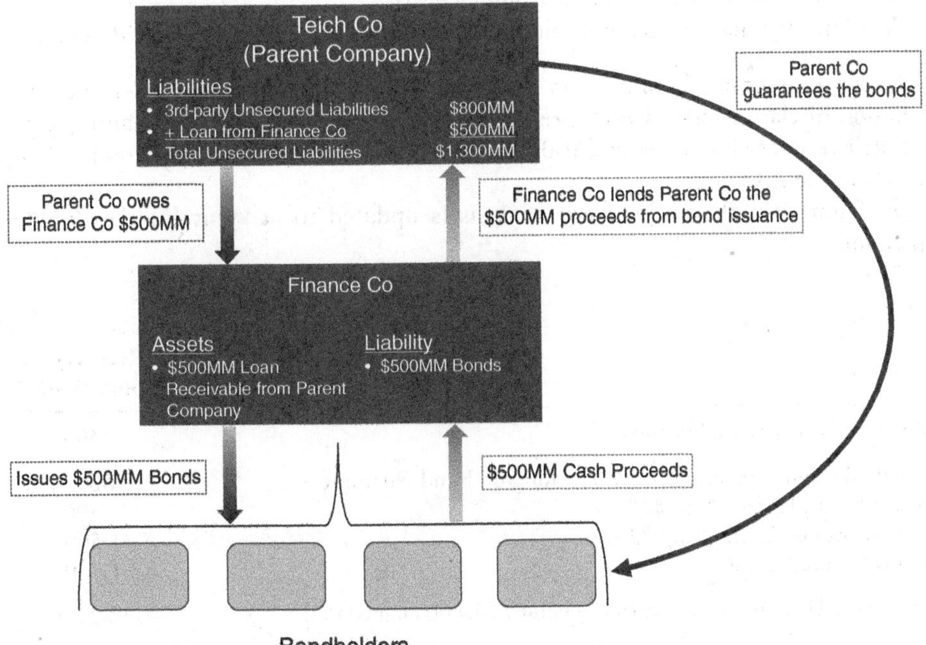

FIGURE 17.18 Teich Inc. Legal Structure

[2]The analysis ignores the bid/ask spread to unwind the trade.

Teich Inc. files for bankruptcy, and residual value for all the unsecured claims after paying administrative, priority, and secured claims is $400 million. Other unsecured claims, excluding any claims from Finance Co, are $800 million. When I ask my students what the recovery to the bonds is, most say 30.8%. Their logic is as shown in Figure 17.19.

	Recovery Amount ($MM)
Value Left for Unsecured Claims	$400
Unsecured Claims, Excluding FinCo Claim and Bond Guarantees	$800
Bonds Issued at FinCo	500
Total Unsecured Claims	$1,300
Recovery to Unsecured Claims Including Bonds ($400 value / $1,300 claims)	30.8%

FIGURE 17.19 Teich Inc. Recoveries

They would be wrong, unless the case is substantively consolidated. Finance Co bondholders enjoy the benefit of two claims against the Parent:

1. Finance Co has a $500 million claim against Parent Co resulting from its intercompany loan. Any recovery from that loan goes to Finance Co bondholders since there are no other claims at Finance Co.
2. In addition, Finance Co bondholders exert a guarantee directly against Parent Co.

Even though the bondholders only lent $500 million, they are entitled to $1 billion of claims against the Parent Co, referred to as a double dip claim. (Note that their recovery is capped at $500 million—that is, they cannot receive more than the amount lent.)

In Figure 17.20, the recovery analysis is updated to account for the double dip claim.

	Recovery Amount ($MM)
Value Left for Unsecured Claims	$400
Unsecured Claims Excluding FinCo Claim and Bond Guarantees	$800
FinCo Loan to Parent ("dip #1")	500
Bond Guarantee Claim ("dip #2")	500
Total Unsecured Claims	$1,800
Recovery to Unsecured Claims ($400 value / $1,800 claims) (%)	22.2%
Recovery to FinCo Bonds (22.2% from FinCo Loan + 22.2% from Parent Guarantee)	44.4%

FIGURE 17.20 Teich Inc. Double Dip Claim Recoveries

The recovery to the Finance Co bondholders is 44.4%, resulting from two claims: they receive a 22.2% recovery from the intercompany loan and a 22.2% recovery from the Parent guarantee.

However, if the case is substantively consolidated, all intercompany receivables and payables will be eliminated, along with the double dip claim. Finance Co recovery will be 30.8% (see Figure 17.19) versus 44.4%.

Lehman Brothers is a classic example of a double dip claim. Before its 2008 bankruptcy filing, Lehman's finance subsidiary, Lehman Brothers Treasury Co BV (LBT), issued approximately $30 billion of bonds with a parent guarantee from Lehman Brothers Holding Inc (LBHI). LBT then lent the proceeds to the parent, LBHI, resulting in a double dip claim for LBT bondholders. The first claim was related to the intercompany loan LBT made to the parent, and the second claim related to the guarantee the parent made to the LBT bondholders. Therefore, LBT bondholders fought to maintain legal separation, while LBHI claim holders fought for sub con.

To simplify what happened, the debtor first tried to file a Plan of Reorganization with a "split-the-baby" approach that offered LBT creditors 50% of their guarantee claim (i.e., they would forgo 50% of one of their double dip claims). The LBT noteholders (including my firm) refused to support this plan. After the lapse of the exclusivity period, two competing plans were filed with the court:

1. A complete sub con plan (supported by LBHI claim holders); and
2. A "non sub con" plan (supported by other LBT holders and us).

After being in bankruptcy for several years, the key players hashed out a negotiated settlement that gave LBT creditors 80% of their second claim against the parent, up from the original debtor proposal of 50%. This resulted in a recovery to LBT creditors of 1.8x higher than the recovery to debt instruments without the double dip claim.

CHAPTER CONCLUSION

While prior chapters have emphasized the importance of collateral when forecasting recovery value, in this chapter you have learned about the power of various forms of subordination to impair or improve your claim. Understanding the potential for subordination of various claims in a Chapter 11 scenario is critical to an investment recommendation for a distressed or bankrupt issuer. Given the nuances and complexities of individual bond indentures, this sometimes requires a third-party legal opinion. The case studies in this chapter illustrate that any legal fees incurred to determine subordination risk more than pay for themselves in better investment decisions.

Our discussion of subordination sets the stage for a deeper dive into legal—if creative—methods used by creditors against one another. In the next chapter, you will learn about techniques used by creditors to maximize their profits by leapfrogging their way to a better position in a bankrupt issuer's capital structure or laying exclusive claim to specific sources of value.

NOTE

i. Weil, Gotshal, and Manges. (October 2005) "Bankruptcy Bulletin." *Current Issues in Restructuring and Reorganization.* Vol 12 no. 10, October 2005.

CHAPTER 18

Liability Management and Creditor-on-Creditor Violence

By now, you probably have concluded that distressed debt investing is not for the faint of heart. However, starting around 2015, new trends emerged that made it even more confrontational. Some argue that this resulted from a long period of economic growth, which led to fewer opportunities for distressed debt investors, forcing them to become more aggressive in pursuit of good returns. But the bigger driver was a structural shift that led to fewer creditor safeguards in loan documents.

Recall from Chapter 12 that loan and bond indentures include covenants that impede lender-unfriendly behavior. While these covenants still exist, historically low interest rates in response to the GFC increased demand for high-yielding debt investments. In this seller's market for corporate loans, issuers negotiated more borrower-friendly terms, especially in broadly syndicated loans (BSLs).

The financial press has focused on the increase in secured loans without any financial covenants ("cov-lite" loans), but lack of covenants was only one aspect of weakened creditor protections. The loan documents that became standardized in the BSL market have fewer creditor safeguards outside of financial covenant protection, including built-in "land mines" that permit borrower-friendly transactions at the expense of the lender, such as asset-stripping. Borrowers and their lawyers euphemistically refer to transactions that rely on weak documents as "liability management." In contrast, many lenders call this "getting screwed by the borrower and/or other creditors." These deals have led to increased "lender-on-lender violence," as some creditors benefit at the expense of others.

More than ever, successful debt investors must know how to spot these loopholes so they are not surprised when liability management occurs. These transactions rely on highly technical interpretations of loan agreements, which you must understand. Additionally, it is critical to learn to identify situations requiring outside counsel. In this chapter, I will simplify some concepts to make them understandable to the layperson (without a law degree) and provide a road map of the types of transactions that can lead to creditor conflicts.

ASSET-STRIPPING, OR GETTING "J. SCREWED"

To illustrate asset-stripping, we'll start with a hypothetical situation. You recommended your firm buy $100 million of a $1.5 billion senior secured loan to SU Corporation, a consumer products company with a great brand. SU is owned by a private equity firm that paid $3.05 billion for the business. The company's capital structure is shown in Figure 18.1.

	Capital Structure	
	Amount ($MM)	% of Capital Structure
Senior Secured Term Loan	$1,500	49.2%
Unsecured Bonds	500	16.4%
Total Debt	2,000	65.6%
Less Cash	–100	–3.3%
Net Debt	1,900	62.3%
Sponsor Cash Equity	1,150	37.7%
Enterprise Value	$3,050	100.0%

FIGURE 18.1 SU Corp Capital Structure

Although SU Corp was underperforming expectations, the senior secured loan's loan-to-value (LTV) of 49.2% based on the sponsor's purchase price ($1.5 billion secured debt / $3.05 billion enterprise value) gave you comfort. This loan was "first in line" since all of SU Corp's assets secured it, meaning the company's value would have to decrease by more than half before the loan was impaired.

Your investment thesis was based entirely on the loan's security position, which in turn relied primarily on SU's brand, which constituted the majority of the company's asset value. This would have been a reasonable thesis, except that you did not carefully review or hire outside counsel to review the 200-page loan document. Instead, you relied on a summary of it.

As SU Corp's performance continues to deteriorate, it requires additional liquidity to fund operating losses. As part of a new financing, SU transfers the asset of the brand from the legal entities that guarantee your loan to a guarantor entity set up for the new lenders, who are now collateralized by SU's brand. Your loan trades down 30 points once the market discovers that the brand no longer secures it.

You have been J. SCrewed.

In 2015, J. Crew raised new debt and exchanged some junior notes using a complex drop-down, or "trap door" transaction. To understand drop-down financings, we must delve deeper into the loan documents. As discussed in Chapter 17, companies are typically made up of many legal entities which are designated as:

1. Credit parties or non-credit parties (also referred to as loan parties and non-loan parties):
   - Credit parties are obligors under the credit facility, either as borrowers or guarantors of the loans.
   - Non-credit parties have no payment obligations to lenders.

   And
2. Restricted subsidiaries or unrestricted subsidiaries:
   - The credit agreement and bond indentures' covenants bind restricted subsidiaries, meaning they must stay in compliance with covenants.
   - Unrestricted subsidiaries are not bound by covenants.

Credit parties are always restricted, and therefore, unrestricted subsidiaries are never credit parties. However, in some cases (primarily foreign subsidiaries), a restricted subsidiary might not be a credit party, meaning it must obey the terms of the loan agreement and/or bond indentures, even though it is not an obligor of the loan and/or bond. Figure 18.2 is a simplified diagram of a hypothetical corporate structure similar to J. Crew.

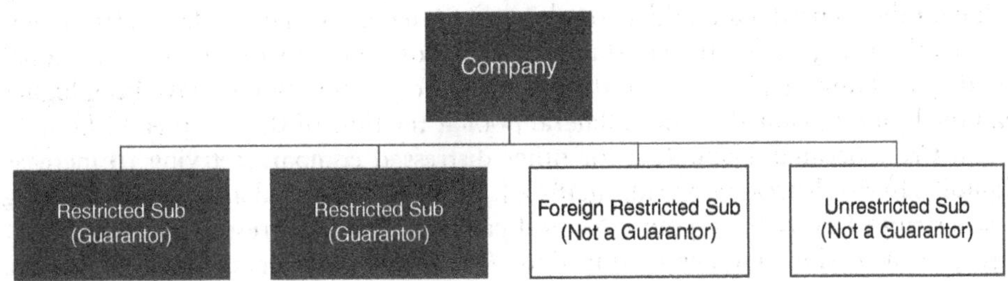

FIGURE 18.2 Hypothetical Corporate Structure—J. Crew Example

Preppy apparel retailer J. Crew was taken private by PE firms TPG and Leonard Green in 2011 for $3 billion. By 2016, the company was facing a liquidity crisis, as $540 million in unsecured PIK notes were coming due with no chance of refinancing them because its unsecured debt was trading well below par. The private equity owners were unwilling to inject more cash into the business as their original investment was underwater. The only financing available to J. Crew was secured debt—but all its assets, including intellectual property, were already pledged to the $1.5 billion term loan. These lenders were unwilling to increase their commitments because they were not comfortable lending at a higher LTV.

Some clever lawyers reviewed the term loan's legal documents and devised a way to strip collateral away from these lenders so that it could be used as collateral for new debt. Section 7.02 of the company's loan agreement allowed for three separate permitted investment baskets. Two critical points allowed the company to "strip assets" away from its existing secured lenders:

1. The permitted investment baskets did not require that the investment (or transfer of assets classified as an investment) be for a new business venture or to support an existing business; and
2. None of the baskets restricted which assets could be used for the investment. In other words, the company could transfer any asset, including its intellectual property, as long as its value did not exceed the allowed baskets.

The company used the above baskets to assign 72.04% of its US trademarks with a value (estimated by the company) of $250 million to IPCo, an unrestricted subsidiary. This intellectual property (i.e., the J. Crew brand) was arguably its most valuable and only significant asset besides its inventory, but the company received a fairness opinion from an independent financial advisor before completing the transaction. Ultimately, creditors sued, arguing that the IP was worth upwards of $1 billion, far exceeding the permitted investments allowed under the loan documents and, in addition, that such amount constituted substantially all of the value of their collateral, which could not be transferred without the consent of each lender.

While litigation was pending on the transfer of the assets, J. Crew started negotiations with the holders of the unsecured PIK notes and the senior secured term loan. Eventually, deals were cut with the vast majority of creditors.

These transactions extended J. Crew's runway, but only delayed the inevitable as it filed for Chapter 11 in 2020. It's impossible to calculate the diminution of recovery value for the secured loan holders resulting from the removal of the brand from their collateral package given the substantial passage of time (not to mention the global pandemic). However, it is certain that their recovery values would have been higher had the brand remained in the collateral pool at the time of the Chapter 11 filing.

J. Crew became a template for other distressed companies trying to increase liquidity. In the distressed world, "getting J. SCrewed" emerged as a term for having assets stripped away from your collateral package. Other distressed companies that have executed similar types of trap door / drop-down financings include Revlon, Travelport, and Cirque du Soleil.

The conclusion is simple: lenders need to read the documents! If the credit agreements have large permitted investment baskets that can be used to move material assets into non-creditor entities without lender consent, you risk having collateral stripped away from your loan.

UPTIERING, OR GETTING "SERTA'D"

Again, we'll use a hypothetical situation to illustrate this type of transaction. Your firm took down $100 million of a $2 billion broadly syndicated loan that financed a $3 billion LBO of PU Corp. After PU Corp's material underperformance, your loan trades down to 65 cents on the dollar. You are concerned about the company's liquidity, but you decide not to sell based on your view of the company's floor/downside case value of $1.5 to $1.75 billion. Even accounting for a priming DIP to fund $100 million of bankruptcy expenses, your recovery would be between 70.0% and 82.5% (see recovery analysis in Figure 18.3), versus the $65 market price. The loan documents included covenants that, in your view, limited PU Corp's ability to incur additional secured debt.

	Recovery Analysis	
Monetary amounts in $MM	**Low**	**High**
Analyst's Downside Valuation of the Company	$1,500	$1,750
Priming Bankruptcy Expenses/DIP	(100)	(100)
Value Left for Senior Secured Loan	$1,400	$1,650
% Recovery (Value left / $2 B loan)	*70.0%*	*82.5%*

FIGURE 18.3 Recovery Analysis for PU Corp

Your recovery value thesis is shattered by a press release announcing that the company obtained consent from a majority (50.1%) of its secured lenders to amend its debt covenants to permit a $200 million capital raise that would prime (come ahead of) the existing loan. This new loan was provided by—you guessed it—the lenders who signed the amendment.

Furthermore, the company announced a plan to exchange the $1,002 million of debt (50.1% of the $2 billion facility) owned by the consenting lenders into $952 million of new debt that would also prime your loan. Your position went from first place in line (subordinated only to a potential DIP) to behind $1.15 billion of debt ($200 million new debt + $952 million exchanged debt). Debt that initially shared your exact security position cut the line to get ahead of you. Your recovery analysis just went from 70%–82.5% (see Figure 18.3) to 24.8%–49.8% (see Figure 18.4), assuming the company utilizes all of its new liquidity. Meanwhile, the consenting lenders stand to receive an effective 95% recovery on their debt ($952 million of exchange debt / $1,002 million of debt exchanged).

	Recovery Analysis	
Monetary amounts in $MM	Low	High
Analyst's Downside Valuation of the Company	$1,500	$1,750
Priming Bankruptcy Expenses/DIP	(100)	(100)
Value Left for Senior Secured Loan	1,400	1,650
New Priming Senior Secured Loan	(200)	(200)
Rolled/Exchanged Loan	(952)	(952)
Value Left for the Non-Rolled Loan	$ 248	$ 498
% Recovery[a]	*24.8%*	*49.9%*

[a]Value Left for the Non-Rolled Loan/$998MM the 49.9% of the loan not rolled

FIGURE 18.4 PU Corp Recovery Analysis after Uptiering Transaction

Your debt trades down, while debt that a day earlier was identical to yours trades up.

You have been Serta'd.

Serta, the US bedding manufacturer, took advantage of a "land mine" in its loan documents to accomplish a non-pro rata exchange, or uptiering transaction.

Generally, it takes a majority of lenders (based on par value, not number of lenders) to amend a loan agreement. However, amendments requiring only majority consent typically cannot adversely affect any lenders without their consent. For instance, 51% of the lenders cannot amend the document to subordinate the other 49%.

In addition, most loan agreements have pro rata sharing provisions, which dictate that all payments made to lenders must be allocated pro rata based on how much debt the lenders own. For instance, if you own 10% of the debt facility, you must receive 10% of every distribution to lenders. This provision cannot be amended without consent from the affected lenders. It is sometimes referred to as one of the "sacred rights" of the loan agreement (see Chapter 12 for a list of all sacred rights). In other words, the company cannot pay back some lenders while leaving other lenders' obligations outstanding; all lenders must get their fair share unless they agree otherwise.

However, the Serta documents included a carve-out for debt-for-debt exchanges on a non-pro rata basis that takes place pursuant to an open market transaction, meaning a transaction that involved secondary buyers and sellers of Serta's debt—even if the company itself is the purchaser. This provision permitted the uptiering transaction in two steps (or so the lawyers for the company argued).

First, a lender group holding more than 50% of the first lien loans ("Participating Lenders") amended the loan agreement to allow the company to borrow new money with priority over the existing secured lenders (priming debt). As this affected all lenders equally, it only required a 50.1% vote. After the amendment, the Participating Lenders made a new $200 million loan, senior to the existing secured loan.

Next, Serta relied on the credit agreement's language permitting "debt-for-debt exchanges on a non-pro rata basis as part of open market transactions" to offer a debt exchange to Participating Lenders in which they rolled their loans into "new" debt that primed those that did not participate. The company structured this as an open market transaction in which Serta bought the Participating Lenders' loans at a discount and gave them priming debt as consideration.

The impact on the first lien minority (non-participating) lenders was devastating. Before the uptiering transaction, they owned a syndicated loan that was first in line to get repaid. After the transaction, they were subordinated to $1.075 billion of priming debt ($200 million of new loans and $875 million of exchanged notes[1]).

The Serta transaction served as a road map for other distressed companies that needed to raise new capital. However, only companies whose original loan documents have the non-pro rata language can execute the uptiering transaction. Other companies that have implemented this strategy include Boardriders, Trimark, and Travelport.

The legal battles around these transactions continue as of the writing of this book. For instance, in the Boardriders case, on October 17, 2022, New York Supreme Court Justice Andrea Masley denied motions to dismiss the minority lender's breach of contract, breach of the implied duty of good faith, and fair dealing claims against the company and participating lenders.[i]

The conclusion is simple: lenders need to read the documents! If the credit agreements have non-pro rata language and you are a minor participant in the loan, you risk subordination to lenders in the same facility. The participating lenders' positions are improved at the expense of the non-participating lenders. Companies with pressing liquidity needs will inevitably interpret the language in their loan documents in the most borrower-friendly manner and team up as necessary with the creditor(s) who offer them the most flexibility to take advantage of loopholes.

CREDIT DEFAULT SWAPS (CDS)—MANUFACTURED DEFAULTS

The last example of creditor-on-creditor violence is probably the most controversial. CDSs are derivatives that enable investors to hedge the risk of default of credit investments they own or bet on the default of a company and the secondary trading levels of that company's securities after default.

The easiest way to understand CDSs is to think of them as insurance against a default. The buyer pays an up-front fee and an annual premium to compensate the seller for taking on the default risk, referred to as "buying protection." The price of the CDS contract incorporates the risk of default at the time of purchase. If an issuer's debt is already trading at a substantial discount to par, the combination of the

[1]Participating lenders "rolled" a portion of their loans into the priming facility. Their remaining exposure was treated like the non-participating lenders'.

up-front fee and annual premium will be much higher than if it is trading close to par. If the company has a "credit event," such as failure to make a principal payment or a bankruptcy filing, the insurance seller pays the buyer par for the underlying bonds, regardless of where they are trading, essentially providing a recovery of 100%.

While CDSs originated as a tool to hedge the risk of a long position in an issuer's debt, they can also be a stand-alone speculative investment (i.e., without a corresponding investment in the debt). CDS sellers are implicitly betting that an issuer will not default—that is, they are synthetically going long the company's credit. The buyer of a CDS contract is betting the company will default—that is, they are synthetically shorting the company's credit.

Let's go through a hypothetical situation. You are evaluating a homebuilder with significant debt maturities over the next three years, which might force the company to file for bankruptcy. Based on your analysis, you are willing to take the other side of the bet—but there isn't sufficient liquidity in the underlying bonds to buy the bonds outright. Instead, you enter into a \$250 million of notional value CDS, thus synthetically creating a long position. You are the seller of the contract, and the buyer on the other side is taking the opposite credit view (i.e., that the company will file). The terms on the CDS are as follows:

- Notional amount (i.e., the amount of par value debt being "insured"/the amount you are synthetically long): \$250 million;
- Up-front fee (paid by the buyer of the CDS contract to you as seller): 17.5% of the notional amount; (conceptually the higher the up-front fee, the higher the implied probability of default, and thus the higher the cost of "insurance");
- Annual premium (also referred to as running spread, paid by the buyer of protection to you): for distressed companies, the running spread is 5% of the notional amount;
- Term: 3 years.

If the company does not have a credit event, you will make \$81.25 million over three years. Figures 18.5 and 18.6 illustrate the proposed CDS transaction.

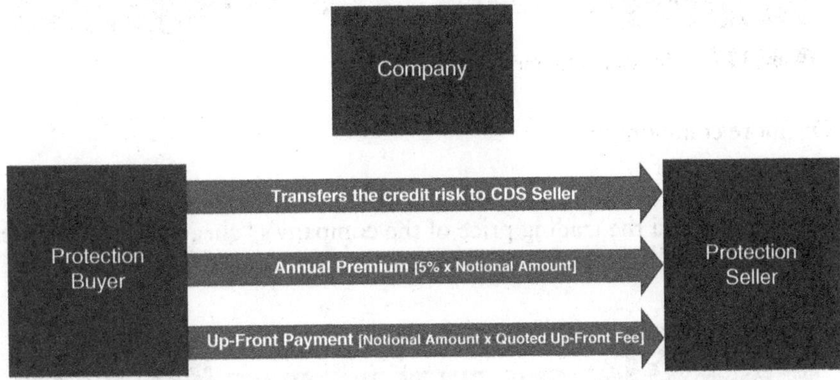

FIGURE 18.5 Overview of CDS Transaction

	CDS P&L ($MM)
Up-Front Fee = $250MM Notional Amount × 17.5%	$43.75
Annual Premium = $250MM Notional Amount × 5.0%	$12.5
× Number of Years on CDS Contract	×3
Total Premiums Earned Over 3 Years	$37.5
Total Profits (Up-front fee plus premiums)	**$81.25**

FIGURE 18.6 CDS Economics and Return

Your investment is working out well 18 months into your trade. The company's performance has improved, and the credit markets have rallied, allowing the company to refinance its near-dated maturity. The fund that took the other side of the bet (purchased the CDS) is not happy in the face of an $81.25 million loss if the company does not default or file for bankruptcy before the end of the contract.

However, your celebration was premature, as the company—notwithstanding the fact that it has ample liquidity to pay its debts as they come due—skips a small coupon payment on a $25 million bond issue that is owed to one of its own affiliates. Put simply, the company decided not to pay back money it owed itself. The missed coupon payment happens to be just large enough to trigger a "credit event" under the CDS contract. Upon a credit event, two things happen. First, the CDS buyer is no longer required to pay the annual premium to the seller. Second, the CDS seller must compensate the buyer in one of two ways:

1. Physical settlement (Figure 18.7): The buyer of protection delivers bonds by buying them in the open market at a price well below par (resulting from the credit event), and the seller of protection pays par for those bonds.

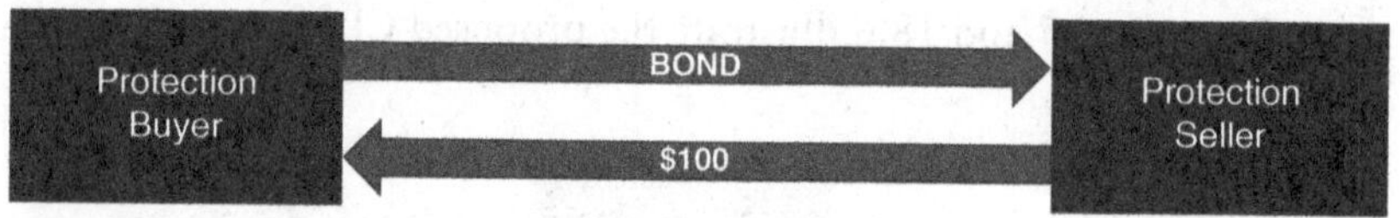

FIGURE 18.7 Physical Settlement

Or (more commonly):

2. Cash settlement (Figure 18.8): The protection seller pays the buyer the difference between par and the trading price of the company's "cheapest to deliver" credit instrument, as determined in a market-wide auction.

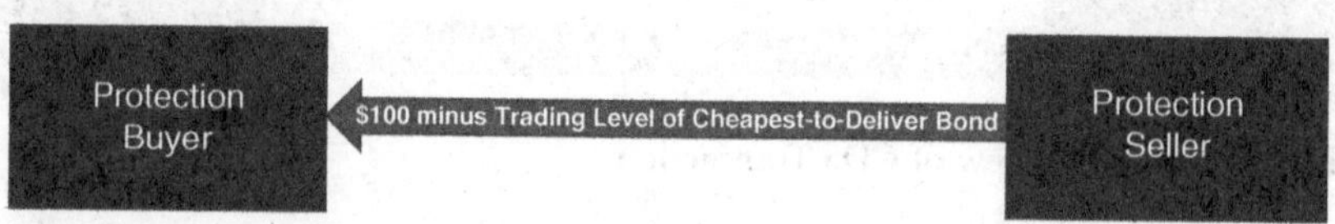

FIGURE 18.8 Cash Settlement

While this credit event is not great for your position, at first blush it is not a disaster. The company is healthy, and your trader tells you its bonds generally trade at 97% of face value. Based on this, you estimate the cash settlement of the CDS is $7.5 million, which as shown in Figure 18.9 takes your estimated profit from the trade down to $55 million, still not a bad return.

	CDS P&L ($MM)
Up-Front Fee = $250MM Notional Amount × 17.5% [A]	$43.75
Annual Premium = $250MM Notional Amount × 5.0%	$12.5
× Number of Years before Credit Event	×1.5
Total Premiums Earned [B]	$18.75
Total Cash Inflows Related to Selling CDS [A + B]	$62.5
Cost of Cash Settlement Due to Credit Event Trigger[a]	-7.5
Revised Profits from the Trade	$55.0

[a] 100%–97% trading level to cheapest to deliver bond × $250MM notional amount.

FIGURE 18.9 Revised CDS Economics and Returns

However, simultaneous with the nonpayment of interest to itself, the company borrowed money from another lender on below-market terms and effectuated a bond exchange to create a new bond that trades at a significant discount to par because of its terms: a 5% coupon with a 22-year maturity. The existing bonds trading at 97% have, on average, a 9% coupon with shorter than ten-year maturities. As you know from Chapter 3, the combination of a lower coupon and longer maturity translates into a substantially lower price of this new bond—55% of face value. Your CDS position is now showing an expected loss of $50 million because the cheapest to deliver security is much cheaper, making the corresponding cost of cash settlement (which you pay the CDS buyer) much higher than if the cheapest to deliver bonds were at $97. The revised P&L is shown in Figure 18.10.

	CDS P&L
Up-Front Fee = $250MM Notional Amount × 17.5% [A]	$43.75
Annual Premium = $250MM Notional Amount × 5.0%	12.5
× Number of Years before Credit Event	×1.5
Total Premiums Earned [B]	18.75
Total Cash Inflows Related to Selling CDS [A + B]	$62.5
Cost of Cash Settlement Due to Credit Event Trigger[a]	-112.5
Revised Profits from the Trade	-$50.00

[a] 100%–55% trading level to cheapest to deliver bond × $250MM notional amount

FIGURE 18.10 Revised CDS Economics and Returns Taking into Account Off-Market Bond

This situation makes no sense to you. As the seller of the CDS, you should be the winner. The company's performance improved; it refinanced its near-maturity bonds; and all of its debt (besides this bizarre off-market bond) trades at or near par. You believe you should be up approximately $81 million; instead, you are now projecting a loss of $50 million, equating to a whopping $131 million swing in profit.

You discover that the CDS buyer, a hedge fund, orchestrated the steps outlined above to transform its loss position into a gain. The hedge fund approached the borrower with an offer it couldn't refuse: below-market financing in exchange for a manufactured default on an inconsequential bond. The default would trigger the payment from the CDS seller to the buyer. The company got below-market financing, and the hedge fund made a handsome net profit, earning considerably more on the CDS contract than it lost on the mark-to-market from the below-market financing it provides.

This is what Solus, a credit-focused hedge fund, accused homebuilder Hovnanian and GSO, another hedge fund, of working together to achieve.

Upon announcement of the contemplated transaction, Solus first sought an injunction in NY Federal Court to block it. The judge denied that request, finding that monetary damages (paid by Hovnanian and GSO) could compensate Solus if she ultimately found the transaction illegal. With the transaction complete, the question shifted to whether the transaction triggered a CDS contract payout from Solus (the CDS seller, betting on Hovnanian's health) to GSO (the CDS buyer, betting on Hovnanian's default). But the CDS market does not treat this type of dispute as a court-litigated matter; instead, a CDS Determinations Committee comprised of 10 sell-side institutions and five buy-side institutions appointed by ISDA (International Swaps and Derivatives Association, the governing body on derivatives contracts) determines whether a CDS credit event has occurred and which debt instruments can be referenced as the cheapest-to-deliver to determine the amounts owed under the CDS contract. In parallel with the ISDA process, the litigation between Solus and GSO continued, with Solus seeking damages for, among other things, market manipulation.

As both sides prepared to make their respective cases to both ISDA and the judge, the novel and aggressive transaction began to attract significant media attention.

Ultimately, the parties settled their disputes on confidential terms before either the court or ISDA weighed in. A year later, ISDA amended its operative documents to make it clear that transactions like this one (deemed "narrowly tailored credit events") would not trigger a CDS payout going forward.

The specific creditor-on-creditor violence strategy pursued in the Hovnanian case may no longer be available thanks to changes in contract language meant to address this type of situation. But the CDS market and its operative documents remain complex and ripe for potential manipulation under the right set of circumstances and with the right counterparties involved.

CHAPTER CONCLUSION

Legal documents matter. Many credit investors never read or engage outside legal counsel to read the entire credit agreement or bond indenture, instead relying on a summary of key terms to evaluate their level of protection. If nothing goes wrong, they clip their coupon and get paid back at or before the maturity date. However, if the company experiences distress, these investors are at a material disadvantage to those who understand every aspect of the legal documents. A sophisticated investor should assume that a company facing a liquidity crisis and its lawyers will take advantage of any loopholes in the underlying documents to wring value out of these situations. Investors who understand what the documents do and don't allow are in a better position to value the underlying debt. While distressed debt investors have a reputation for sharp elbows, they also seek to understand every nuance of the governing documents of their holdings to keep from ending up on the wrong side of liability management transactions.

NOTE

i. Moss, Joel. (October 21, 2022). "Boardriders Lenders Notch Initial Victory Challenging Uptier Transactions." *JD Supra.* https://www.jdsupra.com/legalnews/boardriders-minority-lenders-notch-5910453/.

CHAPTER 19

Making Money in Distressed Situations

Now that we have reviewed all the fundamentals related to investing in credit and layered on the nuances of distress and bankruptcy, we have arrived at the real action: How do distressed investors make money?

While distressed debt investors find opportunities in all types of markets and economic backdrops, market dislocations, such as the Global Financial Crisis in 2008 and the beginning of the Covid-19 pandemic in early 2020, present ideal conditions for the asset class. There is no better time to buy than when others are forced sellers or paralyzed by fear. While this may seem obvious, there are several unique aspects of the corporate credit asset class that compound the opportunities for distressed investors in market downdrafts.

Funds that are sensitive to credit ratings may become forced sellers during economic upheaval. For instance, many investment grade funds must sell a holding if it is downgraded from an investment grade to a high yield rating. Additionally, many CLOs have limits on CCC exposure, so they become forced or incentivized sellers of CCC loans as they approach that threshold. Liquidity needs can also result in selling; when investors become concerned about a downturn, funds can become forced sellers to meet redemptions.

Lastly, a bankruptcy filing is a sell trigger for many investors in "par" high yield bonds and loans. First, they often lack the expertise and resources needed to navigate the bankruptcy process. Second, many institutional investors have restrictions on holding the bonds and loans of defaulted companies.

Even in periods of economic calm, distressed investment opportunities arise from idiosyncratic situations, for example:

1. Self-inflicted wounds such as a poorly planned acquisition;
2. Negative changes in the competitive landscape (e.g., new competitors);
3. Secular business model shifts (e.g., disruptive technology);
4. Over-levered balance sheets structured for growth that does not materialize.

With that backdrop, let's examine eight strategies employed by distressed investors, summarized in Figure 19.1. In addition to discussing real-life examples for each strategy, as promised, we will circle back to JCPenney at the end of the chapter to evaluate trade ideas relevant to its period of distress in 2012.

1) New financing for companies that can't access the traditional credit markets
2) Spread tightening trades
3) Distressed for control trades
4) Fundamental value plays
5) Capital structure arbitrage
6) Trade claims and vendor puts
7) Liquidations
8) Unique special situations trades

FIGURE 19.1 Distressed Debt Investing Strategies

NEW FINANCING FOR COMPANIES THAT CAN'T ACCESS THE TRADITIONAL CREDIT MARKETS

Distressed debt investors make money by providing new capital to a company when traditional lenders will not. These new financings fall into three categories:

1. *Emergency financing*. Lending to a company whose performance has deteriorated and is looking for liquidity for a turnaround that avoids bankruptcy.
2. *Debtor-in-possession (DIP) loans*. Lending to a company that is in bankruptcy. See Chapter 15 for more detail on DIP loans.
3. *Exit financing*. Loans to companies emerging from bankruptcy.

One of the first deals I underwrote was an emergency loan to Party City (PC) in 1999. At the time, the company was the largest specialty retailer of party goods. Approximately half its store base was company-operated, and the other half was franchised. During the Halloween season, the company turned a quarter of its square footage into a "Halloween Costume Warehouse." Halloween was PC's biggest season, making up most of its annual EBITDA.

The company grew explosively, from one store in 1986 to approximately 400 in 1999. It went public in 1996, and the stock hit a high of $35.25 per share in March 1998. However, it missed third quarter estimates that year, and in March 1999, it was unable to get a clean audited opinion due to issues with inventory management.[i] In late May, the company's CFO resigned, and the NASDAQ delisted the stock in July. The lack of an audit constituted a technical default on PC's loan agreement, and its existing lenders froze access to the revolving credit agreement. Without funds to finance inventory purchases, PC was at risk of missing the all-important Halloween season and appeared to be headed for bankruptcy.

Goldman Sachs partnered with Tennenbaum Capital and Gordon Brothers to conduct due diligence on the situation and potentially provide emergency financing. While the company did not have audited financial statements, one of its largest franchisees had clean books and records. Using data from the stores that this franchisee ran, we gained conviction in the concept's profitability and a valuation that covered PC's debt.

Given the dire straits of the company and the lack of competing financing proposals, we obtained very favorable terms: a 13.5% coupon, along with warrants to purchase 6.9 million shares (approximately 25% of the company) at an ultimate exercise price of $1.07 per share. The new financing provided liquidity for the critical Halloween season and an upgrade of information systems to ensure the accounting issues would not recur. In the summer of 2001, the NASDAQ relisted Party City, and in 2005, the company was acquired by Amscan, a private equity–owned supplier of party goods, at $17.50 per share. In addition to the great returns on the investment, I was fortunate to work on the deal with two exceptionally talented investors: Howard Levkowitz, a founding partner of Tennenbaum, and Matt Kahn, the president of Gordon Brothers' private equity group. I would team up with them over the next 20 years on many complex situations.

The Party City saga is not over. In 2012, the company was sold to another private equity firm for $2.7 billion, of which $2.0 billion was debt. In 2022, the company missed forecasts, and on January 17, 2023, it filed for bankruptcy. As of the writing of this book, the restructuring process is playing out, and the outcome is far from certain.

SPREAD TIGHTENING TRADES

A spread tightening trade occurs when an investor believes debt is trading at too low a price and too high a spread/yield relative to the underlying risk of the issuer.

For example, let's say you work for a distressed debt hedge fund that targets 15%–20% yields. Your boss asks you to analyze the bond of a company with a B-/B3 rating, ten-year maturity, and a 6% coupon trading at $84. The yield to maturity of the bond is 8.4%, which corresponds to a 540 bps spread over the 10-year treasury yield of 3.0%. This spread is elevated relative to that of other similarly rated bonds. (Refer back to Chapter 3 for a primer on yields and spreads.)

Your first instinct is that this assignment is a waste of time; a yield of 8.4% is well below the firm's target return. However, your boss believes the market is too pessimistic about the issuer's prospects. She thinks the company could outperform expectations and, within the next two quarters, trade more in line with other single-B rated credits. If this happens, she believes the spread will tighten by 100 bps (from 540 to 440 bps). If she is correct, the bonds will trade up to $90.6, resulting in an IRR of 22.9%.

The profits and IRR, if the trade works out, are shown in Figure 19.2.

	IRR Calculation
	Cash Flows
Buy $1,000 Bonds at a Price of $84	(840)
Sell Bonds in 6 months[a]	936
$ Profits	96
6-month IRR	11.43%
Annualized IRR = 2 × (6-month IRR)	22.86%

[a] 6-month Coupon (1,000 × 3%) Plus Sell Bonds at a Price of $90.60 (1,000 × 90.6%).

FIGURE 19.2 Spread Tightening Trade IRR

Note on annualized IRR:

For simplicity, I annualized the 6-month month IRR calculation by multiplying it by two. Another approach would be to compound the 6-month IRR, resulting in a slightly higher return using the formula $(1 + \text{6-month IRR})^2 - 1$. Furthermore, some firms prefer to use the XIRR[1] function versus IRR. I recommend taking your firm's approach to calculating returns.

Example of a spread tightening trade:

A real-life example of a spread tightening trade is Macy's long-dated bonds during the 2020 pandemic. The pandemic created tremendous volatility in the credit markets; spreads of single-B corporate bonds widened from a pre-Covid low of 335 bps to a pandemic high of 1,189 bps. Department store bonds were especially hard hit as the pandemic shutdown reduced store revenue meaningfully and increased fears about the acceleration of the secular shift away from brick-and-mortar stores.

Macy's was rated investment grade (S&P rating BBB- and Moody's rating Baa3) for most of the decade preceding the pandemic. However, because of the concerns about the department store sector, S&P had already downgraded the debt to BB+ when the pandemic hit. Both ratings had agencies downgraded Macy's to a single-B rating by the end of May 2020. In order to bolster liquidity needed due to Covid-related shutdowns, Macy's replaced its $1.5 billion unsecured revolver with a $2.9 billion asset-backed revolver and raised an additional $1.3 billion in debt secured by a portion of its owned real estate. The company also publicly stated its commitment to return to an investment grade rating by paying down debt and reducing leverage to less than 3x.

By November 2020, there was light at the end of the tunnel, as the Pfizer vaccine had begun phase II clinical trials. Given the company's liquidity and the view that shutdowns would end soon, Macy's bonds presented an interesting spread tightening trade opportunity. Its 5.125% bond due 2042 was trading at $60.20 for a yield to maturity of 9.53% and spread of 823 bps. While this was below Macy's peak Covid spread of 1,095 bps, it was still extremely wide versus its pre-Covid spread of 369 bps. Furthermore, Macy's spread tightening had lagged that of the market and comparable single-B bonds.

This underperformance was partly because Macy's was downgraded from investment grade to high yield. This resulted in an excellent combination for distressed debt investors: forced sellers in investment grade mandates and an absence of new buyers, as high yield investors had only recently started looking at Macy's in depth. Figure 19.3 outlines Macy's bond spread and spread retracement versus major indices, while Figure 19.4 shows Macy's spread retracement versus some of its competitors.

[1]The main difference between Excel XIRR and IRR functions is that IRR assumes all the periods in a series of cash flows are of equal length. XIRR provides the flexibility to assign specific dates to each cash flow.

	Bond Spread & Spread Retracement			
	Spread Over Treasuries			
	November 2020	Pre-Covid	Peak Covid	% Retraced
Macy's 5.125% Bond Due 2042	823	369	1,095	37.5%
BBB Index	148	127	488	94.2%
BB Index	319	186	837	79.6%
B Index	480	335	1,189	83.0%

FIGURE 19.3 Macy's Bond Spread and Spread Retracement versus Indices
Percent Spread Retraced = [(Peak Covid spread – Current spread) / (Peak Covid spread – Pre-Covid spread)]
Sources: Bloomberg and Silver Point traders

	Retracement Comparison
	% Spread Retraced
Macy's	37.5%
Nordstrom	60.0%
Kohl's	72.7%
Dillard's	71.9%
Peer Average	68.2%

FIGURE 19.4 Macy's Spread Retracement versus Other Department Stores

The following is an illustrative scenario analysis of the trade, with corresponding price changes and IRRs shown in Figures 19.5 and 19.6. All scenarios assume Treasury rates stay the same or are hedged, and trade plays out in one year.

- Upside #1: Macy's bond spread retraces by the same percentage as the peer group.
- Upside #2: Macy's bond spread tightens to the average B spread.
- Upside #3: Macy's bond spread tightens to Macy's pre-Covid level.
- Downside: Macy's bond spread widens to its spring 2020 peak.

	Trading Level Scenario Analysis		
As % of Face Value	New Price After Spread Tightens	Original Purchase Price	Change in Price
Upside #1	77.6	60.2	17.4
Upside #2	88.8	60.2	28.6
Upside #3	101.7	60.2	41.5
Downside	48.1	60.2	–12.1

FIGURE 19.5 Change in Trading Levels

$ in 000s	IRR and Cash-on-Cash Calculations				
	Upside Scenarios				
Cash flows	# 1	# 2	# 3	Downside	Description of Cash Flows
Trade Date	(602.000)	(602.0000)	(602.000)	(602.000)	$1 MM bonds at a price of 60.2%
6 months	25.625	25.625	25.625	25.625	$1 MM bonds × coupon/2
1 year	801.625	913.625	1,042.625	500.625	($1 MM bonds × new price) + ($1MM bonds × coupon/2)
Profits	225.250	337.250	466.250	(69.750)	
IRR	35.1%	50.7%	67.5%	-12.2%	IRR function in Excel × 2
Multiple of Money	1.37x	1.56x	1.77x	0.88x	[2 coupons + proceeds from sale of bond] / [Purchase price]

FIGURE 19.6 Profits and IRR on a $1 Million Trade

What happened?

Macy's recovered quickly following the approval of the Pfizer vaccine in December 2020, which unleashed strong consumer demand further catalyzed by record stimulus payments from the federal government. Additionally, the retention of aggressive pandemic-era cost cuts and the tremendous success of its online channel resulted in Macy's exceeding its $2.3 billion 2019 EBITDA, as the company reported 2021 EBITDA of $3 billion. With its excess cash flow, the company prioritized deleveraging, refinancing near-term maturities, and redeeming the high-cost secured debt issued at the pandemic trough by August 2021.

By the end of June 2021, Macy's 2042 senior notes had tightened significantly in spread and traded up to $93. This resulted in an IRR of 63% and a cash-on-cash return of 1.63x.

DISTRESSED FOR CONTROL TRADES

When a distressed debt investor accumulates a position in the debt instrument viewed as the fulcrum security of a company anticipated to file or already in bankruptcy, this is referred to as distressed for control. As discussed in Chapter 16, the fulcrum security is the class of claim entitled to some, but not a full, recovery; it is where "value runs out." This claim is positioned to be converted into the equity of the reorganized company; however, as discussed previously, that typically entails a valuation fight with other creditor classes.

Tailored Brands is a men's apparel retailer that operates under banners such as Men's Wearhouse and Jos A Bank, with 15% of its sales from formal wear rentals (e.g., tuxedos). The company's performance had deteriorated before Covid, driven by a rapidly changing consumer landscape and management distractions due to negotiating and integrating the Jos A Bank acquisition. Despite these issues, the company enjoyed high market share and awareness in its categories and generated $2.9 billion in revenue and $240 million of EBITDA in 2019, as outlined in Figure 19.7.

	Summary Financial Performance		
$ in millions	**FYE Feb 2018**	**FYE Feb 2019**	**FYE Feb 2020**
Net Sales	$3,053	$3,005	$2,881
Sales Growth	−1.5%	−1.6%	−4.1%
Same Store Sales Growth	0.1%	1.2%	−3.0%
Adjusted EBITDA	$343	$327	$240
% Margin	11.2%	10.9%	8.3%
Adjusted EBITDA Growth	3.3%	−4.7%	−26.6%

FIGURE 19.7 Tailored Brands Summary Performance (fiscal year end February)
Source: Adapted from Company filings.

At the end of 2019 (FYE 2/2020), the company had the capital structure outlined in Figure 19.8.

	Tailored Brands Capital Structure		
$ in millions	**Debt Outstanding in Millions**	**LTV (%)**	**Multiple of LTM EBITDA of $242 Million**
$ABL RCF, Net of Excess Cash	$36		
1st Lien TL	882		
Total Secured Debt	918	65.9%	3.8x
Unsecured Bonds	174		
Total Net Debt	1,092	78.4%	4.6x
Equity Market Cap (~ average in 2019)	300		
Enterprise Value	$1,392	100.0%	5.8x

FIGURE 19.8 Tailored Brands Summary Capital Structure

Tailored was forced to close all its stores when the pandemic hit. In July, the company missed its bond coupon payment, and on August 2, 2020, it filed for bankruptcy. The term loan was trading between 30 and 40 cents on the dollar, and the bonds were quoted below 10 cents on the dollar.

This was a situation with tremendous uncertainty. The company was burning cash, and future cash burn was tough to forecast given lockdown uncertainty. Furthermore, Covid had an extreme impact on Tailored's business model since work from home disproportionately reduced demand for business wear, and demand for formal wear plummeted as weddings and other events were put on hold indefinitely.

There was a two-pronged investment thesis for investing in Tailored's term loan:

- *Limited downside even in a Chapter 7 liquidation of the company*. Our credit committee believed the hard assets, inventory, and owned real estate should result in a recovery above the current trading levels of the loan even if all available liquidity was used to fund cash burn (which would increase the amount of priming debt).
- *Tremendous upside in a Chapter 11*. Our credit committee expected the term loan to be the fulcrum security and thus to receive most of the post-emergence equity. We saw significant opportunity for two reasons:
  - We were more optimistic than the market that demand for events would eventually return and the company would benefit from a less crowded competitive landscape as other retailers reduced their footprint or folded.
  - Our committee also believed the business could be significantly improved through the bankruptcy process by retooling certain key contracts, including an expensive licensing agreement that could be renegotiated in Chapter 11, using the threat of rejection to drive a favorable outcome. In addition, bankruptcy would allow the company to rationalize its store base.

Ultimately, the company rejected leases to close its least profitable stores, reducing its store footprint by ~30%, which eliminated the cash burn of these stores while improving the profitability of adjacent stores benefiting from sales recapture. The remaining stores were further bolstered by reduced rents from leases that were renegotiated with landlords during the bankruptcy process.

Below is a back-of-the-envelope analysis for instructional purposes only, to provide an idea of how an investor might look at the upside and downside of the trade.

Upside analysis

We assumed the term loan would receive 85% of the equity. The remaining 15% would be split between a "tip" to entice the unsecured creditors to agree to a consensual deal and a management incentive plan (MIP). To arrive at our valuation, we forecasted stabilized EBITDA and the cash burn required to get there. (Refer back to Chapter 10 for a detailed overview of forecasting.) Figure 19.9 shows a scenario analysis for a range of EBITDA and multiple assumptions.

	Scenario Analysis		
$ in millions	Low	Base	High
Stabilized EBITDA	$150	$215	$275
Multiple	5.0x	5.5x	6.0x
Enterprise Value at Stabilization	750	1,183	1,650
Less Amount of $550MM ABL Outstanding	−150	−150	−150
Less Cash Burn before EBITDA Stabilization	-200	-150	-100
Value Left after Paying Off Priming Debt	400	883	1,400
% allocated to Term Lenders	85%	85%	85%
Value for Term Lenders [A]	$340	$750	$1,190
Term Loan Outstanding	$880	$880	$880
Average Trading Level	40%	40%	40%
Cost of Investment in Term Loan [B]	$352	$352	$352
$ Profit [A-B]	-$12	$398	$838
Multiple of Money [A]/[B]	0.97	2.13	3.38

FIGURE 19.9 Investment Scenario Analysis

In the downside case, the cash burn becomes too much for the assets to support, and/or the EBITDA stabilizes at or below the low case of $150 million. In that draconian downside scenario, the company would liquidate. Based on the liquidation value of the company's $2 billion of assets, we believed the term loan should recover more than our cost basis (i.e., the $40 market price). Later in this chapter, we will go through a liquidation analysis in more detail.

What happened?

After negotiations among the debtor, the term loan lenders, and the unsecured creditors' committee, a consensual plan was agreed upon, and the company emerged from bankruptcy in December 2020. The key terms of the Plan of Reorganization were:

- A subset of the term loan lenders would provide the company with a new $75 million term loan (the proceeds of which would provide extra liquidity after emergence).
- The pre-petition ABL would be replaced with an exit ABL.
- The $880 million of term loans would receive:
  - $365 million of a take-back loan with an L + 8% coupon (with a PIK option to provide further flexibility for the company); and
  - Approximately 93.3% of the equity.
- The bonds and other unsecured claims would be equitized and receive 6.7% of the equity and out-of-the-money warrants.
- 7.5% of the equity would be reserved for a management incentive plan (which would dilute the equity).
- The new shareholders (i.e., the converted term loan lenders) led the process of sourcing and selecting a new board and a new high-caliber management team.

Soon after emergence from Chapter 11, the company required additional liquidity to bridge the extended effects of the Covid-related shutdowns. Within a month, the company started to PIK its exit term loan and embarked on another $75 million capital raise. The shareholders structured a new financing composed of a $25 million add-on to the super senior facility (i.e., the existing $75 million exit term loan) and a $50 million third lien loan mandatorily convertible into equity.

Only two shareholders were willing to fund the new $50 million third lien loan and thus had to invest more than their pro rata share of the deal. Those shareholders demanded extremely attractive terms: a 6% PIK coupon, a 10% backstop fee (also PIK, in additional convertible debt), and a three-year maturity. Furthermore, the third lien would convert into equity at an extremely discounted valuation. The conversion price would have been meaningless if all lenders funded their pro rata share of the third lien because all holders would maintain the same percentage stake. But since a significant number of shareholders did not participate, those who did went from owning 33% of the company before conversion to 92% of the company after conversion.

Despite the immediate need for the post-reorg equity to inject $75 million of additional liquidity, Tailored's performance has dramatically improved as of the writing of this book. The management team has publicly stated that "our business is stronger, more agile, and financially healthier than before the pandemic," due to the release of pent-up consumer demand for apparel, the restructuring actions taken in bankruptcy, and the operational improvements implemented by the new board/management. Sales are currently well above 2019 levels on a same-store basis, and EBITDA is well in excess of pre-pandemic levels.

While Tailored looks like an excellent investment for those who bought the term loan at the Covid trough and participated in the new third lien term loan, distressed debt investors have learned only to celebrate once they have monetized their position. Retail is a tough industry, and time will tell how much of Tailored Brands' recent performance is sustainable versus driven by pent-up demand. I look forward to writing an update on this situation in the next edition of this book.

FUNDAMENTAL VALUE PLAYS

Fundamental value plays are investments driven by a significant difference between an analyst's valuation and the market's. Successful investing requires a contrarian view. If your value estimate is higher than the market's, you "go long"; if it's lower, you "short." The securities of companies in out-of-favor industries in secular decline can trade at levels well below their intrinsic value, sometimes even below liquidation value. These are great long trades; however, the opposite also holds when the market is too optimistic and overvalues a company.

For example, in 2013, many analysts believed that the equity market was not pricing in how dire JCPenney's liquidity situation was and that its stock was trading well above its fundamental value. At the end of this chapter, we will discuss the trade investors put on to position for this point of view.

CAPITAL STRUCTURE ARBITRAGE

Capital structure arbitrage (arb) is a strategy in which an investor purchases one security while shorting another within the same company's capital structure. Some examples:

1. *Liquidity plays.* If you believe that a company has adequate liquidity to attempt a turnaround in the near term but will eventually file for bankruptcy, you can take a long position in its shorted-dated bonds and short its long-dated bonds. This is also referred to as a "curve trade" as it involves arbitraging different instruments on the time-yield curve. This can be a dangerous trade if you are wrong on the timing of a default, as the shorter-term bonds of a distressed issuer typically trade at much higher prices (reflecting the likelihood of repayment) than the issuer's longer-maturity bonds (reflecting recovery value in a bankruptcy). If the company files for Chapter 11, all bonds of the same seniority and security converge to roughly the same (recovery-based) price, and the loss on your long will be more than the gain on your short.
2. *Legal analysis plays.* If you spot legal differences in bond indentures that make one bond in a company's capital structure better than another, you can buy the better bond and short the other one. In 2013, some analysts viewed Safeway (the supermarket chain) as a prime candidate for an LBO. The company had some bonds with a change of control (CoC) put, which gave the owner of the bonds the right to force the company to repurchase those bonds at $101 in an LBO scenario. These bonds would trade up to a price of $101 in an LBO, while the bonds without the CoC put language would "travel" with the company after the LBO and likely trade down meaningfully since an LBO would burden Safeway with meaningful new debt. Hedge funds betting the LBO would happen went long the bonds with a CoC put and shorted bonds without it. If an LBO did not happen, the trade would have negative carry, meaning the cost of the short (the coupon payment on the non-CoC bonds) was greater than the interest earned on the CoC bonds. Since there was reasonable concern about an LBO in the market, investors had started paying up for the CoC bonds, making their yield and spread lower than that of bonds lacking the CoC put.

   Other examples of capital structure arb informed by legal analysis include Enron and Lehman. The complex legal entities at these companies combined with the rapid transition from investment grade to distressed territory meant that many market participants were slow to understand legal nuances at the bond issuer level. Investors who quickly figured out the legal structures, beneficial liability guarantees, and labyrinth of intercompany loans put on multiple capital structure arb trades. We discussed one example of this in Chapter 17; some Lehman bonds had double dip claims that ended up receiving a significantly higher recovery relative to other bonds in the Lehman complex, and investors who figured this out bought these bonds and shorted others.
3. *Insurance / "overheated" market "put" trades.* When the market is overheated, it does not always price risk correctly. For example, in 2006 and early 2007, some market participants believed the spread between a healthy company's secured and unsecured debt was not priced appropriately. Investors who did not view

this spread as adequate compensation for the risk of going from secured to unsecured debt could put on a capital structure arb trade by going long the company's secured debt and shorting the same company's unsecured debt.

Let's say you are analyzing the LBO of an extremely cyclical business with high fixed costs and the capital structure shown in Figure 19.10 in an overheated, frothy market environment (e.g., 2006):

	Capital Structure		
	Debt Outstanding in Millions	LTV (%)	Multiple of LTM EBITDA of $295 Million
$750MM ABL Revolver (L[a] + 250 bps)	$50		
Secured Term Loan (L[a] + 425 bps)	1,200		
Total Secured Debt	$1,250	42%	4.2x
9.5% Senior Unsecured Bond	1,000		
Total Debt	$2,250	76%	7.6x
Less Cash	(150)		
Net Debt	$2,100	71%	7.1x
Sponsor Equity	850		
Total Enterprise Value	$2,950	100%	10.0x

[a]The LIBOR curve averages 4% over the investment period. Note this example uses LIBOR, but as discussed in Chapter 3, in 2020, LIBOR was replaced with SOFR.

FIGURE 19.10 Hypothetical Capital Structure

If the economy continues to expand, you believe the company will produce adequate cash flow to service its debt. However, a recession will lead to cash burn. The difference in yield between the unsecured bond and the secured term loan is 1.25%, which you believe is inadequate compensation for the incremental risk relative to the secured term loan. Hence, you recommend buying $10 million of the secured term loan against a $10 million short of the unsecured bond. Three potential return scenarios for this trade are quantified in Figures 19.11, 19.12, and 19.13:

1. Scenario #1 (Figure 19.11): no recession. You hold the trade for two years and then unwind. You expect the term loan and the bond to continue to trade at par.
2. Scenario #2: a modest recession (Figure 19.12). You believe the term loan will trade down modestly (3 points) since it is secured and only 42% LTV currently (i.e., a significant amount of total enterprise value would have to be eroded before impairment). Since the bond is unsecured and has a much higher LTV and, therefore, a smaller value cushion, you believe it will trade down 10 points.
3. Scenario #3: a severe recession (Figure 19.13). You believe the term loan will trade down 10 points while the bond trades down 65 points. If this is a prolonged, severe recession, the company might file for bankruptcy, in which case the term loan might be the fulcrum, and the bond might be wiped out entirely.

Scenario 1: Trade Profit and Loss (P&L)				
Trade	Instrument	$ Amount	Coupon	$ Coupon
Long	Secured Term loan	10,000,000	8.25%	$825,000
Short	Unsecured Bond	-10,000,000	9.50%	-950,000
Annual Cost of Carry			-1.25%	-$125,000
Expected Hold Time in Years				x 2
2-Year Cost of Carry				-$250,000
Less Transaction Costs to Unwind Trade (25 bps on each side)				-50,000
Cost of Carry for Two Years[a] - Total P&L				-$300,000

[a]The cost of this trade could be higher. Bonds tend to have meaningfully better call protection than loans, so the bond could trade above par (see Chapter 12), versus the loan which is capped modestly above par, resulting in an additional cost (the difference in price between the bond and the loan) to unwind the trade.

FIGURE 19.11 Scenario #1 – No Recession in the Next Two Years

Scenario 2 – Trade P&L				
Trade	Instrument	$ Amount	Price Change	$ P&L
Long	Secured Term Loan	10,000,000	-3.00%	-$300,000
Short	Unsecured Bond	-10,000,000	-10.00%	1,000,000
Profits from Price Chg				$700,000
Cost of Carry for Two Years (from 19.11 above)				-300,000
P&L of the Trade in Modest Recession Scenario				$400,000

FIGURE 19.12 Scenario #2 – Modest Recession in the Next Two Years

Scenario 3: Trade P&L				
Trade	Instrument	$ Amount	Price Change	$ P&L
Long	Secured Term Loan	10,000,000	-10.00%	-$1,000,000
Short	Unsecured Bond	-10,000,000	-65.00%	6,500,000
Profits from Price Chg				$5,500,000
Cost of Carry for Two Years (from 19.11 above)				-300,000
P&L of the Trade in Severe Recession Scenario				$5,200,000

FIGURE 19.13 Scenario #3 – Severe Recession in the Next Two Years

Let's assume the consensus view of the chances of a recession are as outlined in Figure 19.14.

Recession Probability Weighting	
Probability of No Recession (Scenario #1)	80%
Probability of Modest Recession (Scenario #2)	15%
Probability of Severe Recession (Scenario #3)	5%
Total	100%

FIGURE 19.14 Recession Probability

Given these assumptions, the trade's probability-weighted expected P&L is only $80,000 (shown in Figure 19.15). Moreover, 80% of the time, you will lose money; it does not seem like a great use of your firm's capital.

Probability Weighted P&L

Scenario	Est P&L		Probability		Probability Weighted P&L
No Recession	-300,000	×	80%	=	-240,000
Modest Recession	400,000	×	15%	=	60,000
Severe Recession	5,200,000	×	5%	=	260,000
Probability Weighted P&L					$80,000

FIGURE 19.15 Probability Weighted P&L

The opposing arguments are that it is a cheap way to "insure" your portfolio from massive negative returns during recessions and that your firm believes the chances of a recession are much higher than the market is projecting.

I asked my good friend Adam Cohen to explain his philosophy on capital structure trades. I started my career with Adam at Goldman Sachs, and he went on to run Caspian Capital, a $4.5 billion credit hedge fund. Adam's fund massively outperformed the market during the GFC as he had put on many "insurance" capital structure arb trades in anticipation of the downturn. Adam writes the following:

> *To be successful, a capital structure arbitrage trade requires the investor to predict financial stress before it arrives. Obviously, the earlier the investor makes such a trade, the more limited the downside and the greater the upside. In addition, the more complicated a company's capital structure is, the more opportunities may be available. Beyond the basic trades of being long secured versus unsecured or being long senior versus subordinated debt, there are additional nuanced opportunities available such as being long a company's subsidiary versus parent debt or trades in debt with differing collateral packages or covenant protections. These trades require significant legal and financial diligence as well as an understanding of the options available to and likely outcomes for debtholders of companies experiencing distress, undergoing a restructuring, or filing for bankruptcy. In addition, investors may choose to vary the long/short ratio from 1:1 if they have a particular view on recovery values of the instruments.*

Notably, some investors will buy debt coupled with shorting equity of the same company and label this capital structure arbitrage. While there are varying opinions of this type of investment, it loses the limited downside characteristic of traditional capital structure arbitrage trades. Generally speaking, if an investor is short a debt instrument, the worst case is that it matures at par, so the downside is known and quantifiable. As equity has no cap on how high it can trade, the loss on an equity short if the investor is wrong can be infinite.

A good example of a classic capital structure arbitrage trade my firm deployed is Aleris International, a global leader in aluminum rolled products, extrusions and recycling. In 2007, we identified the company for such a negatively biased trade because: (1) it was a highly leveraged LBO, (2) aluminum is a commodity with meaningful price volatility (the company had stopped hedging), and (3) the company was extremely cyclical with meaningful exposure to the housing, auto and aerospace markets. Aleris' capital structure was composed of floating rate domestic and European secured bank facilities, 9% senior unsecured notes and 10% subordinated unsecured notes. We purchased the bank facilities and shorted the notes. As the global financial crisis unfolded, Aleris was one of several commodity-based companies that was forced to file for Chapter 11 in early 2009. In the company reorganization, both sets of unsecured notes received almost no recovery (less than 1%) and were extinguished. The bank debt holders had the opportunity to roll up some of their debt into more senior debt and also wound up with equity ownership of the reorganized company. As the company returned to health, the former bank debt holders were able to take a dividend as the new equity owners, and eventually sold the company to a conglomerate for a meaningful profit.

The Aleris trade is an example of an "insurance/overheated markets" capital structure trade. However, Adam's investment played out much better than expected. Let's examine this trade assuming Adam put on a $10 million long secured term loan position against a $5 million short of the 9% senior unsecured notes and a $5 million short of the 10% subordinated notes. If Aleris did not get into trouble, the carrying cost of the trade would be approximately $260,000 per year, as outlined in Figure 19.16.

Aleris Trade Cost of Carry[a]

Trade	Instrument	Amount	Coupon (%)	$ Coupon
Long	Secured Term Loan	10,000,000	6.9%	690,000
Short	Senior Unsecured Bond	-5,000,000	9.0%	-450,000
Short	Subordinated Bond	-5,000,000	10.0%	-500,000
Annual Cost of Carry[b]				-260,000

[a]The annual cost ignores any potential transaction costs to unwind the trade.
[b]The bank debt had a floating rate coupon. Based on the LIBOR rate when the trade was executed, the coupon was 6.9%.

FIGURE 19.16 Aleris Trade Cost of Carry

The actual P&L on this trade was staggering relative to the annual carrying cost. Adam won on both sides of the trade. Since the unsecured bonds ended up being worth pennies on the dollar, he made almost $10 million of profits on the short alone. And his long position made money as well due to the term loan's above-par recovery. The term loan lenders provided the company with a very lucrative DIP facility. They were also eligible to participate in a below-market rights offering of new equity to fund the emergence from bankruptcy. As a result, the term loan lenders that participated in the DIP and the rights offering ended up owning virtually all the equity in the company when Aleris exited bankruptcy in 2010. As the economy recovered from the 2008–2009 recession, Aleris's performance improved dramatically. After emerging from bankruptcy, the company distributed over $800 million in dividends to its new shareholders, and in 2020 it was sold to Novelis for $2.8 billion.

TRADE CLAIMS AND VENDOR PUTS

Trade claims: When a company files for bankruptcy, the amount owed to trade vendors that shipped before the bankruptcy (the company's pre-petition accounts payable) becomes part of the unsecured claims pool. Therefore, the analysis is similar to valuing the unsecured bonds of a bankrupt company. The difference is in the liquidity of the underlying markets. When you want to buy bank debt or bonds, you call a broker-dealer such as Goldman Sachs to get a quote and transact. But you must source trade claims by calling vendors directly to find the right person to negotiate with, identify a willing seller, and directly negotiate a price along with the associated legal documents. This is a colossal pain in the ass; however, because there is no quoted market, you typically get paid for the excess work by negotiating a price cheap to the pari passu bonds or other comparable financial claims. For instance, in the MCI bankruptcy, we bought trade claims at a 10-point discount to debt with the same priority.

In the early days of Silver Point, I set up and ran our trade claims business. In those days, there was minimal competition in buying trade claims. We had a group of five sourcers whose job was to find vendors interested in selling their claims. When a company files for bankruptcy, its required Schedule F filing lists all unsecured creditors. Our sourcers would "dial for dollars" using the Schedule F, hoping to find vendors interested in selling. Over time, you develop relationships with these vendors, making it less of a cold call in future situations.

Vendor puts: As we developed relationships with vendor accounts receivable/credit departments, we identified another opportunity: providing put options (basically, credit insurance) for vendors. When a vendor becomes concerned about the financial health of a customer, it cuts back its exposure (e.g., by shortening payables from 60 to 30 days or moving to cash on delivery, or COD, terms). In many instances, this tightening of credit negatively impacts vendor sales; vendors could do more business if they were willing to take on more credit risk.

Let's assume a vendor has traditionally shipped $100 million of products with 90-day terms for the holiday season to a troubled department store. This year its credit department is only willing to take $75 million of credit risk, and the retailer will not agree to cash on delivery. The vendor will lose out on $25 million in sales and likely hurt its relationship with an important customer because of its unwillingness to take as much credit risk. A vendor put contract with a notional amount of $25 million keeps risk at $75 million without missing out on the incremental $25 million in sales. Sample terms for a vendor put contract might include:

- Amount of protection (notional amount): $25 million of receivables from the specific retailer;
- Cost quoted in premium per month of protection: 2% (paid up front);
- Time of protection: 3 months;
- Strike price (price at which the vendor can sell its receivable to the put provider upon a bankruptcy filing): 90% of claim.

The put contract would earn $1.5 million as long as the retailer pays the vendor, as outlined in Figure 19.17.

Vendor Put Up-Front Cost	
Notional Amount in Millions	$25.0
Cost per Month	2%
Number of Months of Protection	3
Up-Front Cost (to vendor) / Profit (to fund)	$1.5

FIGURE 19.17 Vendor Put Up-Front Cost

However, if the retailer goes bankrupt, the fund will own $25 million of trade claims at a cost of 84%, as outlined in Figure 19.18.

Cost of Trade Claims in a Bankruptcy Scenario	
Notional Amount in Millions	$25.0
Strike Price	90%
$ Purchase Price of the Receivables	$22.5
Less Premium Earned	-1.5
Cash Cost of Receivables	$21.0
% Cost ($21MM cash cost / $25MM receivables)	84.0%

FIGURE 19.18 Effective Cost of Trade Claims in Bankruptcy

The ultimate trading level of the vendor claim (driven by the claim's recovery value) determines how much you lose on this trade. If the fund sells the trade claim for 60 cents on the dollar, the loss would be $6 million, as outlined in Figure 19.19.

Trade Claim P&L	
Cash Cost of Receivables (from Figure 19.18 above)	$21.0
Less Ultimate Realized Value ($25 × 60% sale price)	-15.0
Loss on the Trade	$6.0

FIGURE 19.19 Trade Claim P&L—Bankruptcy Scenario

Before you can write a vendor put, you must analyze the company's liquidity and the probability of its not paying the vendor. In addition, you must have a view on the ultimate recovery in a bankruptcy if your liquidity analysis is wrong, and the company files for bankruptcy, in which case this payable claim will go into the unsecured creditor pool.

At Goldman, I entered into a regrettable vendor put contract for Kmart in 2001. This vendor had a fourth quarter holiday order for the company that was $50 million greater than its internal Kmart risk limit permitted. We agreed to insure the payment of $50 million of receivables at terms of 1.5% per month for three months with a strike price of 90%. The effective yield on the risk of the put option was approximately 20% (1.5% per month × 12 to annualize / 90% strike price). This was an excellent risk-adjusted return versus Kmart's 9.5% unsecured bond, which was trading close to par, and which we shorted to hedge $20 million of our exposure.

For years, Kmart had struggled to compete with Walmart and Target, but the company's 2001 year-to-date performance was fine, with modest same-store sales growth of 0.4%. Its liquidity (cash plus availability on its revolving credit facility) was robust at $1.5 billion, and its inventory would support an additional $500 million of revolver availability. LTM EBITDA was $1.4 billion, with less than 2x leverage, and LTM free cash flow was positive. There seemed to be an extremely low probability that Kmart would face a liquidity issue in the next three months.

The trade went well until late December of 2001, when rumors started circulating that Kmart's holiday season had been a disaster and that the board had lost confidence in the CEO. Despite these rumors, few thought the company would file for bankruptcy; market consensus was that the company would preannounce poor results in early January along with a $2 billion secured ABL facility to provide confidence to vendors, factors, and the markets.

However, time passed and no announcements were made, and by mid-January, some vendor receivables were not being paid on time. On January 22, 2002, the company filed for bankruptcy after three days of board meetings. Later, it would emerge that Kmart's 2001 performance was a disaster, with *negative* $400 million of EBITDA. Trade claims traded down to 46 cents on the dollar. The loss on the $30 million unhedged portion of our trade was a little under $12 million as outlined in Figure 19.20.

	Kmart Trade
	Trade P&L $ in Thousands
Trading Value of Receivables ($30MM × 46%)	$13,800
Amount of Receivables Put	$30,000
× Strike Price	90%
Price Paid to Vendor	$27,000
Less Premiums Earned Up Front (1.5% × 3 mos × $30MM)	-1,350
Effective Cost of Receivables	$25,650
Loss on the Trade	**-$11,850**

FIGURE 19.20 Kmart Trade Claim P&L

Because Kmart's bankruptcy was a surprise and because of the holiday season timing, most vendors had peak exposure to the credit, and losses were extremely high. Many vendors did not want to continue to ship to Kmart in bankruptcy after recognizing such significant losses. However, post-petition trade claims (trade support provided after a bankruptcy) are significantly lower risk, as they receive administrative priority status (see Chapter 15). Since Kmart filed for bankruptcy with no secured debt outstanding, post-petition claims were next in line to be paid after the DIP facility if the company did not emerge and instead liquidated. After I made the transition to Silver Point, I underwrote Kmart post-petition receivable puts that to this day remain the best risk-adjusted investment I have ever made. Our thesis was that Kmart not only possessed substantial liquidity to attempt a turnaround, but also, more important, even in the event of a liquidation the post-petition receivable claims would maintain their value given the priority status of post-petition vendors. Even using the most draconian assumptions for liquidation value, the claim would have been worth par.

LIQUIDATIONS

As discussed earlier, not all companies in bankruptcy emerge as going concerns; some liquidate and cease to exist. I like investing in liquidations because the market tends to make the most draconian assumptions, which in my experience leads to more upside than downside surprises. Furthermore, in my career, I covered the retail industry, which had many high-profile liquidations including Ames, Caldor, Bradlees, Service Merchandise, Montgomery Ward, Linens N Things, Circuit City, Modell's, Pier 1, Blockbuster, Payless Shoes, Sears/Kmart, Gymboree, Lord & Taylor, and Bed Bath & Beyond. Depending on your age, you might recognize some of these retailers. What they have in common is that they were all extremely successful for a time, and now they are gone.

The liquidation analysis of a retailer is straightforward:

1. List every asset;
2. Perform due diligence on what it would be worth in an orderly sale process, subtracting out the costs associated with the liquidation to get to a distributable value;
3. Estimate the amount owed to creditors and their priority; and
4. Distribute the value based on the priorities of claims, an analysis referred to as a recovery or waterfall analysis.

Figures 19.21 and 19.22 show a liquidation and recovery analysis that we ran on a large retailer. (For confidentiality reasons, I changed the name to Kyle Hayden Alyssa (KHA) Corp and altered some financial information.)

		Retail Liquidation Analysis					
		Est % Recovery			Est $ Recovery		
$ in millions	Book Value	Low	Base	High	Low	Base	High
Inventory	2,850	80.0%	84.0%	88.0%	$2,280	$2,394	$2,508
Receivables	125	92.5%	95.0%	97.5%	116	119	122
Owned Real Estate	NM				438	533	629
Value of Leases	NM				642	738	841
Brands	NM				0	0	50
Other	250	0.0%	10.0%	20.0%	0	25	50
Total Liquidation Value [A]	**NM**				**$3,476**	**$3,809**	**$4,200**

FIGURE 19.21 Liquidation Analysis of KHA Corp

	Waterfall Analysis		
	Est $ Recovery		
$ in millions	Low	Base	High
Total Liquidation Value [A]	$3,476	$3,809	$4,200
Less Current DIP Financing Outstanding	-550	-550	-550
Less Liquidation/Wind-Down Expenses	-89	-96	-105
Less Other Administrative & Priority Claims	-350	-325	-300
Less Secured Pre-Petition Claims	-1,110	-1,110	-1,110
Distributable Value to Unsecured Claims [B]	**$1,377**	**$1,728**	**$2,135**
Unsecured Bonds	$2,277	$2,277	$2,277
Scheduled Pre-Petition Payables	1,000	975	950
Lease Rejection Claims	516	474	430
Other Pre-Petition Unsecured Liabilities	150	150	150
Cushion	100	0	0
Estimate Total General Unsecured Claims (GUCs) [C]	**$4,043**	**$3,876**	**$3,807**
Recovery to Unsecured Claims (%) [B/C]	34%	45%	56%

FIGURE 19.22 Recovery/Waterfall Analysis of KHA Corp

Notes on liquidation analysis of KHA Corp

Inventory Most retailers do not liquidate their own inventory. Instead, they sell their merchandise to an asset disposition firm (liquidator), which agrees on a price for the inventory (sometimes with an upside-sharing arrangement). The liquidator takes over the stores for 8–12 weeks, is responsible for all expenses, runs a going-out-of-business (GOB) sale, and returns the stores "broom-swept" clean. Four liquidation firms dominate the industry: Gordon Brothers, Great American, Hilco Global, and Tiger Group. These firms also provide appraisal services to the asset-based lenders that lend to a company based on a borrowing base formula of the liquidation value of inventory (see Chapter 5 for further discussion of ABL facilities).

Based on the type of retailer, inventory recovery rates tend to range from 70% to 100% of book value. However, the best way to get the most reliable range of values is to get input from one of the major liquidators, as they have an extensive recovery database. In fact, at Goldman, we looked into buying a minority stake in Gordon Brothers; not only was the business extremely profitable, it would also give us a significant competitive advantage in valuing distressed retailers.

Receivables For most retailers, receivables are not a significant source of value. Retail consumers use cash or credit cards, and credit card receivables clear in one to two days. However, recovery rates tend to be extremely high, 90+% of book value. It is more challenging to value receivables in other industries, which requires analyzing the creditworthiness of significant customers, the aging of receivables (how many are past due), and the likelihood of disputes to determine the recovery rates.

Owned real estate It is a competitive advantage if an investment fund has a real estate group to opine on the value of a company's real estate. In the absence of an in-house team, most funds hire an expert to assist in valuation.

There are three basic methods to value real estate. Below is a brief overview of each; however, as with going-concern valuation techniques, there are entire courses and textbooks on real estate valuation approaches.

1. *Replacement cost.* The replacement cost method to value commercial real estate attempts to determine how much it would cost to build the same building today.
2. *Analysis of comparables.* A second method of valuing commercial real estate is to compare the price of a building against other recent comparable sales prices per square foot (PSF). For example, if the property next door sold recently for $200 PSF, then, all else equal (a big assumption), your property could also be sold for $200 PSF. Of course, many factors could affect the ultimate sale price of a building relative to comparables, including building quality, occupancy, type, and location. Appraisers and investors can adjust to account for these factors.
3. *Cap rate methodology.* This approach applies the DCF analysis for valuing a company discussed in Chapter 11 to the real estate's cash flows (also referred to as net operating income, or NOI), which are discounted by the appropriate discount rate (referred to as the property's cap rate). The NOI divided by the cap rate is the resultant estimate of value. Like sales PSF values, cap rates are typically inferred from comparable transactions.

For KHA Corp, our internal real estate team valued owned properties at $438–$629 million using the cap rate methodology, as outlined in Figure 19.23.

	Real Estate Valuation Scenarios		
	Low	Base	High
Number of Owned Properties	93	93	93
Avg. Square Feet per Property (in 000)	95	95	95
Total Owned Square Feet	8,835	8,835	8,835
Estimate Market Rent per Square Foot	$4.0	4.5	5.0
Annual Cash Flow (in $MM) [A]	$35	$40	$44
Divided by the Cap Rate [B]	8.0%	7.5%	7.0%
Value of Owned Stores (annual cash flow / cap rate) (in $MM) [A/B]	**$438**	**$533**	**$629**
Value per Store (in $MM)	$4.7	$5.7	$6.8

FIGURE 19.23 Real Estate Valuation of KHA Corp

Value of in-the-money leases If a company entered into a 30-year lease 10 years ago and rents have increased dramatically, the 20 years of remaining lease payments are significantly below market. While most leases have a non-assignability clause, the bankruptcy code makes those clauses non-enforceable and allows the debtor to assume and assign the lease. There is economic value for the debtor in selling below-market lease rights to another retailer. To estimate the value of the lease, the investor estimates how much savings per year a new tenant would generate by paying the contractual lease rate versus the current market rate and calculates the present value of these savings over the remaining lease term using the appropriate cap rate.

For KHA Corp, our real estate group believed 40%–50% of the leased stores had rents below market. On average, the company was paying $2.5 PSF below market rates for those stores. The leases had ten years remaining, resulting in an in-the-money lease value of $642 to $841 million. The estimated value of the in-the-money leases is shown in Figure 19.24.

	In-the-Money Lease Valuation		
	Low	Base	High
Number of Properties	1,100	1,100	1,100
Less Number Owned	-93	-93	-93
Number of Leases	1,007	1,007	1,007
% That Are in the Money	40%	45%	50%
Number of In-the-Money Leases	403	453	504
Avg. Square Feet per Property (in 000)	95	95	95
Total In-the-Money Square Feet (in 000)	38,285	43,035	47,880
Amount Rent Is Below Market per Square Foot	2.5	2.5	2.5
Annual Rent Savings Rents (in $MM)	96	108	120
Average Number of Years Remaining on Lease	10	10	10
Total Savings (in $MM)	960	1,080	1,200
Cap Rate (%)	8.0%	7.5%	7.0%
In-the-Money Lease Value (present value of lease savings)[a]	642	738	841
Value per In-the-Money Lease	1.6	1.6	1.7

[a] In-the-money lease value is the sum of the PV of the 10 years of annual rent (using the cap rate as the discount rate). For instance, in our "low case" it is the PV Year 1 savings (96/1.08^1) + PV Year 2 savings (96/1.08^2) + . . .

FIGURE 19.24 Value of In-the-Money Leases of KHA Corp

Brands The valuation process for any asset is an art, not a science; however, brands are particularly difficult to value. Some liquidations result in zero value for the brands; others are incredibly valuable. Some questions to consider when thinking through brand value include:

- Does the company have strong brand recognition?
- Is the consumer perception of the brand positive or negative?
- Would someone pay a licensing fee to use the name?

For example, in 2008, Sharper Image filed for bankruptcy and subsequently liquidated when it could not turn the business around. Silver Point bid $30 million for the brand and was outbid by a consortium that paid $49 million.[ii] With 20/20 hindsight, our assumptions were too conservative. The buyer was able to generate significant cash flow by licensing the Sharper Image name, and in 2016, the company was sold to ThreeSixty Group for $100 million.[iii]

We assigned zero value to KHA's brand in the downside and base cases and $50 million in the upside case.

Other There were other miscellaneous assets, including furniture, fixtures, and equipment (FF&E). Our lack of conviction in the worth of these assets led us to assign them a value of 0%–20% of book value.

Liquidation/wind-down expenses The size and complexity of a particular case dictate wind-down expenses. While a small, uncontested liquidation can cost the estate a few million dollars, Lehman Brothers' liquidation set a new record on the upper bound of costs. The Federal Reserve Bank of New York estimated Lehman's wind-down cost at a staggering $6 billion,[iv] a dramatic increase over the previous highwater mark of the 2001 Enron liquidation cost of $1 billion.

For KHA Corp, we had negotiated investment banking fees and commissions of 1%–1.5% of liquidation value. Other expenses were estimated at $2 million per month, and there was an agreed stay bonus for essential employees of $30 million. Figure 19.25 outlines the range of liquidation costs.

	Liquidation Cost Scenarios		
$ in Millions	Low	Base	High
Liquidation Valuation	$3,476	$3,809	$4,200
Investment Banking Fee	1.0%	1.25%	1.5%
Fees [A]	$35	$48	$63
Additional Cost per Month (in $MM)	$2	$2	$2
(x) Months to Wind Down	12	9	6
Costs [B]	$24	$18	$12
Stay Bonuses [C]	$30	$30	$30
Total Wind-Down Costs [A+B+C]	$89	$96	$105

FIGURE 19.25 Liquidation Cost Scenarios for KHA Corp

Other administrative and priority claims Administrative and priority claims are entitled to recovery ahead of any general unsecured claims (GUCs). For KHA, these claims were based on required bankruptcy filings. See Chapter 15 for more details on administrative and priority claims.

Secured pre-petition claims KHA Corp had an ABL facility and a secured term loan with $1.11 billion outstanding. The company had been paying the secured lenders post-petition interest, so there was no accrued interest. The analysis assumes the secured debt will be paid in full with no deficiency claim.

Unsecured bonds KHA Corp had $2.277 billion in unsecured bonds outstanding as of the filing date.

Scheduled pre-petition payables Our estimate of pre-petition payables was based on bankruptcy filings. Differences in our low/base/high estimates related to $50 million disputed payables.

Lease rejection claims As discussed in Chapter 15, leases rejected in bankruptcy have an unsecured claim for lost rent over the remaining lease period, less amounts mitigated by re-leasing. The bankruptcy code limits the landlord's claim to 15% of the remaining undiscounted lease payments, capped at three years of rent. Our real estate team estimated that of the stores not assumed and assigned, approximately 75% would not be re-leased, creating a lease rejection claim. The lease rejection claims are estimated in Figure 19.26.

	Lease Rejection Claim Scenarios		
	Low	Base	High
Total Number of Leased Properties	1,007	1,007	1,007
Less Leases Expected to be Assumed and Assigned	-403	-453	-504
Total Number of Leases to Be Rejected	604	554	503
Percent of Those Leases Not at Market Value Rents	75%	75%	75%
# of Out-of-the-Money Leases [A]	453	416	377
Average Square Feet (000s) [B]	95	95	95
Average Annual Rent per Square Foot ($ PSF) [C]	$4	$4	$4
Max Lease Rejection Not to Exceed 3x [D]	3.0x	3.0x	3.0x
Estimate of Lease Rejection Claims (in $MM) [A × B × C × D]	**$516**	**$474**	**$430**

FIGURE 19.26 Lease Rejection Claim Scenarios for KHA Corp

Other pre-petition unsecured liabilities These were based on court filings.

Non-retail/more complex liquidations

Not all liquidation analyses are as straightforward as KHA Corp. For example, many funds invested in the Madoff, Enron, and Lehman liquidations. These liquidations were extremely complex, and most of the returns came from assets that were challenging to value, including litigation claims against third parties and esoteric derivatives. As of the writing of this book, one of the most interesting and complex potential liquidations working its way through bankruptcy is FTX.

FTX was the second largest cryptocurrency exchange. In October 2017, Sam Bankman-Fried (known as SBF) set up a crypto trading firm, Alameda, to exploit price discrepancies in this opaque market. In May 2019, he launched FTX, a crypto exchange, which he would eventually domicile in the Bahamas, invisible to the watchful eye of the SEC. In early 2022, FTX was valued at $40 billion and had marquee investors such as Softbank, Sequoia Capital, and Blackrock.[v] By the end of 2022, the company had filed for bankruptcy, and SBF had been arrested on fraud charges. The FTX combined entity has more than 100,000 and possibly over 1 million creditors.[vi]

Some distressed debt funds started to focus on FTX when its operations began seizing up. While the company has some assets that are relatively easy to value, such as owned real estate, the bulk of the liquidation value will be in litigation claims against the individuals who ran the company and their advisers, various crypto securities, and venture capital investments. FTX will likely be an exciting case study in the next edition of this book.

UNIQUE SPECIAL SITUATIONS TRADES

There are certain investments that many avoid on the premise of "life is too short." These can generate tremendous risk-adjusted returns for those willing to fight it out to the bitter end. One example is Elliott Capital Management's 14-year battle with Argentina. In 2001 Argentina defaulted on $80 billion of debt. Ninety-three percent of the country's creditors settled for approximately 30 cents on the dollar.[vii] However, Elliott refused to settle. The battle between a "vulture" hedge fund and a sovereign government made international headlines when Elliott won an injunction in the Ghanaian superior court to seize an Argentinian naval ship carrying a crew of 250.[viii] Elliott's persistence paid off, and it received $2.4 billion for a claim Elliott, according to the *Washington Post*, purchased for approximately $115 million—a 20x return.[ix]

Silver Point's investment in Quinn Industries fits this category. It is the most interesting investment I have ever made. This was a very volatile situation, with many unique characters, including some with rumored ties to the former Irish Republic Army. Everyone involved in the negotiations worried about their safety at some point during the process. Rather than give a summary of the situation, in Appendix, I have included a case study that I have taught at Columbia Business School, Harvard Business School, and Fordham's undergraduate business program. If, after reading the case, you're interested in learning more, you can read *Citizen Quinn* by Gavin Daly and Ian Kehoe and *Quinn* by Trevor Birney. And if you want to hear the real behind-the-scenes drama, invite me to guest lecture at your university.

END OF CHAPTER: JCPENNEY TRADE IDEAS—TRADE #1

In Chapter 6, we discussed the events leading to JCP's disastrous 2012 performance, and in the following six chapters, we ran a complete analysis of the company. Now let's utilize that work to make some trade recommendations. The following are examples of trades possible in early 2013 after the release of JCP's dismal fourth quarter 2012 earnings report. The trading prices differ from those in the capital structure table from Chapter 9, as these trades were recommended in different periods in 2013.

JCP trade recommendation #1: Capital structure arb

Buy $10 million 7.125% notes due 11/15/2023 (trading at $89.5) and short $10 million 7.4% notes due 4/1/37 (trading at $82).

Investment thesis for trade recommendation #1:

- Based on our liquidity analysis (Chapter 8), JCP only has 12–24 months to turn its operations around before it runs out of liquidity. This assumes trade vendors continue to support the business at existing terms.
- Therefore, it's likely the company would want to increase its liquidity by raising new debt. JCP has a significant amount of unencumbered real estate that it could pledge as collateral for new financing. The company's 10-K discloses that 429 of its 1,104 stores are owned. In addition, JCP owns nine distribution facilities. Public reports value the owned real estate at $3 billion, which at a 65% loan-to-value could support $1.95 billion in real estate financing.
- However, the company's 10-K discloses one bond (the 7.125% due 11/15/2023) with a restrictive covenant limiting incremental debt:

  We have an indenture covering approximately $255 million of long-term debt that contains a financial covenant requiring us to have a minimum of 200% net tangible assets to senior funded indebtedness (as defined in the indenture). This indenture permits our Company to issue additional long-term debt if we are in compliance with the covenant.

- Based on the definitions in the 7.125% bond indenture, additional debt financing would be limited to approximately $500 million before the covenant is tripped,[2] and this amount will decrease if net tangible assets continue to decline with asset write-downs and/or ongoing shrinkage of the company's book equity with net losses.
- As the 7.125% bond is only $255 million in size, the company might call or tender for it to eliminate the restrictive covenant.

[2]This calculation is an estimate, as the 10-K does not have enough detail to calculate the exact number. The company provided its calculation of net tangible assets to senior funded indebtedness as 304%, greater than what most analysts estimated using the public disclosures. The exact number is not as important as realizing these bonds would severely limit the new debt the company is allowed to raise.

Summary upside/downside analysis for trade recommendation #1

- The downside for this trade is losing the $750,000 premium paid for the bond with the restrictive covenant (paying $89.5 for the long position versus getting $82 for the short position). There are three ways to lose the premium paid:
  - The company does not take out these bonds, and they decline in price to the same level as the shorted bond.
  - The company files, and as a result the 7.125% bonds and the 7.4% bonds trade at the same price.
  - The company turns itself around, meaning both bonds will get paid out at par.

  In addition, there is a $27,500 annual cost of carry on the trade, as outlined in Figure 19.27.

Cost to Carry JCP Trade – in $000s

Trade	Instrument	Amount	Coupon	$ Coupon
Long	7.125% Bond	10,000	7.125%	712.5
Short	7.4% Bond	-10,000	7.400%	-740.0
Annual Cost to Carry JCP Trade			-.275%	-27.5

FIGURE 19.27 Cost to Carry JCP Trade

- However, the upside potential is substantial. The 7.125% bonds are only callable at a very expensive make-whole premium (Treasuries + 20 bps), so the company would likely negotiate a takeout price anywhere from a slight premium to the current trading level to as high as the make-whole price of $165 (par plus 10.5 years of remaining coupons discounted by a rate of Treasuries + 20 bps). Furthermore, if the company took out the 7.125% bond, it would pave the way for significant secured financing using owned real estate as collateral. The analyst believes the remaining unsecured bonds would trade down as the new real estate financing would prime them. If that is correct, the investment wins on both sides of the trade: the price of the long position goes up, and the price of the shorted bond goes down.

A reasonable range of upside scenarios is outlined in Figure 19.28.

$ in 000s	Upside Trade Scenarios #1	#2	#3	#4
Take-Out Price 7.125% Bond	100.0%	120.0%	140.0%	160.0%
Less Today's Trading Levels (%)	89.5%	89.5%	89.5%	89.5%
Price Chg (7.125% Bond)	10.5%	30.5%	50.5%	70.5%
× $10MM Long Position	× 10,000	× 10,000	× 10,000	× 10,000
Profit on Long Position [A]	1,050	3,050	5,050	7,050
New Trading Level 7.4% Bond	82.0%	79.0%	76.0%	72.0%
Less Today's Trading Levels	82.0%	82.0%	82.0%	82.0%
Price Chg (7.4% Bond)	0.0%	-3.0%	-6.0%	-10.0%
× $10MM Short Position	× (10,000)	× (10,000)	× (10,000)	× (10,000)
Profit on Short Position [B]	0	300	600	1,000
Total Profit on the Trade [A+B]	**$1,050**	**$3,350**	**$5,650**	**$8,050**

FIGURE 19.28 Upside Scenarios for JCP Trade

As in the downside scenarios, the trade has an annual negative carry of $27,500.

What happened? Trade recommendation #1:

- This trade ended up being a home run. JCP's first quarter of 2013 disappointed investors, as same-store sales decreased by 16.6%, and adjusted EBITDA was negative $264 million. As liquidity concerns increased, the company tendered for the 7.125% bonds at a price of $145 and raised a five-year, $2.25 billion real estate term loan with a coupon of LIBOR + 5.0%. The 7.4% bond was quoted down $0.5 to $81.5. The P&L on the trade (excluding the annual negative carry discussed above) is outlined in Figure 19.29.

$ in 000s	Trade P&L #1
Take-Out Price 7.125% Bonds	145.0%
Less Trading Level When Trade Was Initiated	89.5%
Price Chg (7.125% bonds)	55.5%
× $10MM Long Position	× 10,000
Profit on Long Position [A]	$5,550
New Trading Level 7.4% Bonds	81.5%
Less Trading Level When Trade Was Initiated	82.0%
Price Chg (7.4% Bonds)	-0.5%
× $10MM Short Position	× (10,000)
Profit on Short Position [B]	50
Total Profit on the Trade [A+B]	**$5,600**

FIGURE 19.29 JCP Trade P&L

END OF CHAPTER: JCPENNEY TRADE IDEAS—TRADE #2

JCP trade recommendation #2: Bullish spread tightening trade

Buy $10 million 6.375% notes due 10/15/2036 (trading at $75)

Investment thesis for trade recommendation #2

- This trade is predicated on a successful turnaround of the business. The rationale for a turnaround thesis is that the damage resulted from an unsuccessful shift in pricing strategy, and the company can simply revert to its prior strategy to reclaim lost customers and EBITDA.
- In 2010, before the pricing strategy change, JCP bonds were rated Ba1 (Moody's) and BB+ (S&P) and traded with an average spread over treasuries of 272 bps. After the disastrous 2012 performance, the bonds are rated Caa1/CCC+, and at $75, the 6.375% bonds now trade at a yield of 8.94% and spread of 594 bps.
- As the turnaround gains traction, the rating agencies will upgrade the bond to single-B, and its spread will tighten by 100–150 bps.
- This is expected to be a 12- to 24-month trade.

Summary upside/downside analysis of trade recommendation #2

- If the company successfully executes its turnaround strategy and the spread on its bond tightens by 100–150 bps, the expected IRR on the trade will be 20%–26% if it plays out in one year and 14%–17% if it plays out in two years.

  The IRR if the trade plays out in one year is shown in Figure 19.30.

$ in 000s	One Year Trade	
Amount Spread Tightens	100 bps	150 bps
Initial Investment on 4/15/2013 (price × $10MM of bonds)	($7,500.00)	($7,500.00)
Six Month Coupon Pmt ($10MM bonds × 6.375% coupon / 2)	318.75	318.75
Six Month Coupon Plus Selling Bond at New Price (84.1 @ 100 bps tightening and 88.9 @ 150 bps)[a,b]	$8,728.75	$9,208.75
$ Profits on a $10 Million Trade	$1,547.5	$2,027.5
IRR in Excel × 2 to Annualize 6 mos. CFs	20.1%	25.9%
Multiple of Money	1.21x	1.27x

[a] Assumes either no change in treasury rates or hedged treasury risk.

[b] Refer to the discussion of yield/spreads in Chapter 3. The prices in the spread tightening scenarios were calculated using Bloomberg.

FIGURE 19.30 One-Year Upside IRR

The IRR if the trade plays out in two years is shown in Figure 19.31.

$ in 000s	Two Year Trade	
Amount Spread Tightens	**100 Bps**	**150 Bps**
Initial Investment on 4/15/2013 (price × $10MM of bonds)	($7,500.00)	($7,500.00)
Six Month Coupon Pmt ($10MM bonds × 6.375% coupon / 2)	318.75	318.75
Six Month Coupon Pmt ($10MM bonds × 6.375% coupon / 2)	318.75	318.75
Six Month Coupon Pmt ($10MM bonds × 6.375% coupon / 2)	318.75	318.75
Six Month Coupon Plus Selling Bond at New Price (84.4 @ 100 bps tightening and 89.1 @ 150 bps)[a,b,c]	$8,758.75	$9,228.75
$ Profits on a $10 Million Trade	$2,215.00	$2,685.00
IRR in Excel × 2 to Annualize 6 mos. CFs	14.1%	16.8%
Multiple of Money	1.30x	1.36x

[a]Assumes either no change in treasury rates or hedged treasury risk.
[b]Refer to the discussion of yield/spreads in Chapter 3. The prices were calculated using Bloomberg.
[c]The selling price of each bond is slightly higher than the one-year trade, despite the same tightening of spread, due to being one year closer to maturity.

FIGURE 19.31 Two-Year Upside IRR

- However, this trade has significant downside if the company files for bankruptcy. Based on market consensus that the bonds would trade at $35 in a bankruptcy, the IRR on the trade would be −59.1% if it plays out in one year and −26.8% if plays out in two years as shown in Figures 19.32 and 19.33.

$ in 000s	One-Year Trade
Initial Investment on 4/15/2013 (Price × $10MM of bonds)	($7,500.00)
Six Month Coupon Pmt ($10MM bonds × 6.375% coupon / 2)	318.75
Company Files and Bond is Sold at $35	$3,500.00
$ Profits on a $10 Million Trade	($3,681.25)
IRR in Excel × 2 to Annualize 6 mos. CFs	-59.1%
Multiple of Money	0.51x

FIGURE 19.32 One-Year IRR in Bankruptcy Scenario

$ in 000s	Two-Year Trade
Initial Investment on 4/15/2013 (price x $10MM of bonds)	(7,500.00)
Six Month Coupon Pmt ($10MM bonds x 6.375% coupon / 2)	318.75
Six Month Coupon Pmt ($10MM bonds x 6.375% coupon / 2)	318.75
Six Month Coupon Pmt ($10MM bonds x 6.375% coupon / 2)	318.75
Company Files and Bond is Sold at $35	3,500.00
$ Profits on a $10 Million Trade	($3,043.75)
IRR in Excel x 2 to Annualize 6 mos. CFs	-26.8%
Multiple of Money	0.59x

FIGURE 19.33 Two-Year IRR in Bankruptcy Scenario

What happened? Trade recommendation #2

JCP's board fired CEO Ron Johnson, the architect of the disastrous change in strategy, and rehired Mike Ullman, the previous CEO. The company did not run out of liquidity over the next two years. However, the business never fully recovered. The bonds traded at approximately $72.6 one year following the trade and $76 on its second anniversary. The IRR on the investment would have been 5.3% if held for one year and 9.1% if held for two. Given the risk-return profile, while not a money loser, this trade was disappointing.

The company and its bonds had many ups and downs after the two-year investment horizon discussed above. In May 2020, JCP became one of many companies that filed for bankruptcy due to the global pandemic. Its bonds traded down to the $30s.

END OF CHAPTER: JCPENNEY TRADE IDEAS—TRADE #3

JCP trade recommendation #3: Fundamental valuation trade

Short $10 million of stock (trading at $15.2/share)

Investment thesis for trade recommendation #3

Based on the liquidity analysis referenced above, there was a disconnect between JCP's stock price and its bond pricing. A liquidity crisis was looming (see Chapter 8 analysis), and the company was at risk of filing for bankruptcy in the next two years, wiping out any equity value. JCP's stock price was too high even in most analysts' upside cases assuming a successful turnaround.

A short position is a bet against the company. The investor borrows shares from a broker-dealer and then sells the shares at the market price. Eventually, the investor must return the borrowed shares by buying the stock in the open market, which is profitable if the share price declines during the short contract period.

Summary upside/downside analysis for trade recommendation #3

A sample upside/downside analysis of JCP stock during this timeframe is presented in Figure 19.34. This analysis uses the forecast from Chapter 10 and the valuation analysis from Chapter 11.

	Bankruptcy	Turnaround Scenarios		
$ in millions, except share price	Scenario	Low	Mid	High
Projected Stabilized EBITDA	NM	800	1,000	1,200
× EBITDA Multiples	NM	5.25x	5.50x	5.75x
TEV at the End of Proj Period (future value)	NM	4,200	5,500	6,900
Less Projected Net Debt Outstanding	NM	(3,590)	(2,914)	(2,477)
Projected Equity Market Cap	0	610	2,586	4,423
Divide by Shares Outstanding	219	219	219	219
Projected Price per Share [A]	0.00	2.78	11.8	20.18
Price of Stock When Shorted	15.20	15.20	15.20	15.20
Projected Price per Share [A]	(0.00)	(2.78)	(11.80)	(20.18)
Profit (Loss) per Share Shorted	15.20	12.42	3.40	(4.98)
Number of Shares Shorted (in MM)	.658	.658	.658	.658
Profit (Loss) in Millions	10.00	8.17	2.24	(3.27)

FIGURE 19.34 Upside/Downside Analysis for JCP Stock

The above analysis might make this trade look like a no-brainer, but short equity positions are extremely risky due to their asymmetric risk profile. The stock cannot go below $0 per share, so your profits are capped at $10MM. However, if your valuation is wrong, or the market is irrational, there is no limit to how high a stock can trade—so while your profits are capped, your losses are not. Compounding that risk, the JCP short was a "crowded trade," meaning a lot of investors had put it on. Any surprisingly good news for the company would drive the stock up and lead short sellers to unwind their positions, which they can only do by "covering their shorts," i.e., buying the stock, which would in turn drive the price up further (referred to as a short squeeze).

What happened? Trade recommendation #3

The two-year stock chart in Figure 19.35 shows that the short trade worked well if it took place between April and September of 2013. However, by October 2013, the investment had played out. The shares traded under $7/share and then, over the next several years, traded in a tight range averaging approximately $8/share.

FIGURE 19.35 Share Price Chart
Source: BitMEX.

The profit on the short for a one-year holding period would be $4.5 million on the $10 million short position, as outlined in Figure 19.36.

$ in millions, except share price	Short Trade P&L
Price of Stock When Shorted	15.20
Average Price One Year Later	(8.3)
Profit (Loss) per Share Shorted	6.9
Number of Shares Shorted (in MM)	.658
Profits (Loss) in Millions[a]	4.54

[a] This analysis ignores any fees the broker-dealer charged on the borrowed shares. The stock loan fee is based on the difficulty of borrowing the shares.

FIGURE 19.36 JCP Stock Short P&L

Interestingly, $8/share is consistent with the valuation analysis performed in Chapter 11. Figure 19.37 shows the probabilities assigned to each scenario and the resultant probability-weighted stock price forecast of $8.19.

	Probability-Weighted Share Price				
$ in millions, except share price	Bankruptcy	Turnaround			Probability
	Scenario	Low	Mid	High	Weighted
Projected Price per Share (from above)	0.00	2.78	11.80	20.18	
Probability Assigned to Each Scenario	30%	10%	50%	10%	
Probability-Weighted Price per Share	0.00	0.28	5.90	2.02	8.19

FIGURE 19.37 Probability-Weighted Share Price

CHAPTER CONCLUSION

As a distressed debt investor, you can break your career progression into three stages:

1. *Early stage.* Provide leverage to your organization with basic analysis and company modeling. More experienced team members use your work to identify good trade ideas.
2. *Middle stage.* Perform analysis and make trade recommendations.
3. *Late stage.* Review others' work and trade recommendations and decide which ones to include in the portfolio.

This chapter is designed to help you transition from stage #1 to stage #2. The examples outlined above represent a comprehensive set of strategies employed by distressed investors, but they are by no means all-inclusive. As an analyst, you must consistently think of creative ways to make money for your organization and translate your analysis into recommendations. Sometimes this is uncomfortable. Not all of your ideas will make it through your firm's investment committee process. And inevitably, some of your recommendations will lose money. To become a great investor, you must take risk; you will have losses, but you will learn from each trade recommendation.

Whenever you analyze a company, force yourself to make trade recommendations. Keep a journal of all your investment ideas. Do a post-mortem every six months. What return would you have had if you put on the trade? Did your investment thesis play out? If not, why, and what did you learn? The transition from stage #2 to #3 requires years, or even a decade, of experience. Your personal "paper" portfolio and track record of ideas will build confidence, experience, and wisdom.

NOTES

i. Party City 1999 10-K. https://www.sec.gov/Archives/edgar/data/1005972/000095012399009019/0000950123-99-009019-index.htm.

ii. Taub, Eric. (January 19, 2009). "Sharper Image Stores Are Dead, but the Brand Goes On." *New York Times.* https://www.nytimes.com/2009/01/19/technology/companies/19sharper.html.

iii. Stech Ferek, Katy. (January 16, 2019). "Fed Says Lehman Brothers Chapter 11 Case I Costliest in History." *Wall Street Journal.*

iv. Griffin, Erin, and David Yaffe-Bellany. (November 11, 2002). "Investors Who Put $2 Billion Into FTX Face Scrutiny." *New York Times.*

v. Sridharan, Harish. (November 16, 2022). "Rise and Fall of Crypto Exchange FTX." Reuters. https://www.reuters.com/markets/currencies/rise-fall-crypto-exchange-ftx-2022-11-10/.

vi. Merle, Renae. (March 29, 2016). "How One Hedge Fund made $2 Billion from Argentina's Collapse." *Washington Post.*

vii. Ibid.

viii. Ibid.

ix. Ibid.

Closing Comment

CHAPTER 20

My Closing Comment

I had two goals when I undertook the ambitious project of writing this book. My first goal was to prepare the reader for a career investing in the leveraged credit markets. My approach is 100 percent vocational and zero percent academic. It gives readers skills to help land a job in the credit markets and outperform their employer's expectations once they do. While this book focuses on the debt markets, I believe the seven-step process applies to any corporate investment whether debt or equity.

My second goal was even more important to me personally. My career in the leveraged credit markets has brought me the kind of professional fulfillment that is increasingly hard to find. Were there late nights? Yes. Were there nasty fights with creditors on the other side of the trade? Yes. But the intellectual challenge of the job, the joy of working with some of the most intelligent people I've ever met (some of whom you've encountered in this book), and the rush of realizing that I've identified something everyone else has overlooked have made any unpleasant parts of the job worthwhile. I hope that this book gave you a sense of what it is like to work in the leveraged credit markets, along with an analytical leg up as you embark on your career.

The credit markets are vast and getting vaster, with many career paths. You could end up working on a sell-side credit trading desk, at a hedge fund, for a CLO manager, at a "par" high yield bond mutual fund, or on the investment banking/advisory side of the business. No matter your career path, I am confident you can rely on the practices outlined in this book to perform superior credit analysis and either improve your prospects in your existing career or prepare yourself for a new one.

I wish you well in your journey, and look forward to quoting some of you in future editions as you become the next generation of practitioners on the front lines of credit cycles to come.

Please feel free to contact me with any questions, comments, or suggestions at gatto@creditinvestorshandbook.com or connect with me on LinkedIn.

Appendix

Appendix: The Quinn Case Study

12/11/2013 – An oil tanker was rammed into the headquarters of the Quinn Group.

This case study has been provided for instructional purposes only and references only publicly available information, including bankruptcy filings and press coverage. Certain financial data was re-created or altered solely for instructional purposes.

Use the questions below to frame your reading and put yourself in the shoes of the Investment Group as they evaluate their options in mid-2014.

FRAMING QUESTIONS

1. If this were a "normal situation" in which management could run a formal sale process, what would you pay for the Tranche B debt? Do not take into account the exogenous factors of unrest in the community.
2. Taking into account this exogenous factor, what would you pay for the Tranche B debt?
3. Do you think Sean Quinn is a hero or a villain?

4. Evaluate management's plan to appease "the community" by selling the Building Products and Packaging divisions to QBRC backed by Endless Capital. Would you support it? What are the pros and cons of this plan?
5. If you do not support management's plan to engage with QBRC, what would you advise the distressed debt funds to do?

CASE

The Quinn story is a legend in Ireland. In 1973, Sean Quinn, a high school dropout, borrowed £100 and embarked on his first business venture extracting and washing gravel from his family's farm in remote Derrylin, which he sold to local construction firms in the Derrylin/Ballyconnel border region between Northern Ireland and the Republic of Ireland. Sean grew his gravel business into cement production and expanded exponentially, quickly becoming one of the largest cement producers in Ireland and building what would become the cornerstone of his business empire, the Quinn Group.

Sean established a reputation for investing in the highest specification equipment and green-fielding large investments in mature, low-margin industries. Sean competed with established players on both quality and price, taking advantage of chronic under-investment by the competition. By 2006, the Quinn Group consisted of a large Manufacturing Group with divisions including Building Products (cement, foam insulation, roof tiles, etc.), Glass, Radiators, Plastics and Packaging, an Insurance Group with a large Irish and UK discount insurance underwriter, and an expansive international real estate portfolio in far-flung countries such as Russia, India, and Ukraine.

At the peak of his career, Sean was regarded as a near demigod in Derrylin and across Ireland. He'd brought thousands of jobs and real industry to the underdeveloped border region through his massive, debt-financed investments in two state-of-the-art cement plants and a world-class glass factory underwritten by Anglo Irish Bank, a "Celtic Tiger" that had grown precipitously on the heels of the Irish property boom, and a large group of bondholders, primarily based in the US.

Sean ruled his expansive empire with an iron fist, amassing a significant amount of wealth in the process. In 2008, *Forbes* reported that the Quinn family was worth $6 billion, making them by far the wealthiest people in Ireland. Sean's nearly four decades of ever-increasing success in business fueled a predilection for risk-taking, increasingly so with his own personal investment portfolio, which ultimately would be his Achilles' heel.

From 2005 to 2007, Sean built a 28 percent equity stake in Anglo Irish, largely through derivative instruments, which allowed him to leverage the investment, providing more economic exposure for less up-front capital. To make these investments, Sean was required to post collateral, which he did in part by providing a pledge of his family's equity in the Quinn Group, thus tying the financial prospects of his business empire to that of Anglo Irish. Sean also borrowed from Anglo Irish to build his large international property portfolio.

By late 2008, Anglo Irish's share price was falling as the Irish real estate market collapsed, and by January 2009, the bank had been nationalized. Over the following two years, Sean and Anglo Irish attempted to negotiate an out-of-court restructuring.

At the same time, Sean and his associates pursued a variety of complicated, illicit, and possibly illegal transactions to maneuver Quinn Group's assets out of the reach of Anglo Irish's creditors. Once these actions came to light, a court-appointed receiver took control of the family's equity interest (pledged as collateral to Anglo Irish) in April 2011, completely removing Sean and his family from their ownership stake and management role.

The Quinn Manufacturing Group ultimately restructured via a UK Company Voluntary Arrangement ("CVA") in early December 2011, resulting in a new capital structure. The pre-petition debt was divided into two tranches:

i. Tranche A, consisting of a €450 million OpCo term loan with a first lien on all of the manufacturing assets and an 8.5% cash coupon; and
ii. Tranche B, consisting of a €900 million HoldCo term loan with a 7.5% PIK coupon and stapled equity such that the Tranche B holders controlled the company and could vote on any major corporate actions, including the hiring and firing of management.

Tranche A was viewed as a relatively safe investment that did not trade and was held by large international banks. Tranche B largely traded into the hands of distressed hedge funds following the completion of the CVA.

Tranche B holders put in place a new leadership team for the Manufacturing Group, led by Paul O'Brien, a seasoned executive familiar with the border region. The ouster of Sean and his family caused great distress in the community but was welcomed by the international bondholders who had watched the market price of their debt fall to extremely low levels and were concerned that the Quinn family, under Sean's direction, was siphoning off collateral and misrepresenting the health of the business.

Over the next few years, Paul O'Brien, his new management team, and the business itself experienced threats, sabotage, and attacks from individuals in the community upset by the treatment of the Quinn family. Some of the more severe attacks included Paul O'Brien's car being set on fire at his home, an oil tanker being driven into the packaging plant in an attempt to explode the factory, and a bullet being sent in the mail to a potential acquirer of one of the Quinn businesses. This period of instability, along with discrepancies discovered in the business, made Quinn's debt very volatile, and resulted in opportunities to buy at prices significantly below par.

By late 2013, the new management team had stabilized the Manufacturing Group, rebranded "Aventas," and was attempting to execute a recovery strategy for the international bondholders, many of whom had acquired the debt at significant discounts to face value. Despite the relative stability in the underlying Aventas businesses and the large pool of potential buyers for the company's other businesses, O'Brien faced roadblocks in monetizing these assets individually, as Aventas was subject to an ongoing and escalating level of attacks and threats that impeded its ability to execute asset disposals. In one circumstance, the CEO of Lagan Group, a potential acquirer of the Building Products division, received a threatening letter in the mail accompanied by a bullet, leading Lagan to back out of its proposal to acquire the division. Despite enhanced security, by mid-2014, Aventas had experienced 70+ attacks, and the company's Tranche B debt had traded to a low of 8 cents on the dollar and suspended cash interest payments.

In early 2014, the local press announced that a new entity named Quinn Business Retention Corp ("QBRC") had been formed by a local politician and several local businessmen, including the former CEO, CFO, and COO of the Quinn Group, with the intent of acquiring all former Quinn Group businesses, reportedly to preserve employment in the local area. John McCartin, a local politician and founding member of QBRC, made clear its plan to keep the Quinn Group intact, contrary to Aventas management's plan, stating: "As we all know, the Quinn businesses are critical to the viability of this region . . . We are not acting out of any self-interest, but at the urging of our business and community peers who want to see the businesses held intact, nurtured and expanded locally for future generations." Despite the involvement of former senior Quinn Group executives, according to McCartin, "[QBRC] will be financed by our financial backers, not the Quinn family." Unfortunately for Aventas' investors and management, there was no clear way to determine whether QBRC was simply a front for Sean Quinn.

In July 2014, after threats received by potential acquirers thwarted an attempted sale of the Packaging business, Aventas notified its bondholders that it had entered into a letter of intent ("LOI") to sell the Building Products and Packaging divisions to QBRC, which had backing from a UK private equity firm, Endless Capital, for €85 million. To complete the sale, Aventas required the approval of a majority in par value of the Tranche B debt. Three distressed debt funds (together, the "Investment Group," or IG) owned more than the required 50% stake in aggregate.

The Aventas management team noted that while a competitive auction was not possible given the community unrest, the proposed transaction represented an opportunity to gain goodwill and secure peace in the local community while Aventas pursued a sale of the substantially larger Glass division. This business had also been subject to sabotage, attacks, and threats by local community members since the April 2011 restructuring of the Quinn Group. Aventas believed it had identified a separate private equity buyer for the Glass business, but the transaction would be subject to demonstrating peace in the local community.

In addition, Aventas believed it could sell the Radiators and Plastics divisions within the next six months regardless of the state of the community given their locations outside of the Irish border region. Finally, there was speculation that Aventas management would resign if they did not obtain approval for these contemplated sales, leaving the company rudderless against a backdrop of growing discontent and violence in the community.

The Investment Group needed to determine whether to sign on to management's plan to sell the individual businesses, and if not, an alternative plan given management's potential resignations, escalating community unrest, and the looming maturity of the Tranche A debt.

Aventas Current Capital Structure (Millions of €)	Principal O/S	Maturity	Cash Coupon	PIK Coupon	Trading Price
Tranche A Debt – OpCo	€ 450	9/30/15	8.50%	0.00%	97.0
Tranche B Debt – HoldCo	€ 900	12/2/16	0.00%	7.50%	8.0
Total	€ 1,350				

Aventas Division Summaries

Glass

- € 60 million LTM EBITDA;
- Glass provides full life-cycle production and filling of glass bottles for the beverage industry with blue-chip customers such as Jameson's Whiskey;
- Potential acquirers: Ardagh, Vidrala, KKR or other large private equity firm.

Trading Comps	LTM EBITDA Multiple
Zignano Vetro	6.1x
O.I.	6.3x
Vidrala	6.5x

Plastics

- € 15 million LTM EBITDA;
- Plastics primarily makes various forms of plastic sheet (acrylic and polycarbonate) but is in a relatively weak position given it is not vertically integrated; the Plastics division is located in Western Europe and primarily serves that market;
- Potential Acquirers: Evonik, Arkema, Lucite, Sabic, Bayer.

Trading Comps	LTM EBITDA Multiple
Arkema	7.5x

Building Products

- € 13 million LTM EBITDA;
- Building Products primarily produces cement and cement-related products and insulation for the building industry in Ireland and the UK;
- Building Products has been disproportionately impacted by community violence, customer departures out of loyalty to Sean Quinn; however, these headwinds are offset by improving economic tailwinds including increasing demand for homes in Ireland and the UK and more favorable FX trends;
- Potential Acquirers: Lafarge, CRH, Lagan, Holcim, Cemex, Kingspan.

Trading Comps	LTM EBITDA Multiple
Heidelberg	8.3x
Holcim	8.5x
Lafarge	10.0x
CRH	8.5x
Kingspan	9.0x

Packaging

- € 2 million LTM EBITDA;
- Packaging primarily produces thermoformed trays and trays for the food industry; the business is well-capitalized, but small;
- Potential Acquirers: Other strategics looking to build scale, small private equity fund.

Trading Comps	LTM EBITDA Multiple
RPC Group	7.9x
Sonoco	8.8x
Huhtamaki	9.0x

Radiators

- € 0 million LTM EBITDA;
- Radiators produces home radiators for the UK market, generating roughly €60+ million in revenue. The factory is world-class, but profitability has been impaired by significant imports of radiators from subsidized Turkish companies. Hilco (a global liquidation firm) can liquidate the assets for proceeds of € 17.5- 22.5 million net of expenses.
- Potential Acquirers: Limited, likely a financial player;
- Trading Comps: N/A.

Index